The Protection of the Underwater Cultural Heritage

Before and After the 2001 UNESCO Convention

edited by
ROBERTA GARABELLO
and
TULLIO SCOVAZZI

MARTINUS NIJHOFF PUBLISHERS
LEIDEN/BOSTON

Published by:
Brill Academic Publishers
P.O. Box 9000, 2300 PA Leiden, The Netherlands
cs@brill.nl
http://www.brill.nl

A C.I.P. Catalogue record for this book is available from the Library of Congress.

Printed on acid-free paper

ISBN 90-411-2203-6

Brill Academic Publishers incorporates the imprint Martinus Nijhoff Publishers

Typeset by BookEns Ltd, Royston, Herts
Printed and bound in Great Britain by Antony Rowe Limited.

THE PROTECTION OF THE UNDERWATER CULTURAL HERITAGE: BEFORE AND AFTER THE 2001 UNESCO CONVENTION

Publications on Ocean Development

Volume 41

A Series of Studies on the International, Legal, Institutional and Policy Aspects of Ocean Development

General Editor: Vaughan Lowe
Chichele Professor of Public International Law and Fellow of All Souls College, Oxford University

The titles published in this series are listed at the end of this volume.

CONTENTS

DOCUMENTS

FOREWORD

On 6 November 2001 the UNESCO Convention on the Protection of the Underwater Cultural Heritage was signed by the Director-General of UNESCO and the President of the UNESCO General Conference. The Convention was adopted with 87 affirmative votes, 4 votes against and 15 abstentions. It will enter into force three months after the date of the deposit of the twentieth instrument of ratification.

The editors of this book consider the Convention to be a major achievement in the field of international law and a remarkable improvement on the regime established by the United Nations Convention on the Law of the Sea as regards archaeological and historical objects found at sea. They are confident that this impression is confirmed by the reading of the contributions included in the volume, which relate to both the present regime and the regime that will apply once the Convention will be in force. An appendix containing a number of relevant documents is included.

*

The editors had the opportunity to participate in the negotiations for the Convention and wish therefore to thank the Italian Ministry of Foreign Affairs. They are also grateful to the "Consiglio Nazionale delle Ricerche" (the Italian Council for Scientific Research) which financed a research project on new trends of international law relating to the protection of underwater cultural heritage, carried out within the "Dipartimento Giuridico delle Istituzioni Nazionali ed Europee" of the University of Milano-Bicocca. Special thanks go to Susan Phillips Clavarino, who took care of the linguistic revision of the English texts, and to the publisher Giuffrè Editore of Milan, which authorized the reprint of the paper by A. Gonzalez.

Milan, 28 April 2003

Roberta Garabello
Tullio Scovazzi

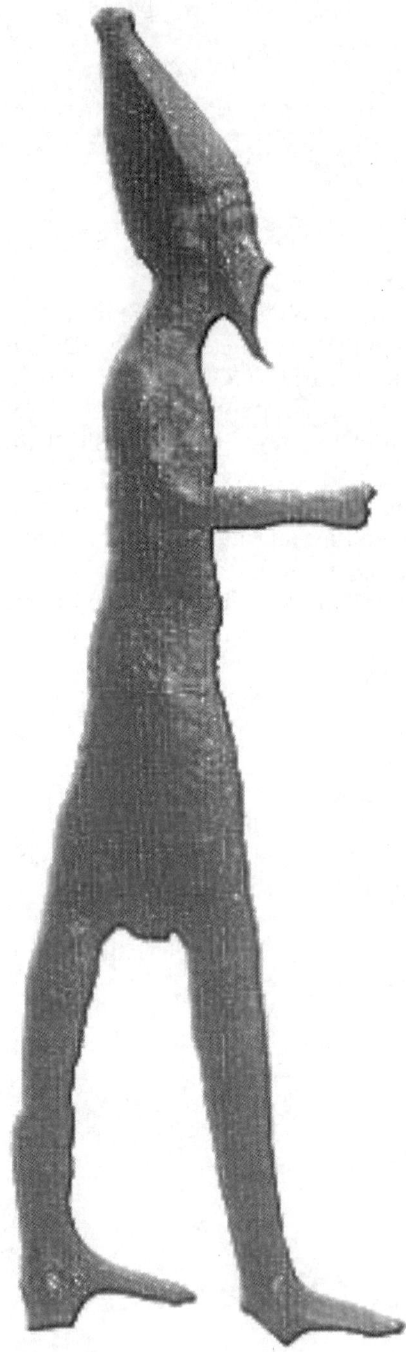

Bronze statue of a Syro-Palestinian divinity, so-called Melqart of Sciacca (XI–X century B.C.): see Chap. 2, para. 2.

ABBREVIATIONS

AJIL	*American Journal of International Law*
C-VLA JL & A	*Columbia-VLA Journal of Law and the Arts*
D.Md	United States District Court for the District of Maryland
E.D.Va	United States District Court for the Eastern District of Virginia
ERM	*Espaces et ressources maritimes*
F.2d	Federal Reporter, Second Series
F.3d	Federal Reporter, Third Series
F. Supp.	Federal Supplement
ICLQ	*International and Comparative Law Quarterly*
IJCP	*International Journal of Cultural Property*
IJECL	*International Journal of Estuarine and Coastal Law*
IJMCL	*International Journal of Marine and Coastal Law*
IJNA	*International Journal of Nautical Archaeology*
IJNAUE	*International Journal of Nautical Archaeology and Underwater Exploration*
ILM	*International Legal Materials*
JMLC	*Journal of Maritime Law and Commerce*
MP	*Marine Policy*
OCLJ	*Ocean and Coastal Law Journal*
ODIL	*Ocean Development and International Law*
RDI	*Rivista di diritto internazionale*
RGDIP	*Revue générale de droit international public*
S.D.Fla	United States District Court for the Southern District of Florida
TMLJ	*Tulane Maritime Law Journal*
UM	*Underwater Magazine*
U.S.	United States Supreme Court Reports
U.S. App. LEXIS	United States Court of Appeals (district courts and federal circuits)
U.S. Dist. LEXIS	United States District Court
VJIL	*Virginia Journal of International Law*
WLSJ	*Widener Law Symposium Journal*

PART I

THE REGIME OF UNDERWATER CULTURAL HERITAGE BEFORE THE 2001 UNESCO CONVENTION

Chapter 1

A CONTRADICTORY AND COUNTERPRODUCTIVE REGIME

*Tullio Scovazzi**

1. An Unexpected Obstacle

On 6 November 2001 the Convention on the Protection of the Underwater Cultural Heritage[1] was signed in Paris with UNESCO. It will apply to "all traces of human existence having a cultural, historical or archaeological character which have been partially or totally under water, periodically or continuously, for at least 100 years" (Art. 1, para. 1, a).

The CPUCH, which is the outcome of a longlasting negotiation, was adopted by vote (87 States in favour, 4 against[2] and 15 abstentions[3]). The lack of consensus at the moment of its adoption should not be considered as an irreparable flaw. Not only did the great majority of developing countries vote in favour, but also several

* Professor of International Law, University of Milano-Bicocca.

1 Hereinafter: the CPUCH.

2 Namely, the Russian Federation, Norway, Turkey and Venezuela. The observer delegate of the United States, who was not entitled to vote (the United States not being a member of UNESCO), regretted that his delegation could not accept the CPUCH because of objections to several key provisions relating to jurisdiction, the reporting scheme, warships, and the relationship of the convention to UNCLOS. The negative vote of Turkey and Venezuela was due to disagreement on the CPUCH provisions on peaceful settlement of disputes (Art. 25) and reservations (Art. 30).

3 Namely, Brazil, Czech Republic, Colombia, France, Germany, Greece, Iceland, Israel, Guinea-Bissau, Netherlands, Paraguay, Sweden, Switzerland, United Kingdom, Uruguay. The abstentions were based on different, and sometimes opposite, reasons. For instance, the Greek delegate stated *inter alia* that "despite the fact that throughout the negotiations at UNESCO the majority of governmental experts were in favour of extending coastal rights over underwater cultural heritage on the continental shelf, the Draft Convention does not even mention the term "coastal State". According to the French delegate, "la France est en désaccord avec le projet sur deux points précis: le statut des navires d'Etat et les droits de juridiction, dont nous considérons qu'ils sont incompatibles avec les dispositions de la Convention sur le droit de la mer".

Roberta Garabello and Tullio Scovazzi (eds.), The Protection of the Underwater Cultural Heritage, 3–17.

among the industrialized countries were satisfied with the final outcome of the negotiations.[4]

To explain the merit of the CPUCH a basic consideration must be made. Any attempts to deal with the cultural heritage at sea have inevitably to face an unexpected obstacle, that is Art. 303 of the United Nations Convention on the Law of the Sea.[5] This provision is not only incomplete, but also counterproductive. It can be understood in a sense that undermines the very objective of protecting the underwater cultural heritage. Such a clearcut assumption about the deficiencies of Art. 303 requires some elaboration.

2. The Unclos Regime

A) Two General Obligations

The UNCLOS regime relating to the underwater cultural heritage is based on the following scheme.

Art. 303, para. 1, sets forth two very general obligations which apply to all archaeological and historical objects, wherever at sea they are found:

> States have the duty to protect objects of an archaeological and historical nature found at sea and shall co-operate for this purpose.

Due to its rather broad content, Art. 303, para. 1, does not say very much. Nevertheless, some legal consequences can be drawn from it. A State which knowingly destroyed or allowed the destruction of elements of the underwater cultural heritage would be responsible for a breach of the obligation to protect it.

A State which persistently refused any request by other States to establish some forms of cooperation aiming at the protection of the underwater cultural heritage could also be held responsible of an internationally wrongful act. An obligation to cooperate is not devoid of legal meaning. It implies a duty to act in good faith in pursuing a common objective and in taking into account the situation of the other interested States. As remarked by the International Court of Justice in the judgement of 20 February 1969 on the *North Sea Continental Shelf* cases,

> the parties are under an obligation to enter into negotiations with a view to arriving at an agreement, and not merely to go through a formal process of negotiation as a sort of a prior condition for the automatic application of a certain method of delimitation in the absence of agreement; they are under an obligation so to conduct themselves that the negotiations are meaningful,

---

4 For example, Australia, Canada, China, Japan, New Zealand, the Republic of Korea voted in favour. Among the member States of the European Community, Austria, Belgium, Denmark, Finland, Ireland, Italy, Luxembourg, Portugal and Spain voted in favour, while France, Germany, Greece, the Netherlands, Sweden and the United Kingdom abstained.

5 Hereinafter: the UNCLOS.

which will not be the case when either of them insists upon its own position without contemplating any modification of it.[6]

B) Cigarette Smugglers, Clandestine Immigrants and Infectious Patients

While underwater cultural heritage located within internal maritime waters, archipelagic waters and territorial sea is subject to the jurisdiction of the coastal State,[7] Art. 303, para. 2, UNCLOS specifically relates to archaeological and historical objects located within the 24-mile zone set forth by Art. 33 UNCLOS (the contiguous zone):

> In order to control traffic in such objects, the coastal State may, in applying article 33, presume that their removal from the sea-bed in the zone referred to in that article without its approval would result in an infringement within its territory or territorial sea of the laws and regulations referred to in that article [= customs, fiscal, immigration or sanitary laws and regulations].

Art. 303, para. 2, does give some rights to the coastal State. But the content of these rights is far from being clear, as the wording of the provision gets entangled in mysterious complications. As provided for in Art. 33, in the contiguous zone, which is located between the external limit of the territorial sea (12 n.m., in the case of most States) and 24 n.m., the coastal State may exercise control for customs, fiscal, immigration or sanitary purposes. If literally understood, para. 2 suggests that the removal of archaeological and historical objects located in the contiguous zone can determine a violation of domestic provisions relating to matters which have little or nothing to do with the cultural heritage, such as smuggling, public health and immigration. Under the UNCLOS logic, it is only as a consequence of the competences that it can already exercise in the fight against cigarette smugglers, clandestine immigrants and infectious patients that the coastal State can exercise some other competences for the protection of the underwater cultural heritage located within 12 n.m. from the shore! The wisdom of such a logic, that implies that underwater cultural heritage cannot be protected *per se*, is not fully convincing, to say the least.

Other problems arise from the wording of para. 2, if literally understood. The

---

6 I.C.J., *Reports*, 1969, para. 85 of the judgment. According to the arbitral award rendered on 16 November 1957 in the *Lake Lanoux* case (France v. Spain), the obligations to negotiate an agreement "take very diverse forms and have a scope which varies according to the manner in which they are defined and according to the procedures intended for their execution; but the reality of the obligations thus undertaken is incontestable and sanctions can be applied in the event, for example, of unjustified breaking off of the discussions, abnormal delays, disregard of the agreed procedures, systematic refusals to take into consideration adverse proposals of interests, and, more generally, in cases of violation of the rules of good faith" (*International Law Reports*, 1957, p. 128).

7 The question of the regime of State vessels and aircraft will not be discussed here (but see *infra*, the paper by R. Garabello). According to certain States, such as the United States, the flag State retains title indefinitely to its sunken craft, wherever it is located, unless title has been expressly abandoned or transferred by it.

coastal State, which is empowered to prevent and sanction the "removal from the sea-bed" of objects of an archaeological and historical nature, is apparently defenceless if such objects, instead of being removed, are simply destroyed in the very place where they have been found.[8] Again, it is difficult to subscribe to the logic of such a conclusion. All the textual complications of Art. 303, para. 2, are probably due to the obsession of the drafters to avoid any words that might give the impression of some kind of coastal State jurisdiction beyond the territorial sea (*horror jurisdictionis*, to say it in Latin). Rather than laying down a substantive regime to deal with a new concern, such as the protection of the underwater cultural heritage, the UNCLOS seems more interested in playing with abstractions, like the preservation of the right balance between the jurisdiction of the coastal State and the freedom of the other States.

In any case, even if the spectre of cigarette smugglers, clandestine immigrants and infectious patients does not seem the ideal way to transmit the message, from Art. 303, para. 2, the conclusion may be drawn that the coastal State can establish a 24-mile so-called archaeological zone where it can apply its legislation for the aim of protecting the relevant objects.[9]

C) The Benefit of Mankind as a Whole

A specific provision of the UNCLOS (Art. 149) deals with the underwater cultural heritage found on the seabed and ocean floor beyond the limits of national jurisdiction (the so-called Area):

> All objects of an archaeological and historical nature found in the Area shall be preserved or disposed of for the benefit of mankind as a whole, particular regard being paid to the preferential rights of the State or country of origin, or the State of cultural origin, or the State of historical and archaeological origin.

Art. 149 appears rather vague in its content and devoid of details that could ensure its practical application. It however shows a preference for those uses of archaeological and historical objects that promote the "benefit of mankind as a whole". Private interests, such as the search for and use of the objects for trade and personal gain, are given little weight, if any.

Some categories of States which have a link with the objects (namely, the State of cultural origin, the State of historical and archaeological origin, the State or country of origin *tout court*[10]) are given preferential rights, although Art. 149 does not specify the content of these rights and the manner in which they should be harmonized with the concept of "benefit of mankind as a whole".

---

[8] Destroyed by a company holding a license for oil exploitation, for instance.

[9] In fact, a number of countries have already created such a zone.

[10] The wording of Art. 149 gives rise to some textual doubts. Should the State of historical origin be at the same time also the State of archaeological origin to get preferential rights? What is the meaning of the word "country" in the expression "State or country of origin"? Why is "country" not used in the cases of cultural, historical and archaeological origin?

D) A Legal Vacuum

While two UNCLOS provisions apply to the space within 12 (or 24) n.m. and to the Area, there is no clarification in the UNCLOS about the regime relating to the archaeological and historical objects found on the continental shelf or in the exclusive economic zone,[11] that is the space located between the 12-mile limit (or 24-mile limit if an archaeological zone has been established) and the Area. It is however clear that the rights of the coastal State on the continental shelf are limited to the exploration and exploitation of the relevant "natural resources", as explicitly stated in Art. 77, para. 1, of UNCLOS, and cannot be easily extended to man-made objects,[12] such as those belonging to the underwater cultural heritage.[13]

This legal vacuum greatly threatens the protection of cultural heritage, as it brings into the picture the abstract idea of freedom of the seas.[14] It could easily lead to a "first come, first served" approach. Availing himself of the principle of freedom of the sea, any person on board any ship could explore the continental shelf adjacent to any coastal State, bring the archaeological and historical objects to the surface, become their owner under a domestic legislation (in most cases, the flag State legislation[15]), carry the objects into certain countries and sell them on the private market. If this were the case, there would be no guarantee that the objects are disposed of for the public benefit rather than for private commercial gain or personal benefit. Nor could a State which has a direct cultural link with the objects prevent the continuous pillage of its

---

11 The reference to the exclusive economic zone seems redundant (and will be hereinafter omitted), as the objects of archaeological or historical nature are more likely to lie on the seabed than to float in the waters of the exclusive economic zone. However, during the negotiations for the CPUCH, the highly hypothetical example was made of a bottle containing a message by the Italian national hero, Mr. Giuseppe Garibaldi, which is found floating in the exclusive economic zone of the United States or Uruguay, countries where Mr. Garibaldi had lived in certain periods of his life. Embarking on another effort of imagination, one could also think of an ancient little statue which has been eaten by a fish or cetacean swimming in the exclusive economic zone.

12 As also stated by the International Law Commission in the commentary to the relevant provision of the draft Convention on the continental shelf: "It is clearly understood that the rights of the coastal State do not cover objects such as wrecked ships and their cargos (including bullion) lying on the seabed or covered by the sand and the subsoil" (U.N., *Yearbook of the International Law Commission*, 1956, vol. 2, p. 298).

13 It seems too eccentric to assume that archaeological and historical objects which are found embedded in the sand or encrusted with sedentary living organisms can be likened to natural resources. See, however, *infra*, the paper by T. Scovazzi on *The Application of "Salvage Law and Other Rules of Admiralty" to the Underwater Cultural Heritage: Some Relevant Cases*, para. 6 C.

14 Art. 59 UNCLOS (*Basis for the resolution of conflicts regarding the attribution of rights and jurisdiction*), that is the provision on the so-called residual rights in the exclusive economic zone, should also be taken into consideration. Under Art 59, "in cases where this Convention does not attribute rights or jurisdiction to the coastal State or to other States within the exclusive economic zone, and a conflict arises between the interests of the coastal State and any other State or States, the conflict should be resolved on the basis of equity and in the light of all the relevant circumstances, taking into account the respective importance of the interests involved to the parties as well as to the international community as a whole". If this were the case, the CPUCH regime could be seen as the application of UNCLOS Art. 59, as far as the underwater cultural heritage within the exclusive economic zone is concerned.

15 The problems posed by flags of convenience should also be taken into consideration.

historical heritage. The danger of freedom of fishing for underwater cultural heritage is far from being merely theoretical, as a number of instances show.[16]

During the negotiations for the UNCLOS some countries were ready to extend, under certain conditions, the jurisdiction of the coastal State to the underwater cultural heritage found on the continental shelf. For instance, an informal proposal submitted in 1980 by Cape Verde, Greece, Italy, Malta, Portugal, Tunisia and Yugoslavia provided as follows:

> The Coastal State may exercise jurisdiction, while respecting the rights of identifiable owners, over any objects of an archaeological and historical nature on or under its continental shelf for the purpose of research, recovery and protection. However, particular regard shall be paid to the preferential rights of the State or country of origin, or the State of cultural origin, or the State of historical and archaeological origin, in case of sale or any other disposal, resulting in the removal of such objects out of the Coastal State.[17]

The rejection of this kind of proposal, due to the already mentioned fear of creeping jurisdiction by coastal States (*horror jurisdictionis*),[18] led to the legal vacuum resulting from the present UNCLOS regime.

E) An Invitation to Looting

The danger of uncontrolled activities is aggravated by Art. 303, para. 3, UNCLOS, which subjects the general obligations of protection of archaeological and historical objects and international cooperation to a completely different set of rules:

> Nothing in this article affects the rights of identifiable owners, the law of salvage and other rules of admiralty, or laws and practices with respect to cultural exchanges.

In fact, salvage law and other rules of admiralty are given an overarching status by the UNCLOS. If there is a conflict between the objective to protect the underwater cultural heritage, on the one hand, and the application of salvage law and other rules of admiralty, on the other, the latter prevail, as they are not affected by any of the paragraphs of Art. 303.[19]

There is no clarification in the UNCLOS about what the expression "the law of salvage and other rules of admiralty" means. In many countries, the notion of salvage ("sauvetage", in French) is only related to the attempts to save a ship or property carried by it from imminent marine peril on behalf of its owners. But it has

---

16 See *infra*, the paper by T. Scovazzi on *The Application of "Salvage Law and Other Rules of Admiralty" to the Underwater Cultural Heritage: Some Relevant Cases.*

17 Informal proposal by Cape Verde, Greece, Italy, Malta, Portugal, Tunisia and Yugoslavia (UN doc. A/CONF.62/C.2/Informal Meeting/43/Rev. 3 of 27 March 1980).

18 *Supra*, para. 2 B.

19 Luckily enough, the drafters of the UNCLOS did not subject to salvage law and other rules of admiralty the heritage found in the Area which falls under Art. 149.

never been intended to apply to submerged archaeological sites or to ancient sunken ships which, far from being in peril, have been definitively lost. On the contrary, in a minority of other countries of common law tradition the concept of salvage law has been enlarged by some court decisions to cover activities which have very little to do with the traditional sphere of salvage. Several cases decided by domestic courts in the United States of America give the idea of the result that the application of this kind of rules is likely to determine. As specifically clarified elsewhere in this book,[20] "the law of salvage and other rules of admiralty" (including the law of finds), simply means the application of a first-come-first-served or freedom-of-fishing approach which can only serve the interest of private commercial gain.

The fact remains that the bodies of "the law of salvage and other rules of admiralty" are today typical of a few common law systems, but are complete strangers to the legislation of other countries. Yet, because of the lack of corresponding concepts, the very words "salvage" and "admiralty" cannot be properly translated into languages different from English. In the French official text of the UNCLOS they are rendered with expressions ("droit de récupérer des épaves et (...) autres règles du droit maritime") which have a broader and different meaning.

This worsens the already sad picture of Art. 303 of the UNCLOS. Does this provision, while apparently protecting the underwater cultural heritage, strengthen a regime which results in the destination of much of this heritage for commercial purposes? Does Art. 303 give an overarching status to a body of rules that cannot provide any sensible tool for the protection of the heritage in question? The doubt is far from being trivial.

F) Prospects for a Better Regime

It would be difficult to find elsewhere so many obscurities and contradictions as can be found in the UNCLOS regime of the underwater cultural heritage.[21] If the protection of the underwater cultural heritage is to be achieved "for the benefit of mankind as a whole" (as stated in Art. 149), why are salvage law and the other rules of admiralty, which only serve the purpose of private benefit and commercial gain, granted an overarching status (as stated in Art. 303, para. 3)? If the underwater cultural heritage is to be protected everywhere (as stated in Art. 303, para. 1), why is an evident gap left open as regards the heritage located on the continental shelf?[22]

---

[20] See the paper by T. Scovazzi on *The Application of "Salvage Law and Other Rules of Admiralty" to the Underwater Cultural Heritage: Some Relevant Cases.*

[21] "The regimes for underwater archaeology resulting from the Convention are complicated and not complete" (Nordquist, Rosenne & Sohn, *United Nations Convention on the Law of the Sea 1982 – A Commentary*, vol. V, Dordrecht, 1989, p. 161).

[22] The fact that the UNCLOS regime is far from being satisfactory seems implicitly acknowledged in the declaration made by the Netherlands on 28 June 1996 on ratification of the UNCLOS: "Jurisdiction over objects of an archaeological and historical nature found at sea is limited to articles 149 and 303 of the Convention. The Kingdom of the Netherlands does however consider that there may be a need to further develop, in international cooperation, the international law on the protection of the underwater cultural heritage".

As a further surprise, it may be added that prospects to find some remedy to the unsatisfactory regime of the UNCLOS could be drawn from para. 4 of Art. 303 itself. Under this paragraph, Art. 303 does not prejudice "other international agreements and rules of international law regarding the protection of objects of an archaeological and historical nature".[23] There is no reason why future agreements, such as the CPUCH, should not be covered by this provision. In other words, the UNCLOS itself seems to allow the drafting of more specific treaty regimes which can ensure a better protection of the underwater cultural heritage. The UNCLOS itself seems to encourage the filling of the gaps and the solution of the contradictions that it has generated.

3. The CPUCH as a Defensive Tool

Many States feel today that the CPUCH is a reasonable defensive tool against the results of the contradictory and counterproductive regime of the UNCLOS. The basic elements of such a defensive strategy are three, namely: the elimination of the undesirable effects of the law of salvage and finds; the exclusion of a "first come, first served" approach for the heritage found on the continental shelf; the strengthening of regional cooperation.

A) The Rejection of the Law of Salvage and Finds

While most countries participating in the negotiations for the CPUCH concurred in the rejection of the application of the law of salvage and finds to underwater cultural heritage, a minority of States were not prepared to accept an absolute ban. To achieve a reasonable compromise, Art. 4 (*Relationship to law of salvage and law of finds*) of the CPUCH provides as follows:

> Any activity relating to underwater cultural heritage to which this Convention applies shall not be subject to the law of salvage or law of finds, unless it:
> (a) is authorized by the competent authorities, and
> (b) is in full conformity with this Convention, and
> (c) ensures that any recovery of the underwater cultural heritage achieves its maximum protection.

This provision is to be understood in connection with Art. 2, para. 7, of the CPUCH ("underwater cultural heritage shall not be commercially exploited") and with all the rules contained in the annex, which form an integral part of the CPUCH. In particular, under Rule 2 of the Annex,

[23] Under para. 3, Art. 303 does not affect salvage law and other rules of admiralty. Under para. 4, Art. 303 is without prejudice to other international agreements regarding the protection of objects of an archaeological and historical nature. If there is a conflict between salvage law and an international agreement covered by para. 4, which one would prevail? To try to give an answer to the question, which is a consequence of the plethora of contradictions embedded in Art. 303, does not seem a sensible exercise.

the commercial exploitation of underwater cultural heritage for trade or speculation or its irretrievable dispersal is fundamentally incompatible with the protection and proper management of underwater cultural heritage. Underwater cultural heritage shall not be traded, sold, bought or bartered as commercial goods.

The practical effect of the CPUCH regime is the prevention of all the undesirable effects of the application of the law of salvage and finds. Freedom of fishing for archaeological and historical objects is definitely banned. This seemed generally acceptable to all the States participating in the negotiation.

B) The Exclusion of a "First Come, First Served" Approach for the Heritage Found on the Continental Shelf

The majority of the countries participating in the negotiation were ready to extend the jurisdiction of the coastal State to the underwater cultural heritage found on the continental shelf or in the exclusive economic zone. However, a minority of States assumed that the extension of the jurisdiction of coastal States would have altered the delicate balance embodied in the UNCLOS with respect to the rights and obligations of the coastal State and the other States beyond the limit of the territorial sea. Such a difference of positions proved to be a thorny question.

During the negotiations, the chairman of Working Group 1 of the Group of Governmental Experts, trying to find a way out of the deadlock rather than merely recording the statements and re-statements of the opposing positions,[24] undertook to produce a tentative proposal.[25] It was based on a three-step procedure: reporting of planned activities or discoveries, consultations on how to ensure the effective protection of the underwater cultural heritage, provisional protection measures. The coastal State was entitled to coordinate the consultations among the States which declared their interest,[26] unless it invited another State to act as coordinating State. Pending the outcome of the consultations, all States Parties had to comply with the provisional protection measures adopted by the coordinating State.

During the same session, a "non-paper" was proposed by three unnamed delegations as a basis for discussion. Although different for several aspects from the

---

[24] See *Final Report of the Third Meeting of Governmental Experts on the Draft Convention on the Protection of Underwater Cultural Heritage*, UNESCO doc. CLT-2000/CONF.201/CLD.7, para. 4 of Annex 1.

[25] UNESCO doc. WG1-NP3 of 6 July 2000 (reproduced also in the doc. quoted *supra*, note 24).

[26] To avoid the ghost of jurisdiction (*horror jurisdictionis*), the coastal State was not called coastal State, but was given a special responsibility under the following wording: "Taking into account its interest in avoiding unjustified interference with the exercise of sovereign rights and jurisdiction in its exclusive economic zone or on its continental shelf in accordance with international law, a State Party has a special responsibility for the co-ordination of activities directed at the underwater cultural heritage and for the protection of any discoveries made in its exclusive economic zone or on its continental shelf" (Art. D, para. 2, of the tentative proposals of the chairman of Working Group 1).

proposal of the chairman of Working Group 1, the non-paper was also based on reporting and consultation.[27] It introduced two important elements, namely: that the States entitled to participate in the consultations were those which had a "verifiable link" with the underwater cultural heritage concerned; and that the coastal State[28] was entitled to impose requirements not in its own interest but on behalf of all States Parties as a whole.

Both proposals were based on a spirit of compromise and showed an effort to find reasonable solutions based on procedural mechanisms, without insisting on a mere extension of the jurisdiction of the coastal State. Both proposals led to the present Arts. 9 and 10 of the CPUCH. It is regrettable that, despite all the efforts to reach a reasonable compromise, a consensus could not be achieved.

It would be a difficult task to dwell upon all the nuances of provisions, such as Arts. 9 and 10, resulting from a stratification of proposals, counter-proposals, last-minute changes and "constructive ambiguities" which do not lead to an easily readable text. The essence of the regime is the three-step procedure (reporting, consultations, urgent measures) it sets forth.[29]

As regards reporting, the CPUCH bans secret activities or discoveries.[30] States Parties shall require their nationals or vessels flying their flag to report activities or discoveries to them. If the activity or discovery is located in the exclusive economic zone or on the continental shelf of another State Party, the CPUCH sets forth two alternative solutions:

(i) States Parties shall require the national or the master of the vessel to report such discovery or activity to them and to that other State Party;
(ii) alternatively, a State Party shall require the national or master of the vessel to report such discovery or activity to it and shall ensure the rapid and effective transmission of such report to all other States Parties (Art. 9, para. 1, b).[31]

While the wording leaves a certain margin of ambiguity, the "State Party" mentioned in sub-para. (ii) is to be understood as the State to which the "national" belongs or the State of which the "vessel" flies the flag.[32] This interpretation is in

[27] UNESCO doc. WG.1/NP.1 of 5 July 2000 (reproduced also in the doc. quoted above, note 24).

[28] Again, the expression "coastal State" was not used in the "non-paper" either.

[29] Under Arts. 11 and 12 CPUCH a similar (although not identical) three-step procedure applies to the underwater cultural heritage found in the Area.

[30] For obvious reasons, the principle of transparency of information is limited to the competent authorities of States Parties: "Information shared between States Parties, or between UNESCO and States Parties, regarding the discovery or location of underwater cultural heritage shall, to the extent compatible with their national legislation, be kept confidential and reserved to competent authorities of States Parties as long as the disclosure of such information might endanger or otherwise put at risk the preservation of such underwater cultural heritage" (Art. 19, para. 3).

[31] On depositing its instrument of ratification, acceptance, approval or accession, a State Party shall declare the manner in which reports will be transmitted (Art. 9, para. 2).

[32] The ambiguity lies in the fact that the "State Party" in question could be understood as the coastal State.

conformity with the preparatory works of the CPUCH.[33] Information is also notified to the Director-General of UNESCO who shall promptly make it available to all States Parties (Art. 9, paras. 4 and 5).

As regards consultations, the coastal State[34] shall consult all States Parties which have declared their interest in being consulted on how to ensure the effective protection of the underwater cultural heritage in question (Art. 10, para. 3, a, and Art. 9, para. 5). The CPUCH provides that any State Party may declare its interest in being consulted and that "such declaration shall be based on a verifiable link, especially a cultural, historical or archaeological link, to the underwater cultural heritage concerned".[35]

The coastal State[36] shall coordinate the consultations, unless it expressly declares that it does not wish to do so, in which case the States Parties which have declared an interest in being consulted shall appoint another coordinating State (Art. 10, para. 3, b). The co-ordinating State shall implement the measures of protection which have been agreed by the consulting States and may conduct any necessary preliminary research on the underwater cultural heritage (Art. 10, para. 5).

As regards urgent measures, Art. 10, para. 4, CPUCH provides as follows:

> Without prejudice to the right of all States Parties to protect underwater cultural heritage by way of all practicable measures taken in accordance with international law to prevent immediate danger to the underwater cultural heritage, including looting, the Coordinating State may take all practicable measures, and/or issue any necessary authorizations in conformity with this Convention and, if necessary prior to consultations, to prevent any immediate danger to the underwater cultural heritage, whether arising from human activities or any other cause, including looting. In taking such measures assistance may be requested from other States Parties.

The right of the coordinating State to adopt urgent measures is the cornerstone of the CPUCH regime. It would have been illusory to subordinate this right to the conclusion of consultations that are normally expected to last for some time. It would also have been illusory to grant this right to the flag State, considering the

---

33 See *infra*, the paper by R. Garabello. A draft resolution submitted by the Russian Federation and the United Kingdom and endorsed by the United States tried to clarify the point by proposing the following wording: "When the discovery or activity is located in the exclusive economic zone or on the continental shelf of another State Party: (i) a State Party shall require its national or the master of a vessel flying its flag to report such discovery or activity to it and to that other State Party; (ii) alternatively, a State Party shall require its national or the master of a vessel flying its flag to report such discovery or activity to it and shall ensure the rapid and effective transmission of such reports to all other States Parties" (UNESCO doc. 31 C/COM.IV/DR.5 of 26 October 2001). The draft resolution was not adopted.

34 Here and everywhere else, the CPUCH avoids the words "coastal State" (because of the already mentioned *horror jurisdictionis*) and chooses other expressions, such as the "State Party in whose exclusive economic zone or on whose continental shelf" the activity or discovery is located.

35 The attempt to define what is a "verifiable link" was not made.

36 See above, note 34.

risk of activities carried out by vessels flying the flag of non-Parties or a flag of convenience.[37] By definition, in a case of urgency a determined State must be entitled to take immediate measures without losing time in any procedural requirements.[38]

The CPUCH clearly sets forth that in coordinating consultations, taking measures, conducting preliminary research and issuing authorizations, the coordinating State acts "on behalf of the States Parties as a whole and not in its own interest" (Art. 10, para. 6). Any such action shall not in itself constitute a basis for the assertion of any preferential or jurisdictional rights not provided for in international law, including the UNCLOS.

In any case, "a State Party in whose exclusive economic zone or on whose continental shelf underwater cultural heritage is located has the right to prohibit or authorize any activity directed at such heritage to prevent interference with its sovereign rights or jurisdiction as provided for by international law including the United Nations Convention on the Law of the Sea" (Art. 10, para. 2, CPUCH). This could mean that the coastal State can exercise broader rights if a wreck is embedded in the sand or is encrusted with oysters, molluscs or other sedentary living resources over which it already exercises sovereign rights under the UNCLOS provisions on the continental shelf.[39]

C) The Strengthening of Regional Cooperation

The CPUCH devotes one of its provisions (Art. 6) to bilateral, regional or other multilateral agreements:

> 1. States Parties are encouraged to enter into bilateral, regional or other multilateral agreements or develop existing agreements, for the preservation of underwater cultural heritage. All such agreements shall be in full conformity with the provisions of this Convention and shall not dilute its universal character. States may, in such agreements, adopt rules and regulations which would ensure better protection of underwater cultural heritage than those adopted in this Convention.

---

37 The present experience of the regulation of fisheries proves the dangers posed by vessels flying flags of convenience and engaging in so-called IUU (illegal, unreported, unregulated) fishing.

38 On the contrary, the draft resolution submitted by the Russian Federation and the United Kingdom and endorsed by the United States (quoted above, note 33) subordinated the right to adopt measures to prevent immediate danger to a specific condition: "(...) but in any event prompt assistance shall be requested from the State Party that is the flag State of the vessel engaged in such activities".

39 The majority of countries participating in the negotiation rejected the assumption, put forward by the United States of America, that the only possibility for the coastal State to protect the underwater cultural heritage was based on its right to prevent interferences with its sovereign rights or jurisdiction as provided for by international law. This assumption is in principle unacceptable, as it implies that oysters and other equally respectable living resources are more important than the cultural heritage. It is also dangerous, as it can be interpreted in the sense that the salvor can retain the wreck after having given all the oysters to the coastal State!

2. The Parties to such bilateral, regional or other multilateral agreements may invite States with a verifiable link, especially a cultural, historical or archaeological link, to the underwater cultural heritage concerned to join such agreements.[40]

Art. 6 opens the way to a multiple-level protection of underwater cultural heritage. This corresponds to what has already happened in the field of the protection of the natural environment where treaties having a world sphere of application are often followed by treaties concluded at the regional and sub-regional level. The key to coordination between treaties applicable at different levels is the criterium of the better protection, in the sense that the regional and sub-regional treaties are concluded to ensure better protection than those adopted at a more general level.

The possibility to conclude regional agreements should be carefully considered by the States bordering enclosed or semi-enclosed seas which are characterized by a particular kind of underwater cultural heritage, such as the Mediterranean, the Baltic, the Caribbean. For instance, in a declaration adopted in Siracusa, Italy, on 10 March 2001,[41] the participants to an academic conference stressed that "the Mediterranean basin is characterized by the traces of ancient civilisations which flourished along its shores and, having developed the first seafaring techniques, established close relationships with each other" and that "the Mediterranean cultural heritage is unique in that it embodies the common historical and cultural roots of many civilizations". They consequently invited the Mediterranean countries to "study the possibility of adopting a regional convention that enhances cooperation in the investigation and protection of the Mediterranean submarine cultural heritage and sets forth the relevant rights and obligations".

4. Concluding Remarks

It is not likely that any sensible prospects for protecting the underwater cultural heritage may be drawn from the contradictory and counterproductive regime embodied in the UNCLOS, at least if it were literally read. The drafters of the UNCLOS could not forecast the subsequent progress in underwater technologies and the diffusion of treasure hunting activities in many seas of the world. They probably did not feel that the protection of the underwater cultural heritage was to be considered an urgent need.

For its innovative and pragmatic character, the CPUCH is a major step forward in the progressive development of international law. It has been criticized for the

[40] Under Art. 6, para. 3, the CPUCH "shall not alter the rights and obligations of State Parties regarding the protection of sunken vessels, arising from other bilateral, regional or other multilateral agreements concluded before its adoption, and, in particular, those that are in conformity with the purposes of" the CPUCH.

[41] Text in this volume, document No. 17.

reason that, irrespective of Art. 3,[42] it departs from the regime embodied in the UNCLOS.[43] Perhaps it partially departs. But it must also be stressed that the UNCLOS regime is so insufficient that it was impossible to protect the underwater cultural heritage without partially departing from it.

Variations from the UNCLOS regime are not a novelty. After the adoption of the UNCLOS, two multilateral treaties have been concluded which apparently "implement" the UNCLOS, namely the 1994 Agreement Relating to the Implementation of Part XI of the UNCLOS and the 1995 Agreement for the Implementation of the Provisions of the UNCLOS Relating to the Conservation and Management of Straddling Fish Stocks and Highly Migratory Fish Stocks. In fact, as both agreements depart from the UNCLOS, the politically prudent label of an "implementing agreement" can be considered as a euphemism for the word "amendment" which would have been more correct from a substantial point of view. The reality is that, as it is itself a product of time, the UNCLOS cannot stop the passing of time. It is therefore subject to a process of evolution in the light of subsequent international practice.

The establishment of an effective protection regime for the underwater cultural heritage cannot be seen as an encroachment on the principle of the freedom of the sea. Nor is it the creation of other jurisdictional zones. It is difficult to see how rules and entitlements on the underwater cultural heritage found on the continental shelf could affect navigation in the superjacent waters. The concept of freedom of the sea is today to be understood not in an abstract way, but in the context of the present range of marine activities and in relation to the other potentially conflicting uses and interests. Also the idea that the coastal State can exercise rights on the oil found in its continental shelf corresponded, when it was initially proposed,[44] to an encroachment on the freedom of the high seas. Evident encroachments on the freedom of fishing on the high seas can easily be found in the above mentioned 1995 Straddling and Highly Migratory Fish Stocks Agreement, which introduces the most innovative idea that States which persistently undermine the measures agreed upon by the others can be excluded from an activity taking place on the high seas. In this case, a new regime was considered a necessary tool to promote the conservation and sound management of living marine resources and, as such, was found reasonable by the great majority of States. Abstract principles and fears of creeping jurisdiction (*horror jurisdictionis*) were not sufficient to prevent the evolution of international law of the sea and the drafting of reasonable legal responses to emerging needs.

---

[42] "Nothing in this Convention shall prejudice the rights, jurisdiction and duties of States under international law, including the United Nations Convention on the Law of the Sea. This Convention shall be interpreted and applied in the context of and in a manner consistent with international law, including the United Nations Convention on the Law of the Sea".

[43] See, for example, the intervention made on 28 November 2001 by the delegate of the Russian Federation, Mr. Tarabrin, at the United Nations General Assembly.

[44] See the Presidential Proclamation concerning the policy of the United States with respect to the natural resources of the subsoil and seabed of the continental shelf, adopted on 28 September 1945 (the so-called Truman Proclamation).

Similarly effective solutions are today required with respect to the underwater cultural heritage. The protection of the underwater cultural heritage is endangered by an increasing number of unreported and unregulated activities which are the consequence of the improvement of underwater instruments and technologies. Should there remain a freedom-of-fishing-type regime for objects of an archaeological and historical nature? Do they deserve less protection than fish? The CPUCH provides sensible answers to both questions.

Chapter 2

THE APPLICATION OF "SALVAGE LAW AND OTHER RULES OF ADMIRALTY" TO THE UNDERWATER CULTURAL HERITAGE: SOME RELEVANT CASES

Tullio Scovazzi

1. A RATHER UNCONVINCING STATEMENT (TO SAY THE LEAST)

In 2001, Mr. Patrick Griggs, in his capacity of President of the Comité Maritime International (CMI), wrote a letter to Mr. Koïchiro Matsuura, the Director General of UNESCO. Referring, *inter alia*, to Art. 4 ("Relationship to law of salvage and law of finds") of the draft Convention on the Protection of the Underwater Cultural Heritage, that at that time was being negotiated, Mr. Griggs made the following remarks:

> We support the intent of Article 4, which deals with the relationship of the law of salvage to the Draft Convention. The CMI is firmly of the opinion that the law of salvage is not incompatible with the goals of the Draft Convention. In our view, there is no reason why the law of salvage should be deemed a threat to the protection and preservation of underwater cultural heritage. The law of salvage has long had international recognition and is explicitly recognized in Article 303 of the Law of the Convention. Although we support Article 4, we are concerned that Article 4(a) is ambiguous as to what entity may be deemed "the competent authority" and that Article 4 could be applied to restrict legitimate salvage operations which are otherwise in conformity with international law.
>
> I would be most grateful if you could advise the delegates to the General Conference of our concerns.[1]

[1] The letter is reproduced in Comité Maritime International, *Yearbook*, 2001, p. 620.

Roberta Garabello and Tullio Scovazzi (eds.), The Protection of the Underwater Cultural Heritage, 19–79.

As requested, the letter by the President of the CMI was duly brought to the attention of the delegates to the UNESCO General Conference. However, it produced no tangible results. Art. 4 of the draft Convention remained unchanged.[2] The great majority of delegates, with all due respect to be paid to the CMI, were unable to agree with the statement that "there is no reason why the law of salvage should be deemed a threat to the protection and preservation of underwater cultural heritage".

Yet the statement made by the CMI seems rather unconvincing, to say the least. Most of the instances hereunder presented show how many reasons there are to believe that the law of salvage and the other rules of admiralty law do correspond to a serious threat to the protection of the underwater cultural heritage.

2. The Melqart of Sciacca

In January 1955 a 38 cm high bronze statue accidentally became entangled in nets being dragged by the *Angelina Madre*, a fishing vessel flying the Italian flag. The recovery of the artefact occurred on the Italian continental shelf, at about 20 n.m. from the Italian coast south of the island of Sicily.[3]

At first the statue was not attributed importance. Without dissent of any sort, it was taken by one of the sailors, Mr. Santo Vitale, to his home in the city of Sciacca. It was then displayed for some months in a small grocery shop managed by Mr. Calogero Vitale, father of the sailor. It was later sold to a neighbour, Mr. Giovanni Tovagliari, or perhaps (the point has never been clarified) bartered for some flasks of wine. Mr. Tovagliari was the first to wonder whether the statue might be of historical importance and submitted it for examination to Mr. Stefano Chiappisi, an expert in history. Mr. Chiappisi's research ascertained that the statue was a very rare historical relic of the Phoenician civilization (9th to 11th century B.C.), representing a deity that was probably Melqart, the god of the sea. It was similar, but perhaps more precious because of its greater height, to the only two other examples in existence in the world: the Adad, or Ba-Al, of Minet el Beida, found in Syria and now exposed in the Louvre in Paris; and the Addad of Pelizeus, or Resef, preserved in the museum of Hildesheim, Germany.

Learning of the fortunate finding, the Superintendent of Antiquities of the Province of Agrigento requested that the Melqart of Sciacca (as the statue came to be called) be handed over to him, as the property of the State. Under Italian legislation, all objects belonging to the cultural heritage which are fortuitously found belong to the State.[4] But Mr. Tovagliari, to ensure the Melqart for the city's cultural heritage, donated it to the Municipality of Sciacca. The Municipality accepted the

---

2 See below the paper by Garabello.

3 On the statue see Camerata Scovazzo, *Presentazione della statuetta bronzea di Reshef (Melqart)*, in Li Vigni & Tusa (a cura di), *Strumenti per la protezione del patrimonio culturale marino – Aspetti archeologici*, Milano, 2002, p. 1.

4 Law 1 June 1939, No. 1089, and (today) Legislative Decree 29 October 1999, No. 490 (*Gazzetta Ufficiale* suppl. to No. 302 of 27 December 1999). The finder is entitled to a reward.

donation and entrusted the Melqart to a respected clergymen, Mgr. Aurelio Cassar, who jealously cared for the statue in the historical section of the municipality's library, opposing any requests of the Superintendent.

At this point, Mr. Michele Scaglione, the owner of the *Angelina Madre*, intervened in the matter. He maintained that the sphere of application of the Italian legislation on the cultural heritage was limited to the Italian territory and territorial sea (which was, at that time, 6 n.m. in breadth). Relying on what could be considered a sort of law of finds, he asked that the Melqart be declared his property, as a *res nullius* having been found by his vessel on the high seas.

The subsequent litigation to determine the ownership of the statue involved, on opposing sides, the State, the Municipality of Sciacca, Mr. Scaglione and the heirs of Mr. Tovagliari (the latter maintaining that Mr. Tovagliari, who in the meantime had died, had not donated the Melqart to the Municipality but had only entrusted it for safekeeping). The case was settled on 9 January 1963[5] by an interesting, albeit questionable, decision whereby the Tribunal of Sciacca found that the Melqart belonged to the State.

The Tribunal held that a ship flying the Italian flag is to be considered as a part of the Italian territory. The nets of a fishing vessel flying the Italian flag are a part of the vessel and, consequently, also a part of the Italian territory. This meant that the Melqart, having been enmeshed in the nets of an Italian fishing vessel, was to be treated as if it had been found in the Italian territory with the consequent application of the Italian legislation which granted to the State the ownership of all the cultural heritage fortuitously found.

Taking into consideration the public interest in protecting the cultural heritage,[6] the practical result obtained by the decision can be appreciated. In facing a case for which no precedents were available, the Tribunal avoided the application of a first-come-first-served or freedom-of-fishing approach which would have only served the private interests of the shipowner.

However, looking at the general aspects of the matter, the legal principles applied by the Tribunal can hardly be subscribed. If the Melqart had been recovered by the nets (or whatever other machinery) of an American treasure hunting vessel, the United States legislation, that is the law of finds, would have become applicable and would have played for the benefit of the treasure hunter and his auction house.[7]

3. The Dutch East India Company Vessels

A) The Agreement between Australia and the Netherlands

In the 17th and 18th centuries the ships of the Dutch East India Company (*Vereenigde Oostindische Compagnie*, VOC) used to sail from Europe to the East

---

5 The decision can be read in *Il Foro Italiano*, 1963, I, p. 1317.

6 Today the Melqart can be found at the Regional Archaeological Museum of Palermo.

7 See below, paras. 6 and 7.

Indies (Indonesia) using the quickest route.[8] After doubling the Cape of Good Hope, they followed an east-bound route to take advantage of the winds. In the vicinity of the western coast of Australia, the ships steered north to reach the East Indies. Some of the VOC ships became wrecked off the Australian coast.

In principle, the Netherlands, which under Art. 247 of the Constitution of the Batavian Republic of 1789 is the legal successor of the VOC, claims to retain title over the VOC vessels and wrecks, wherever they are located. However, on 6 November 1972 it signed an Agreement with Australia concerning old Dutch shipwrecks, followed by an Arrangement setting out the guiding principles to determine the disposition of material from the shipwrecks of VOC off the coast of Western Australia.[9] The Arrangement specifically refers to four ships, namely the *Batavia*, the *Vergulde Draeck* (*Gilt Dragon*), the *Zuytdorp* and the *Zeewijk*, which sank respectively in 1629, 1656, 1712 and 1727.

Under the Agreement, all legal titles to the VOC wrecks lying off the coast of the state of Western Australia (a member state of Australia) are transferred from the Netherlands to Australia:

> The Netherlands, as successor to the property and assets of the V.O.C., transfers all its right, title and interest in and to wrecked vessels of the V.O.C. lying on or off the coast of the State of Western Australia and in and to any articles thereof to Australia which shall accept such right, title and interest (Art. 1).

The Netherlands, as the State of historical origin, is granted a "continuing interest" in the articles recovered from the wrecks:

> Australia recognizes that the Netherlands has a continuing interest, particularly for historical and other cultural purposes, in articles recovered from any of the vessels referred to in Art. 1 of this Agreement (Art. 4, para. 1).

Australia is bound to set up a Committee, composed of two persons nominated by each contracting party, "to determine the disposition and subsequent ownership of the recovered articles between the Netherlands, Australia and the State of Western Australia" (Art. 4, para. 2).

Under the Arrangement, the articles removed from the wrecks are distinguished in three categories, depending on whether they are abundant samples (such as coins, bricks, pottery, elephant tusks), less abundant samples (such as cannons, anchors, cannon balls) or rare and even unique objects (such as articles possessed by crew members or passengers, like barber's instruments, navigational instruments, ornaments). The Arrangement aims at the fulfilment of those "historic, educational, scientific and international considerations" which "make the deposition of

---

8 The information given in this paragraph is taken from Johnson, *The Agreement between Australia and the Netherlands Concerning Old Dutch Shipwrecks*, in Camarda & Scovazzi (eds.), *The Protection of Underwater Cultural Heritage – Legal Aspects*, Milano, 2002, p. 21.

9 For the texts see Prott & Srong (eds.), *Background Materials on the Protection of the Underwater Cultural Heritage*, Paris, 1999, p. 19 and 76; also in this volume, document No. 9.

representative collections in the museums of the Netherlands and Australia most desirable". In this regard, it provides as follows:

> In its deliberations the Committee will have, as its general aim, the purpose of ensuring that representative series of statistical samples and sufficient examples of the rarer objects will be deposited in the museums of the Netherlands and Australia to convey the variety and contents of each wreck to both the public and to scholars while, at the same time, ensuring that major projects of scholarly research will not be impeded by over fragmentation of the collection.

Neither the Agreement nor the Arrangement specify the precise legal meaning of the generic expression "off the coast of Western Australia". However, it appears that the *Zuytdorp*, one of the wrecks mentioned in the Arrangement, is approximately located "40 miles north of the mouth of the Murchison River".[10] This implies that the Agreement applies also to the VOC wrecks found on the Australian continental shelf, beyond the limit of the Australian territorial sea.

In 1976 Australia enacted the *Historic Shipwrecks Act* which explicitly applies to the remains of ships of historical significance situated in the "Australian waters" or "in waters above the continental shelf of Australia".[11] Under the Act, the Minister for Communications and the Arts may declare certain shipwrecks and relics to be historic and declare protected zones (not exceeding 100 hectares) around them. Except in accordance with a permit, nobody can damage, interfere with, dispose of or remove a historic shipwreck or relic.

The 1972 Agreement is probably the first international treaty specifically devoted to underwater cultural heritage. It was concluded by two States which had a verifiable link with the heritage in question (the coastal State and the flag State) and which were both committed to its preservation for public research and appreciation. Nowhere does the Agreement pay any consideration to salvors. Yet salvage activities and the consequent first-come-first-served or freedom-of-fishing approach are implictly excluded by the Agreement as radically incompatible with its basic aim.

B) The Salvaging of the Geldermalsen

A different story may be told as regards the materials removed from the wreck of what was later identified as the *Geldermalsen*, a vessel of the VOC which sank in 1752.

As reported in a book written by the salvor himself, Capt. Michael Hatcher[12] (a British national), the wreck was found in the spring of 1985 on Admiral Stellingwerf Reef:

---

[10] This location is given in Schedule 2 annexed to the *Historic Shipwrecks Act 1976* of Australia (in Prott & Srong, *supra* note 9, at 3).

[11] *Ibidem*. The Act does not prejudice the special regime applying to the VOC wrecks off Western Australia under the 1972 bilateral agreement, which is set out as Schedule 1 to the Act.

[12] Hatcher, de Rham & Thorncroft, *The Nanking Cargo*, 1987 (the quotations are taken from the excerpts that are reproduced in Prott & Srong, *supra* note 9, at 83).

> It is in international waters but irritatingly close to Bintan, an island that is now part of Indonesia. It gets its name from a Dutch ship which had hit the Reef in the nineteenth century, but its roll call of victims stretches up to modern times. (...) The dangerous section is not much more than two hundred yards long where, at both ends, the Reef rises almost to the surface. You can stand on the two pinnacles, gazing out to sea as far as your eyes can travel before a wave knocks you off. It is these peaks, some five feet below the surface, which have claimed the lives of so many vessels and so many men.[13]

The wreck of a big vessel, about 36 m long and 10 m wide, was located by the divers.[14] It soon became apparent that she carried large quantities of plates, bowls, tea pots and mugs. The salvor returned to Singapore, the city from which he had previously sailed, taking with him some samples:

> James Spencer, a Christie's Chinese ceramics expert, was summoned to identify the finds. He immediately recognized them as eighteenth-century porcelain".[15]

The salvage operations were soon resumed. The find was amazing:

> The first loose pieces of porcelain (...) came from chests that had been smashed open by the falling cannon. But most of the chests were firmly intact. Indeed they had to be prised open. The first revealed tea bowls and saucers packed very tightly in some brown glutinous substance. It did not take too long for the divers to realize that this was, appropriately enough, tea. As they later learned, tea was the most valuable commodity, and the eighteenth-century merchants had thrown in the porcelain, not as ballast exactly, but very much as run-of-the-mill back-up. (...)
>
> The miracle was that the cargo had remained virtually intact. This was thanks to the tea as much as to the slow sinking of the vessel.[16]

Most of the divers' work was done with the airlift, a machine like a vast vacuum cleaner which sucked out the sand and coral and marine detritus from the crates and the loose porcelain. One diver operated the airlift and another carried the objects by the armful to the lift (a one-meter-square steel box):

> To try and liven up this exhausting work the divers competed to see which pair could pack up the most porcelain in one fifty-minute stint. The record was twelve baskets full of dinner plates, seven hundred pieces in all.[17]

Although rewarding, the work was tedious and exhausting:

> Sometimes, when the airlift had pumped away all the debris, they discovered a

---

13 *Ibidem*, p. 84.

14 The salvor "gave a crew lecture on security: there were to be no letters home. Already his operations on the Reef had attracted gangs of Australian rivals" (*ibidem*, p. 84).

15 *Ibidem*, p. 85.

16 *Ibidem*, p. 86 and 87.

17 *Ibidem*, p. 86.

chest that had been hit by a falling cannon, breaking every single plate or bowl with an identical crack. All the shards were ignored as were most slightly broken objects. There were more than enough in perfect condition. So up they came, the tea bowls and saucers, the soup plates and butter tubs, the jugs and the tureens, virtually all made of blue and white porcelain and covered with the familiar Chinese scenes, of fishermen and pagodas, pine trees and peonies. It became tedious as well as exhausting".[18]

Moving from the cargo hull to the cabins, the salvors discovered better quality porcelain. The officers of the *Geldermalsen* marketed these goods at home through individual sales or presented them to their loved ones. The efforts and the thoughts of the hard-working salvors are very vividly described in the book by Capt. Hatcher:

> By this time they were working hurriedly, hardly examining the chocolate cups and queer-shaped bowls which were later to divide the experts – were they chamber pots or vomit cups? As the weather deteriorated so did the working conditions.[19]

Law scholars are perhaps interested to know that the discoveries promoted the spontaneous elaboration of legal rules by the salvors to deal with the finds:

> Early on, they had learned to be very careful as they washed the porcelain on the barge. Out of mugs and jars could tumble jewels and small statues and glasses. It was agreed that nothing should be held back: everything was to be auctioned. If a diver was fond of a particular object he had found, he could bid for it later. Only the cracked pieces could be retained. In the event most of the divers now have small, but select, collections from the wreck.[20]

Finally, also 126 ingots of gold were found and recovered:

> The gold was the perfect icing on the cake. It proved to be Chinese gold of an hitherto unknown shape, and individual ingots were eventually to sell for over £50,000, well in excess of their bullion value of nearer £2,000. The romance of its discovery, and its unique shape, made it desirable to collectors.[21]

The salvor chose Christie's auction house in Amsterdam to organise the sale of gold ingots and the about 170,000 pieces of Chinese porcelain coming from the wreck, an unprecedented quantity put on the market. Christie's gave to the whole find the name of the "Nanking Cargo". The reasons behind such a name are interesting:

---

18 *Ibidem*, p. 87.

19 *Ibidem*, p. 87.

20 *Ibidem*, p. 87.

21 *Ibidem*, p. 88. "Hatcher was very lucky here. Dutch East Indiamen carried gold on the return to Europe for just twenty-five years after 1735 and only two lost ships had gold on board – the *Enkhuizen* and the *Geldermalsen*" (*ibidem*, p. 90). However, according to the ship's papers, the *Geldermalsen* should have carried 171 ingots. When the 32 survivors of the wreck reached the Netherlands, they were suspected of hiding the gold.

> In the eighteenth century such a cargo of porcelain would be advertized in European cities as coming from Nanking, even though specialists now know it was made further inland in China. Also Nanking had a reassuring oriental sound without being too specific about the actual origin of the porcelain.[22]

The catalogue for the sale was published in December 1985 by Christie's of Amsterdam under the title "The Nanking Cargo: Chinese Export Porcelain and Gold, European Glass and Stoneware, Recovered by Captain Michael Hatcher from a European Merchant Ship Wrecked in the South China Seas". In the meantime, Christie's submitted the porcelain for examination to Dr. Christiaan J.A. Jörg, a historian of the university of Groningen and a recognized authority on the Dutch East India Company porcelain trade. Dr. Jörg found documents in the Dutch archives, including the original packing lists and purchase orders, about a Dutch East Indiaman, the *Geldermalsen*, which was likely to be the wreck salvaged by Capt. Hatcher:

> More to the point, if the wreck could be conclusively proved to be the *Geldermalsen*, the planned sale would go that much better: it really would be the identifiable past come to life again.[23]

Under the advice of Dr. Jörg, a second, speedy dive was undertaken to recover the ship's bell and two bronze cannons, which confirmed the identification of the wreck as the former *Geldermalsen*. Capt. Hatcher was generous enough to donate the ship's bell to a Dutch museum.

Two months before the auction, which took place in April 1986, Dr. Jörg was able to publish a book on the wreck, its history and the objects recovered.[24] The auction was a complete success. The final yield was $16,000,000. Many pieces brought from 10 to 15 times the estimated value in the catalogue.

The objects salvaged from the *Geldermalsen* were dispersed around the world. For example, Bloomingdale's department store purchased over 3,000 pieces of the "Nanking Cargo" to be later advertised and sold to its clients:

> It's a rare opportunity to bring museum quality artifacts into your home. Look for the Nanking Cargo Shop, starting today on the second floor.[25]

The story of wreck of the *Geldermalsen* is one of the best examples of the results that may be expected if the law of salvage and the other rules of admiralty, based on a first-come-first-served or freedom-of-fishing approach, are applied to the underwater cultural heritage. Instructive lessons can be drawn from it.

In 1987 the archaeologist George L. Miller published, under the self-explanatory title "The Second Destruction of the *Geldermalsen*", a review of Dr. Jörg's book.[26]

---

[22] *Ibidem*, p. 88.

[23] *Ibidem*, p. 88.

[24] Jörg, *The Geldermalsen History and Porcelain*, Groningen, 1986.

[25] Advertising by Bloomingdale's in the *Boston Globe* of 21 November 1986.

[26] The review by Miller is published in *The American Neptune*, 1987, p. 275 and is reprinted in Prott & Srong, *supra*, note 9, p. 94.

The reviewer makes a number of considerations "about wrecks and those who destroy such resources either by stripping the artifacts from them or making it profitable by marketing or purchasing objects from such operations".[27] He adds some quite appropriate comments about the salvor and those who also played a role in the game, namely the auction house and the purchasers:

> Hatcher's strip-mining operation had nothing to do with archaeology other than it destroyed a significant site.[28]
>
> The second player, and perhaps the major force in the destruction of the *Geldermalsen* was Christie's of Amsterdam. Hatcher is only responding to opportunities that Christie's and other auction houses provide.[29]
>
> The third player is those who purchase objects ripped from archaeological contexts".[30]

Also the role performed by Dr. Jörg, despite the information about the *Geldermalsen* cargo he gave in his book, is not immune from criticism:

> Some archaeologists and nautical scholars will not have anything to do with looted materials and with those who destroy archaeological resources. An argument in favour of that position is that documentation and identification adds to the monetary value of the objects and thus encourages further looting.[31]

For understandable reasons, Capt. Hatcher does not seem to very much like dealing with governments.[32] He and other professional salvors – "the explorers, the risk-takers, the creators, the achievers"[33] – might feel it is too frustrating and too expensive to cooperate with government archaeologists and academics, who move "slowly, carefully, methodically, with a programme over many seasons".[34]

Besides, as Mr. Miller also suggests, there are some aspects of the auction sale that raise interesting questions. Nowhere in the auction catalogue is it specified where the objects had been salvaged, what the name of the wrecked ship was and who was her owner.

As Capt. Hatcher tells us, the Admiral Stellingwerf Reef, which was struck by the *Geldermalsen*, "is in international waters but irritatingly close to Bintan, an island that is now part of Indonesia".[35] What does the expression "irritatingly close" mean?

---

[27] *Ibidem*, p. 95.

[28] *Ibidem*, p. 96.

[29] *Ibidem*, p. 97. Mr. Miller recalls that the April 1987 issue of *Auction News from Christie's* opens with the following sentence: "Over the years, Christie's Amsterdam has established itself as the most significant venue in the world for disposal at public auction of artifacts and cargos recovered from sunken vessels".

[30] *Ibidem*.

[31] *Ibidem*, p. 95.

[32] "You [referred to 'professional salvagers'] also have to be able to negotiate with fickle, nervous, and sometimes venal third world Governments" (*ibidem*, p. 93).

[33] *Ibidem*, p. 92.

[34] *Ibidem*, p. 92.

[35] Above, note 12.

It seems that, after having struck the reef, the ship drifted for about 5 n.m. before sinking.[36] The lack of information about the precise location of the wreck and the relevant salvaging activities is regrettable. If it had been within the limit of the Indonesian territorial sea (or archipelagic waters), a regime different from a mere first-come-first-served or freedom-of-fishing approach would have been applicable.

Elaborating further on the idea that also some States may have had connections with the wreck of the *Geldermalsen*, the position of China should also be noticed. Does China have some verifiable cultural links with such a huge cargo of seventeenth century Chinese porcelain?[37] It is a truism to give am affirmative answer, even though nobody actually cared about that when the wreck was found and its cargo auctioned.

But the perfect icing on the cake of the story of the *Geldermalsen*, which indeed marks the triumph of the destination of underwater cultural heritage for the exclusive aim of private commercial gain and quick financial return, may be found in the position of the Netherlands. A British salvor and a Dutch auction house made a fortune out of the sale of the artefacts removed from the wreck of a VOC vessel. All this occurred in the city of Amsterdam, the capital of the State which claims to be the legal successor to the VOC and to retain title over the VOC vessels and wrecks, wherever they are located![38]

4. The British Warships

A) "Women and Children First" (The Birkenhead)

The British warship *Birkenhead*, under the command of Capt. Robert Salmond, was employed as a troopship, transporting men and their families to and from the Cape Colony. Her last voyage ended on 26 February 1852, when she followed a route too close to the South African coastline and suddenly struck an unchartered rock at about 1,500 m from the shore.

As the inrush of water flooded the lower troopdeck, many soldiers were instantly drowned. All the surviving officers and men went up on deck and kept order on board. The few available lifeboats were filled with women and children, launched and rowed away. Then the captain shouted that everyone could save himself by

---

[36] See Miller, *supra* note 26, at 96.

[37] The Regulations of China concerning the administration of the work for the protection of the underwater cultural heritage, promulgated under Decree No. 42 of 20 October 1989 (text, in English translation, in Prott & Srong, *supra* note 9, at 26), provide that the State of China has ownership and exercises jurisdiction on cultural relics located in Chinese inland waters, territorial sea or in waters under the Chinese jurisdiction (this expression should refer to the exclusive economic zone). They also provide that the State has "the right to identify the owners" of "cultural relics of Chinese origin that remain in sea outside the territorial waters of any foreign country but under the jurisdiction of a certain country, or in the high seas" (Art. 2, para. 3, and Art. 3). This last provision may apply to the artifacts of Chinese cultural origin, like the porcelain carried by the *Geldermalsen*.

[38] See above, para. 3 A.

jumping into the sea and swimming to the lifeboats. But the soldiers' commanding officers, who realized that such a rush might mean that the lifeboats would be swamped and the women and children further endangered, asked the men not to listen to this suggestion. Nobody moved and everybody went down with the *Birkenhead*. Of the 638 people on board only 193, but including all the women and children, survived.

It is difficult to find a more splendid lesson of self-discipline and devotion to the weakest. The men of the *Birkenhead* set the precedent of "women and children first" as a naval rule throughout the world.

To ensure the proper treatment of the human remains and the objects related to such a wreck,[39] the two States concerned, South Africa and the United Kingdom, made an exchange of notes in Pretoria on 22 September 1989.[40] By this instrument, which was concluded without prejudice to the respective legal positions of the two governments (para. 7), the parties reached a settlement to limit and control the application of salvage law to activities taking place on the wreck.

On the one hand, the United Kingdom renounces its right to conclude salvage contracts on its own:

> The British Government shall not enter into any salvage contract in respect of the *Birkenhead* and shall not object to the South African Government maintaining its existing salvage arrangements in regard to the wreck under the applicable South African legislation.

On the other, South Africa is responsible for ensuring that the behaviour of the salvors acting under the arrangements it has made does not exceed certain limits:

> The wreck of the *Birkenhead* shall, as a military grave, continue to be treated at all stages with respect. In particular, the South African Government shall seek to ensure that the salvors treat reverently and refrain from disturbing or bringing to the surface any human remains which may be discovered at the site of the wreck or in its vicinity (para. 2).

The United Kingdom is granted some rights on the objects found, including temporary access for historical purposes:

> The South African Government shall as far as possible ensure that representative examples of the salvaged artefacts identifiable with a particular British regiment or institution are offered without charge to that regiment (or its successor) or to such institution (para. 3).
>
> If any gold coin (apart from the coins considered to have been in private ownership) were to be recovered, such coin (after deduction of the share due to salvors in accordance with the existing salvage arrangements) would be shared equally between our two Governments" (para. 5).

---

[39] According to a legend which has never been verified, the *Birkenhead* carried £240,000 in gold secretly stored in the powder-room.

[40] Text in Prott & Srong, *supra* note 9, at 59; also in this volume, document No. 10.

British military historians shall have temporary access for research purposes to salvaged artefacts designated for South African museums (para. 2).

The common feeling that salvage activities on objects having a historical character is something that, if ever allowed, should not take place under a first-come-first-served or freedom-of-fishing approach is implied in a provision on monitoring included in the exchange of notes:

> In order to facilitate the implementation of these arrangements [= existing salvage arrangements], consultations shall be held as necessary between representatives of our two Governments, the salvors and other South African institutions concerned.

B) The Search for the Erebus and the Terror

On 19 May 1845, Sir John Franklin, a distinguished British naval officer and polar explorer, sailed from England to search for the North-West Passage.[41] He was in command of two ships, the *Erebus* and the *Terror*, provisioned with food thought to be enough for three years.

On 26 June, the two ships were seen by the crew of a whaling ship off Baffin Island, in the Canadian Arctic archipelago. Then the whole expedition disappeared. It was later found that the two ships wintered in 1845–46 in the lee of Beechey Island, close to the much bigger Devon Island. In the summer of 1846 the ships, after having passed through the Peel Sound (between Somerset Island and Prince of Wales Island) and the Franklin Strait (between Prince of Wales Island and the Boothia Peninsula), entered the Victoria Strait (between Victoria Island and King William Island), where they were trapped in the pack ice.

The *Erebus* and *Terror* remained imprisoned for 19 months, during which 21 men, including Franklin,[42] died. Due to the exhaustion of supplies, the 105 survivors, led by Capt. Francis Crozier, were forced to abandon the ships and travel south on foot. The desperate attempt to seek refuge at Fort Resolution on the Great Slave Lake (nearly 2,000 km to the south) failed. All the members of the expedition progressively fell by the way, the last ones in the summer of 1848 at Starvation Cove on the Adelaide Peninsula, leaving behind them a wake of graves, skeletons and relics.[43]

The *Erebus* and *Terror* have not been found as yet, despite the many expeditions that set out to rescue the members of the Franklin expedition and, later, to solve the mystery of the location of the wrecks. One of the abandoned ships is believed to have foundered in Victoria Strait. The other seems to have drifted to O'Reilly Island, where she was plundered by Inuits before sinking.

---

41 See Cyriax & Wordie, *Centenary of the Sailing of Sir John Franklin with the Erebus and Terror*, in (1945) *The Geographical Journal* 169; MacInnis, *Fire on the Ice: Men of the Erebus and Terror*, in (1978) *Canadian Geographical Journal* 52.

42 Sir John Franklin died on 11 June 1847 and was presumably buried beneath the ice in Victoria Strait.

43 In 1858 a boat was discovered that the survivors had dragged on the ice, hoping to reach open waters.

Despite the fact that their precise location is still unknown, the two lost ships have been designated by the Minister of Canadian Heritage to be National Historic Sites. On 5–8 August 1997, Canada and the United Kingdom concluded a memorandum of understanding on the "activities surrounding the exploration, recovery and disposition of the *HMS Erebus* and *HMS Terror*".[44]

Unlike in the *Birkenhead* exchange of notes, salvors and salvage activities are not even mentioned in the *Erebus* and *Terror* memorandum. Yet, both parties are committed to promote "proper archaeological research and disclosure" and disregard the "interests of financial gain and media coverage":

> The Parties desire to ensure the commemorative integrity of the wrecks through the orderly and scientific exploration, recovery and disposition of the wrecks and their contents. The Parties further intend that proper archaeological research and disclosure shall prevail over interests of financial gain and media coverage (Art. 1).[45]

Under the prudent wording of the memorandum, the United Kingdom, without prejudice for its position of principle, agrees to limit some of the rights it may have claimed, as the owner of the wrecks, under the doctrine of immunity of State vessels:

> Britain, as owner of the wrecks, hereby assigns custody and control of the wrecks and their contents to the Government of Canada, and acknowledges Canada as its agent for the purposes of this Understanding. In so doing, Britain does not waive ownership or sovereign immunity with respect to the wrecks or their contents while they are on the seabed, but accepts that any site investigation, excavation or recovery of either of the wrecks or their contents will be under Canada's control (Art. 2).

Canada is granted a broad margin of discretion as regards the actions to be taken. But it is bound to ensure that activities be carried out only by approved organizations in accordance with an approved plan and procedure:

> In exercising custody and control, Canada has the discretion to take any actions with respect to the wrecks and their contents that it considers appropriate. Canada may accordingly deny at any time permission for investigation, excavation or recovery of the wrecks or their contents, and will seek to ensure that any such permission will only be granted to approved organizations or persons in accordance with an approved plan and procedure (Art. 3).

This wording excludes by itself the risk of first-come-first-served or freedom-of-fishing salvage activities. Canada is also bound to ensure the proper conservation and public display of the objects recovered:

---

[44] Text in this volume, document No. 12.

[45] The assumption that there is a conflict between "proper archaeological research and disclosure" and the "interests of financial gain and media coverage" is implied in Art. 1.

Canada will seek to ensure that any recovered contents are dealt with in accordance with applicable Canadian law and with a plan and procedures approved by marine archaeologists of the Government of Canada, and are properly conserved and made available for public display or other museological purposes, education or research. British historians and archaeologists will be given reasonable access for research purposes to information derived from site investigations, to artifacts raised, and to all reports produced" (Art. 5).

The United Kingdom retains ownership over some of the objects that could be found:

Once either of the wrecks has been positively located and identified, Britain will assign to Canada ownership of everything recovered from that wreck and its contents, except that

a) any gold recovered from the wrecks, apart from coins considered to have been in private ownership, will after deduction of any share which may by law be due to any third party be shared equally between Canada and Britain, and
b) any recovered artifacts identified by Britain as being of outstanding significance to the Royal Navy will be offered to Britain for display in an appropriate museum. Britain will assume responsibility for all reasonable costs associated with the recovery, conservation and transportation of such artifacts" (Art. 4).[46]

Under Art. 7 of the memorandum, Canada will keep the United Kingdom apprised on a regular basis of developments relating to the recovery of the *Erebus* and the *Terror* (should they ever be found).

5. The United States Warships

A) The First Ironclad Ship (the Monitor)

The battle between the *Monitor*, launched by the Navy of the United States of America on 30 January 1862, and the Confederate warship *Virginia*, is recorded as the first battle ever fought between ironclad ships. This happened on 9 March 1862, during the American Civil War,[47] off the coast of Norfolk, Virginia. The two

[46] Canada is also bound to ensure the proper respect due to human remains: "Canada will seek to ensure that anyone dealing in any way with either of the wrecks and their contents treat reverently, and refrain from disturbing or bringing to the surface, any human remains that are discovered at the sites of the wrecks or in their vicinity. Any human remains that must be removed in order to conduct archaeological work, or that are inadvertently recovered, will be re-interred with proper respect and reverence, and in consultation with Britain" (Art. 6).

[47] Indeed, the American Civil War is very interesting for its naval aspects. The *Hunley*, a ship of the Confederate Navy which was one of the first submarines, has recently been found at about 7 km off the coast of South Carolina and brought to the surface with the utmost care. It is at present being restored. As regards the story of the *Alabama*, see below, para. 5 B.

enemies exchanged cannon fire for hours, but neither was able to prevail over the opponent.

A few months later (31 December 1862), the *Monitor* sank in a storm, while being towed by a paddlewheel steamer of the United States Navy. The wreck was found in 1973 by an expedition organized by Duke University, lying under 230 feet (70 m) of water at about 16 n.m. off Cape Hatteras Lighthouse, North Carolina. It is thus located on the continental shelf of the United States, beyond the limit of the territorial sea.

Many discussions on the fate of the ship took place among federal, state and local authorities, as well as historians and the public. On 30 January 1975, on the basis of the *Marine Protection, Research, and Sanctuary Act* of 1972, the United States Secretary of Commerce adopted regulations to establish the Monitor National Marine Sanctuary, the first sancturary established under the act. It consists "of a vertical water column in the Atlantic Ocean one mile in diameter extending from the surface to the seabed, the center of which is at 35°00′23″ north latitude and 75°24′32″ west longitude". The regulations prohibit a number of activities which could be detrimental for the wreck.[48] Access to the sanctuary is limited to scientific research conducted under a permit issued by the United States National Oceanic and Atmospheric Administration.

Having a rather broad purpose, the above mentioned 1972 United States legislation on marine sanctuaries, as subsequently amended, can be used to protect also wrecks of cultural relevance. It applies to the "marine environment", defined as "those areas of coastal and ocean waters, the Great Lakes and their connecting waters, and submerged lands over which the United States exercises jurisdiction, including the exclusive economic zone, consistent with international law". It provides that the Secretary of Commerce may designate any discrete area of the marine environment as a national marine sanctuary and promulgate regulations implementing the designation if he determines, *inter alia*, that the area "is of special national significance due to its conservation, recreational, ecological, historical, scientific, cultural, archaeological, educational, or aesthetic qualities". Another condition for the designation is that "existing State and Federal authorities are inadequate or should be supplemented to ensure coordinated and comprehensive conservation and management of the area, including resource protection, scientific research, and public education".

Once the designation is made, it is unlawful for any person to "destroy, cause the loss of, or injure any sanctuary resource" and "possess, sell, offer for sale, purchase,

[48] "Except as may be permitted by the Director, the following activities are prohibited and thus are unlawful for any person to conduct or to cause to be conducted within the Sanctuary: (a) Anchoring in any manner, stopping, remaining, or drifting without power at any time; (b) Any type of subsurface salvage or recovery operation; (c) Diving of any type, whether by an individual or by a submersible; (d) Lowering below the surface of the water any grappling, suction, conveyor, dredging or wrecking device; (e) Detonating below the surface of the water any explosive or explosive mechanism; (f) Drilling or coring the seabed; (g) Lowering, laying, positioning or raising any type of seabed cable or cable-laying device; (h) Trawling; or (i) Discharging waste material into the water in violation of any Federal statute or regulation".

import, export, deliver, carry, transport, or ship by any means any sanctuary resource".

The application *ratione personae* of the *Marine Protection, Research, and Sanctuary Act* does not seem fully clear. The regulations issued under the act

> (...) shall be applied in accordance with generally recognized principles of international law, and in accordance with treaties, conventions, and other agreements to which the United States is a party. No regulation shall apply or be enforced against a person who is not a citizen, national, or resident alien of the United States, unless in accordance with
> (1) generally recognized principles of international law;
> (2) an agreement between the United States and the foreign state of which the person is a citizen; or
> (3) an agreement between the United States and the flag state of a foreign vessel, if the person is a crewmember of the vessel.

This provision should be sufficient to prevent a first-come-first-served or freedom-of-fishing approach to the wrecks protected under a marine sanctuary designation, at least as far as American citizens or assimilated persons are concerned. In 2002 the NOAA (National Oceanic and Atmospheric Administration) and the United States Navy recovered the revolving gun turret of the *Monitor*, which was brought to the Mariner's Museum in Newport News, Virginia, for conservation.

B) The Bell of the Alabama

A painting by Edouard Manet, dedicated to "The battle between the *Kearsarge* and the *Alabama*", is on display at the Philadelphia Museum of Art. "The *Kearsarge* at Boulogne" is the subject of two other works of Manet, a watercolour to be found in the *Musée des Beaux-Arts* of Dijon, and an oil on canvas, given in 1999 as a bequest to the Metropolitan Museum of Art of New York.

Indeed, there is a link between one of the greatest European artists and the American Civil War. In 1864, like many people who came from as far as Paris, also Manet was attracted by an extraordinary event. This was a naval battle between the *Kearsarge*, a ship of the United States of America, and the *Alabama*, a ship of the Confederate States of America, which took place in the vicinity of the French coast.

The *Alabama* had been built in Liverpool in 1862 to order by the Confederate Navy. She was armed with guns and ammunition in Terceira, Azores Islands, Portugal, to avoid the legal consequences of the status of neutrality of Great Britain that would have prevented the construction and the arming in British territory of warships for a belligerent power.[49]

[49] The attempt was unsuccessful. After the end of the Civil War, the United States claimed compensation for the damages caused by the Confederate vessels constructed or armed in British ports and engaged in military operations. An arbitral award rendered on 14 September 1872 granted to the United States the sum of $ 15,500,000 dollars, as compensation to be paid by Great Britain.

Resort to privateer activities was the way in which the Confederacy reacted to the blockade of the coasts of the South, decided by the Union on 19 April 1861. Under the command of Capt. Raphael Semmes, the *Alabama* was used for privateer actions and become the scourge of the merchant marine of the United States:

> (...) the *Alabama* roamed the Atlantic Ocean, the Gulf Coast, the African Cape, and the China Sea for two years destroying or capturing at least 62 American merchant and whaling ships. According to one source, the work of the Confederate cruisers and privateers, in addition to their effect on individual ships, raised insurance rates, caused hundreds of American vessels to fly the British flag to avoid capture, and generally gave the American merchant marine a setback from which it did not recover until the time of the first World War.[50]

In 1864 the *Alabama* was docked for repairs and supplying at the French port of Cherbourg. But, positioned in international waters, the *Kearsarge*, a corvette of the Navy of the United States put under the command of Capt. John Winslow, was waiting for her departure. On 19 June 1864, Capt. Semmes decided to set sail from the port and engage in the battle. Capt. Semmes and Capt. Winslow knew each other well, as in 1847 they had shared a cabin on board an American warship that took part in the war against Mexico.[51] The battle off Cherbourg lasted an hour and ten minutes and ended with the sinking of the *Alabama*,[52] before the eyes of many people who lined the harbour to watch the event.

Many years later, in 1936, the diver William Lawson salvaged a brass bell bearing the inscription "C.S.S. Alabama". It is reported that Mr. Lawson traded the bell for drinks with the owner of a bar in the British island of Guernsey. The bell hung on the bar until World War II, when the place was destroyed by a bombing raid. After that, the bell passed from hand to hand and was acquired by an English antique dealer, who sold it in 1978 to an American colleague, Mr. Richard Steinmetz, in exchange for other antique items having a value of approximately $12,000.

Mr. Steinmetz took the bell to the United States. He offered it to the Naval Academy which was however unwilling to purchase it. In 1990 he decided to place the bell in a gallery for auction. At that time, the United States claimed entitlement to the bell. But Mr. Steinmetz resisted.

The case was decided on 13 May 1991 by the United States District Court, District of New Jersey.[53] Incidentally, the hearing turned out to be also a celebrative occasion. The *Alabama* bell was displayed to schoolchildren and the historical events behind it

---

50 *United States of America v. Richard Steinmetz*, 973 F.2d 212, 214 (3rd Cir., August 21, 1992).

51 Yet several distinguished officers engaged in the American Civil War had already served in the military expedition to Mexico (for example, Ulysses Grant, George McClellan and George Meade, on the Union side, Jefferson Davis, Robert Lee and Thomas Jackson, called "Stonewall", on the Confederacy side).

52 Capt. Semmes was picked up by an English yacht and taken to England, where he was set free.

53 763 F. Supp. 1293. On the case see Acquaviva, *The Case of the Alabama – Some Remarks on the Policy of the United States towards Underwater Cultural Heritage*, in Camarda & Scovazzi, *supra* note 8, 31.

were recounted by one of the district judges of New Jersey, Mr. Winslow Bissell, who, for a rare coincidence, was a descendant of Capt. Winslow himself:

> The final encounter of the *CSS Alabama* was recalled. Each student in the sixth grade of Maplewood's Middle School struck the bell bringing forth once again the vibrant tone heard many times at sea during the years 1862 to 1864.[54]

The District Court found that the United States was the owner of the bell. The judgment was fully affirmed in a decision rendered on 21 August 1992 by the United States Court of Appeals for the Third Circuit.[55] Both courts rejected the application of a first-come-first-served or freedom-of-fishing approach.

The Court of Appeals acknowledged that the legal issues raised by the case "appear to be of substantial interest to numerous persons beyond the United States and Steinmetz".[56] On the one hand, a number of associations representing individuals who, either as a hobby or as a business, had a financial interest in Confederate military equipment, assumed that their potential loss of ownership rights to the relevant artefacts "would have a significant chilling effect on their efforts to expand our knowledge of Civil War history through discovery and preservation of its physical relics".[57] On the other, several associations of historians and archaeologists argued that recognition of United States ownership of Confederate property would ensure "that the United States maintains the right and ability to protect and preserve historic artifacts which would be otherwise subject to damage or loss through inappropriate retrieval and disposition and will remove the economic incentives for individuals to remove artifacts from their historical contexts for personal financial gain".[58] The Court of Appeals, as the District Court had done before, based its decision on three legal grounds.

First, the Court of Appeals excluded that the *Alabama* could be considered as a privately owned ship engaged in piracy:

> Without some facts to contradict the clear evidence that the Confederacy owned the *Alabama* and that Captain Semmes, although obviously given considerable autonomy on the high seas, was understood by the United States and the Confederate government to be an agent of the Confederacy, there is no material question of fact as to whether the Confederacy owned the *Alabama* when it sank in 1864. Thus, we conclude that the *Alabama* was not a piratical vessel.[59]

Second, the Court of Appeals maintained that, at the end of the Civil War, all the properties of the Confederacy passed to the United States:

---

54 *Ibidem*, p. 1294.
55 See decision quoted *supra* note 50.
56 *Ibidem*, p. 217.
57 *Ibidem*, p. 217.
58 *Ibidem*, p. 217.
59 *Ibidem*, p. 219–220.

(...) whether or not historians would regard the international law of succession as applicable here, the succession doctrine, as explicated and applied by the United States Supreme Court with respect to the Civil War, entitled the United States to all property acquired by the Confederacy. Therefore we hold that, as a matter of law, the United States acquired title to the *Alabama* after the Civil War ended.[60]

Third, the Court of Appeals dismissed the argument by Mr. Steinmetz that the United States had abandoned the wreck because it never asserted ownership of it and never showed any interest in its salvage. In this respect, the Court applied Art. IV, Sect. 2, Clause 2, of the Constitution of the United States.[61] This provision was interpreted "to mean that the United States cannot abandon its own property except by explicit acts":

> The Government, which holds its interests here as elsewhere in trust for all the people, is not to be deprived of those interests by the ordinary court rules designed particularly for private disputes over individually owned pieces of property.[62]

The final remarks of the judgment dwell upon the future functions of the bell:

> Steinmetz, of course, is free to present his case to sympathetic congressional representative who may introduce a private bill. As we noted at the outset, our function is to decide the law, and thus decide for whom the *Alabama's* bell tolls after 128 years: it tolls for the United States.[63]

In the meantime, the wreck of the *Alabama* had been located in 1984 by French divers at about 7 n.m. off the coast, at a depth of 180 feet (55 m). The wreck lies on the bed of the French territorial sea, whose breadth was enlarged in 1971 from 3 to 12 n.m.[64]

France and the United States avoided any potential conflict between the rights claimed by the coastal State and those claimed by the flag State by signing in Paris on 3 October 1989 an Agreement concerning the wreck of the *CSS Alabama*.[65] This instrument is sufficient to prevent any risk of salvage or looting activities by private organizations.

In the preamble of the Agreement the parties recognize the historical and archaeological importance of the wreck and express their wish to cooperate to ensure

---

[60] *Ibidem*, p. 221–222.

[61] "The Congress shall have Power to dispose of and make all needful Rules and Regulations respecting the Territory or other Property belonging to the United States; and nothing in this Constitution shall be so construed as to Prejudice any Claims of the United States, or of any particular State".

[62] *Ibidem*, p. 222.

[63] *Ibidem*, p. 223. Today, the bell of the *Alabama* is on display in Washington, at the Naval Historical Center.

[64] Law No. 71-1060 of 24 December 1971 (U.N., *National Legislation and Treaties Relating to the Law of the Sea*, New York, 1976, p. 17).

[65] Text in U.N., *Law of the Sea Bulletin*, No. 20, 1992, p. 26. See Roach, *France Concedes United States Has Title to CSS Alabama*, in (1991) *AJIL* 381.

the protection and study of it. The Agreement sets up a Scientific Committee composed, on a basis of equality, of two representatives of each party and of governmental experts. The Committee is entrusted with significant powers:

> Any measure related to scientific activities or any project concerning the development of the wreck of the *CSS Alabama* shall be reviewed by the Scientific Committee, which shall make its decisions by agreement of the representatives of both governments (Art. 2).

France, as the State in whose territorial sea the *Alabama* is located, is granted the rights to establish a protection zone around the wreck and to take urgent action:

> The provisions adopted by the French Government to establish a zone of protection around the wreck of the *CSS Alabama* shall remain in force for the term of this agreement, unless the Parties decide otherwise. The competent French authorities may amend these provisions, as necessary. Neither Party shall take measures adversely affecting the wreck or its associated artifacts without the agreement of the other Party.
>
> If the conservation of the wreck is compromised, the competent French authorities may take, on their own authority or at the request of the United States authorities, the conservation measures necessitated by the situation. In the event such urgent action is taken by the French authorities, they will notify the United States authorities promptly of the full details regarding such action (Art. 3).[66]

The special position of the United Kingdom, the country where the warship had been built, is also recognized:

> The Scientific Committee shall agree upon, as necessary, the procedure governing the participation of the Government of the United Kingdom of Great Britain and Northern Ireland in the operations that are undertaken (Art. 8).

6. The Saga of the Spanish Galleons

A) The Nuestra Señora de Atocha

The Spanish galleon *Nuestra Señora de Atocha* (in brief, the *Atocha*), en route from Havana to Cadiz, sank in 1622 off the Marquesas Keys, Florida. The disaster, which caused the loss of about 550 lives, has been described as follows:

> This case dates back to the early 17th century, when Spain was using the riches of the New World to finance her European military adventures. On September 4, 1622, a fleet of 28 ships, known as the Tierra Firme Flota, commanded by the Marquis of Cadereita, set sail from Havana for Cadiz laden with bullion,

[66] It is also provided that "proposals adopted by the Scientific Committee will be submitted to the French Minister of Culture, who shall grant the necessary authorizations with due regard for the procedures provided for by French law" (Art. 4).

spices, and tobacco for King Philip IV. As the ships entered the Florida Straits in search of the favourable Gulf Stream currents, bad weather set in, and the vessels soon found themselves in the midst of a hurricane. The destructive winds from the northeast stripped the vessels of their masts, sails, and standing rigging. The winds then shifted to the south and eight of the ships were driven towards the dangerous waters of the lower Florida Keys, where they were soon lost. The remaining vessels limped back to Havana. One of the eight ships that went down was the *Nuestra Señora de Atocha*. When the *Atocha* set sail from Havana, she was carrying in excess of one million pesos of registered bullion and specie. Her hold contained a treasure worthy of Midas: 160 gold bullion pieces, 900 silver ingots, over 250,000 silver coins, 600 copper planks, 350 chests of indigo and 25 tons of tobacco.[67]

A first attempt of salvage was immediately made by the Spaniards. The *Atocha* was located intact in 55 feet of water. But only two bronze cannons were retrieved, as the divers were unable to enter the holds containing the treasure. The first salvors placed surface buoys to mark the position of the wreck, but a hurricane shattered the *Atocha* and buried her beneath the sands. The buoys were also removed by the storm and nobody was able to relocate the vessel. In late 1623 the Spaniards abandoned the search.[68]

Only in 1971 was the wreck of the *Atocha* found by two Florida corporations, Treasure Salvors, Inc., and Armada Research Corp., formed by Mr. Mel Fisher and his professional salvaging group.[69] They entrusted a historian with the task of conducting a thorough research with the Archive of the Indies in Seville where documentary evidence about the exact location of the wreck was found.[70] The wreck was finally located on the continental shelf of the United States, 9.5 n.m. West of the Marquesas Keys and 40 n.m. West of Key West, beyond the limit of the territorial sea which, at that time, was fixed at 3 n.m. The relevant environment has been described as follows:

> (. . .) a shallow-water wreck site found off the coast of Florida lies in or on the continental shelf, in or on shoals or keys, on bedrock or covered by many feet of overburden such as sand, mud or seagrass. The waters are relatively shallow and lend themselves to scuba diving and modern techniques of recovery. In some shallow water wrecks the hull or significant portion of a lost vessel has been found, but research has brought recognition that over 350 years a wooden galleon disintegrates, is dispersed and passed along the shoals and shallow

---

[67] *Florida Department of State v. Treasure Salvors, Inc.*, 621 F.2d 1340, 1341-42 (5th Cir, July 24, 1980).

[68] The commander of the fleet, the Marquis of Cadereita, personally supervised the fruitless search. This is recalled by the very name of the keys where he set his camp, which were called "Cayos del Marqués" (Marquesas Keys).

[69] In 1963 Mr. Mel Fisher, owner of a scuba diving shop, came to Florida from California, where he formed different salvaging groups (see also below, para. 6 B).

[70] This shows that, in certain cases, diving in the dust of archives may prove to be more fruitful than diving in the depths of the sea.

> waters, driven by the hurricanes that visit the area, the currents and natural phenomena, which would result in substantial dispersal or "scatter" of the wreck site. Actually, the dispersal usually takes the form of a corridor from which quantities of artifacts are found, including ballast or cargo, as well as pieces of wood, metal fasteners, hooks, anchors and other artifacts of ship and cargo. It may well be that a given wreck over a 350 year period can produce more than one scatter pattern over thousands of yards each, and therefore more than one corridor caused by the travel left from the initial impact, subsequent dispersal and later impact areas.[71]

The finders, who expended in the search and salvaging operations more than $ 7 million, retrieved gold, silver, artefacts and armament which were in 1981 valued at $ 8 million.[72]

As regards the legal aspects of the case, the finders brought an action for possession and confirmation of title before the United States District Court for the Southern District of Florida. They assumed that, where a vessel has been abandoned, the finder in possession becomes the owner of it. The United States counterclaimed, contending that objects of antiquity recovered by persons subject to its jurisdiction are the property of the people of the country as a whole, and not of the finders alone.

The District Court, by an order of summary judgment rendered on 3 February 1976,[73] found that possession and title were rightfully conferred upon the finder of the wreck, which was to be considered as *res derelicta*. The District Court added that both the relevant domestic legislation and the Convention on the Continental Shelf (Geneva, 1958) applied only to mineral resources in and under the continental shelf and could not be extended to cover wrecks.

The decision was confirmed by a judgment of 13 March 1978 by the United States Court of Appeals, Fifth Circuit. The Court concluded, *inter alia*, that the District Court had correctly applied the law of finds, according to which "title to abandoned property vests in the person who reduces that property to his or her possession".[74] The Court of Appeals dismissed the argument by the United States that no marine peril existed as regards the wreck of the *Atocha* and that, consequently, the conditions for the application of salvage did not exist in the specific case. According to the Court, the concept of marine peril includes more than the threat of storm, fire or piracy. It can also lie in the mere fact that a vessel has been lost.

A passage in the decision reveals all the admiration that the Court of Appeals nurtured with respect to the finders:

---

71 *Treasure Salvors, Inc. v. The Unidentified Wrecked and Abandoned Sailing Vessel Nuestra Señora de Atocha*, 546 F. Supp. 919, 924-25 (S.D.Fla, July 2, 1981).

72 This is an estimation made by the decision of 2 July 1981 (*supra* note 71). But at that time it was also estimated that only 5% of the artefacts of the ship and cargo and only 3% of the silver coins had been recovered.

73 *Treasure Salvors, Inc. v. The Unidentified Wrecked and Abandoned Sailing Vessel believed to be Nuestra Señora de Atocha*, 408 F. Supp. 907 (S.D.Fla, February 3, 1976).

74 *Treasure Salvors, Inc. v. The Unidentified Wrecked and Abandoned Sailing Vessel believed to be Nuestra Señora de Atocha*, 569 F. Supp. 330, 337 (5th Cir., March 13, 1978).

> The case also presents the story of a triumph, a story in which the daring and determination of the colonial settlers are mirrored by contemporary treasure seekers.[75]

A subsequent litigation arose when the finders claimed the restitution of a number of artifacts removed from the wreck and held by the Division of Archives of the State of Florida (a member State of the United States of America). In fact, the finders began their operations pursuant to a contract with Florida, under which they were entitled to 75% of the total appraised value of all materials recovered and Florida to 25%. The contract was made in the belief that Florida was entitled to rights on the portion of the United States continental shelf where the wreck had been found. But in 1975 the United States Supreme Court, in deciding a litigation on the rights relating to oil exploitation, held that the part of the continental shelf on which the *Atocha* was resting had never been owned by Florida.[76]

As a consequence of the Supreme Court's judgment, the United States District Court for the Southern District of Florida, by a decision rendered on 21 August 1978,[77] held that the contract between the finders and Florida was invalid from the time of its execution, because of a mutual mistake of material fact, and that Florida was wrongfully witholding a number of artefacts of the *Atocha*. Besides celebrating the glorious deeds of the treasure finders, the District Court also severely blamed the greed of the officials of the Florida Division of Archives who flimsily attempted to keep the objects for the State:

> The finding of a great treasure from the days of the Spanish Main is not a cherished dream of only the United States and Florida citizens; countless people from other lands have shared such thoughts. It would amaze and surprise most citizens of this country, when their dream, at the greatest of costs, was realized, that agents of the respective governments would, on the most flimsy of grounds, lay claim to the treasure. (...) The zeal of the United States in claiming the salvaged articles of the *Atocha* has been exceeded by the agents of the State of Florida. Although occasionally state employees are faulted for failure to protect state property, certainly this does not apply to the personnel of the Division of Archives who, in their unstinting efforts to claim property belonging to Treasure Salvors, have reacted as though Treasure Salvors were attempting to steal the old Capital Building as well as the great Seal of the State.[78]

The holding of the District Court was affirmed by a decision made on 24 July 1980 by the United States Court of Appeals, Fifth Circuit,[79] and by a decision made on 1 July 1982 by the United States Supreme Court.[80]

---

75 *Ibidem*, p. 333.

76 *United States v. Florida*, 420 U.S. 531 (Supreme Court, March 17, 1975).

77 *Treasure Salvors, Inc. v. The Unidentified Wrecked and Abandoned Sailing Vessel believed to be Nuestra Señora de Atocha*, 459 F. Supp. 507 (S.D.Fla, August 21, 1978).

78 *Ibidem*, p. 511.

79 See decision quoted *supra* note 67.

80 *Florida Department of State v. Treasure Salvors, Inc.*, 458 U.S. 670 (Supreme Court, July 1, 1982).

The *Atocha* and her artefacts were the subject of a third kind of litigation, which took place between Treasure Salvors, Inc., and Armada Research Corp., on the one hand, and a different treasure salvor group based in Key West, on the other. In fact, incidents had occurred between the competing salvors which included gunshots fired into the air as warnings. In a decision rendered on 2 July 1981, the United States District Court, Southern District of Florida,[81] found that to allow others to come in and reap the benefits that are bestowed upon a finder or a salvor would constitute irreparable harm and injury for which there would be no adequate remedy at law. The District Court added that,

> in terms of public interest, the dedicated archaeological and historical efforts by the plaintiffs [= Treasure Salvors, Inc., and Armada Research Corp.] in preservation of the wreck sites unqualifiedly suggest that the public can be best served by allowing these plaintiffs to continue their efforts further.[82]

To preserve the rights of the salvor in possession, the District Court prohibited the competing salvors from interfering with his activities within a 13.3 square-mile area located around the wreck.

The promising consequences of the several American decisions on the wreck of the *Atocha* and its cargo can be seen also today. It is reported that a museum at Key Largo, Florida, exhibits materials, such as gold bars and silver ingots, taken from the Spanish galleons *Atocha* and *Concepción*. The shop of the museum "offers authentic coins and artifacts".[83] Elsewhere, fake coins have been cast from silver bars salvaged from the wreck of the *Atocha*.[84]

B) The Apotheosis of Salvors (the Admiral Ship of the 1715 Plate Fleet)

The story of the Spanish galleons which in 1715 sailed back from the American colonies to their mother country deserves to be fully reported:

> In the early eighteenth century, Spain's dominions extended over one third of the known world. The King of Spain annually sent two fleets of ships to the New World to bring back the wealth of the Americas. One fleet picked up the gold, emeralds, and pearls unearthed from Peruvian mines, at the port of New Granada – present day Cartagena Colombia; the other boarded delicate pottery and china shipped from the Orient, and Mexican silver, cochineal and

81 See decision quotes *supra* note 71.

82 *Ibidem*, p. 929.

83 Johnston, *Treasure Salvage, Archaeological Ethics and Maritime Museums, in International Journal of Nautical Archaeology and Underwater Exploration*, 1992, reprinted in Prott, Planche & Roca-Hachem, *Background Materials on the Protection of the Underwater Cultural Heritage*, Paris, 2000, p. 398.

84 "Seasonal gift catalogues in the United States (and possibly elsewhere) have begun to offer "pieces-of-eight" earrings and jewellery pendants from the wreck of the Spanish galleon *Atocha*. However, these coins are not original: they were "cast from actual silver bars salvaged from the wreck. The molten silver was poured into casts made from the original coins. Each piece is numbered and includes a certificate of authenticity" (*ibidem*, p. 399).

indigo dyes, at Veracruz, Mexico. Each year the two fleets met in Havana, Cuba to voyage homeward together across the Atlantic. This afforded the treasure laden galleons some measure of protection from the pirates of the Caribbean who were well aware of the sailing dates of the fleet and the richness of the prize that was theirs if they could but capture one of these vessels.

Normally, the combined fleet sailed by May or June on order to clear the Straits of Florida before the treacherous hurricane season set in, but in the summer of 1715, the fleet of General Don Juan Esteban de Ubilla and General Don Antonio de Echeverz was delayed due to trade problems and the late arrival of four ships from Veracruz.

The Governor General of Havana was painfully aware of the Spanish monarch's critical need for the immense treasure of gold, silver and precious jewels secured in the King's treasure chests awaiting shipment. The Royal Treasury was exhausted by the cost of fighting the war of the Spanish Succession and the failure of the fleet to sail the preceding year. So, notwithstanding that it was the heart of the danger season of the high winds, a treasure fleet of twelve ships departed from Havana Harbor on July 24, 1715.

According to historical accounts, it was an occasion for celebration with brighty colored flags whipping briskly in the breeze and the booming of ceremonial cannon fire ringing in the ears of the throngs of excited citizens crowding the docks. Few of those present, and certainly none of the over two thousand men aboard the ships, had any inkling of what lay ahead on their fateful voyage. Before the week was out, over half their number would be dead and all of their mighty ships, save one, would lie entombed in a water grave forever.

The galleons sailed northward through the Straits of Florida and past the Florida Keys under a clear and cloudless sky. Their chartered course, and one that they traditionally followed, took them along the east coast of Florida to a point past Cape Canaveral, then following the Gulfstream until it veered eastward to a point north of Bermuda where the fleet would catch the prevailing winds that carried them across the Atlantic to Spain.

By noon of Tuesday, July 30, 1715, a strange calmness had settled in, punctuated by occasional gusts of strong wind that whipped the waves into ever mounting heights of whitecapped water. By mid-afternoon the sky had darkened and the wind was gusting steadily, whipping spray from the breaking waves over the doomed fleet.

In the early morning hours of July 31st, the wind suddenly shifted to the east-northeast, and the hurricane struck with all its fury. The ships, gripped in the incredible force of the crashing waves and mighty winds of nature's most awesome phenomena, were lifted like matchsticks on mountainous crests to be plummeted in the next instant into deep troughs of the ocean. Tons of seawater crashed over the railings of the galleons and, with the shriek of the wind, drowned out the screams of the seamen washed overboard to their death.

Huge anchors were dropped in a desperate attempt to bring the bows of the ships around into the wind and hold them in the deeper waters offshore. As the wind howled and the hurricane increased in intensity, the panic stricken sailors watched the thick anchor lines snap, one by one. Second, and sometimes third, anchors were dropped as the tempestuous sea pounded the ships relentlessly closer and closer to the jagged reefs and shoals. Ultimately, as the oaken hulls of the once proud and mighty Spanish Treasure Fleet were ripped by the cruel coral of the Florida coast, the seawater poured into the smashed ships and they heeled over and sank.

For the wretched survivors, the hurricane had inflicted an incredible measure of death and destruction; one thousand persons perished, eleven galleons sunk, and fourteen million pesos of treasure lost. Only one vessel survived, under the masterful seamanship of its captain, to limp back to Havana with news of the disaster. Destiny brought the ghosts of these Spanish Galleons, that had set sail bravely from Havana Harbor July 24, 1715, to a rendezvous in an Admiralty Court at the United States Courthouse in Key West, Florida, two hundred and sixty-six years later on July 27, 1981.[85]

On 17 August 1979, Cobb Coin Company, Inc., a corporation established in Florida, United States of America, and formed by Mr. Mel Fisher and his professional salvaging group,[86] filed a complaint in admiralty before the United States District Court for the Southern District of Florida versus an unidentified, wrecked and abandoned sailing vessel. Cobb Coin had located at a few hundred feet from the shore of Florida, under fairly shallow waters and underneath 6 to 22 feet of sand, the wreck site of a vessel which was believed to be one of the Spanish galleons sunk in 1715. The remains were believed to belong to the admiral ship of the 1715 Plate Fleet, known to the Spanish by two names (*San Christo del Valle* or *Nuestra Señora de la Concepción*). The claimant asked the Court to determine either that he owned as a finder the artefacts retrieved from the wreck site or that, by virtue of his services as a successful salvor, he was entitled to an appropriate salvage award. Three days after the complaint Cobb Coin retrieved a cannon from the wreck site.

The State of Florida intervened in the procedure and sought a preliminary injunction preventing Cobb Company from continuing to salvage from the wreck. Florida contended that, under its statutes, in particular the 1967 *Archives and History Act*, it owned all wrecks within the limit of the territorial waters and asked restitution for the items that the plaintiff had salvaged. On 12 October 1979 the Court denied Florida's application for injunction. Pending the decision on the merit, the Court ordered that Cobb Coin was to allow agents of Florida to come on board its salvage vessels solely to catalogue and authenticate articles brought up from the wreck site.

During the salvage season of 1980 and 1981 many artefacts were salvaged from the vessel. Cobb Coin retrieved over 1,000 silver coins, 14 gold pieces (including 8

---

[85] The description is taken from the introductory paragraphs of the injunctive order rendered on 2 October 1981 by the United States District Court for the Southern District of Florida in the case *Cobb Coin Company, Inc. v. The Unidentified, Wrecked and Abandoned Sailing Vessel*, 525 F. Supp. 186.

[86] See above, para. 6 A, note 69.

royal escudos), silver containers, bronze forks, magnificent timbers complete with dead eyes and hundreds of historic items.[87]

But in June 1981 the Florida marine patrol officers boarded the salvage vessel and a criminal citation was issued against the captain for having violated the State legislation against unauthorized exploration and salvage. For this reason Cobb Coin asked the Court to issue a preliminary injunction prohibiting Florida from interfering with its ongoing salvage operations.

During the procedure, the opposing positions of the two litigants were clearly put forward. On the one side, Florida relied on its own statute and administrative regulations, according to which objects of historic value and interest to the public which had been abandoned on state-owned submerged lands belonged to the State. Potential salvors were required to obtain a license from the State and received a percentage award allocation of the sunken artefacts recovered, in accordance with contracts entered into by the State. In fact, the wreck site where, without any license, Cobb Coin was engaging in its salvage activities was, at the time of the lawsuit, the subject of a lease between Florida and another private company, Quest Corporation.

On the other side, Cobb Coin relied on the traditional principles of maritime law which regulated salvage activities. It asserted that any impediment to its ongoing work would cause irreparable damage and extreme economic hardship, considering the investment of thousands of dollars it had made in salvage equipment and manpower.

In deciding the case, the Court proved to be fully sympathetic with the position of the salvor. Indeed, the decision rendered by the District Court can be considered as an almost absolute triumph of the assumption that the best use of underwater cultural heritage is for private commercial gain (or, to repeat the lofty expression used in this kind of cases, for "successful return to the mainstream of commerce").

The District Court made some preliminary remarks which were intended to clarify the scope of the "traditional maritime principles", as they were considered applicable to the specific case. The fact that the teredos[88] and the passage of time had eroded the vessel structure, leaving a load of cargo scattered on an expanse of ocean floor, could not diminish the rights and remedies available to the salvor:

> The absence of a hull (...) does not affect the traditional maritime right of a salvor to uninterrupted salvage operations where such salvor, in conducting his operations on an identifiable wreck site, does so in a manner demonstrating

[87] As pointed out in the decision of 31 August 1982 (*Cobb Coin Company, Inc. v. The Unidentified, Wrecked and Abandoned Sailing Vessel*, 549 F. Supp. 540, 547), "during the brief 1979 salvage season, Cobb Coin retrieved only pottery fragments, ballast stones, nails, and the cannon; it found no 'high value' items, such as gold or silver. In 1980, the plaintiff recovered 734 individual silver coins, two gold discs, 10 clumps of inseparable silver coins, and 300 pieces of 'encrusted objects'. In 1981, it recovered 25 or 30 'encrusted objects', 300 silver coins, and 12 Royal Eight Escudo gold coins. The Royal Eight Escudos are in 'fairly good shape'. Many of the silver coins are pieces of eight, minted in 1713; the value of one is now estimated at $500.00 to $600.00. The value of a Royal Eight Escudo is estimated to range between $5,000.00 and $12,000.00, depending on the quality of the coin".

[88] The teredos, called also ship worms, are molluscs that bore ships.

that degree of dominion and control which is appropriate under the circumstances.[89]

The salvor, who was not required to have an actual or "manual" possession of the lost or abandoned property, could take advantage of a situation of "constructive possession":[90]

The law does not always require that one who discovers lost or abandoned property must actually have it in hand before he is vested with a legally protected interest. The law protects not only the title finally acquired by one who finds lost or abandoned property but also the right of the person who discovers such property, and is actively and ably engaged in reducing it to possession, to complete this project without interference from another. The courts have recognized that in order to acquire a legally cognizable interest in lost or abandoned property, a finder need not always have "manual" possession of the thing. Rather, a finder may be protected by taking such constructive possession of the property as its "nature and situation" permit.[91]

Following the precedent of the *Atocha* case,[92] the District Court attributed itself the role of a traffic policeman who had been granted (incidentally, by whom?) the duty to establish priorities among salvors competing for wrecks located in all the oceans and seas of the world. Any doubts about such an extravagant and exorbitant role to be played by the American courts could be dispelled by the magic endowment of two Latin expressions (*in rem*, *in personam*):

One law should govern salvor's rights, whether the winds of fate have dashed a particular ship's hopes on the New England rocks, on the coral reef, in the Bermuda Triangle or in the sandy bottom near Florida's Sebastian Inlet. And certainly, the rules governing a salvor's rights to search and be rewarded should not depend upon the historical accident whereby a ship's remains and cargo – often, over two centuries before – have come to rest either inside or outside what later became a particular state's three-mile territorial boundary.[93]

In summary, then, once a salvor who discovers and brings up an artifact from an identifiable wreck site initiates suit by taking that object into federal court, the court acquires jurisdiction not only to adjudicate the disposition of the article already within its territorial jurisdiction, but maritime jurisdiction (based on *in personam* principles) to adjudicate disputes between competing salvors, and *in rem* jurisdiction (coupled with *in personam* jurisdiction over the claimants) to dispose of all articles therefore brought up from that site. The filing of such a suit is, as here, an open invitation (either at that time, or such

[89] See decision quoted *supra* note 85, p. 195.

[90] In another case quoted in the decision (p. 195), constructive possession was acquired by a salvor who had placed his boat over the wreck, with the means and persistent efforts to raise its valuables.

[91] *Ibidem*, p. 195

[92] Above, para. 6 A.

[93] See decision quoted *supra* note 85, p. 210.

time as an applicable interest may thereafter arise) for claimants and competing salvors to come before the court and make their alleged interests known.[94]

Any possible rights of the King of Spain, the "original owner" of the artefacts, and his successors were bluntly disregarded. The King "indeed attempted to salvage his wrecked ships, but abandoned the effort in 1716".[95] No attention was given to the question whether the ships of the 1715 Plate Fleet had the status of State owned ships and, as such, enjoyed some kind of State immunity. The King and the State of Spain were treated as unsuccessful salvors.

The District Court did not deny the right of Florida to attempt to preserve cultural and historic heritage by the exercise of its police powers. However Florida itself was treated by the District Court as an unsuccessful salvor:

> But it is hard to view the items before the Court as "public property used and employed for governmental purposes", when they have lain serenely in their two-hundred-sixty-plus-year habitat, with the State having only recently taken mere verbal action to claim (and no positive steps of its own to locate or raise) these artifacts from the ocean bottom.[96]

The District Court followed the principle that admiralty rules must govern the exploration and salvage of artefacts under the ocean, irrespective of the statute and administrative regulation enacted by Florida. Such a first-come-first-served or freedom-of-fishing-for-underwater-cultural-heritage approach was seen by the District Court as a "fundamental adjunct to the American principle" of freedom of the high seas:

> Florida's statutory scheme violates the maritime law, which permits any potential salvor to search and explore the open waters for salvageable goods. The right so to search is a fundamental adjunct to the American principle that the high seas be freely navigable to all seafaring persons to navigate for pleasure or commerce, or otherwise to ply their trades.[97]
>
> The requirement that one be licensed to be able to explore the ocean for abandoned property at the bottom contravenes the maritime law principle that potential salvors be free to explore the open waters. While salvage law will permit one whose salvage efforts are continuous and reasonably diligent to work a wrecksite, once discovered, to the exclusion of others, (...) until discovery and subsequent dominion of the site occurs, no one may be restricted from exploring the navigable waters for salvageable sites. In this aspect, the Florida act and regulations are contrary to established maritime law.[98]

Florida's legislation, although designed to acquire and preserve objects of historic

---

[94] *Ibidem*, p. 197.
[95] *Ibidem*, p. 198.
[96] *Ibidem*, p. 199.
[97] *Ibidem*, p. 203.
[98] *Ibidem*, p. 203.

value and interest to the public, was seen by the District Court as inconsistent with the fundamental principles of maritime law. The salvor's preliminary approval, the requirement of a lease, the safeguarding of the granted rights during the period of the lease regardless of the salvor's subsequent success, or lack thereof, were all elements

> contrary to admiralty's "diligence" ethic, which underlies a policy of encouraging the careful, effective, and expeditious retrieval of goods which have been abandoned at sea.[99]

In particular, Florida's legislation, which provided that all sunken artefacts retrieved belonged to the State, and the contracts entered into by Florida with the leaseholder Quest Corporation, providing that Quest was to be compensated according to a 3/4 ratio of the value of such artefacts, conflicted "with the maritime law's flexible and equitable approach to compensating salvors".[100] Any kind of legislative and administrative burden

> (...) works material prejudice to the characteristic features of the maritime law which allows freedom to explore the high seas, requires diligence on the part of salvors working a site, and rewards salvage efforts on a case by case basis depending on the circumstances of the particular salvage services.[101]

Yet, "in the case of abandoned property, the entire value of the salved property may be awarded a salvor".[102]

In the opinion of the District Court, freedom to be granted to private salvors could not be limited by the exercise of police powers by public entities, such as Florida. States' police powers were traditionally confined to "land or to health, safety or other concerns",[103] such as (to repeat the examples given in the decision) the maintenance of the sponge fishery, vessel safety and seaworthiness, the prevention of pollution. On the contrary,

> the regulation of recovery of ancient artifacts is not as traditional a matter within states' police power as are health and safety. Although the Supreme Court has recognized historic preservation as a valid state concern, a state may not enact legislation in that area in such a way as to interfere, as do portions of Florida's licensing statute, with the uniformity required by maritime law.[104]

As it can be seen, in the opinion of the District Court, a State can limit the freedom of fishing for sponges, as this corresponds to the exercise of a police power. But a State cannot prevent a salvor from availing himself of the freedom of recovering ancient artefacts (or, in a less lofty language, the freedom-of-fishing for underwater cultural heritage), as this would conflict with the overarching principles

---

[99] *Ibidem*, p. 206.
[100] *Ibidem*, p. 207.
[101] *Ibidem*, p. 211.
[102] *Ibidem*, p. 207.
[103] *Ibidem*, p. 211.
[104] *Ibidem*, p. 212.

of maritime law. No doubt, such principles could only play in favour of the salvor Cobb Coin:

> Under the prevailing "American" rule regarding ownership of lost or abandoned property, in the absence of an express statutory claim by the sovereign, abandoned goods successfully recovered become the property of the salvor.[105]

In fact, the District Court made a total confusion between the need of culture and the interests of commerce. It treated both historical research and market value collected from the artefacts as if they were the same thing. Moving from these assumptions, the District Court reached the surprising, but consistent, conclusion that the best defenders of culture are the salvors themselves:

> The interest recognized on behalf of the State is not one which would bar a proper salvage award for the plantiff's services in restoring to the mainstream of commerce and culture these historically invaluable goods left abandoned to the sea.[106]
>
> Implicit in the State's interest in acquisition and preservation is that the removal of artifacts be accomplished with scrupulous care. The historic value of each artifact is enhanced by careful monitoring of archaeological provenience, the exact location at which each item is found in terms of coordinates on the ocean, the depth under the water, the extent buried beneath the ocean bottom, and the geographical relationship to other items found. This information is not only important for the historical information it provides, but was shown at the hearing to be essential to the intrinsic value of salved items for purposes of resale to interested buyers. If salvage on an ancient shipwreck is conducted without proper regard for this essential information, both the historic and market value of the artifacts are substantially diminished.
>
> (...) The plaintiff demonstrated to the Court's satisfaction that it adequately documents archaeological provenience in its salvage operations on the Corrigan Site. Because of Cobb Coin's accurate record keeping, the State's interest in acquiring and preserving historic and archaeological information will be fully served if the injunction issues.[107]

In conclusion, the motion by Cobb Coin for a preliminary injunction was granted under the order rendered by the District Court on 2 October 1981. Florida was specifically enjoined from interfering with the plaintiff's ongoing salvage operations or arresting the plaintiff's officers, agents and employees. The previous order of 12 October 1979, which permitted the State to maintain an inspection agent aboard the

---

[105] *Ibidem*, p. 213. The District Court following the precedent of the *Atocha* case (above, para. 6 A), found that no express statutory claim existed, as the relevant legislation (*Continental Shelf Lands Act*) had to be interpreted in the sense that the United States' ownership interest pertained only to natural resources, and not to historic wreck sites, discovered on the continental shelf (*ibidem*, p. 215).

[106] *Ibidem*, p. 216.

[107] *Ibidem*, p. 218.

salvage vessel for the purpose of cataloguing and authenticating recovered artefacts, was reaffirmed.

The treatment of private salvors could not have been more triumphal than that! Freedom-of-fishing for cultural heritage was seen by the District Court as a "fundamental adjunct to the American principle" of freedom of the high seas. Anything that could have impaired salvage activities was seen by the Court as intrinsically immoral and contrary to "admiralty's diligence ethic". The public interest in the historical heritage was confined to cataloguing and authenticating objects to be subsequently given to salvors and sold to private buyers. Indeed, the order rendered on 2 October 1981 by the United States District Court for the Southern District of Florida is the bible of the ethic of salvage for underwater cultural heritage, as celebrated by some American courts!

The final award on the merits of the case, rendered on 31 August 1982 by the same United States District Court for the Southern District of Florida,[108] is a logical consequence of the principles embodied in the previous order. On the basis of the public policy underlying salvage awards in admiralty courts, which is to provide a continuing incentive to undertake the physical and financial risks entailed in salvage operations and to bring the property thus recovered into court for a salvage determination, the District Court applied the proper elements in establishing the salvage award.[109] In the specific case, Cobb Coin's expenses were evaluated at $ 288,012.60 and the value of the property saved was approximately $ 451,050. Cobb Coin was granted all the artefacts it had recovered since the inception of the lawsuit, "as compensation for its expenses and an award for superlative salvage services".[110] The award was given *in specie*, "because the property saved is uniquely and intrinsically valuable beyond its monetary value".[111]

No artefacts were granted to the State of Florida for the purpose of exhibiting the property for the people's benefit. The District Court found that the State already possessed numerous artefacts from leaseholders who saved the 1715 wrecks in the previous two decades and that a significant portion of them were already displayed in museum exhibits around the State.[112]

In an effort to consider the various aspects of the issue, the District Court devoted

108 See decision quoted *supra* note 87.

109 These elements are: "the labor expended by the salvors in rendering the salvage service; (2) the promptitude, skill and energy displayed in rendering the service and saving the property; (3) the value of the property employed by the salvors in rendering the service and the danger to which such property was exposed; (4) the risk incurred by the salvors in securing the property from the impending peril; (5) the value of the property saved; and (6) the degree of danger from which the property was rescued" (*ibidem*, p. 557).

110 *Ibidem*, p. 561.

111 *Ibidem*, p. 561.

112 However, the finding of the Court was without prejudice to the right of Florida "to intervene in future salvage award determinations before this court (...) to assert an interest on behalf of its citizenry to particular artifacts recovered which are not represented in its present inventory and which it feels are essential to the preservation of the people's heritage" (*ibidem*, p. 562).

some attention also to the opinion of some "archaeologists for the State" who believed that the wrecks were in no peril at all:

> Archaeologists for the State testified that in their opinion ancient shipwrecks buried under the sand are in no "peril" at all; they are undisturbed "time capsules" rich with archaeological, anthropological and historical data. They felt that salvage on old wrecks actually created a "peril" for these artifacts by disturbing their tranquil existence.[113]

But this assumption was considered as irrelevant by the District Court:

> These artifacts were recovered from under many feet of ocean sand through the plaintiff's skilled and laborious efforts. Had they not been saved, they likely would still be lying on the ocean bottom subject to further rearrangement and, perhaps, loss from weather condition. Further, if not recovered, they would be threatened by pirates who might have disturbed the site and removed the articles without the supervision of the Admiralty Court.[114]

The idea that salvors are the main defence against the threats posed by pirates (are State officials and archaeologists also included in this category?) is the final touch which completes the masterpiece created by the United States District Court for the Southern District of Florida in deciding the case of the objects removed from a Spanish galleon sunk in 1715.

C) Being Embedded in the Sand (the Santa Rosalea and Others)

In the second half of the 18th century three Spanish ships, the *Santa Rosalea*, the *San Lorenzo de Escoral* and the *Santa Clara*, sank in the Atlantic Ocean off the shore of Ocean City, Maryland, United States of America, as a consequence of a fierce hurricane. They were carrying a gold altarplate and other riches. In 1981 two American corporations, Subaqueous Exploration & Archaeology, Ltd.,[115] and Atlantic Ship Historical Society, Inc.,[116] instituted *in rem* actions before the United States District Court, District Maryland, against four unidentified, wrecked and abandoned vessels, believed to be the three above mentioned Spanish ships and the *Royal George*, an English privateer believed to contain Spanish treasure. On the basis of admiralty jurisdiction and law, the plaintiffs sought title to the abandoned vessels or, alternatively, full and liberal salvage awards to compensate them for their efforts to recover the vessels and their cargo. The Court entered orders directing that warrants for arrest of the vessels be issued and appointed Subaqueous as substitute custodian of them. When the actions were instituted no objects had been recovered from the wrecks which were all located within a 3-

---

[113] *Ibidem*, p. 560.
[114] *Ibidem*, p. 561.
[115] Hereinafter: Subaqueous.
[116] Hereinafter: Atlantic.

mile distance from the coast of Maryland (a member State of the United States of America).

After publication of the notices of the actions, the State of Maryland filed motions to vacate the arrests of the vessels. Maryland contended that the vessels were its property pursuant to the federal legislation (*Submerged Lands Act* of 1953) and a statute of Maryland, the *Natural Resources Article*. It also contended that the District Court lacked jurisdiction on the ground of the Eleventh Amendment to the United States Constitution. The *Submerged Lands Acts* provides that the seaward boundary of each original coastal State of the United States is a line three miles distant from the coast line and vests in the States "title to and ownership of the lands beneath navigable waters within the boundaries of the respective States, and the natural resources within such lands and waters". Under the Maryland's *Natural Resources Article*, "any object or material of historical or archaeological value or interest found on an archaeological site or land owned or controlled by the State is the property of the State" (Sect. 2-309). The Eleventh Amendment to the United States Constitution provides that "the judicial power of the United States shall not be construed to extend to any suit in law of equity, commenced or prosecuted against one of the United States by Citizens of another State, or by Citizens or Subjects of any Foreign State". It applies to actions brought against a State by its own citizens as well.

Subaqueous and Atlantic argued that Maryland lacked a colorable claim of ownership of the vessels and their cargo. They added that the Maryland statute constituted an unconstitutional intrusion into the exclusive federal regulations of admiralty and maritime matters, including salvage operations.

The United States District Court, District Maryland, by a judgment rendered on 21 December 1983,[117] granted the Maryland's motions to vacate arrests. The decision is particularly notable for the acknowledgment that the preservation of the cultural heritage constitutes a public interest. The District Court moved from the premise that "a state's police powers may be exercised to preserve and regulate the use of resources necessary for the public welfare" and that "cultural or aesthetic interests are proper objects of public welfare which the state may protect pursuant to its police powers".[118] It consequently found that

> the State of Maryland's public policy of protecting and preserving historical and archaeological objects found on its lands (...) falls within the range of public welfare interest protectable under its police powers.[119]
>
> The defendant vessels and their cargo, when they are successfully recovered, promise to provide the public with an invaluable opportunity to learn about the culture of people who explored or travelled to the shores of the United States two centuries ago.[120]

---

[117] *Subaqueous Exploration & Archaeology, Ltd., v. The Unidentified, Wrecked and Abandoned Vessels*, 577 F. Supp. 597 (D. Md, December 21, 1983).

[118] *Ibidem*, p. 609.

[119] *Ibidem*, p. 609.

[120] *Ibidem*, p. 610.

As regards the weight to be given to admiralty law, the Court found that a State "may enact laws on matters of local concern pursuant to its police powers which incidentally affect maritime affairs without impermissibly intruding upon federal regulation of admiralty or maritime matters".[121] More precisely,

> the state regulations under challenge herein address themselves exclusively to objects of archaeological or historical value found on lands owned or controlled by the State of Maryland. Given their narrow geographic scope of applicability, the Court finds that such statutes, insofar as they may affect salvage operations directed towards objects of historical and archaeological value, merely have an incidental effect upon or supplement federal maritime laws or powers, and, consequently, do not impermissibly intrude into federal laws.[122]

Particularly relevant is the analysis made by the Court on the historical origin and proper scope of salvage law, which was seen as strictly limited to ships and property in peril and having nothing to do with objects belonging to the cultural heritage:

> The admiralty law of salvage was developed in pertinent part to encourage seamen to render assistance to maritime property in imminent peril. (...). However, the defendant vessels in these proceedings have been resting on the ocean floor under an undetermined amount of sand for hundreds of years. (...) The Court finds that the defendant vessels are not reasonably in peril of being lost through the elements since they are impervious to weather conditions above the surface of the sea, with the sand preventing deterioration under water. (...)
>
> The Court, therefore, finds under the circumstances that the traditional public policy concerns underpinning the federal law of salvage are insufficiently implicated, if at all, when the objects to be rescued are marine antiquities which have been undisturbed for centuries. The challenged sections of Maryland's Natural Resources Article clearly do not interfere with the rescue of recently wrecked or damaged vessels. Moreover, the state statutes at issue here should not impair the uniformity of admiralty salvage laws. Maryland's laws apply only to recovery operations directed toward historical or archaeological items found within its territorial waters.[123]

Firmly departing from the disagreeable jurisprudence established in the *Atocha* and *Cobb Coin* cases,[124] the judgment of the Maryland District Court is particularly meaningful in excluding a first-come-first-served or freedom-of-fishing approach where the cultural heritage and a public welfare interest are at stake.

---

[121] *Ibidem*, p. 610.
[122] *Ibidem*, p. 611.
[123] *Ibidem*, p. 611.
[124] "This forum declines to follow the recently developed rule in the Fifth Circuit that an ancient, abandoned shipwreck constitutes a marine peril for purposes of stating a valid salvage claim" (*ibidem*, p. 611). See above, paras. 6 A and 6 B.

The same judgment is also relevant for being a precedent of an assumption which is common also today in the United States legislation and jurisprudence. According to this assumption, the underwater cultural heritage can be assimilated to the "natural resources" of the seabed.

Plaintiffs Subaqueous and Atlantic contended that the objective of the *Submerged Lands Act* was to permit the coastal States to manage and develop the exploitation of "natural resources", that is the ore resources contained within the 3-mile limit, without encompassing the right to regulate the recovery of abandoned shipwrecks. Yet, the Act provides the following definition:

> The term "natural resources" includes, without limiting the generality thereof, oil, gas, and all other minerals, and fish, shrimp, oysters, clams, crabs, lobsters, sponges, kelp, and other marine animal and plant life but does not include water power, or the use of water for the production of power (Sect. 1301).

The Court found that the plaintiffs' contention was unduly narrow and declined to adopt it. In particular,

> although Congress' primary intention in enacting the Submerged Lands Act may have been to allow the states to regulate the exploration of ore resources within their submerged lands, as plaintiffs contend, the Act plainly granted the coastal states far broader powers. While the Act expressly vested ownership in the states of natural resources within the submerged lands, the Act also expressly vested title and ownership of the submerged land themselves in the states (...), as well as the right and power to manage, develop, and use such lands. (...)
>
> It appears to the Court that a state's regulatory rights respecting its submerged lands would include the power to regulate objects found in, on, or buried beneath such submerged lands, including abandoned shipwrecks and their cargo. Furthermore, even though the ships and their cargo are "man-made" or objects not created exclusively through the forces of nature, those marine antiquities can be characterized as "natural resources" within the meaning of the Submerged Lands Act. By its plain terms, the definitional section of natural resources within that Act is not all-inclusive. The remains of abandoned, two hundred year old shipwrecks, which have lain undisturbed for centuries under an undetermined amount of sand, reasonably can be characterized as natural resources for purposes of the federal Act.[125]

Yet, the assimilation of man-made objects to natural resources seems hardly acceptable. Even if broadly interpreted, a concept cannot become equivalent to its very contrary. The underwater cultural heritage deserves to be protected for itself, and not as a mere consequence of its being embedded in the sand or encrusted by oysters or other forms of marine life. It is however evident that the District Court was mainly inspired by the objective of ensuring the protection of a public interest

[125] *Ibidem*, p. 612–613.

which was put at risk by the impending activities of salvors. Failing a specific federal enactment, the District Court adapted to such a deserving objective a piece of United States legislation which had very little to do with historical wrecks, whether embedded in sand or not. It also asked the question "whether there are a sufficient number of ancient abandoned shipwrecks lying within the territorial waters of the coastal states so as to warrant uniform regulation by the Congress".[126]

The United States Congress responded to the question with the *Abandoned Shipwreck Act* of 1987.[127] Under the Act,

> the United States asserts title to any abandoned shipwreck that is
> (1) embedded in submerged lands of a State;
> (2) embedded in coralline formations protected by a State on submerged lands of a State; or
> (3) on submerged lands of a State and is included in or determined eligible for inclusion in the National Register" (sect. 6, a).[128]

The title so asserted is transferred by the United States to the States in or on whose submerged lands the shipwreck is located. Such States shall carry out their responsibilities under the Act "to develop appropriate and consistent policies so as to (A) protect natural resources and habitat areas; (B) guarantee recreational exploration of shipwreck sites; and (C) allow for appropriate public and private sector recovery consistent with the protection of historical values and environmental integrity of the shipwrecks and the sites" (sect. 4, a, 2). In managing the resources subject to the Act, "States are encouraged to create underwater parks or areas to provide additional protection for such resources" (sect. 4, b).

Particularly interesting is the regime that the Act reserves to the law of salvage and the law of finds:

> The law of salvage and the law of finds shall not apply to abandoned shipwrecks to which section 6 of this Act applies (sect. 7 a).

This means that the 1987 United States legislation preserves from a first-come-first-served or freedom-of-fishing approach all abandoned shipwrecks which are located within a certain distance from the national coasts.

D) The Revenge of Spain (the Juno *and the* La Galga*)*

Two naval vessels of the Kingdom of Spain, the *La Galga* and the *Juno*, were lost off the shores of Virginia, United States of America, in 1750 and 1802 respectively. As

---

[126] *Ibidem*, p. 611.

[127] Text in Prott & Srong, *supra* note 9, at 31.

[128] The term "embedded" means "firmly affixed in the submerged lands or in coralline formations such that the use of tools of excavation is required in order to move the bottom sediments to gain access to the shipwreck, its cargo, and any part thereof" (Sect. 3, a). The "National Register" is the National Register of Historic Places maintained by the Secretary of the Interior under the National Historic Preservation Act (Sect. 3, b).

recalled in the decision rendered on 21 July 2000 by the United States Court of Appeals for the Fourth Circuit,

> *La Galga* ("The Greyhound") was a fifty-gun frigate commissioned into the Spanish Navy in 1732. *La Galga* left Havana on its last voyage on August 18, 1750, in order to escort a convoy of merchant ships to Spain. It carried the Second Company of the Sixth Battalion of Spanish Marines, Spanish Royal property, and English military prisoners. On August 25, 1750, the convoy encountered a hurricane near Bermuda that scattered the ships and forced them westward toward the American coast. *La Galga* eventually sank off the coast of the Maryland/Virginia border. Most of the crew and passengers reached land safely. When Captain Daniel Houny attempted to salvage items from the wreck, he found that local residents had already begun looting the vessel. He secured the assistance of Governor Ogle of Maryland, but any further salvage efforts ended when a second storm came and broke up what was left of the ship. *La Galga* remained undisturbed until the recent salvage efforts by Sea Hunt.[129]
>
> The *Juno*, a thirty-four gun frigate, entered the service of the Spanish Navy in 1790. On January 15, 1802, *Juno* set sail from Veracruz bound to Spain. On board *Juno* were the soldiers of the Third Battalion of the Regiment of Africa, their families, and various civilian officials. The *Juno* was beset by a ferocious storm and began taking on water. It encountered the American schooner *La Favorita*. The two ships sailed together trying to reach an American port before *Juno* succumbed to her leaks. As *Juno* continued to take on water, the Captain ordered his passengers and crew to begin transferring to *La Favorita*. But only seven persons were able to transfer before the storm picked up and *Juno* was lost in heavy fog. *La Favorita* could come close enough to hear the anguished cries for help as *Juno* went under. At least 413 sailors, soldiers, and civilians perished in the sinking of *Juno*. Spanish authorities ordered an investigation into the sinking, but the location of the wreck was not discovered until Sea Hunt's recent efforts.[130]

A few years ago Virginia asserted ownership over the wrecks and issued permits to conduct salvage operations and recover artefacts pursuant to the *Abandoned Shipwreck Act*[131] to Sea Hunt, Incorporated, a maritime salvage company based in Virginia. Sea Hunt spent about a million dollars in conducting remote sensing, survey, diving and identification operations and succeeded in locating both ships off the coast of Virginia, within the territorial sea of the United States. In 1998 it initiated an admiralty action, seeking a declaratory judgment that the shipwrecked vessels had never been subject to the sovereign prerogative of Spain and were subject to admiralty's laws of abandonment and the law of finds. Sea Hunt also asked that

---

[129] *Sea Hunt, Inc. v. Unidentified Shipwrecked Vessel or Vessels*, 221 F.3d 634, 638-639 (4th Cir., July 21, 2000).

[130] *Ibidem* , p. 639.

[131] See above, para. 6 C.

any items it had salvaged from the wrecks be distributed pursuant to the permits issued by Virginia.

In response, Spain moved to intervene and filed a claim stating that it

> "was and still is the true and bona fide owner of the vessels *Juno* and *La Galga* (...) and that title and ownership interest in said vessels has never been abandoned or relinquished or transferred by the Kingdom of Spain". Spain put forth affidavits and exhibits showing that at the time of their sinking both ships were serving as vessels of the Royal Navy, that both vessels are currently on the register of the Spanish Navy, and the transfer or abandonment of the vessels would require formal authorization by the government of Spain.[132]

In a verbal note sent to the United States on 18 May 1998, Spain stated its wish that "the remains of these vessels be treated as maritime graves and that their salvage not be authorized at this time".[133]

On 27 April 1999 the District Court for the Eastern District of Virginia, Norfolk Division,[134] found that Spain had abandoned its claim to *La Galga* under Art. XX of the definitive treaty of peace between France, Great Britain and Spain, signed on 10 February 1763. But the District Court held that Spain had not expressly abandoned its title to *Juno*. By a subsequent order rendered on 25 June 1999,[135] the same District Court found that Sea Hunt could not rightfully claim a salvage award for the salvage services conducted on *Juno* because Spain had expressly refused such services:

> It is the right of the owner of any vessel to refuse unwanted salvage. Sea Hunt knew before bringing this action that the *Juno* was a Spanish ship and that Spain might make a claim of ownership and decline salvage. Before conducting any salvage operations pursuant to this Court's Orders, Sea Hunt received an express communication of refusal of salvage from Spain. Because Sea Hunt had express knowledge of Spain's ownership interests and had reason to expect Spain's ownership claim and refusal to agree to salvage activity on *Juno*, Sea Hunt can not be entitled to any salvage award. The Court realizes that this holding places a substantial burden on Sea Hunt, and places on potential salvors the risk of expending significant time and resources in salvaging sunken objects for which they will not receive compensation. However, such is the risk inherent in treasure salvage.[136]

The judgment of 27 April 1999 was appealed by Spain, as regards *La Galga*, and by Sea Hunt and Virginia, as regards *Juno*.

---

[132] See decision quoted *supra* note 129, p. 640.

[133] *Sea Hunt, Inc. v. Unidentified Shipwrecked Vessel or Vessels*, 1999 U.S. Dist. LEXIS 21752, 9 (E.D.Va., June 25, 1999).

[134] *Sea Hunt, Inc. v. The Unidentified, Shipwrecked Vessel or Vessels*, 47 F. Suppl. 2d 678 (E.D.Va, April 27, 1999).

[135] See decision quoted *supra* note 133.

[136] *Ibidem*, p. 13.

The United States Court of Appeals for the Fourth Circuit, by a judgment rendered on 21 July 2000,[137] found that both vessels remained the property of Spain and, consequently, reversed the finding of the district court that Spain had abandoned *La Galga*.

On the question on whether, under the *Abandoned Shipwreck Act*, abandonment could be implied, the Court stated that "sovereign vessels must be treated differently from privately owned ones" and that "an implied abandonment standard would seem least defensible where, as here, a nation has stepped forward to assert ownership over its sovereign shipwrecks".[138] In the case of Spain, an express abandonment standard was required by Art. X of the 1902 treaty of friendship between Spain and the United States, providing that, in the case of shipwreck, each party was bound to afford to the vessels of the other "the same immunities which would have been granted to its own vessels in similar cases".[139] Following the precedent of the *Alabama* case,[140] the Court held that Art. IV of the Constitution of the United States precluded a finding of implied abandonment of State property. In the statement of interest submitted to the Court on 18 December 1998, the United States Department of State emphasized that its policy was "to recognize claims by foreign governments – such as in this case by the Government of Spain regarding the warships *Juno* and *La Galga* – to ownership of foreign warships sunk in waters of the United States without being captured, and to recognize that title to such sunken warships is not lost absent express abandonment by the sovereign".[141]

As regards *La Galga*, the Court held that Art. XX of the 1763 treaty of peace[142] did not contain clear and convincing evidence of express abandonment. The language of the provision did not mention vessels or shipwrecks, nor did it refer to Spanish property in the sea or on the seabed.[143] The view that no abandonment had taken place was confirmed by the positions taken by the two parties concerned,

---

137 See decision quoted *supra* note 129.

138 *Ibidem*, p. 641.

139 The United States Department of State remarked in the statement of interest submitted to the Court on 18 December 1998 that this provision was unique in that no other "friendship, commerce and navigation (FCN) treaty of the United States contains such a broadly worded provision applying to State ships entitled to sovereign immunity" (*ibidem* p. 642).

140 Above, para. 5 B.

141 See decision quoted *supra* note 129, p. 643.

142 "His Catholick Majesty cedes and guaranties, in full right, to his Britannic Majesty Florida, with Fort St. Augustin, and the Bay of Pensacola, as well as all that Spain possesses on the continent of North America, to the East or to the South East of the river Mississippi. And, in general, every thing that depends on said countries and lands, with the sovereign property, possession and all rights, acquired by treaties or otherwise. (...)".

143 With reference to the words "on the continent of North America" (Art. XX of the 1763 treaty), the Court noted that "in the light of the eighteenth century understandings, this 'on the continent' language would hardly amount to clear and convincing evidence of an express abandonment of property in coastal waters. In fact, the three-mile coastal belt, well recognized today, had no clear counterpart in eighteenth century international law. Ownership of the three-mile belt in the eighteenth century was but a nebulous suggestion" (see decision quoted *supra* note 129, p. 645).

namely by Spain, during the whole procedure, and by the United Kingdom, in a diplomatic note issued after the judgment of the District Court. The United States itself, acting in the procedure as *amicus curiae*, strenuously defended Spain's ownership over the two wrecks:

> The United States "is the owner of military vessels, thousands of which have been lost at sea, along with their crews. In supporting Spain, the United States seeks to ensure that its sunken vessels and lost crews are treated as sovereign ships and honoured graves, and are not subject to exploration, or exploitation, by private parties seeking treasures of the sea".[144]

The conclusion reached by the Court of Appeal confirms the impression that commercial salvors should have little to do with historic shipwrecks, at least if such wrecks fall under the category of State vessels:

> It bears repeating that matters as sensitive as these implicate important interests of the executive branch. Courts cannot just turn over the sovereign shipwrecks of other nations to commercial salvors where negotiated treaties show no sign of abandonment, and where the nations involved all agree that title to the shipwrecks remains with the original owner.[145]

The official position taken on the question of sunken warships was reaffirmed by a statement made in 2001 by the President of the United States:[146]

> Pursuant to the property clause of Article IV of the Constitution, the United States retains title indefinitely to its sunken State craft unless title has been abandoned or transferred in the manner Congress authorized or directed. The United States recognizes the rule of international law that title to foreign sunken State craft may be transferred or abandoned only in accordance with the law of the foreign flag State.
>
> Further, the United States recognizes that title to a United States or foreign sunken State craft, wherever located, is not extinguished by passage of time, regardless of when such sunken State craft was lost at sea.
>
> International law encourages nations to preserve objects of maritime heritage wherever located for the benefit of the public.
>
> Those who would engage in unauthorized activities directed at sunken State craft are advised that disturbance or recovery of such craft should not occur without the express permission of the sovereign, and should only be conducted in accordance with professional scientific standards and with the utmost respect for any human remains.
>
> The United States will use its authority to protect and preserve sunken State craft of the United States and other nations, whether located in the waters of the United States, a foreign nation, or in international waters.

---

144 *Ibidem*, p. 647.
145 *Ibidem*, p. 647.
146 *Sunken Warships*, The White House, Office of the Press Secretary, January 19, 2001.

The statement makes a precise reference to the risks posed by salvors, treasure hunters and others:

> Thousands of United States government vessels, aircraft and spacecraft ("State craft"), as well as similar State craft of foreign nations, lie within, and in waters beyond, the territorial sea and contiguous zone. Because of recent advances in science and technology, many of these sunken government vessels, aircraft and spacecraft have become accessible to salvors, treasure hunters and others. The unauthorized disturbance or recovery of these sunken State craft and any remains of their crews and passengers is a growing concern both within the United States and internationally. In addition to deserving treatment as gravesites, these sunken State craft may contain objects of a sensitive national security, archaeological or historical nature. They often also contain unexploded ordnance that could pose a danger to human health and the marine environment if disturbed, or other substances, including fuel oil and other hazardous liquids, that likewise pose a serious threat to human health and the marine environment if released.

Under the American position, which is shared by some other naval powers as well, sunken State craft seem definitely preserved from a first-come-first-served or freedom-of-fishing approach. The repetition of cases such as *Atocha* and *Cobb Coin*[147] is not likely to occur today. But the condition of the sunken cultural heritage which does not belong to any State is quite different, as the following instance shows.

7. The Saga of the *Titanic*

A) The Loss and the Discovery

In 1912 the passenger liner *Titanic*,[148] at that time the largest ship in the world[149] and the largest man-made object ever moved, set out on her maiden voyage.

The *Titanic*, which flew the British flag, had been built in Belfast by the shipyard Harland & Wolff. It was owned by the British company *White Star Lines*, belonging in 1912 to a shipping trust substantially controlled by American interests. On April 10 the liner, under the command of Captain Edward J. Smith, sailed on her first and last voyage from Southampton, England, en route to Cherbourg, France. In the two

---

[147] Above, paras. 6 A and 6 B.

[148] Information on the history of the *Titanic* and the location of the wreck is taken from the fascinating book by Ballard & Archbold, *The Discovery of the Titanic*, 2nd ed., Toronto, 1998.

[149] The *Titanic* (269 m of length, 28 m of width, 53 m of height from keel to the top of funnels, 46,329 tons of gross tonnage) was the largest ship in the world together with her sister ship *Olympic*, launched in 1910 and retired in 1935, after 24 years of fully satisfactory service. A third sister ship, the *Britannic*, was launched in 1914. During World War I, it was converted into a hospital ship and sunk by German mines in 1916. The wreck lies under 395 feet of water in the Greek territorial sea in the vicinity of the island of Kea. In 1995 it was explored by an expedition led by Mr. Ballard (see Ballard & Archbold, *Lost Liners*, Toronto, 1997, p. 116).

ports the liner was boarded by the passengers, most arriving on the boat-trains from London and Paris. She then left for Queenstown, Ireland, from where she departed on April 11 for the transatlantic crossing to New York, United States. The estimated number of passengers and crew on board was 2,228.

In the night between 14 and 15 April, other ships warned the *Titanic* of heavy ice pack and icebergs. The warnings were overlooked by the captain, who did not reduce speed, and by the *Titanic* wireless operators, who were busy with passengers' traffic of messages. At 11,40 p.m. of April 14, with the *Titanic* moving at a speed of 20.5 knots, the lookouts suddenly saw an iceberg about 500 yards ahead towering some 60 feet above the water. The officer in charge immediately gave the order to stop the engines and steer full astern. The *Titanic* began to veer to port, but the iceberg struck the starboard bow side and brushed along the side of the ship. Thirty-seven seconds elapsed from the sighting to the collision.

The *Titanic* was divided by 15 transverse bulkheads into 16 compartments that were said to be watertight. However, if more than four holds were flooded, the water would spill from one compartment into the next and so on. After the collision, five watertight compartments began to take on water. At that time the captain knew on the basis of mathematical calculations that the ship could stay afloat for about one-and-a-half hours only. He ordered distress calls to be made for assistance and the lifeboats to be uncovered. But in the 20 lifeboats there was only enough room for 1,178 people.[150]

At 2,17 a.m. of April 15 Capt. Smith told the crew members "it's every man for himself" and returned to the bridge to await his end. At 2,18 the ship broke in two and the bow section sank. At 2,20 the broken-off stern section righted itself for a few moments and slowly sank into the sea.

In the disaster of the *Titanic* 1,523 people died.[151] The inquiry conducted by the British Board of Trade recommended "more watertight compartments in ocean-going ships, the provision of lifeboats for all on board, as well as a better lookout".

In the meantime, the legend of the *Titanic* had begun:

> In the popular imagination the events of the night of April 14, 1912, have distilled themselves into a powerful morality play about overweening pride leading inevitably to a tragic fall. A great passenger ship, the largest and most luxurious yet built, sets out on her maiden voyage. She is widely believed to be "unsinkable" – although her builders and owners never make such a claim – and there are not enough lifeboats. Aboard are gathered a glittering array of the wealthy set of England and America, the celebrities of an age that worshipped old money and blue blood. In command is a veteran captain whose lack of self-doubt epitomizes his rich passengers' confidence in the world they control. Despite a number of warnings of ice ahead, he does not slow down and takes only the minimum precautions. He has made this passage countless times before and, besides, there is often ice in April.

[150] This was due to outdated British regulations on safety.

[151] Except for one, all 29 first and second class children were saved. However, 53 out of 76 third class children died.

> The ship hits an iceberg at full speed, a glancing blow but a fatal one, and begins to sink. The passengers are at first simply curious, turning the event into a diversion from shipboard routine. But as the ship begins to show a pronounced tilt at the bow and a slight but definite list to starboard they begin, reluctantly, to enter the lifeboats, many of which leave not even half full. Less than three hours later, the great ship has vanished beneath the freezing water of the North Atlantic.[152]

In 1985 an expedition to locate the wreck of the *Titanic* was jointly organized by Robert D. Ballard of the Woods Hole Oceanographic Institution, United States, and Jean-Louis Michel of IFREMER (*Institut Français de Recherche pour l'Exploitation de la Mer*), France. On 1 September 1985, Mr. Ballard discovered and photographed a boiler of the *Titanic* at a depth of 12,460 feet (3,798 m) on the ocean floor southeast of Newfoundland, Canada. Mr. Ballard made use of very advanced deepwater technology, namely a research vessel (*Knorr*), an unmanned submersible (*Argo*), loaded with video cameras and towed by a long fiber-optic cable, and a robot (*Jason*), attached to *Argo* on a tether and equipped with lights and stereo cameras.[153]

In 1986, Mr. Ballard led a second expedition under the sponsorship of the Woods Hole Oceanographic Institution,[154] but without French cooperation. This time he used a research vessel (*Atlantis II*) and a manned deepwater submersible (*Alvin*)[155] which was linked to a remotely controlled underwater robot (*Jason Junior*). The second expedition explored and photographed both the bow and the stern sections of the wreck, located about 1,970 feet away one from the other, and the vast field of debris scattered in the vicinity of the stern.[156]

The exact position of the wreck was not disclosed until the publication of a book by Mr. Ballard in 1987.[157] But a quite accurate indication of the location of the *Titanic* had already been given on 3 September 1985 by the *Evening Telegram*, a newspaper published in St. John's, Canada. Yet, the distance from the Canadian coast of the area where the wreck of the *Titanic* has been found is not univocally reported. The American judges locate it at about 368 n.m. from the coast, on what

[152] Ballard & Archbold, *The Discovery cit., supra* note 148, p. 10.

[153] *Jason* had its own propulsion system and was able to roam into risky places, gather specimens and take close color images.

[154] Mr. Ballard's activities, both in 1985 and 1986, were primarily funded by the United States Navy.

[155] *Alvin* could carry three people.

[156] "The contents of the *Titanic*'s kitchens were laid out on the sea floor, copper pots and pans (and lids) polished to a sheen by the current, serving dishes, plates, cups, and even a copper sink. One pan even had a big piece of pink floor covering sitting in it. There was a wine and spirit cellar that would have fetched a fortune laid out before us – including champagne bottles, many with the corks intact. Soon it became difficult to keep track: porcelain chamber pots, white enameled metal bed headboards, ornate wrought iron supports from the wooden deck benches, rusting bathtubs, faucets marked hot and cold, sinks, brightly colored red-and-white floor tiles – even a spittoon" (Ballard & Archbold, *The Discovery cit., supra* note 148, p. 148).

[157] This was the first edition of the book quoted above, note 148. The position is 41° 43′ 57″ Lat N, 49° 56′ 49″ Long W (bow section) and 41° 43′ 35″ Lat N, 49° 56′ 54″ Long W (stern section).

they assume is the bed of the high seas.[158] However, the agreement finalized (but not signed) in 2000 by Canada, France, the United Kingdom and the United States[159] locates the wreck "325 miles southeast of Newfoundland", "on the Canadian continental shelf". This could be the case in the light of the new and extremely complex definition of continental shelf given by Art. 76 of the United Nations Convention on the Law of the Sea, according to which the continental shelf can extend, beyond the distance of 200 n.m. from the coast, up to the outer edge of the continental margin. It appears that the *Titanic* is located well inside a line drawn 60 n.m. from the foot of the Canadian continental slope and within both the alternative limits provided by Art. 76, namely 100 n.m. from the 2500 m isobath and 350 n.m. from the baselines of the Canadian territorial sea.[160]

B) The R.M.S. Titanic Memorial Act of 1986

The story of the legal developments which followed the discovery of the wreck of the *Titanic* is both amazing and disappointing. It may justify Mr. Ballard's pessimistic remark about "the high-seas carnival that has unfolded at the *Titanic* wreck".[161]

Yet, the first chapter of the story, that is the specific legislation enacted in 1986, aimed at a promising objective. On 21 October 1986, the United States adopted the *R.M.S. Titanic Memorial Act of 1986*,[162] "to encourage international efforts to designate the shipwreck of the R.M.S. Titanic as an international maritime memorial and to provide for reasonable research, exploration, and, if appropriate, salvage activities with respect to the shipwreck" (as stated in the preamble). The findings of the Act specify that

> (1) The R.M.S. Titanic, the ocean liner which sank on her maiden voyage after striking an iceberg on 14 April 1912, should be designated as an international maritime memorial to the men, women, and children who perished aboard her;
> (2) The recent discovery of the R.M.S. Titanic, lying more than 12,000 feet beneath the ocean surface, demonstrates the practical applications of ocean science and engineering;
> (3) The R.M.S. Titanic, well preserved in the cold, oxygen-poor waters of the deep North Atlantic Ocean, is of major national and international cultural and historical significance, and merits appropriate international protection; and
> (4) The R.M.S. Titanic represents a special opportunity for deep ocean scientific research and exploration.

Under sect. 6 of the Act,

---

[158] See, for example, *R.M.S. Titanic, Inc. v. The Wrecked and Abandoned Vessel believed to be the R.M.S. Titanic*, 9 F. Supp. 2d 624, 629 (E.D.Va, June 23, 1998).

[159] See below, para. 7 B.

[160] See the thorough study by Ruffmann, Townsend Gault & Vanderzwaag, *Legal Jurisdiction over the Titanic*, in 37 (1988) *Lighthouse* 23.

[161] Ballard & Archbold, *supra* note 149, at 217.

[162] Text in U.N., *Law of the Sea Bulletin*, No. 9, 1987, p. 36.

(a) The Secretary [= the Secretary of State] is directed to enter into negotiations with the United Kingdom, France, Canada, and other interested nations to develop an international agreement which provides for:
(1) The designation of R.M.S. Titanic as an international maritime memorial; and
(2) Research on, exploration of, and if appropriate, salvage of the R.M.S. Titanic consistent with the international guidelines developed pursuant to section 5 and the purposes of this Act.[163]

The Act does not explain why four States are singled out as potential parties to the agreement envisaged. However, the United Kingdom, France, Canada seem to be the countries which, together with the United States, have the closest links with the wreck. Other "interested nations" (but interested why?) are entitled to become parties as well.

The Act sets forth what provisional regime should apply pending the conclusion of the international agreement. This regime specifically prevents salvage activities:

It is the sense of Congress that research and limited exploration activities concerning the R.M.S. Titanic should continue for the purpose of enhancing public knowledge of its scientific, cultural, and historical significance: Provided that, pending adoption of the international agreement described in section 6 (a) or implementation of the international guidelines described in section 5, no person should conduct any such research or exploration activity which would physically alter, disturb, or salvage the R.M.S. Titanic (sect. 7).

The Act also contains a clause on "disclaimer of extraterritorial sovereignty" over the marine areas where the wreck is located:

By enactment of this Act, the United States does not assert sovereignty, or sovereign or exclusive rights or jurisdiction over, or the ownership of, any marine areas or the R.M.S. Titanic (sect. 8).

It is surprising to see how some American courts have failed to apply the Act,[164] and in particular its sect. 7. In 1994, the United States District Court for the Eastern District of Virginia, Norfolk Division, granted exclusive salvor rights to R.M.S. Titanic, Inc. (RMST), a corporation incorporated in Florida. In 1998 the same District Court set aside the Act with the following remarks:

No treaty, as envisioned by the Act, has ever been negotiated. The Executive Branch invited other nations to enter into such negotiations but received no

[163] Under sect. 5 of the Act, the Administrator of the National Oceanic and Atmospheric Administration (NOAA) is directed to enter into consultations with the United Kingdom, France, Canada, and other interested nations to develop international guidelines for research on, exploration of, and if appropriate, salvage of the R.M.S. Titanic.

[164] The remark that federal district courts "failed to apply the clear prescriptions of Congress" is made by Nafziger, *The Evolving Role of Admiralty Courts in Litigation Related to Historic Wreck*, paper submitted to the International Bar Association Conference (Durban, 2002), p. 10.

> interest. (...) Moreover, it does not appear that negotiations will ever begin. Twelve years have gone by since the Act was passed and no negotiations have ensued. Meanwhile, the wreck is in international waters and no country or combination of countries has territorial jurisdiction over it. The only law that governs is the internationally recognized principles of admiralty and maritime law (including the law of salvage).[165]

In fact negotiations for the drafting of an "agreement concerning the shipwrecked vessel R.M.S. Titanic" were conducted between 1997 and 2000 by Canada, France, the United Kingdom and the United States. The text of an agreement was finalized on 5 January 2000 and annexed to the final minute of the negotiations. But the national procedures for the signature of the agreement have not been completed yet.[166]

C) The Granting of Salvor Rights

In 1987 the deep-sea submersible *Nautile* of IFREMER returned on the wreck of the *Titanic* on behalf of the British-registered consortium Oceanic Research and Exploration Ltd. More than 300 objects were recovered for preservation and display in exhibitions.

Also Titanic Ventures, a limited partnership, explored the wreck of the *Titanic*, bringing up approximately 1,800 artefacts. It then sold its interests in the salvage operations and the artefacts to RMST.[167] On 27 August 1993, RMST presented to the District Court a wine decanter salvaged from the *Titanic*, requesting to be awarded the sole and exclusive salvage rights for the wreck.

In September 1993, notice of the procedure was provided to other potential salvors by publication in three newspapers (*The Virginian-Pilot*, *The Wall Street Journal* and *The Journal of Commerce*). This means that, "for admiralty law purposes, the whole world had notice that rights to the wreck of the R.M.S. *Titanic* were litigated" in the Court.[168] Only Liverpool and London Steamship Protection and Indemnity Association, the former insurer of the *Titanic*, filed a claim, which was later dismissed, following an agreement concluded by the insurer and RMST.

On 7 June 1994, the District Court entered an order conferring to RMST the salvor-in-possession status. The wording of the order deserves to be reproduced:

> RMS Titanic, Inc., is the salvor in possession of the wreck and wreck site of the *RMS Titanic*, including without limitation, the hull, machinery, engine, tackle, apparel, appurtenances, contents and cargo, and that RMS Titanic, Inc., is the true, sole and exclusive owner of any items salvaged from the wreck of the defendant vessel in the past and, so long as RMS Titanic, Inc., remains salvor

---

[165] See decision quoted *supra* note 158, p. 639.

[166] The text of the agreement can be read on the Internet. Due to its uncertain legal status it will not be analyzed here.

[167] Mr. Ballard has nothing to do with Titanic Ventures, RMST and their shareholders.

[168] See decision quoted *supra* note 158, p. 634.

in possession, items salvaged in the future, and is entitled to all salvage rights, and that default judgment is entered against all potential claimants who have not yet filed claims and such claims are therefore barred and precluded so long as RMS Titanic, Inc., remains salvor in possession".

The order, as stated by the District Court itself in a subsequent decision, was "designed to adjudicate rights in specific property against all of the world".[169] It was issued on the promise, made by the counsel for RMST, that it was RMST's intention "to display these artifacts and to try to get money back out of admissions to the display rather than selling them off".

For its salvage operations, RMST and its predecessor Titanic Ventures chartered a research vessel and a deepwater submersible (*Nautile*) from IFREMER. Following the expeditions made in 1987, 1993, 1994, 1996, 1998, 2000, more than 6000 artefacts were recovered from the wreck site to be exhibited in a number of countries.[170] While no artefacts have been put on the market so far, RMST began selling to the public the coal retrieved from the vessel,[171] on the assumption that the coal is a natural substance and not a man-made artefact. RMST financed its salvage operations through royalties from ticket sales at the artefact exhibits, sale of licenses for artefact replicas, photographs, videos, clothes and other products. In 1996 RMST planned to raise a piece of the hull lying on the seabed. The attempt failed for technical reasons.[172] But it succeeded in 1998.

D) The Salvor against the Competing Salvor

In 1996, a competing salvor, Mr. John A. Joslyn, filed a motion requesting that the District Court rescind its 1994 order. Mr. Joslyn put forward that RMST had failed to salvage the *Titanic* diligently and lacked the financial capacity to undertake further salvage operations.

By an order of 10 May 1996, the District Court dismissed the motion. The District Court took into consideration not only the time, effort and money that RMST had invested in the salvage operation, as well as its chances of success, but also the salvor's preservation efforts of a vessel of historic importance. But the merits of RMST went beyond preservation of the *Titanic*:

> Finally, RMST has done more than merely preserve the site and the artifacts; it has made the artifacts available to the public through exhibitions, thereby

---

[169] *R.M.S. Titanic, Inc. v. The Wrecked and Abandoned Vessel believed to be the R.M.S. Titanic*, 920 F. Supp. 96, 97 (E.D.Va, April 1, 1996).

[170] An exhibition is presently being held in Paris from March to August 2003 (see the catalogue published by RMST: *Trésors Titanic*, Gand, 2003).

[171] The coal is sold in small pieces, contained in a display case with an accompanying plaque.

[172] "In late August of 1996, I followed the progress, with a mixture of fascination and dismay, of the salvagers attempting to raise a piece of hull plating from the *Titanic* debris field. (...) At the last minute, the cables that attached the floats to the salvaged section of the *Titanic*'s hull parted and it dropped back to the ocean bottom where it belongs" (Ballard & Archbold, *Lost Liners supra*, note 149, p. 214).

benefiting the public more than the requisite at-site-archaeological preservation could do.[173]

E) The Salvor against the Photographer

A few months later, Mr. Joslyn, who had also planned to conduct an expedition solely to photograph the wreck, was defeated for the second time. By an order of 13 August 1996, the District Court found that RMST had "the exclusive right to take any and all types of photographic images of the *Titanic* wreck and wreck site". In particular,

> the Court is of the opinion that photographs can be marketed like any other physical artifact and, therefore, the rights to images, photographs, videos, and the like belong to R.M.S. Titanic.[174]
>
> Therefore, if R.M.S. Titanic is not selling artifacts like traditional salvors, it must be given the rights to other means of obtaining income. The Court finds that, in a case such as this, allowing another "salvor" to take photographs of the wreck and wreck site is akin to allowing another salvor to physically invade the wreck and take artifacts themselves.[175]

F) The Salvor against the Tour Operator

In 1998, a commercial venture was planned by Deep Ocean Expeditions, a British Virgin Islands corporation headquartered on the Isle of Man, Great Britain, to provide tourists with the opportunity to view and photograph the wreck of the *Titanic* for $32,000 per person. The expedition was to be organised in cooperation with the Shirshov Institute of Oceanology of the Russian Academy of Sciences in Moscow, using Soviet made MIR submersibles supported by a mother ship (the *Akademik Keldysh*). The promotional material pointed out that the organizers of the expedition "will categorically avoid any collection of artifacts or pieces of the wreck, neither interfacing with nor damaging the wreck in any way" and acknowledged that "there is a salvor in possession claim recognized by an American Court under Admiralty Law, awarded to a U.S. company R.M.S. Titanic, Inc.".

On a motion filed by RMST, the District Court issued on 23 June 1998 an order that enjoined all the parties interested in the expedition[176] from interfering with the rights of RMST, as salvor in possession of the wreck and the wreck site, including the right of obtaining any image, video or photograph of the wreck or wreck site.

---

173 *R.M.S. Titanic, Inc. v. The Wrecked and Abandoned Vessel*, 924 F. Supp. 714, 723 (E.D.Va, May 10, 1996).

174 *R.M.S. Titanic, Inc. v. The Wrecked and Abandoned Vessel*, 1996 U.S. Dist. LEXIS 22227, 3 (E.D.Va, August 13, 1996).

175 *Ibidem*, p. 5.

176 Including Mr. Christopher S. Haver who had signed to pay Deep Ocean Expeditions $32,000 for transportation to the wreck, where he intended to take photographs and videotapes solely for his own personal use.

In the order the District Court also gave the geographical coordinates of the points delimiting a 168-square-mile zone of rectangular shape, the so called "wreck site", where anyone was forbidden to enter with the intention of performing acts which would interfere with the rights granted to RMST.[177] The District Court acknowledged that "international waters – or the high seas – are free to all States, (...) and no state may exercise sovereignty over any part of the high seas". But it added that the rules of international law "must be harmonized with the internationally recognized rules of salvage"[178] and that "restricting freedom of navigation over a few square miles of the vast North Atlantic Ocean is hardly a significant intrusion".[179]

The order of 23 June 1998 was reversed by a judgment rendered on 24 March 1999 by the United States Court of Appeals for the Fourth Circuit.[180] The Court of Appeals found that the law of salvage does not extend to the vesting of exclusive rights to visit, view and photograph a wreck and a wreck site:

> To award, in the name of salvage service, the exclusive right to photograph a shipwreck, would, we believe, also tend to convert what was designed as a salvage operation on behalf of the owners into an operation serving the salvors. The incentives would run counter to the purpose of salvage. Salvors would be less inclined to save property because they might be able to obtain more compensation by leaving the property in place and selling photographic images or charging the public admission to go view it. Even if we were to assume that the salvors had full title to the yet to be recovered shipwreck, as would be the case if the law of finds were applied, it is doubtful that such title to property lying in international waters would include the right to exclude others from viewing and photographing it while in its public site. Exclusive viewing and photographing of property is usually achieved by exercising exclusive possession and removing the property to a private or controllable location where it cannot be viewed or photographed except under conditions controlled by the owner. But a property right does not normally include the right to exclude viewing and photographing of the property when it is located in a public place.[181]

The Court of Appeals also disagreed with the District Court's exclusion of persons from entering a specific area on the high seas, as it conflicted with the principle of freedom of navigation:

> The district court's August 1996 injunction also prohibited anyone from entering within a 10-mile radius of the wreck site to search, survey, or obtain any image of the wreck or wreck site, and the court's June 1998 order prohibited anyone from

---

[177] Nothing in the order was to be constructed "as restricting customary rights of surface navigation on the high seas which do not otherwise violate the specific restrictions set forth" in the order itself.

[178] See decision quoted *supra* note 158, p. 634.

[179] *Ibidem.*

[180] *R.M.S. Titanic, Inc. v. Haver*, 171 F.3d 943 (4th Cir., March 24, 1999). The text of the decision is reprinted in (1999) *ILM* 796.

[181] (1999) *ILM* 815.

> entering, for a similar purpose, a rectangular area around the wreck computed to be 168-square miles. Neither prohibition is justified by the law of salvage or allowed by the law of free navigation on the high seas. For the same reasons that we gave in denying exclusive viewing and photographing rights – that to do so would alarmingly expand salvage law and interfere with the right of free navigation – we also reverse these aspects of the district court's orders.[182]

The Court of Appeal's decision is particularly interesting in the passages where it seeks to clarify what "admiralty law", as well as its components of "salvage law" and "law of finds", are. The Court of Appeals moves from Art. III of the Constitution of the United States, which extends the judicial power of federal courts to "all Cases of admiralty and maritime Jurisdiction", and reaches the following conclusions:

> The body of admiralty law referred to in Article III did not depend on any express or implied legislative action. Its existence, rather, preceded the adoption of the Constitution. It was the well-known and well-developed "venerable law of the sea" which arose from the custom among "seafaring men" (...), and which enjoyed "international comity" (...). Nations have applied this body of maritime law for 3,000 years or more. Although it would add little to recount the full history here, we note that codifications of the maritime law have been preserved from ancient Rhodes (900 B.C.E.), Rome (Justinian's *Corpus Juris Civilis*) (533 C.E.), City of Trani (Italy) (1063), England (the Law of Oleron) (1189), the Hanse Towns or Hanseatic League (1597), and France (1681), all articulating similar principles. And they all constitute a part of the continuing maritime tradition of the law of nations – the *jus gentium*.[183]

The Court of Appeals also assumes that admiralty law, as administered by the American courts, can receive an extra-territorial application:

> The exercise of admiralty subject matters has never been limited to maritime causes arising solely in the United States territorial waters. On the contrary, maritime causes arising from matters on the high seas anywhere in the world have traditionally been brought to courts of admiralty, subject only to a discretionary exercise of the doctrine of *forum non conveniens*.[184]

The Court of Appeals recalls that admiralty law includes both a law of finds and a law of salvage, which must be applied one to the exclusion of the other. As regards the former,

> under the law of finds, a person, who discovers a shipwreck in navigable waters that has been long lost and abandoned and who reduces the property to actual or constructive possession, becomes the property's owner.[185]

---

[182] *Ibidem*, p. 816.
[183] *Ibidem*, p. 807.
[184] *Ibidem*, p. 808.
[185] *Ibidem*, p. 808.

As regards the latter,

> the principles of salvage law are intended to encourage persons to render prompt, voluntary, and effective service to ships in peril or in distress by assuring them compensation and reward for their salvage efforts.[186]
>
> Upon rendering salvage service, a salvor obtains a lien in the saved property by operation of law to secure payment of compensation and award due from the property owner. (...) This lien attaches to the property to the exclusion of all others, including the property's true owner. And to facilitate enforcement of the lien, the salvor enjoys a possessory interest in the property until the salvor is compensated. (...) Because the salvor's lien is exclusive and prior to all others, so too, the salvor's possessory interest in the *res* is enjoyed to the exclusion of all others, including the *res*' true owner. By rendering salvage service, the salvor thus acquires a limited property interest in the goods saved – a first lien and exclusive possession – until the salvor has been paid or his right against the property has been enforced. (...) While this interest attaches only to saved property, to protect a salvor's general salvage rights, a court of admiralty will protect the inchoate right of salvors in yet-to-be-saved property for a reasonable period.[187]

The Court of Appeals remarks that, "because the law of finds deprives the true owner of a property right, the courts of admiralty disfavor its application and prefer to apply the law of salvage in its stead. (...). Accordingly the law of finds is most often applied in the context of long-lost shipwrecks".[188]

G) The Salvor against the United States

In 2000 the negotiations for the "agreement concerning the shipwrecked vessel R.M.S. Titanic"[189] were drawing to their conclusion. This prompted the RMST to file a motion against the United States Secretary of State, the Secretary of Commerce and the Administrator of the National Oceanic and Atmospheric Administration, seeking a declaration that the defendants, by virtue of their efforts to implement the Act, were unlawfully interfering with the exclusive salvage rights of the plaintiff. By an order of 15 September 2000, the District Court denied the motion, remarking that "plaintiff may renew its motion when and if an international Agreement is agreed to and signed by the parties to the Agreement, final guidelines are drafted, and Congress passes implementing legislation".[190]

---

186 *Ibidem*, p. 809.
187 *Ibidem*, p. 810.
188 *Ibidem*, p. 809.
189 See above, para. 7 B.
190 *R.M.S. Titanic, Inc. v. The Wrecked and Abandoned Vessel believed to be the R.M.S. Titanic*, 2000 U.S. Dist. LEXIS 20140, 3 (E.D.Va, September 15, 2000).

H) The Titanic Artefacts Will be Sold

After the 1999 decision of the Court of Appeals,[191] RMST started to maintain that the refusal to give it exclusive visitation and photographic rights had a substantial adverse impact on its income and impaired its ability to finance further salvage operations. In November 1999 the management of RMST changed and a new business plan was articulated "to maximize shareholder value while still protecting the archaeological and historical value of the wreck". While the previous management had focused on earnings generated through the exhibition of artifacts, the new strategy included also "the possible disposition of artifacts to increase revenues".

On 28 June 2000, the District Court issued *sua sponte* an order, directing RMST not to sell, or otherwise dispose of, any artefacts recovered from the wreck. The order restated that RMST had been continued as salvor-in-possession on the understanding that it would have exhibited to the public the artefacts in question. The order was modified on 30 April 2001, to reflect the fact that RMST remained free to sell or encumber any coal it had recovered from the wreck site. Other orders were made by the District Court on 26 September and 19 October 2001, recognizing that "circumstances change and it becomes necessary to change plans and approaches". This could mean that the District Court was ready to consider plans for the sale of artefacts recovered by RMST from the wreck, provided that they were sold as a collection and not as individual artefacts.[192]

RMST decided to appeal the 2001 orders. It maintained that, under the 1994 order appointing it as salvor-in-possession,[193] it had become the absolute owner *in specie* of the artefacts, free and clear, and was entitled to sell them, notwithstanding its earlier expressions to the court of an intent not to do so. It pointed out that the 1994 order did not contain contingencies or exceptions and that admiralty law does not permit the imposing of restrictions on the disposition of artefacts for some perceived public benefit. Such restrictions would equate to a taking of private property.

The Court of Appeals, by a decision rendered on 12 April 2002,[194] rejected the arguments of RMST and affirmed the orders of the District Court. The Court of Appeals found that "RMST's arguments are grounded on a fundamental misunderstanding of its role as salvor-in-possession".[195] Surprisingly enough, only in 2002 did it appear that, in rendering the 1994 order, the District Court made an ambiguous, if not completely mistaken, application of admiralty law by confusing salvage law with the law of finds!

---

[191] Above, para. 7 F.

[192] Yet, in April 2001 RMST pointed out that two organizations, the Titanic Foundation and the Museums and Galleries of Northern Ireland, had expressed interest in purchasing some or all of the *Titanic* artefacts.

[193] Above, para. 7 B.

[194] *R.M.S. Titanic, Inc. v. The Wrecked and Abandoned Vessel believed to be the R.M.S. Titanic*, 2002 *U.S. App. LEXIS* 6799 (4th Cir., April 12, 2002).

[195] *Ibidem*, p. 2.

As the Court of Appeals remarks, a salvor is someone who voluntarily saves life or property at sea. However,

> by saving property at sea, salvors do not become the property's owner; rather, they save it for the owners and become entitled to a reward from the owner or from its property. (...) The reward provides an incentive for rendering salvage services at sea, and courts of admiralty have long enforced claims to this award against owners.[196]
>
> The principal method of enforcing a salvor's award is through the recognition of a salvor's lien in the property saved. (...) The maritime lien arises from the moment salvage service is performed (...) and, as with any other lien, secures the payment of the as-yet-to-be-determined salvage award. Such liens are a temporary encumbrance of the property saved, lasting only until payment of a salvage award can be made. (...) The process begins when the salvor commences an *in rem* proceeding in admiralty against the property. (...) The salvor must provide notice of the *in rem* proceeding to the owner, other lienholders, and potential claimants to the property. (...) If the owner appears and pays the salvage award determined by the court, the lien is discharged and the owner takes the property clear of the salvage lien. (...) On the other hand, if the owner does not appear, then the case continues as an *in rem* action, and the court determines the award, sells the property, and, from the proceeds, pays the salvor. (...) Any remainder from the sale is remitted to the owner. If the owner is no longer living, the court presumably pays the excess to the owner's heirs, and, if there are no heirs, to the state according to its escheat law. If the sale of the salvaged property yields too little to satisfy the salvor's lien for a reward, then all of the proceeds from the sale of the salvaged property are paid to the salvor. Courts have held that an award cannot exceed the value of the property itself.[197]

As a rule, the salvor does not have a direct right to title in the property. However, admiralty courts may, as a matter of discretion, award the salvor title to the property in lieu of the proceeds of the sale, if it becomes apparent to the court that the proceeds from the sale would clearly be inadequate to pay the salvor its full reward. Once the reward is paid, whether in money or in kind, "the reward becomes the property of the salvor to do what it wants".[198] But the salvor's interest to remain in business as a viable company is an issue devoid of any relevance for the court.

According to the Court of Appeals, the ambiguity of the 1994 District Court

---

[196] *Ibidem*, p. 21–22.

[197] *Ibidem*, p. 23–26. The six factors to be considered in determining the award are: 1) The labour expended by the salvors in rendering the salvage service; 2) The promptitude, skill and energy displayed in rendering the service and saving the property; 3) The value of the property employed by the salvor in rendering the service; 4) The risk encurred by the salvors in securing the property from the impending peril; 5) The value of the property saved; 6) The degree of danger from which the property was rescued.

[198] *Ibidem*, p. 28. To do what the salvor wants includes – the question may be asked – destroying the objects of historical value that he has recovered?

order lies in the fact that it "uses both salvage language and finds language", giving RMST property rights and taking them away at the same time.[199] But the true intent of the order was to give RMST the role of salvor, not of finder:

> It appears to give ownership of the artifacts to RMST – declaring RMST the "true, sole and exclusive owner" – but then in the same sentence states that RMST "is entitled to all salvage rights" as long as it maintains its role as salvor. Indeed, the lead-in to the same sentence also states that RMST is the salvor-in-possession – not the finder – of the wreck and the wreck site. Because the court was clearly applying the law of salvage and not the law of finds, it could only convey possession, not title.[200]

This means that RMST, being a salvor and not a finder, has still to complete the salvage service that it intends to perform and have its reward determined by the court. Only after the reward is determined can RMST seek to enforce its lien against the artefacts themselves. An example made by the Court of Appeals shows what could become the fate of the objects recovered from the wreck of the *Titanic*:

> Thus, hypothetically, if RMST were to recover an artifact valued at $50 million (we know, for instance, that paintings have at times sold for more) and the court were to determine that the appropriate salvage award was $5 million, the court could not give the property to RMST in satisfaction of its salvage lien because the lien exists only to the extent of $5 million. The court instead would have to sell the property and remit to RMST $5 million from the proceeds. On the other hand, if RMST were to recover an artifact valued at $2 million (a historic vase, for example) and the court were to determine, again, that the appropriate salvage award was $5 million, a sale would be useless. In lieu of a sale to foreclose the salvage lien, the court could simply convey title in the $2 million vase to RMST, essentially providing RMST what is analogous to a "deed in lieu of foreclosure".[201]

In conclusion, commercial evaluation and commercial sale, either individually or as a collection, are the likely destiny of the artifacts removed from the wreck of the *Titanic*. The non-commercial value of such a historic ship has no relevance whatsoever.

I) Mr. Ballard's View

The elements of the legal saga undergone by the wreck of the *Titanic* speak for themselves. Time will tell about the future developments, as the saga has not yet come to an end.

A very sensible evaluation about the performance of salvage law (or was it law of

---

[199] *Ibidem*, p. 34–35.
[200] *Ibidem*, p. 36.
[201] *Ibidem*, p. 27–28.

finds?), as it was applied to the *Titanic* by the American courts, comes from the discoverer of the wreck. Writing some years after his second and last expedition, Mr. Ballard makes some bitter remarks about what subsequently happened:

> My simple wish is that any who do mount new expeditions to visit the wreck will respect the site as I have.[202]
>
> Since my last visit in 1986, six expeditions have sent robots or submarines down to the wreck site, either to film it or to salvage relics. And there seems little prospect that this ongoing high-seas drama will conclude any time soon. (...) The wreck and the debris field have been picked over by salvagers who profess respect for the site's historical importance but more often demonstrate careless disregard.[203]

Mr. Ballard reveals that he personally resisted the temptation to engage in salvage activities and supply his cellar with a bottle of "*Titanic*" champagne:

> Maritime collectors around the world would have paid thousands of dollars for a piece of the ship. And artifacts could have been easily recovered with *Alvin's* powerful robot arm designed to collect biological and geological samples in the deep sea. How I would have loved a bottle of *Titanic* champagne for my own wine cellar. But from all our discussions it became clear the *Titanic* has no true archaeological value. Although it is tempting to make the comparison, the *Titanic* is not a pyramid of the deep. We knew exactly how the ship was built and what was on board. Recovering a chamber pot or a wine bottle or a copper cooking pan would really just be pure treasure-hunting. My major funder, the Navy, wasn't interested in using taxpayers' money for this purpose. Nor was I.[204]

Under Mr. Ballard's view, the wreck should and could be preserved *in situ*:

> The *Titanic*'s salvagers argue that they are preserving for posterity pieces of wreck that will otherwise decay into rubble, but this need not be the case. The technology for arresting the decline of this and other great lost ships already exists. We could clean the *Titanic*'s hull and repaint it underwater, if there was an agreement to maintain it the way we found it in 1985.[205]

Equally unequivocal are the opposition of Mr. Ballard to the salvaging of important modern wrecks and his desire for an appropriate international agreement:

> My opposition to the salvage of the *Titanic* and other important modern wrecks is well known, and I won't review my arguments here, but the fate of the *Titanic* since our 1985 discovery demonstrates the need for some sort of international agreement to govern the treatment of historically significant

[202] Ballard & Archbold, *The Discovery supra* note 148, at 210.
[203] *Ibidem*, p. 213.
[204] *Ibidem*, p. 138.
[205] Ballard & Archbold, *Lost Liners supra* note 149, at 214.

shipwrecks – whether they lie in the deep ocean or in more accessible shallow waters. What with the confusion between jurisdictions and the competing agendas of those interested in treasure and those determined to preserve history, the current situation borders on chaos.[206]

8. The Skerki Bank Deep Sea Project

Mr. Ballard was adamant enough against the salvaging of the *Titanic* and left the bottles of *Titanic* champagne where they had been found. But it is astonishing to see how, without raising any doubt about consistency, Mr. Ballard himself was ready to remove artefacts from ancient shipwrecks located in the Mediterranean:

> There are many true unopened "pyramids" in the deep sea. For example, thousands and thousands of ships were lost in the deep basins of the Mediterranean and wait to be discovered, ships of real archaeological worth. Their cargoes merit documentation, recovery, and preservation.[207]
>
> In the summer of 1997, I will lead an expedition to the Mediterranean that will perform the first-ever excavation of a wreck in deep water. To accomplish this we plan to mount a powerful pumping system on the U.S. Navy nuclear-powered *NR-1* submarine that will vacuum away two thousand years of sediment from three ancient Roman wrecks.[208]

Four expeditions to locate shipwrecks and retrieve artefacts were undertaken in the period between 1988 and 1997. As it appears from an article published by Mr. Robert Ballard,[209] one of the expeditions, called Skerki Bank Deep Sea Project, utilised a support ship (*Carolyn Chouest*), a nuclear-powered research submarine of the United States Navy (*NR-1*) and a remotely operated vehicle (*Jason*).[210] Ancient shipwrecks were located in an area on the Mediterranean continental shelf beyond the limit of the territorial seas of the coastal States.[211] It seems that no previous official information about the expedition was given to any of the Mediterranean coastal States.

---

[206] Ballard & Archbold, *Lost Liners supra* note 149, at 214.

[207] Ballard & Archbold, *The Discovery supra* note 148, at 138. On the results of the first project that took place in 1989 on a Roman wreck (called *Isis*) found in an area of the Mediterranean high seas about 60 n.m. off Tunisia and 75 n.m. off Italy, see McCann & Freed, *Deep Water Archaeology: A Late-Roman Ship from Carthage and an Ancient Trade Route near Skerki Bank off Northwest Sicily*, Ann Arbor, 1994.

[208] Ballard & Archbold, *The Discovery supra* note 148, at 221. "In subsequent years, I hope to explore the Black Sea, a busy trade route in ancient times. If our hypothesis is right, any wrecks we find in that oxygen-poor inland sea will be amazingly well preserved" (*ibidem*).

[209] Ballard, *High-Tech Search for Roman Shipwrecks*, in 4 (1998) *National Geographic* 32.

[210] The project was supported in part by the United States National Geographic Society, the Office of Naval Research and the J.M. Kaplan Fund.

[211] This area includes the Skerki bank and is located along a navigational route which crossed the Mediterranean in ancient times. Several archaeological discoveries of objects pertaining to the Phoenician, Greek and Roman civilizations have been made there.

Mr. Ballard reported removing more than 150 artifacts (amphorae, glassware, anchors) from the seabed. When asked about the concern that his expeditions had raised,[212] Mr. Ballard relied on the principle of freedom of the sea: "I do not like being wrongly accused. (...) I was well outside 12-mile limit.[213]

Mr. Ballard pointed out that the objects removed from the Mediterranean "were protected by the non-profit Sea Research Foundation which would not allow their exploitation". This implies that the Sea Research Foundation is supposed to be the owner of the objects in question.

Surprisingly enough, Mr. Ballard himself complained of the lack of rules to deter the looting of the underwater cultural heritage:

> Far from being a plunderer, he said, he was worried about others who would try to loot the ancient ships with no international laws to deter them.[214]

The removed artefacts are now in the United States of America:

> The artifacts we bring home from our first deep-sea excavation in 1997, after carefully mapping the wrecks we excavate, will be put on display in the brand new Institute for Exploration in Mystic, Connecticut, due to open in April 1999.[215]

---

[212] "The underwater exploration programme at Woods Hole Oceanographic Institution is built on US Navy and NASA sponsorship of techniques which will enable the recovery from deep water of crashed or lost craft or equipment; for field expeditions, however, the project leader, Robert Ballard, has had to win additional support from transmitting, inserting into educational programmes, and publishing stories of wide general interest, such as the search for *Titanic* or *Bismarck*; his Mediterranean cruises of 1988–89, which studies undersea volcanoes and ancient archaeological sites in deep water, were likewise partly committed to bringing home a story. To make the archaeology more immediate, and, indeed, to understand the objects found, it was desirable to clear, move and even raise items lying in deep-water wrecks. This objective clashed with the principle of conservation of the archeological resource which is now widely incorporated in guidance notes and professional rules for archaeologists, and which discourages anyone from disturbing deep-water wrecks which are under no apparent threat. That material was raised from both dispersed scatters and a coherent wreck led, in the period after the 1989 expedition to criticism which came from more than one quarter, and to which both Ballard and McCann (his archaeological director) are, naturally sensitive" (Parker, *Late Roman Trade in Deep Water*, in (1996) *Journal of Roman Archaeology* 560).

[213] *The Times*, 6 August 1997. For a different view see Blackman, *Is Maritime Archaeology on Course?*, in (2000) *American Journal of Archaeology* 596: "(...) I wonder whether it has been realized in the United States how much offense has been caused to their sensibilities by American archaeological operations in deep water in the Mediterranean". The sensibilities in question are those of the Mediterranean countries.

[214] *Ibidem*. Incidentally, Mr. Ballard's attitude of mind may seem in contradiction with the spirit of the recent Agreement between Italy and the United States concerning the imposition of import restrictions on categories of archaeological material representing the pre-classical, classical and imperial Roman periods of Italy (Washington, 19 January 2001; text in (2001) *ILM* 1031). Under the Agreement, "both Governments agree that, in order for United States import restrictions to be most successful in thwarting pillage, the Government of the Republic of Italy shall endeavor to strengthen cooperation among nations within the Mediterranean Region for the protection of the cultural patrimony of the region, recognizing that political boundaries and cultural boundaries do not coincide; and will seek increased cooperation from other art-importing nations to restrict illicit imports, in the effort to deter further pillage" (Art. II, D).

[215] Ballard & Archbold, *The Discovery supra* note 148, at 221.

9. Conclusion (Why It May Be Better if Columbus' Wrecks are not Found)

The relevance of wrecks for research and the cultural progress of mankind in general can hardly be denied. In the last few years, diving equipment and deep water technologies have been developed which were unimaginable before.[216] As water can preserve organic remains (such as food, clothes and wood) better than they would survive on land, a wreck becomes a time-capsule of the past.

The instances selected in the preceding pages are only a part of the cases that could have been mentioned to show the importance of the preservation of the underwater cultural heritage. Nothing has been said about wrecks such as the *Vasa*,[217] the *Lusitania*,[218] the *Estonia*,[219] the *La Belle*.[220] Nor have the caravels lost by Christopher Columbus, and never found as yet, been evoked.[221]

To tell the truth, if the law of salvage or the law of finds were to be applied, it would be better if the Columbus' caravels remained lost for ever.[222] The application

---

[216] On the evolution of underwater exploration techniques see Blackman, *Underwater Cultural Heritage*, in Council of Europe, Parliamentary Assembly, *Maritime and Fluvial Cultural Heritage*, Doc. 8867, Appendix of 12 October 2000, p. 13.

[217] On 10 August 1628 the *Vasa*, the admiral ship of the Swedish fleet, sailed from Stockholm for her maiden voyage. But she capsized and sank in the harbour after having covered a distance of 1,300 meters. The ship was located in 1956, raised in 1959, and then restored and displayed in the splendid Vasa Museum in Stockholm. Yet, from the legal point of view, the *Vasa* is the easiest case that can be imagined: a warship which sank in the maritime internal waters of the flag State without having visited, and established links with, any other State.

[218] On 7 May 1915 the British liner *Lusitania* was hit off the Irish coast by a torpedo launched by a German submarine. She sank in 18 minutes with a loss of 1,195 human lives. In 1993 the wreck, which lies in 295 feet of water, was explored by an expedition led by Mr. Ballard (see Ballard & Archbold, *Lost Liners supra* note 149, at 63). As stated in the regulations adopted by Ireland (*Underwater Heritage Order – Wreck of the Lusitania* No. 14 of 1995), "the wreck is situated approximately 12 miles south of the Old Head of Kinsale". The order defines the site of the wreck, including the debris field, as a restricted area where no person is allowed to "tamper with, damage or remove any part of the wreck".

[219] The motorship *Estonia* sank on 24 September 1994 in the Baltic Sea on her way from Talinn to Stockholm. By an Agreement made on 23 February 1995 (U.N., *Law of the Sea Bulletin*, No. 31, 1996, p. 62), Estonia, Finland and Sweden agreed that the *Estonia* shall not be raised (Art. 3) and that the wreck and the surrounding area "shall be regarded as a final place of rest for victims of the disaster, and as such shall be afforded appropriate respect" (Art. 1). The Parties also agreed to institute legislation "aiming at the criminalization of any activities disturbing the peace of the final place of rest, in particular any diving or other activities with the purpose of recovering victims or property from the wreck or the seabed" (Art. 4, para. 1). The wreck of the *Estonia* may be too recent to be already considered as underwater cultural heritage.

[220] The *La Belle*, a vessel of the French royal navy, sank in 1686 in what is now the territorial sea of the United States, off the coasts of Texas. An agreement to ensure the protection of the wreck has very recently been signed by France and the United States (in this volume, document No. 13).

[221] Yet the navigator lost a number of ships in his voyages to the Indies: the *Santa Maria* off the coast of Haiti in 1492; two or three ships in the bay of La Isabela, island of Hispaniola, in 1495; four ships during his fourth voyage in 1502-1504 (see Taviani, *L'avventura di Cristoforo Colombo*, Bologna, 2001).

[222] "The greatest problem facing Caribbean underwater cultural heritage remains the lure of Spanish treasure. (...) Countries that have permitted treasure-hunting ventures are learning that profits are seldom achieved, and irreplaceable cultural resources can be lost forever" (Leshikar-Denton, *Problems and Progress in the Caribbean*, reprinted in Prott, Planche & Roca-Hachem, *supra* note 83, at 316).

of these kinds of rules would be an insult to the genius of the man who, after having sailed to the Eastern Mediterranean and the Northern Atlantic, concentrated his restlessness in the Spanish and Portuguese islands of the Atlantic (the Azores, Madeira, the Canaries, Cape Verde) to realize that the west-bound winds of a southern route would have brought him to the Indies and the east-bound winds of a northern route would have brought him back to Europe.

Should these and other wrecks be returned to "the mainstream of commerce"? Should they be subject to "admiralty's diligence ethic" or to a "venerable law of the sea" that is said to have been preserved from ancient Rhodes (900 B.C.E.), Rome (Justinian's Corpus Juris Civilis) (533 C.E.), City of Trani (Italy) (1063), England (the Law of Oleron) (1189), the Hanse Towns or Hanseatic League (1597), and France (1681), all articulating similar principles" and that is applied today by some American judges to every sea and ocean in the world?[223]

The fact remains that the body of the law of salvage and the law of finds is today typical of a few common law systems, but is a complete stranger to other domestic legal systems.[224] For instance, no Italian lawyer (with the laudable exception of a few scholars) would today know what the law of salvage and the law of finds are, despite the fact that the cities of Rome and Trani, which are said to have contributed to these masterpieces of the "venerable law of the sea", are located somewhere in the Italian territory.[225] Nor is it clear how a "venerable" body of rules, that is believed to have developed in times when nobody cared about the underwater cultural heritage, could provide today any sensible tool for dealing with the protection of the heritage in question.

The concrete results of the application of such a "venerable" legislation are summarized as follows in a paper presented by the Archaeological Institute of America:

> In recent decades treasure salvage has been added as an element of marine salvage under admiralty law. From an archaeological perspective, salvage law is a wholly inappropriate legal regime for treating underwater cultural heritage. Salvage law regards objects primarily as property with commercial value and rewards its recovery, regardless of its importance and value as cultural heritage. It encourages private-sector commercial recovery efforts, and is incapable of ensuring the adequate protection of underwater cultural heritage for the benefit of mankind as a whole (...).
>
> Treasure hunting, or private sector commercial recovery, has never been able to convincingly demonstrate that it can operate in a way that satisfies the archaeological and preservation interests. Commercial recovery frequently

---

223 Also the personification of a ship, that is the admiralty's fiction of convenience that a ship is a person against whom suits can be filed and judgments entered, leaves room for doubt.

224 See also, in this volume, the paper by Scovazzi on *A Contradictory and Counterproductive Regime*.

225 Yet, because of the lack of the corresponding concepts, the very words of "salvage" and "admiralty" cannot be properly translated in languages different from English. In the French official text of Art. 303, para. 3, of the United Nations Convention on the Law of the Sea they are rendered with expressions ("droit de récupérer des épaves et (...) autres règles du droit maritime") which have a broader and different meaning.

> results in the destruction of underwater cultural resources as systematic archaeological recording, excavation, and conservation are sacrified in the interests of expedient recovery of marketable property. Even commercial projects that are regulated by state authorities have an abysmal record in terms of professional standards of performance, preservation, and dissemination of information. The aims, methods, and practices of treasure hunters are fundamentally at odds with those of archaeologists and preservationists.[226]

Leaving aside other relevant comments,[227] the conclusion can be taken that all the lofty and almost theological expressions employed by the supporters of the law of salvage and the law of finds ("return to the mainstream of commerce", "admiralty's diligence ethic", "venerable law of the sea", etc.) are doubtful euphemisms. They dissimulate a first-come-first-served or freedom-of-fishing approach based on the destination of underwater cultural heritage for the exclusive purpose of private commercial gain.

Yet, there is no need to spend much time in studying what this very mysterious body of law of salvage and law of finds is. It is sufficient to assess the results of its application to the underwater cultural heritage[228] and draw two evident conclusions from the instances examined in the preceding paragraphs. First, the application of these kinds of provisions, which has proved to be especially beneficial for the pockets of a few private individuals, paves the way to the pillaging of the historical heritage of many countries of the world. Second, the exclusion of the law of salvage and the law of finds is a prerequisite for any attempt to ensure the preservation of the underwater cultural heritage.[229]

More or less the same conclusions were reached in the decision rendered on 26

---

[226] *The Archaeological Institute of America (AIA) Comments on the UNESCO/UN Division on Ocean Affairs and the Law of the Sea Draft Convention on the Protection of the Underwater Cultural Heritage*, reproduced in Prott & Srong, *supra*, note 9, p. 176.

[227] "Treasure hunting in Florida bloomed in the early 1960s, with the discovery of the 1715 plate fleet of Vero Beach. What had been a relatively genteel weekend hobby as practiced in the keys in the early days of SCUBA diving, became a gold rush, with its attendant cast of profit-minded adventurers. (...) The emerging economies of most small Caribbean islands can't even afford decent education systems and health care, much less archaeology and museums. As a result, they are wide open to the blandishments of salvors. (...) Florida treasure hunting sprang from a blooming get-rich-quick society that has little historical past. (...) Today's salvors are no more aware of the cultural material they destroy than the peasant farmers who rob tombs for a living in Sicily or Colombia. (...) Today's treasure hunts are promoted on Wall Street and the Vancouver Stock Exchange. Their investors include some of the wealthiest men in the world. What we are seeing today is an assault on antiquity by an industry, not by a bunch of small-time adventurers. In scale it is larger and better financed than any assault on antiquities in history" (Throckmorton, *The World's Worst Investment: The Economics of Treasure Hunting with Real Life Comparisons*, paper published in *Underwater Archaeology Proceedings from the Society for Historical Archaeology Conference*, 1990, and reprinted in Prott & Srong, *supra* note 9, at 181).

[228] Under Art. 30, para. 1 *a*, of the International Convention on Salvage, adopted in 1989, any State party may reserve the right not to apply the provisions of that convention "when the property involved is maritime cultural property of prehistoric, archaeological or historic interest and is situated on the sea-bed".

[229] Incidentally, this conclusion might diverge from the views expressed by the distinguished members of the Comité Maritime International (above, para. 1).

July 1994 by the High Court of Ireland in a case relating to three wrecks of the Spanish *Armada*, the galleons *La Lavia*, *Juliana* and *Santa Maria de la Visión*,[230] lost in a storm in 1588 and discovered in 1985 very close to the Irish coast at Streedagh. The High Court disregarded the application of salvage law and held that "maritime archaeological wrecks and related artefacts found on or under the sea bed in Irish territorial waters, like similar objects discovered on land, are property of the State which holds them for and on behalf of the people of Ireland as part of the historical and cultural heritage of the nation".

A last quotation, which is taken from a passage of the Irish decision, seems the best way to end this paper:

> If counsel for plaintiff's submission is well founded that admiralty law applies to all derelicts, however ancient, then it follows that, for example, should the remains of a viking ship be found by a salvor in Irish maritime waters then his rights and obligations, statutory and at common law, would be the same as those which apply to the salvaging of a ship which had recently foundered and where the identity of the owner is known. The reality is that the circumstances of each are profoundly different. The latter is in essence a commercial transaction involving the salvor, the owner of the vessel and/or indemnifier of the loss. It entails the assessment of appropriate reward for the salvor based upon, inter alia, the commercial value of the salved property. The salving of a viking ship on the other hand entails a transaction between the salvor and the State which by law is deemed the owner of the wreck. The antiquity of the find precludes the possibility of tracing ownership from the time when the vessel was lost. The discovery of such a ship on the sea bed is an archaeological find which has important historical implications. If salved, it has no commerical value per se, because it belongs to the State as custodian of the national heritage and, because of its antiquity and historical importance, it is not a saleable object. Its significance derives from its importance as an addition to the historical treasury of the nation and of Europe.

[230] *Irish Reports*, 1999, vol. 3, p. 413. The *La Lavia* was a Venetian ship embargoed by Spain at Lisbon. The *Juliana* was a Sicilian but originally a Ragusan (the present Dubrovnik) ship embargoed in Sicily. The *Santa Maria de la Visión* was another Ragusan ship embargoed in Naples.

PART II

THE 2001 UNESCO CONVENTION

Chapter 3

NEGOTIATING THE CONVENTION ON UNDERWATER CULTURAL HERITAGE: MYTHS AND REALITY

*Ariel W. Gonzalez**

Participants to an international negotiation are usually equipped with a set of preconceived ideas on various aspects, including the nature and consequences of the instrument to be negotiated. The ensuing debates allow to confront and to contrast these preconceptions, which can be qualified as "myths". Most of them are gradually – and tacitly – abandoned; the way for consensus is thus paved.

The recently adopted Convention on the Protection of Underwater Cultural Heritage proved to be no exception to these non-written rules. On the contrary, the myths over the draft of such Convention endangered its very existence at the beginning of the negotiations.

But which are exactly those myths? This contribution will briefly highlight three of them, the ones whose perpetuation could be considered most risky in terms of the outcome of the negotiations on the draft Convention.

1. First Myth: On the Nature of the Convention

It is interesting to recall that, when a first meeting of governmental experts was convened in June/July 1998 to examine a draft text prepared by the UNESCO Secretariat,[1] there were almost no signs of the confrontational tone that, unfortunately, permeated afterwards the negotiations related to this text. In fact, most Member States of the Organization viewed such meeting essentially as the appropriate forum to discuss how to translate the technical rules contained in the

* Permanent Delegation of Argentina to UNESCO. The opinions expressed in this contribution are of the exclusive responsibility of its author.

1 Built on a previous work of the International Law Association (ILA), which can be traced at least back to 1994.

Roberta Garabello and Tullio Scovazzi (eds.), The Protection of the Underwater Cultural Heritage, 83–88.

Charter adopted by the International Council on Monuments and Sites (ICOMOS)[2] into an international mechanism for the protection of underwater cultural heritage.

This common understanding is evidenced by the overwhelming support provided by the 29th General Conference of UNESCO (November 1997) to the proposal of starting the process of preparation of the draft convention under the auspices of the Organization.[3] It also explains why at the first meeting in 1998, technical experts (marine archaeologists; experts in the protection of cultural property) easily outnumbered representatives having a legal or political background (foreign ministries' officials; international lawyers). In fact, one of those experts – Mr Carsten Lund, from Denmark – was preferred to chair the meeting.

The general wisdom, then, expected the future Convention to be similar in nature to the other treaties for the protection of heritage adopted under the auspices of UNESCO – *i.e.*, the 1954 Hague Convention on protection of cultural property in armed conflict; the 1970 Convention on protection against illicit trafficking of cultural property; and the 1972 Convention on the protection of world heritage. More than that, it would *reinforce* those instruments, ensuring that the protection of cultural property did not depend on the location of such property -whether on dry land or in the sea.

In the preceding context, it is understandable the confusion – and even disappointment – created by the preconception on the nature of the Convention that some of the participants brought to the 1998 meeting. According to such preconception, *the draft Convention has to do, exclusively, with the Law of the Sea*: its purpose is to specify the legal status of archaeological and historical objects found at sea – an issue only generally regulated in the final clauses of the United Nations Convention on the Law of the Sea of 1982 (UNCLOS).[4] The immediate corollaries of this notion are easily identifiable: the need for the protection envisaged by the Convention is subjected to its strictest conformity to UNCLOS; any attempt to elaborate the mechanism required for such protection beyond a mere repetition of the text of Art. 303 of UNCLOS is therefore resisted; the very role of UNESCO in the negotiation of the instrument is put into question.

In spite of the many efforts to bring the debate on the nature of an instrument for the protection of underwater cultural heritage to its proper terms, the myth of the Convention as an appendix to UNCLOS grew in force, particularly at the second meeting of experts in April 1999. Its most frustrating consequence has been the transformation of a technical exchange of views – in which experts, inspired by a common objective, worked in an atmosphere of cooperation – into a sort of political confrontation where issues so alien as nuclear submarines or cable-lying mix up repeatedly with the true purpose of the Convention. Suddenly, an exchange of views on how best to protect the underwater cultural heritage – one of whose multiple

---

2 ICOMOS International Charter on the Protection and Management of the Underwater Cultural Heritage, known as the "Sophia Charter ".

3 Resolution 29C/21, adopted by acclamation by the plenary of the Conference, on the basis of the report of its Fourth Commission (Culture).

4 Article 303 – Archaeological and historical objects found at sea.

aspects is, of course, *who* is objectively better placed to protect it – became a debate on who owns and/or can administer such heritage according to UNCLOS. It was as if the negotiators of the 1954 Hague Convention on the protection of cultural property in armed conflict had decided to focus in which conflicting party, in accordance with the Geneva Conventions and their Protocols,[5] has the right to defend the property in question.

2. Second Myth: On the Object of the Protection

It may be considered as an unfortunate coincidence that, about the same time that negotiations on underwater cultural heritage started at UNESCO, the Legal Committee of the International Maritime Organisation was working on a draft instrument on wrecks.[6] Unfortunate, because it allowed to develop in the minds of at least some of the negotiators an intimate connection between "wrecks" and "underwater cultural heritage". This connection is at the basis of another preconception contributing to muddle the negotiations on the future Convention: *the idea that the same institutes and body of law applicable to wrecks can be automatically transposed to underwater cultural heritage.*

Again, some corollaries can be derived from this preconception. Paramount among them is the notion that underwater cultural heritage, like a wreck, is the property of someone unless it has been expressly abandoned. Title to property either: a) has been vested and is not lost with the passage of time, or b) is acquired through discovery.

Under the first assumption, some negotiators fiercely opposed, at least during the first and second meeting of experts, the application of the Convention to all underwater cultural heritage. Such negotiators, in fact, considered that the rests that could still be identified as having been part of a warship or other State vessel used only on government and non-governmental service, were subjected to the principle of sovereign immunity codified in UNCLOS.[7] It made no difference whether the rests in question belonged, for instance, to a Spanish warship sunken two months ago as a result of a collision with other vessel or to a 16th century galleon. With some interpretative leeway, this reasoning leads to the awkward conclusion that, since most of the underwater cultural heritage are technically rests of warships or State ships, the application of the Convention *ratione materiae* is very limited.

The second assumption simply provides the rationale for automatically applying to underwater cultural heritage the law of salvage and the law of finds. Thus, even

---

5 The four Geneva Conventions of 1949 codifying humanitarian law, and the two Additional Protocols of 1977 which updated such codification.

6 Draft Convention on Wreck Removal, that the Committee started to consider in substance at its 77th session (1998)

7 Arts. 32 and 236 of UNCLOS. The complete formula with which the object of protection is usually defined is: "any warship, naval auxiliary or other vessel or aircraft owned or operated by a State and identifiable as such, and used, at the time of the sinking, only on government and non-commercial service".

now several experts uphold what they interpret to be the right of anyone to recover and take commercial profit from any cultural object discovered in the sea and not having any identifiable owner. Such opinions seem to ignore that the negotiations on the draft Convention arouse precisely out of an urgent need to stop the looting of cultural property at sea.

Furthermore, the referred myth on the object of the protection proved to be contradictory with the intrinsic value that even UNCLOS recognizes to "objects of an archaeological or historical character", by establishing a specific obligation to protect them.[8] For some negotiators, the notion of "significance" seems to be the way out of this contradiction. The argument would be as follows: underwater cultural heritage are wrecks; they may be subject to a special regime only when they reunite certain characteristics which justify such differential treatment – *i.e.*, when they are significant. This reasoning, however, disregards the fact that – unlike what happens with almost all cultural property on the dry land – it is very difficult in practice to evaluate whether a given rest is underwater cultural heritage or not until an activity has been directed at such heritage.

3. Third Myth: On the Role of the Convention

Standard-setting instruments tend to be highly valued by the international community, particularly because they perform two important roles. For States having an incomplete national legislation – or not regulation at all – on the same subject matter, they represent a *model*. For States engaging in bilateral or regional agreements on the same subject matter, they constitute a *framework of action*.

This second role is particularly relevant in the case of an international instrument of this nature that, like the Convention recently adopted at UNESCO, fixes a minimum standard of protection. After ratifying or adhering to such instrument, States can then devise, either bilaterally or regionally, schemes of protection which may be more strict *but cannot be more flexible* than the minimum standard.

It is interesting to note, in this context, the preconception that some negotiators brought particularly to the third meeting of experts, as regards the role of the future Convention *vis-à-vis* bilateral or regional instruments on the same subject. *Under this preconception, States could celebrate arrangements regarding underwater cultural heritage at the bilateral or regional level which are totally or partially distinct from the minimum standard set in the Convention – particularly, in its Annex*. The process of formation of an overarching scheme of protection of underwater cultural heritage is thus reverted: instead of setting it "from above", an anarchic development "from below" is encouraged.

The problem with such reversal is that it conspired against the effectiveness of the Convention. This instrument would, in fact, become a sort of "orientation guide" which State Parties may o may not decide to follow in their respective regions. Moreover, relatively less developed countries would lack recourse to a sound

[8] Article 303, paragraph 1.

normative reference in order to safeguard their interests in a bilateral negotiation related to underwater cultural heritage in their jurisdictional waters. In both cases, the main objective of protecting such heritage would be undermined. *And, being this objective of a global nature, even if countries of a given region – to put an example, the Mediterranean – managed to set up a scheme with high levels of protection, their historic or cultural objects would be not totally safe from activities of third States following distinct standards from those of the Convention.*[9] As with other domains, selfish attitudes regarding underwater cultural heritage are ill rewarded and counterproductive.

4. Back to Reality?

Following the non-written rules referred to at the beginning of this contribution, the long and intense negotiations on the draft Convention contributed gradually – and painfully – to dilute the abovementioned three myths. It can be reckoned – not with some hope – that the third meeting of experts held in July 2000 was a turning point in this sense.

In fact, it was at this meeting that, looking for a way out of the deadlock that represented the issues of jurisdiction in the Convention, the negotiators dared to think mainly in terms of schemes of protection. This could not – and should not – be interpreted as a departure from the Law of the Sea as stated in UNCLOS and other relevant norms of international law. On the contrary, there was an awareness that we were working in the framework of UNCLOS and that the rights and duties recognized in this instrument – for example, the rights associated to the sovereignty of each State on its continental shelf – would not affected by the future Convention. In other words, *UNCLOS began to be an assumption, and not a constraint, of the Convention.*

Things were less easy as regards the object of protection. As it was explained before, some negotiators at the third meeting still viewed underwater cultural heritage as wrecks, acting accordingly. Some developments could be identified, though. For instance, there was a tacit recognition that referring to issues of property in the text of the Convention was not a way out of the negotiating deadlock: it was more useful, instead, to imagine practical arrangements under which a State having a verifiable link to a given underwater cultural heritage should not be excluded from decisions regarding the protection of such heritage. With the same spirit, there was hope of some recognition that the law of salvage could not be applied in contradiction to the principles and purposes of the Convention, and that questions of significance could be only posed after – and not before – an underwater cultural heritage is discovered.[10]

---

9 As an example which may be of special interest for this meeting: commercial uses of Roman statues recovered from the Mediterranean waters by the ship of a non-Mediterranean country, which are not tolerated by the Convention but are accepted by the regional agreement to which the non-Mediterranean country is Party.

10 And even then, the question of *who* is competent to decide whether a given underwater cultural heritage is significant – with the danger of subjectivity it entails – remains open.

Finally, at the end of the third meeting there appeared to be a consensus overruling the preconception regarding the role of the Convention. Most negotiators, in fact, seemed convinced of the value of ensuring that regional and bilateral agreements are not used to bypass such international instrument.

The identification and understanding of these three myths by most negotiators at the second part of the Fourth Meeting of Experts (Paris; July 2001) engendered the critical momentum leading to the final approval of the Convention by the General Conference of UNESCO in November that year. Time tends to be the best remedy against myths: let us expect, then, that the gradual dissemination, comprehension and implementation of the Convention will confirm its status as a realistic international scheme for the protection of our underwater cultural heritage.

Chapter 4

THE NEGOTIATING HISTORY OF THE CONVENTION ON THE PROTECTION OF THE UNDERWATER CULTURAL HERITAGE

*Roberta Garabello**

1. Introduction. Overview of the Negotiation Process

On November 2, 2001 the 31st General Conference of the UNESCO[1] adopted, by 87 affirmative votes, four votes against[2] and 15 abstentions,[3] the UNESCO Convention on the Protection of the Underwater Cultural Heritage.[4] The Convention was signed on November 6 by the Director-General of UNESCO and the President of the General Conference. This was the last step of a very long negotiating process which had lasted almost ten years.

In 1991 the 29th General Conference adopted a resolution[5] which requested the Director General to make a report on the reinforcement of UNESCO's action for the protection of the world cultural and natural heritage.[6] Two years later the Executive Council asked the Director General a more specific task: to consider the feasibility of an international instrument on the protection of the underwater cultural heritage. Both technical progress – which it made possible to recover even wrecks lying in deep

---

* Faculty of Law, University of Milano-Bicocca (Italy). Member of the Italian delegation at the Fourth Meeting of Governmental Experts on the Draft Convention on the Protection of Underwater Cultural Heritage (UNESCO, Paris). The opinions expressed are solely those of the author.

1 United Nations Educational, Scientific and Cultural Organization.

2 The Russian Federation, Norway, Turkey and Venezuela.

3 Brazil, Colombia, Czech Republic, France, Germany, Greece, Iceland, Israel, the Netherlands, Paraguay, Sweden, Switzerland, United Kingdom, Uruguay (Guinea Bissau, too, abstained, but actually it had no right of vote because it was behind with its financial contributions to the organization).

4 (2002) *ILM* 40-56.

5 Resolution 29C/3.9.

6 *Decision on the Report by the Director-General on the Reinforcement of UNESCO's Action for the Protection of the World Cultural and Natural Heritage*, UNESCO doc. 141 EX/SR 15 par.15.

Roberta Garabello and Tullio Scovazzi (eds.), The Protection of the Underwater Cultural Heritage, 89–192.

international waters – and the inadequacy of the existing legal regime regulating underwater archaeology, preventing looting and ensuring the protection and conservation of the underwater cultural heritage, made the drafting of a new, specific, international instrument on the topic an urgent matter.

In the meanwhile and since 1988, the International Law Association, a private organization, had been working on a draft convention on this issue. In 1994 the draft was finalized and adopted in Buenos Aires.[7] This document was forwarded to UNESCO, which was considered the most appropriate organization to examine and eventually adopt it. The ILA draft was indeed taken into consideration in the feasibility study carried out by the Director General of UNESCO and adopted in 1995,[8] which analysed the most contentious aspects of a new international instrument: its form (recommendation, convention, amendments to existing conventions etc.), its main object, its urgency, the problem of which protection regime to establish, the relationship with salvage law, the standards of archaeological protection, etc.

On the basis of the feasibility study – which received comments by some States[9] the Executive Board decided to convene a group of experts, acting in their personal capacities.[10] Such a decision was agreed by the General Conference.[11] The task of the group of experts was to debate the main issues of the proposal and to report to the following General Conference. The group of experts – composed by people nominated by UNESCO, IMO (International Maritime Organization) and DOALOS (United Nations Division of Ocean Affairs and Law of the Sea)[12] and

---

[7] Resolution 8 on Cultural Heritage Law adopted by the International Law Association at its sixty-sixth Conference, Buenos Aires, 1994.

[8] *Feasibility Study for the Drafting of a New Instrument for the Protection of the Underwater Cultural Heritage*, Paris, 23 March 1995, UNESCO doc. 146 EX/27.

[9] Germany, Greece, Italy, the Netherlands, the Philippines, Spain, Turkey, the United Kingdom, Australia, Colombia, France, the United States. Also the United Nations Division of Ocean Affairs and Law of the Sea (DOALOS) made some comments. They are published in the Annex to the doc. 28C/39 and in doc. 28C/39 Add.

[10] UNESCO doc. 146 EX/27.

[11] *Preliminary Study on the Advisability of Preparing an International Instrument for the Protection of the Underwater Cultural Heritage*, Paris, 4 October 1995, UNESCO doc. 28C/39.

[12] The role of DOALOS in the negotiations is rather controversial. Initially it was, together with UNESCO, the co-sponsor of the new Convention. At the beginning it participated in the meetings and put forward comments on the topics dealt with, in particular in the field of the law of the sea. It appears as the co-author of the first draft of 1998. But since the Second Meeting it no longer actively participated in negotiations. It has been suggested (Boesten, *Activities Affecting Archaeological and/or Historical Valuable Shipwrecks in International Waters, Public International Law and What it Offers*, The Hague, 2002, p. 148) that this was due to the DOALOS' decision not to support the draft Convention. Such a decision would have been a consequence of a letter sent by the United States to the United Nations Legal Council, where it was stated: "We believe the DOALOS role in assisting in the development of such a Draft was inappropriate and beyond its mandate [... We request] that the DOALOS dissociate itself from the text of the Draft Convention" (United States Department of State, Bureau of Oceans and International Environmental and Scientific Affairs, March 9, 1999). The reference was to the potential inconsistency between the UNESCO draft and the UNCLOS, a very sensitive point for the United States. There is no confirmation that this interpretation of the DOALOS' attitude towards the UNESCO negotiations is true. It has been informally denied by UNESCO.

by observers sent by some States – met in May 1996. Unanimity was reached on the issue of the necessity of a new international instrument, while all other aspects proved to be very contentious.[13] As a result, the Director General recommended to prepare a draft convention and, to that end, to convene a meeting of governmental experts and representatives of the competent international organisations.[14]

A total number of four meetings were organized by UNESCO in its headquarters in Paris during the subsequent five years. The first took place in June 1998 and it represented the official beginning of negotiations.[15] The second session was held in April 1999; the third in July 2000. The fourth was a double session – in March/April and in July 2001 – because of the lack of time to finalise all the issues still open during the first round.

At the first meeting Carsten Lund, from Denmark, was elected chairman of the meeting. He maintained this role up to the end of the negotiations. It is worthwhile to note the increasing participation of States in the negotiations. If only 58 States were represented in the first meeting of 1998 (122 experts), 82 were present in the second (171 experts), 84 in the third (209 experts), close to 90 in the fourth (nearly 300 experts); also several international organisations – both governmental and non-governmental – were present (such as the International Law Organization, the International Maritime Organization, the World Underwater Federation, the International Centre for Conservation, the International Council on Monuments and Sites, etc.).

The nature of the meeting of governmental experts deserves some remarks. It was not, generally speaking, a proper diplomatic conference. Delegates represented their respective governments and they did negotiate on behalf of States, but they had no competence to adopt a convention. They could just prepare a draft to be submitted to the General Conference, which had still the power to change the draft and finally adopt it.

Anyway, despite some attempts to pass new amendments, the text of the Convention eventually adopted by the General Conference was that already approved by governmental experts. Indeed, on July 8, 2001, the governmental experts – unable to reach *consensus* on the whole text, as specifically requested by the Director General[16] – approved the draft convention by vote (49 affirmative votes, 4

---

13 *Report of the Meeting of Experts for the Protection of Underwater Cultural Heritage*, Paris, 22–24 May 1996, UNESCO doc. CLT-96/CONF.605/6.

14 *Report by the Director-General on the Findings of the Meeting of Experts concerning the Preparation of an International Instrument for the Protection of the Underwater Cultural Heritage*, Paris, 12 March 1997, UNESCO doc. 151 EX/10. See also *Report by the Director-General on Action taken Concerning the Desirability of Preparing an International Instrument for the Protection of the Underwater Cultural Heritage*, Paris, 5 August 1997, UNESCO doc. 29C/22.

15 *Final Report of the First Meeting of Governmental Experts on the Draft Convention on the Underwater Cultural Heritage*, Paris, 29 June–2 July 1998, UNESCO doc. CLT-98/CONF.202/7.

16 "It is my earnest wish that during this meeting all outstanding issues will be resolved by consensus, after the many meetings which have been held . . . In a spirit of compromise, I invite you all – I urge you all – to decide at this meeting, now, collectively what is acceptable to as many States as possible, and not what would be ideal for you or your State individually" (address by Mr. Koïchiro Matsuura, Director-General of the UNESCO on the occasion of the opening of the Fourth Meeting of

against and 8 abstentions). Strong opposition to the regime established by the Convention – considered as a radical and unjustified departure from the delicate balance established by the United Nations Convention on the Law of the Sea (hereinafter: UNCLOS) – was expressed by the Russian Federation, Norway and the United States (even if they had no right of vote[17]). The contrary vote of Turkey and Venezuela was due to the dispute settlement regime adopted within the Convention, similar to that of UNCLOS, to which these States are not Parties. As far as abstentions are concerned, they are due to the jurisdictional regime for underwater cultural heritage, considered insufficient to ensure an effective protection by one State (Greece), while too revolutionary and incompatible with UNCLOS by most of the others.

The approval of the draft Convention made it possible to forward it to the 31st General Conference which opened in October 2001.[18] Here the draft was first considered in Commission IV on Culture on October 29. A final amendment was proposed by the Russian Federation and the United Kingdom and endorsed by the United States but it did not receive the majority of votes; France withdrew an amendment previously proposed. After declarations by many States, the draft Convention was finally approved with 94 votes in favour, 5 against and 19 abstentions and transmitted to the plenary. Here the final adoption took place on November 2, as explained above. The Convention on the Protection of Underwater Cultural Heritage is now the fourth international instrument dealing with cultural heritage adopted by UNESCO and the first one specifically dealing with underwater cultural heritage existing at the international level. The process of ratification is now open.[19]

* * *

Here the negotiating history of the Convention will be examined. No official written proceedings of debates of the meeting of governmental experts exist;

---

cont.

Governmental Experts on the Draft Convention on the Protection of Underwater Cultural Heritage, UNESCO, 26 March 2001, UNESCO doc. DG/2001/32). The method of *consensus* was also explicitly indicated in the Rule of Procedure of the Meeting of governmental experts: "Participants shall make any effort to take decisions by *consensus*. If *consensus* cannot be reached, decisions shall be taken by voting [. . .] The decisions shall be taken by a simple majority of the participants present and voting" (Art. 11 of the Rules of procedure).

17 The United States was a simple observer and not a member of UNESCO, therefore it had no right of vote. In September 2002 the United States announced its return to UNESCO

18 If no text was agreed in July 2001 – as it seemed possible during the last hours of the negotiations because of the still persisting divergence of views among States on the most sensitive issues under debate – the result would have been not to have any convention until 2003, when a new General Conference would be convened. This time challenge explains all the efforts and the pressure that was exerted in order to ensure the approval of a draft in July 2001 (double sessions of the last meeting of experts, long negotiating rounds till late at night, numerous informal meetings on the most sensitive issues, approval of the convention on 0h35 of July 8).

19 The signatures by the Director General of UNESCO and by the President of the General Conference replace signatures by States. Therefore, States only have to ratify the Convention, if they so wish.

therefore personal notes taken during debates will be used. Most of the preparatory documents – in particular Working Papers, final reports of the meetings of experts, unofficial papers distributed during negotiating sessions, comments by States etc. – will be used as basic documentation to outline the negotiating history of each provision of the Convention. The four drafts produced before and during negotiations will constitute the reference points. They are the following:

1. 1994 ILA draft Convention on the Protection of the Underwater Cultural Heritage (hereinafter: ILA draft);
2. Draft Convention on the Protection of the Underwater Cultural Heritage (with explanatory comments), Paris, April 1998, UNESCO doc. CLT-96/CONF.202/5 (hereinafter: first UNESCO/DOALOS draft);
3. Draft Convention on the Protection of the Underwater Cultural Heritage, Paris, July 1999, UNESCO doc. CLT-96/CONF.202/5/Rev.2 (hereinafter: second UNESCO draft);
4. Single Negotiating Text (presented by the President as a working document), Paris, 1st March 2001 (reproduced in the consolidated working paper: UNESCO doc. CLT-2001/CONF.203/INF.3) (hereinafter: SNT)

2. Preliminary Questions

2.1 Need for an International Instrument and its Form

[Preparatory documents:

a) Comments by States:
   - General remarks by Mr. Hans W. Longva, Director General, Department of Legal Affairs, Royal Norwegian Ministry of Foreign Affairs, 19 April 1999
   - Remarks presented by the Government of Italy (July 2000)
b) Other documents:
   - Feasibility Study for the Drafting of a New Instrument for the Protection of the Underwater Cultural Heritage, Paris, 23 March 1995 (UNESCO doc. 146 EX/27), paras. 10-11 and 39-44
   - Preliminary Study on the Advisability of Preparing an International Instrument for the Protection of the Underwater Cultural Heritage, Paris, 4 October 1995 (UNESCO doc. 29C/39,), paras. 7-10 and 38-43
   - Report of the Meeting of Experts for the Draft Convention on the Protection of Underwater Cultural Heritage, Paris, 22–24 May 1996 (UNESCO doc. CLT-96/CONF.605/6,), paras. 7-8
   - Resolution n. 21 of 29th General Conference, 1997]

The starting point of the UNESCO action to protect underwater cultural heritage was the remark about the urgency of the situation: as the existing international regime was insufficient to grant effective protection to submerged treasures, it was urgent to do something at the global level to prevent further looting. Both in the feasibility study and in the preliminary study this situation is presented as the main argument to justify the drafting of a new legally binding instrument. In these documents UNESCO analysed what best form for such an instrument could be. Neither an amendment to UNCLOS nor to the UNESCO World Heritage Convention[20] were considered a good solution, in that the first mainly deals with the law of the sea and not with the protection of the cultural heritage and the second only concerns heritage of outstanding universal value. A new convention was therefore considered the best solution. At the Meeting of Experts of 1996 the question was raised as to whether, because of the urgency of the situation, a recommendation by UNESCO should precede a Convention in order to save time. The secretariat explained that an identical amount of time was necessary according to UNESCO procedures for making either a Convention or a standard-setting Recommendation. The desirability of an international instrument in the form of a binding convention was also recognised by the General Conference in 1997.

At the Second Meeting of Experts of 1999 – when a draft had already been produced and negotiations developed – Norway called into question the necessity for an international convention:

> [W]e are not persuaded that information on existing possibilities that can be derived from international law have been sufficiently disseminated. Nor we are convinced that these possibilities have been the object of satisfactory implementation at a national level. Before discussing the need for new normative developments in the form of additional instruments of international law, it would be useful to focus more fully on existing and underutilized, and in disturbingly many cases unutilized, possibilities.[21] [...] At the present stage our attention should be focused on the regulatory needs and enforcement issues at a national level within the existing international legal framework.[22]

The opposite view was expressed by Italy, which considered that the dangerous gap left by UNCLOS in the regulation of underwater cultural heritage between 24 n.m. from the coast and the beginning of the Area, needed to be filled as soon as possible. The continuing looting of ancient artefacts meant that the drawing up of a new international instrument on the protection of underwater cultural heritage, as specifically allowed by Art. 303, para. 4 of UNCLOS was urgent:

> [T]he UNCLOS allows for the drafting of more specific treaty regimes which can ensure a better protection of the underwater cultural heritage. In other words, the

---

20 *UNESCO Convention concerning the Protection of the World Cultural and Natural Heritage*, Paris, 29 October 1972, (1972) *ILM* 1358.

21 Norway meant for example the declaration of the contiguous zone, the possible adoption of a Code of Conduct for the protection of underwater cultural heritage in a resolution by the United Nations General Assembly, etc.

22 General remarks by Mr. Hans W. Longva, Director General, Department of Legal Affairs, Royal Norwegian Ministry of Foreign Affairs, 19 April 1999.

UNCLOS itself fully encourages the future filling of the gaps that it has left open, which are particularly evident in the case of the cultural heritage found on the continental shelf. This opportunity should not be lost by States participating in the present UNESCO negotiations.

2.2 Role of UNESCO

[Preparatory documents:
a) Comments by States:
- General remarks by Mr. Hans W. Longva, Director General, Department of Legal Affairs, Royal Norwegian Ministry of Foreign Affairs, 19 April 1999

b) Other documents:
- Report of the Meeting of Experts for the Draft Convention on the Protection of Underwater Cultural Heritage, Paris, 22–24 May 1996 (UNESCO doc. CLT-96/CONF.605/6), paras. 7-8]

When drafting the project of the Convention, ILA consulted several governmental and non governmental organizations, such as the Comité Maritime International, the International Council for Monuments and Sites (ICOMOS), the International Maritime Organization (which replied it was interested in wrecks only as dangerous obstacles to navigation), the DOALOS (which did not reply). It was UNESCO that finally asked ILA to submit its draft Convention to it for consideration.[23] At the 1996 Meeting experts unanimously agreed that UNESCO was the appropriate forum for the adoption of a convention on the protection of underwater cultural heritage. Not so Norway, but three years later. In a written remark presented at the Second Meeting of Expert, it stated:

> Norway also reserves her position with regard to whether or not UNESCO is the appropriate forum for the negotiation and adoption of such a convention. Norway is concerned by the proliferation of negotiating processes and decision-making in a number of international bodies, as well as the conclusion of new international agreements with direct relevance to the international order of the seas. Norway is persuaded that the General Assembly of the United Nations should, through the discussion of the agenda item on the law of the sea, provide necessary guidance and coordination.

3. Negotiating History of the Individual Articles

Preamble

The General Conference of the United Nations Educational, Scientific and Cultural

---

[23] See *Report. Draft Convention on the Protection of Underwater Cultural Heritage*, in *ODIL*, 1994, p. 391, at 392.

Organization, meeting in Paris from 15 October to 3 November 2001, at its thirty-first session,

Acknowledging the importance of underwater cultural heritage as an integral part of the cultural heritage of humanity and a particularly important element in the history of peoples, nations, and their relations with each other concerning their common heritage,

Realising the importance of protecting and preserving such underwater cultural heritage and that responsibility therefore rests with all States,

Noting growing public interest in and public appreciation for underwater cultural heritage,

Convinced of the importance of research, information and education to the protection and preservation of underwater cultural heritage,

Convinced that the public's right to enjoy the educational and recreational benefits of responsible non-intrusive access to *in situ* underwater cultural heritage, and the value of public education to contribute to awareness, appreciation and protection of that heritage,

Aware of the fact that underwater cultural heritage is threatened by unauthorised activities directed at it, and of the need for stronger measures to prevent such activities,

Conscious of the need to respond appropriately to the possible negative impact on underwater cultural heritage of legitimate activities that may incidentally affect it,

Deeply concerned by the increasing commercial exploitation of underwater cultural heritage, and in particular by certain activities aimed at the sale, acquisition or barter of underwater cultural heritage,

Aware of the availability of advanced technology that enhances discovery of and access to underwater cultural heritage,

Believing that cooperation among States, international organizations, scientific institutions, professional organizations, archaeologists, divers, other interested parties and the public at large is essential for the protection of underwater cultural heritage,

Considering that survey, excavation and protection of underwater cultural heritage necessitate the availability and application of special scientific methods and the use of suitable techniques and equipment as well as a high degree of professional specialisation, all of which indicate a need for uniform governing criteria,

Realising the need to codify and progressively develop rules relating to the protection and preservation of underwater cultural heritage in conformity with international law and practice, including the UNESCO Convention on the Means of Prohibiting and Preventing the Illicit Import, Export and Transfer of Ownership of Cultural Property of 14 November 1970, the UNESCO Convention concerning the Protection of the World Cultural and Natural Heritage of 16 November 1972, and the United Nations Convention on the Law of the Sea of 10 December 1982,

Committed to improving the effectiveness of measures at international, regional and national levels for the preservation *in situ* or, if necessary for scientific or protective purposes, the careful recovery of underwater cultural heritage,

Having decided at its twenty-ninth session that this question should be made the subject of an international convention,

Adopts this second day of November, 2001 this Convention.

[Preparatory documents:

a) Working Papers:
  - WP 30, 2 April 2001 (Amendments proposed by small drafting group mandated by Chairman)
  - WP 30rev., 5 July 2001 (Amendments proposed by small drafting group mandated by Chairman)
  - WP 35, 2 April 2001 (Amendments proposed by Mexico and Portugal)

b) Drafts:
  - ILA draft (Preamble)
  - second UNESCO draft (Preamble)
  - SNT (Preamble)]

According to the Vienna Convention on the Law of the Treaties (Art. 31, para. 2) the preamble is part of the context within which a treaty is to be interpreted. The preamble offers general principles guiding interpretation of the whole treaty. The 2001 UNESCO Convention preamble enshrines all the major principles subsequently developed in specific articles: the importance of the underwater cultural heritage, the responsibility of all States in its protection, the public interest in it, the need for non-intrusive access to it, the need to prevent activities directly or incidentally affecting it, the concern for commercialization, the need of co-operation between different subjects to protect it, the will to codify and progressively develop international law in this field, the priority of *in situ* conservation of the underwater heritage.

Notwithstanding the importance of the preamble, it was debated by governmental experts only during the last double session of 2001. This fact is somehow logical considering that most of the principles had to be debated and worked out in depth when negotiating specific articles before being summarized at the beginning of the Convention. When the opposite process was tried (first establishing the general principles, then working them out in specific terms within articles) some obstacles were found. The drafting of the preamble depends on the content of the whole convention.

A comparison of the different drafts of the Convention shows that no drastic changes were made from the ILA draft of 1994 to the final text of 2001. While in the first UNESCO draft the preamble was almost the same as in the ILA draft, because no comment on it was provided by States up to 1998, the second UNESCO draft added two important points: the awareness of increasing commercialization of items of the underwater cultural heritage (permitted by advances in technology) and the consciousness of growing threats to that heritage caused by legitimate activities such as the exploitation of natural resources, laying of cables, construction of artificial islands etc. These two important additions reflect intensive debates among delegates on crucial issues: how to deal with the commercialization of archaeological and historical objects and the need to introduce a distinction between activities directed at the heritage and activities incidentally affecting it (a distinction initially proposed by Canada). In the SNT of 2001 a stronger emphasis was placed on the issue of commercialization in order to condemn it as a real threat to the heritage. It is also interesting to note changes in the qualification of the underwater cultural heritage. According to the ILA draft, it belongs to the "common heritage of humanity"; in the first UNESCO draft it is stated that the underwater cultural heritage "should be preserved for the benefit of humankind", an expression that remained unchanged in the second UNESCO draft and in the SNT, but that was deleted in the final text, where – as in all the previous drafts – it is only acknowledged that the underwater cultural heritage is an integral part of the cultural heritage of humanity. It is likely that this expression was preferred in order to avoid any analogy with the concept of "common heritage of mankind" as codified by UNCLOS, where it is confined to mineral resources of the Area.

During the Fourth Meeting (first session) of Governmental Experts a small working group was created to draw up a revised draft of the preamble in order to take into account the debates that had already taken place during the plenary on the preamble. With minor changes still proposed in subsequent negotiations in plenary, the results of the working group (*WP30* and *WP30rev*) were incorporated in the final text of the Convention. In comparison with the SNT, further additions were made: the need for non-intrusive access to the underwater cultural heritage, specific reference to the advance in technology, double reference to the preference for *in situ* conservation. Other changes in the order of the paragraphs reflect slight changes in the "philosophy" of the Convention: for example, the concept of the responsibility of all States in the protection and conservation of the underwater cultural heritage, which was only the ninth paragraph in the SNT, became the second paragraph in the final text.

During the last meeting negotiations about the preamble were particularly difficult on three points. First, there was no agreement on "who" had to be envisaged in paragraph 10, that is to say who has the duty to co-operate to protect the underwater cultural heritage. In the ILA draft the following categories were indicated: "States, salvors, divers, their organizations, marine archaeologists, museums and other scientific institutions"; the same, but in a different order, were considered in the 1999 UNESCO draft and in the 2001 SNT. When negotiations opened on the preamble on 29 March 2001, Italy suggested cancelling "salvors". It was deemed inconsistent to strongly limit, if not ban, salvage in the Convention but to ask the co-operation of salvors in protecting the underwater cultural heritage in its preamble. Italy also argued that in the preamble the main protagonists of underwater archaeology were to be considered, while salvors, as fishermen, would only be incidentally involved. This position was shared by Greece and Portugal, while opposition was manifested by the United Kingdom which attributed to salvors a specific role in the protection of the underwater cultural heritage, and by France that regarded their co-operation as a key issue for the successful implementation of the Convention. Spain, too, supported by Libya and Tanzania, did not want to see salvors included in the list, but with a different argument: since this was an international convention, only subjects of international law – and therefore no private individuals or associations – had to be envisaged.

The working group responsible for the drafting of the preamble did not reach *consensus* on this issue. The text of the working group compromise still presented several squared brackets:

> *Believing* that cooperation among States, their scientific institutions and professional organizations, relevant [recognised] international organizations, and the involvement of [stakeholders], [[salvors], divers, [dredgers], archaeologists, their respective organizations] and the public at large is essential for the protection of underwater cultural heritage (*WP30)*

In July Italy reiterated that salvors, like dredgers, had to be deleted for the same reason that fishermen were not included. According to Greece priority had to be given to the category of archaeologists. No further discussions were held on this issue: the paragraph was simplified, and "salvors" deleted; only "archaeologists" and "divers", with a general reference to "other interested parties", were retained at the end.

The second major issue at stake in the preamble was the reference to other international instruments and in particular to the United Nations Convention on the Law of the Sea of 1982. The relationship between the UNESCO Convention and UNCLOS was a thorny issue which led to intense debate throughout the negotiations. It was not surprising that even in the preamble, which enshrines general principles, the question retained considerable attention. The UNCLOS – two articles of which (Art. 149 and Art. 303) deal with the underwater cultural heritage – was already referred to in the ILA draft. The SNT widened the reference to international law and practice in the field of the protection of underwater cultural heritage, to include not only UNCLOS, but also existing UNESCO Conventions concerning cultural heritage: this solution had a very precise aim, that is to say to underline that the 2001 UNESCO Convention was not to be considered a simple appendix to UNCLOS (and therefore it was not a Convention only dealing with the law of the sea), but it belonged to the "family" of the UNESCO Conventions on cultural heritage. In the July 2001 Meeting, the United Kingdom, France and Spain asked for a clearer and more meaningful reference to UNCLOS, while Argentina was contrary.

A few days later Norway proposed a new paragraph in the preamble, to read as follows: "Affirming that matters not regulated by UNCLOS or by this Convention continue to be governed by the rules and principles of general international law". Since there is no generally accepted principle of customary international law concerning the protection of underwater cultural heritage, it is likely that the principles referred to in the Norwegian proposal were those well established in the law of the sea. Norway's aim was to present the UNESCO Convention as an appendix to UNCLOS, as such unable to modify the 1982 Convention. In such a perspective, it was inconceivable for Norway that a new convention should develop the UNCLOS. Italy, supported by Argentina and by the Chairman of the Meeting, argued that the proposal was not legally correct: there are matters which are neither regulated by the 2001 UNESCO Convention nor by UNCLOS but which are regulated by other international instruments.[24] In the end the Norwegian proposal was rejected by the plenary and this contributed to this State's negative vote to the Convention.

The third highly debated issue of the preamble dealt with activities incidentally affecting underwater cultural heritage. While the ILA draft simply referred to the exploitation of natural resources and construction activities as possible threats to the submerged heritage, the first UNESCO draft was more detailed in listing activities which can jeopardise the underwater cultural heritage:

> Conscious also of growing threats to underwater cultural heritage from various other activities, namely exploitation of natural resources of various maritime zones, construction, including construction of artificial islands, installations and structures, laying of cables and pipelines,

It seems that the cable laying industry strongly reacted to this draft, arguing that its activities do not damage underwater cultural heritage.[25] Also Canada in commenting the draft argued that this paragraph unduly labelled as "growing threats" activities such as laying of cable. Perhaps, in comparison with cable laying, bottom trawl nets are even more dangerous, but they were not mentioned in the draft. In the 1999 draft the paragraph is unchanged. In the SNT only exploitation of natural resources and construction are envisaged as potential threats. The draft of the *ad hoc* working group was even more cautious: it generally speaks of "possible impact on underwater cultural heritage of legitimate activities that may incidentally affect it". The plenary, briefly negotiating on this point, decided to add "negative" impact and to move the paragraph up in the preamble.

Article 1 – Definitions

> For the purposes of this Convention:
> 1. (a) "Underwater cultural heritage" means all traces of human existence having a cultural, historical or archaeological character which have been partially or totally underwater, periodically or continuously, for at least 100 years such as:
>   (i) sites, structures, buildings, artefacts and human remains, together with their archaeological and natural context;
>   (ii) vessels, aircraft, other vehicles or any part thereof, their cargo or other contents, together with their archaeological and natural context; and
>   (iii) objects of prehistoric character.
>
>   (b) Pipelines and cables placed on the seabed shall not be considered as underwater cultural heritage.
>
>   (c) Installations other than pipelines and cables, placed on the seabed and still in use, shall not be considered as underwater cultural heritage.

---

24 The Chairman mentioned, for example, the *European Convention on Archaeological Heritage*.

25 O'Keefe, *Shipwrecked Heritage: A Commentary on the UNESCO Convention on Underwater Cultural Heritage*, Leicester, 2002, p. 37.

2. (a) "States Parties" means States which have consented to be bound by this Convention and for which this Convention is in force.
   (b) This Convention applies *mutatis mutandis* to those territories referred to in Article 26 paragraph 2(b) which become Parties to this Convention in accordance with the conditions set out in that paragraph, and to that extent "States Parties" refers to those territories.
3. "UNESCO" means the United Nations Educational, Scientific and Cultural Organization.
4. "Director-General" means the Director-General of UNESCO.
5. "Area" means the seabed and ocean floor and subsoil thereof, beyond the limits of national jurisdiction.
6. "Activities directed at underwater cultural heritage" means activities having underwater cultural heritage as their primary object and which may, directly or indirectly, physically disturb or otherwise damage underwater cultural heritage.
7. "Activities incidentally affecting underwater cultural heritage" means activities which, despite not having underwater cultural heritage as their primary object or one of their objects, may physically disturb or otherwise damage underwater cultural heritage.
8. "State vessels and aircraft" means warships, and other vessels or aircraft that were owned or operated by a State and used, at the time of sinking, only for government non-commercial purposes, that are identified as such and that meet the definition of underwater cultural heritage.
9. "Rules" means the Rules concerning activities directed at underwater cultural heritage, as referred to in Article 33 of this Convention.

[Preparatory documents:
a) Working Papers and comments by States:
   - Comments of the United States of America on UNESCO Draft Convention on the Protection of the Underwater Cultural Heritage (April 1999)
   - WG1 WP1, 4 July 2000 (Amendment to Article 1 proposed by USA)
   - WG1 WP2, 4 July 2000 (Amendments to Article 1, New Paragraph proposed by Denmark)
   - WG1 WP3, 4 July 2000 (Amendment to Article 1 proposed by Tunisia)
   - WG1 WP4, 4 July 2000 (Amendment to Article 1 proposed by Australia)
   - WG1 WP5, 4 July 2000 (Amendment to Article 1 proposed by Japan)
   - WG1 WP6, 4 July 2000 (Amendment to Article 1 proposed by India)
   - WG1 WP7, 4 July 2000 (Amendment to Article 1 proposed by Greece)
   - WG1 WP8, 4 July 2000 (Summary of changes proposed by Canada)
   - WG1 WP9, 4 July 2000 (Amendment to Article 1 proposed by Argentina)
   - WG1 WP10, 4 July 2000 (Amendment to Article 1 proposed by The Republic of Korea)
   - WG1 WP11, 4 July 2000 (Amendment to Article 1 proposed by Hungary)
   - WG1 WP12, 4 July 2000 (Amendment to Article 1 proposed by Malta)
   - Comments of the United States of America on Selected Articles being considered in Working Group One, Paris, 4 July 2000

- WG1 WP22, 5 July 2000 (Amendment to Article 1 proposed by Malta)
- WG1-NP2, 6 July 2000 (Tentative proposals of Chairman of Working Group 1)
- WG1 WP41, 6 July 2000 (Proposal by Belgium)
- Non-paper, July 2000 (Poland)
- WP 1, 27 March 2001 (Danish proposal for amendments to the Informal Draft Negotiating Text)
- WP 19, 29 March 2001 (Chairman's proposal)
- WP 20, 29 March 2001 (Chairman's proposal)
- WP 21, 29 March 2001 (Amendments to definition proposed by Australia and seconded by Canada)
- WP 23, 29 March 2001 (Proposal by Australia seconded by Belize)
- WP 27, 30 March 2001 (Proposal presented by Spain, Portugal and Peru)
- WP 29, 2 April 2001 (Amendment proposed by Sweden)
- WP 34, 2 April 2001 (Amendment proposed by Finland, Germany, Japan, the Netherlands, Norway, the Russian Federation, Spain, Sweden, the United Kingdom and endorsed by the United States)
- Non-paper by Spain, 22 June 2001
- Non-paper by the United States, 1 July 2001
- Non-paper 3, 3 July 2001 (State vessels and aircraft, Single Article proposed by UK)
- WP 57, 5 July 2001 (Report of the informal sub-group of the warships working group)

b) Drafts:
- ILA Draft (Art. 1)
- first UNESCO/DOALOS draft (Art. 1)
- second UNESCO draft (Art. 1)
- SNT (Art. 1)

c) Other documents:
- Preliminary Study on the Advisability of Preparing an International Instrument for the Protection of the Underwater Cultural Heritage, Paris, 4 October 1995 (UNESCO doc. 29C/39), paras. 7-9
- Report of the Meeting of Experts for the Draft Convention on the Protection of Underwater Cultural Heritage, Paris, 22-24 May 1996 (UNESCO doc. CLT-96/CONF.605/6), paras. 9-21
- Observations by States on the Report of the Meeting of Experts jointly organised by UNESCO, the United Nations Law of the Sea Office of Legal Affairs and the International Maritime Organization (Annex II to UNESCO doc. 151 EX/10, Paris, 12 March 1997)
- Final Report of the First Meeting of Governmental Experts on the Draft Convention on the Protection of Underwater Cultural Heritage, Paris, 29 June–2 July 1998 (UNESCO doc. CLT-98/CONF.202/7), para. IV
- Final Report of the Second Meeting of Governmental Experts on the Draft Convention on the Protection of Underwater Cultural Heritage , Paris, 19-24 April 1999 (UNESCO doc. CLT-99/CONF.204, Paris, August 1999), para. V

- Final Report of the Third Meeting of Governmental Experts on the Draft Convention on the Protection of Underwater Cultural Heritage, Paris, 3-7 July 2000, Annex I (UNESCO doc. CLT-2000/CONF.201/7, Paris, 21 August 2000)]

Definitions are always delicate in an international convention. The 2001 UNESCO Convention is not an exception in this respect. In particular, paragraph 1 was the result of a longstanding debate, begun as early as the idea itself of drafting a convention on the underwater cultural heritage. Indeed, what was to be included in the convention was not very clear. Some of the questions to be answered were: whether the convention should apply only to maritime waters or also to inland waters; what is considered a wreck; whether sites are also to be considered as underwater cultural heritage to be covered by the convention; whether the convention would apply only to abandoned shipwrecks and what "abandoned" means; what is an archaeological or historical object; whether an artificial time-limit should be considered, so as to clearly define the scope of the convention; whether only significant artefacts should be covered by the convention or also any other archaeological and historical items.

Categories of Underwater Cultural Heritage

Since the beginning, in the preliminary study on the advisability of preparing an international convention, it was felt that, while historic shipwrecks (and their artefacts) are the main body of material constituting the underwater cultural heritage, attention should also be devoted to human settlements submerged by erosion (such as the medieval English town of Dunwich), bradyseism (such as some areas of the ancient city of Pozzuoli in Italy) or earthquake (such as Port Royal in Jamaica) or to prehistoric lake settlements. The ILA draft already shared this view. According to its Article 1, para. 1:

1. "Underwater cultural heritage" means all underwater traces of human existence including:
   a. sites, structures, buildings, artifacts and human remains, together with their archaeological and natural contexts; and
   b. wreck such as a vessel, aircraft, other vehicle or any part thereof, its cargo or other contents, together with its archaeological and natural context.

During the Meeting of Experts of May 1996 it was suggested to include not only shipwrecks and sites, but also landscapes of great importance for the understanding of history, such as the site of the *Titanic*. It was replied that most landscapes are already covered by domestic legislation and the idea was not raised again. According to a Greek proposal of July 2000 (*WG1 WP7*) also natural property had to be covered. Neither of the suggestions was retained in the final text, but – as already stated in the ILA draft – the natural context of both sites and wrecks is included in the definition of underwater cultural heritage.

It may be useful to bear in mind that the inclusion of sites in the definition of underwater cultural heritage represents a novelty in international law. The only existing global instrument dealing with this issue, the UNCLOS, only covers historical and archaeological objects.[26] The same can be said of some domestic legislation, such as the Australian *Historic Shipwreck Act 1976*, the English *Protection of Wrecks Act 1973* and the American *Abandoned Shipwreck Act 1987*. As far as the 1985 draft Convention on the underwater cultural heritage drawn up by the Council of Europe (never signed)[27] is concerned, sites are not explicitly listed in the definition of the underwater cultural heritage, but they can be covered as a "trace of human existence". Art. 1, para. 1 of the draft 1985 European Convention reads as follows:

> 1. For the purposes of this Convention all remains and objects and any other traces of human existence located entirely or in part in the sea, lakes, rivers, canals, artificial reservoirs or other bodies of water, or, recovered from any such environment, or washed ashore, shall be considered as being part of the underwater cultural heritage, and are hereinafter referred to as underwater cultural property.

The inclusion in the definition of objects of a prehistoric character in Art. 1, para. 1, (a) (iii) of the UNESCO Convention, was inserted for the first time among the tentative proposals by the Chairman of Working Group 1 (*WG1-NP2*), an *ad hoc* working group created during the third Meeting to debate Article 1 to 7.[28] However in letter (a) (iii) of the WG1 Chairman's proposal also objects of palaeontological character were considered, as requested by Greece (*WG1 WP7*).[29] Besides, "sites with spiritual associations for indigenous people" were envisaged. This reflected a specific amendment proposed by Australia at the Third Meeting of Governmental Experts (*WG1 WP4*) and reiterated at the fourth Meeting (*WP 21*). This issue was dealt with in plenary at the last Meeting in July 2001, but it was not possible to debate it intensively. While some agreed with the Australian proposal (for example France, which includes spiritual sites in its legislation), it was decided to delete the reference to spiritual sites in the final text.

As far as shipwrecks are concerned, a little change can be noted from the second UNESCO draft to the SNT (but already present in the WG1 Chairman's proposals of July 2000) in (ii) of Art. 1, para. 1. The sentence "wrecks such as a vessel, aircraft, other vehicle etc." was changed to "vessels, aircraft, other vehicles etc.". The word "wreck" ("épave" in French) was deleted at the request of some delegates because it is a technical term of salvage law and includes more than shipwrecks: because of the

---

[26] But one author (Strati, *The Protection of the Underwater Cultural Heritage: An Emerging Objective of the Contemporary Law of the Sea*, The Hague, 1995, p. 182), holds that, as a consequence of the general duty of protection of the underwater cultural heritage established at Art. 303, para. 1 of the UNCLOS, such a restrictive interpretation is not correct and, even if the Convention explicitly deals only with objects, also sites are covered.

[27] Council of Europe, *Ad Hoc* Committee of Experts on the underwater cultural heritage, Doc. CAHAQ (85) 5, Strasbourg, 23 April 1985. See also the comment to the draft by the Council of Ministers, Doc. CM (85) 212, of 28 October 1985.

[28] It was chaired by Mr. Scovazzi (Italy).

[29] But this reference to palaeontological objects disappeared in the SNT of March 2001.

difficult and longstanding negotiations on the issue of the relationship between the Convention and salvage law, it was preferred to avoid any reference to the word "wreck".

Time Limit

A crucial point of the definition is the indication of a time limit, that is to say a practical criterion to fix a boundary between what is underwater cultural heritage covered by the Convention and what is not. While in the Convention one will not find any clear definition of what is "archaeological" and what is "historical" – simply because to establish a clear demarcation line between the two concepts was not useful at all – it was necessary, in order to make it easy to practically implement the Convention, to clearly state up to when an object can be considered archaeological and historical. It was decided not to make reference to a specific date. A more flexible principle was preferred: the trace of human existence must have been underwater for at least 100 years. This is an arbitrary cut-off figure which has several advantages: it is clear, easy to be interpreted and allows a progressive enlargement of the scope of the Convention (because when 100 years are elapsed, an item automatically comes under the scope of the Convention). Such a criterion is not new either in international law or in domestic law. While the UNCLOS avoided establishing any time limit,[30] the principle of 100 years was already enshrined in the 1985 Council of Europe draft, but in that case the object had to be at least 100 years *old*. In the ILA draft, as finally in the UNESCO Convention, the object or the site must have been *underwater* for at least 100 years (Art. 2, para, 1). This point was not extensively debated during the UNESCO negotiations. Just at the beginning, when the idea of convention was considered, some argued that it could be decided to protect everything dating before the twentieth century; archaeologists stressed that there is no such thing as a specific time limit in archaeology. During the first phase of negotiations it was felt that a reasonable compromise could be found in the ILA draft, where the 100 years limit was not mandatory, in that any State could decide to extend the protection provided for by the Convention also to items which had been submerged for less than 100 years. This provision was retained during all the preparatory works, up to the SNT, but then deleted in the final text,[31] despite the fact that it was still recalled in some of the last amendments proposed.

Abandonment

A thorny issue was the question of "abandonment". Some domestic laws, such as the American one, only apply to abandoned shipwrecks. But no agreed definition of

[30] According to Oxman (*The Third United Nations Conference on the Law of the Sea: The Ninth Session (1980)*, in (1981) *AJIL* 241) Art. 303 of the UNCLOS can only be applied to objects previous to the modern era, which starts in 1453 (fall of Constantinople), or, probably, in 1492 (voyage of Columbus), in 1521 (fall of Tenochtitlán), or in 1533 (fall of Cuzco).

[31] The reason why the provision was deleted is that, should a State decide to apply the Convention to items submerged for less than 100 years, this State could, as a consequence, easily exercise title over military vessels flying a foreign flag recently wrecked.

abandonment exists at the international level. The ILA draft, as well as the first UNESCO draft of 1998, limited its scope to abandoned underwater cultural heritage and two different situations were included in the meaning of "abandonment":

> Underwater cultural heritage shall be deemed to have been "abandoned":
> a. whenever technology would make exploration for research or recovery feasible but exploration for research or recovery has not been pursued by the owner of the heritage within 25 years after discovery of the technology; or
> b. whenever no technology would reasonably permit exploration for research or recovery and at least 50 years have elapsed since the last assertion of interest by the owner in the underwater cultural heritage.[32]

As it can be seen, a difference was made according to the availability of technology necessary to recovery the shipwreck. But this definition was contested, also in literature.[33] What is more important is that already in the first Meeting of Experts some delegations, in particular some from Latin America, pointed out that the concept of abandonment did not exist in their domestic law; indeed this concept is only familiar in countries of common law. Moreover, making reference to abandonment meant to introduce into the Convention the question of ownership of the underwater cultural heritage, while it was generally agreed that, as it was a convention of public international law, it was better not to deal with the thorny issue of property. The suggestion by the Chairman to eliminate the term "abandoned" from the draft, made during the first Meeting, was finally approved in the second Meeting. Therefore now the Convention applies to any underwater cultural heritage, irrespective of its property regime.

The "Significance" Criterion

The very crucial issue regarding the definition of the underwater cultural heritage, which represented a major obstacle in reaching *consensus* on this point, was the question of the *significance* of the heritage to be protected according to the Convention. The debate was not new. It is worthwhile here to remember that the same issue had been on stage in the Eighties during negotiations at the Council of Europe for the European Convention.[34]

Whether to introduce a criterion of *significance* was already discussed during the 1996 Meeting of Experts: some, in particular archaeologists, were in favour of the so-called *blanket protection* – that is to say a protection afforded to any kind of ancient artefact – on the basis of three main arguments. First, because archaeologists have no right to say what is important and what is not and any item is considered to be

---

32 Art. 1, para. 2 of the ILA draft.

33 Cfr. Dromgoole & Gaskell, *Draft UNESCO Convention on the Protection of the Underwater Cultural Heritage 1998*, in (1999) *IJMCL* 180; Bederman, *The UNESCO Draft Convention on Underwater Cultural Heritage: A Critique and Counter-Proposal*, in (1998) *JMLC* 334.

34 Cfr. Prott & O'Keefe, *Rapport final sur la protection juridique du patrimoine culturel subaquatique*, Annexe II au *Patrimoine culturel subaquatique*, Rapport de la commission de la culture et de l'éducation (Rapporteur M. John Roper), Strasbourg, 1978 (Doc. 4200-F), p. 66.

significant for the study of humanity. Second, because in any case it was necessary to recover and study an artefact before deciding whether it is significant or not. Third, because from a legal point of view it would have been difficult to give a clear definition of significance and the implementation of the Convention in a specific case would have entailed a subjective judgment, while legal certainty was required. The experience of Australia was also remembered: when the *Historic Shipwrecks Act* was adopted in 1976 it was established that protection could be afforded only after a specific declaration of historical significance had been made by the competent Minister. This method proved to be completely ineffective because the declaration was usually made too late and in the meantime the shipwreck in question was looted. In 1985 the *Historic Shipwrecks Act* was amended in order to allow blanket protection for all shipwrecks older than 75 years, including shipwrecks not yet discovered.

The first UNESCO draft, like the ILA draft – upon which it was based – applied to "all traces of human existence"; no changes were made in the second draft. But some States and first of all the United States reacted strongly, arguing that this definition was too broad and suggesting the new wording "objects of a prehistoric, archaeological, historical or cultural significance found underwater on or under the seabed, and which have been underwater for at least 50 years".

As it has already been said, the issue of the definition of the underwater cultural heritage was more attentively debated in Working Group 1 created during the third Meeting of Experts. Here, the United States still suggested the insertion of the word "significant" (*WG1 WP1*); Japan and the Republic of Korea proposed the more neutral word "nature" (respectively *WG1 WP5* and *WG1 WP10*). The Chairman of the Working Group, in an effort of compromise, suggested a new solution: the Convention would apply to underwater cultural heritage of historical and archaeological character. The advantage of this solution was that a reasonable limit was set into the scope of the Convention, so as to avoid its application to items of no importance but located underwater for at least 100 years,[35] but at the same time all archaeological and historical objects, irrespective of their indefinable importance, would be included. In commenting this solution, the United States still made several criticisms: it was felt that most States would be unable to comply with a legal obligation to manage and protect all underwater cultural heritage simply because they lack the management capacity to do so. Moreover, "most existing historic resource management regimes routinely provide for a process to categorize resources in terms of their relative archaeological or cultural significance. Such a process, which enables managers to focus preservation efforts where they are most needed, is critical to the effective implementation of the Convention".[36] The opposite comment was provided by Poland, according to which "all the remains of human activity situated underwater for a specific period of time should be covered by automatic

[35] The example was made of a can thrown out of a boat.

[36] Comments of the United States of America on Selected Articles being considered in Working Group One, Paris, 4 July 2000.

legal protection until it is determined that they do not have any archaeological, historical, artistic or scientific value" (*Non-paper, July 2000*).

During the last Meeting of Experts the question was still intensively debated. Portugal, Argentina, Greece, Colombia, and ICOMOS (which represented the archaeological community) were strongly against any "significance" criterion. The word "character" was considered a good compromise by Spain, Russia, Italy, Japan and most other States (even the United Kingdom that had previously expressed some criticisms on the point) and the paragraph was adopted. But the question was not closed. When negotiating two other articles of the Convention, States in favour of the "significance" criterion tried to introduce it again into the Convention. This was the case of Article 8 of the SNT on internal waters, archipelagic waters and territorial sea and Article 31 on the Rules of the Annex. As far the first is concerned, it was the Chairman who first proposed inserting a new paragraph into the Article, which read: "Any State Party may decide to afford protection in accordance with this Convention under this Article only to underwater cultural heritage having specific cultural or archaeological significance" (*WP19*): this was a sort of compromise, in that a "significance" criterion was not inserted in the general definition of the underwater cultural heritage but at the same time States would be allowed to apply it to underwater cultural heritage located in waters under their sovereignty. This proposal was agreed upon by the United Kingdom; according to the United States, the Chairman's proposal should have taken the form of a declaration at the time of ratification. This was considered very dangerous by ICOMOS: it would have been a real reservation which could jeopardise the very meaning of the Convention. At the end, no provision of this type was inserted in the final text.

Another of the Chairman's proposals (*WP 20*) concerned Article 31: the Rules of the Annex had to be applied to underwater cultural heritage "with regard to the cultural or archaeological significance of the heritage in question". Most States (Spain, Italy, Greece, Libya, Mexico, India, Argentina, France and Australia) intervened to reject it, arguing that it would be quite strange to adopt a definition and then insert a principle at odds with this definition. Norway, the United Kingdom and the United States agreed with the Chairman's proposal; the United Kingdom stressed that it would be too expensive to protect *in situ* the entire underwater heritage and it would be wise to concentrate only on the most significant artefacts.[37]

[37] This position was already clearly stated in a letter by Margaret Prythergch (Head of International Matters and Underwater Archaeology Branch, Dep. for Culture Media and Sport, United Kingdom): "I can confirm that the Convention will not be acceptable to the UK unless the concept of significance is allowed for in some way. [...] [T]here are thousands of wreck sites around the UK coasts, possibly amounting to half a million wrecks. It is not possible to extend statutory protection to them all and to enforce and police that protection. In the UK we prefer to concentrate our resources on the most significant sites and we have no plans to change that approach. [...] An alternative approach would be to allow some flexibility in the operation of the Convention in territorial waters, such that States would be free to decide which wrecks are to be afforded statutory protection in their own territorial waters. [...] Whilst the UK has no wish to impose its own approach on others, we trust that other States will respect our right to follow the approach which we believe to be the most practical in our own territorial waters". It is useful to remember here that in the United Kingdom Art. 1, para. 1, of the *Protection of*

At this point Ireland proposed a compromise: "In applying the Rule of the Annex, States Party may have regard to priority in management of underwater cultural heritage". Only Japan agreed with this solution, which was finally rejected.

Therefore, despite several attempts to introduce a criterion of significance, the Convention finally guarantees a blanket protection. During its statement on vote in Commission IV on Culture (20 October 2001), the United Kingdom came back on this issue and declared:

> [T]he text obliges signatory States to extend the same very high standards of protection to all underwater archaeology over 100 years old. It is estimated that there are probably about 10,000 wreck sites on the seabed under the United Kingdom territorial sea and it would neither be possible nor desirable to extend legal protection to all of them. The United Kingdom believes that it is better to focus its efforts and resources on protecting the most important and unique examples of underwater cultural heritage. It would simply be impossible to enforce the application of the rules in the Annex to every one of the thousands of wreck sites.

This seems to be a questionable assertion. The Convention will not be applied to *all* underwater objects. The word "character" was retained into the final text precisely in order to reasonably limit the scope of the Convention.

Activities Regulated by the Convention

Paragraphs 6 and 7 of Article 1 deal with the activities regulated by the Convention. It was only at a late stage in the negotiations that it was felt that they had to be included in the definition. In the 1999 UNESCO draft the definition of "activities directed at underwater cultural heritage" appeared for the first time. It was Canada which took the initiative in seeking to restrict the scope of the Convention by drawing a distinction between activities directed at underwater cultural heritage and those incidentally affecting it. Indeed it was felt by this country that it would be impossible for a cultural convention to deal with and regulate all activities which can affect the underwater heritage (i.e. fishery and the use of bottom trawl nets, tourism, laying of cables etc.). In the SNT this distinction was made explicit and adopted with minor changes. Sweden would have liked to see in the Convention a new paragraph stating that "Public access and activities that do not disturb or otherwise damage cultural heritage, including viewing and photography that meet these criteria, are not activities directed at underwater cultural heritage" (*WP 29*). Such a provision was not included, because, as noted by Spain and agreed upon by Belgium and Canada,

---

cont.

Wrecks Act 1973 reads as follows: "If the Secretary of State is satisfied with respect to any site in United Kingdom waters that: a) it is, or may prove to be, the site of a vessel lying wrecked on or in the sea bed; and b) *on account of the historical, archaeological or artistic importance* of the vessel, or of any object contained or formerly contained in it which may be lying on the sea bed in or near the wreck, the site ought to be protected from unauthorised interference, he may by order designate an area round the site as a restricted area" (emphasis added).

it goes without saying that the Convention is intended to regulate only activities which can physically disturb the heritage, while non-intrusive activities are automatically excluded.

Following a Danish proposal for amendment of the SNT (*WP 1*), letter c) of Article 1, para.1 was inserted in order to exclude from the definition of the underwater cultural heritage installations placed on the seabed and still in use. Similarly, during the last Meeting it was agreed to exclude also pipelines and cables.

State Vessels and Aircraft

Paragraph 8 deals with the definition of State vessels and aircraft. This was another thorny and highly contended issue. Indeed, one of the main reasons for the lack of *consensus* on the overall text of the Convention was the regime for State and military vessels. As it was decided to establish a different regime for State vessels, their definition was a crucial point: the more extensive their definition, the larger the exception to the general regime provided for by the Convention and the smaller the number of wrecks rigorously protected according the general scheme. It was not a minor problem: during negotiations a clear dividing line appeared, with some traditional maritime powers such as Spain, the Netherlands and the United Kingdom, whose military vessels in past centuries sailed across oceans on one side, while on the other were past colonies (in particular in the Americas) on whose coasts most of those vessels wrecked. The former delegations sought a broad definition of State and military vessels so as to ensure that the vessels flying their flag in past centuries would not come under a regime where the coastal State was going to have substantive powers. The opposite was true for the others, which argued that there was no justified reason to establish two different regimes and all shipwrecks of any kind had to be protected in the same way.

When negotiations started at UNESCO, the approach chosen was to exclude warships from the scope of the Convention, as suggested by the ILA. As the negotiations developed it became clear that a Convention excluding military vessels would have been a weak one, since a large number of shipwrecks are indeed warships. In the SNT a specific Article (Art. 2) – specifically dealing with warships – appeared for the first time. There were two problems: how to define them and what regime to establish for them. A solution emerged during the Meeting of March/April 2001: in the absence of an agreed definition of warships in international law, Art. 29 of the UNCLOS could be considered a reference point[38] and entirely adopted (*WP 41*). Subsequently it appeared that this solution presented two defects. On the one hand, some felt that this definition did not fit ancient vessels and would not be accepted by archaeologists. On the other, traditional maritime powers insisted upon a larger definition including also State vessels. The United Kingdom proposed the

[38] "For the purposes of this Convention, "warships" means a ship belonging to the armed forces of a State bearing the external marks distinguishing such ship of its nationality, which was, at the time of sinking, under the command of an officer duly commissioned by the government of the State and whose name appears in the appropriate service list or its equivalent, and was manned by crew under regular armed forces discipline".

following definition: "State vessels and aircraft means warships, naval auxiliaries and other vessels or aircraft owned or operated by a State and used, for the time being, only on governmental non-commercial service. Sunken State vessels and aircraft include the remains of the sunken State vessels or aircraft and their content" (*Non-paper 3, 3 July 2001*). Despite the fact that such a definition was considered too broad by some delegations, among which Italy, Egypt and Argentina, it became the basis for any subsequent proposals.[39] In the final version adopted, the definition had to meet three cumulative conditions, according to proposals put forward by several delegations also in previous debates.[40] The said vessels or aircraft: (i) must be owned or operated by a State and used only for government non-commercial purposes, (ii) be identified as such, (iii) meet the definition of underwater cultural heritage.

National

During the last Meeting of Experts the question was raised by some delegations as to whether it was necessary to add a definition of "national". This term was indeed extensively used in some key articles of the Convention, in particular in Articles 9-12 where the regime for the underwater cultural heritage on the continental shelf and in the Area was drawn up. Spain and the United Kingdom argued that such a definition was not necessary, because international law already provides it. Not so for Portugal, Italy and the United States. These delegations stressed that a general and theoretical definition of "national" was not needed. Rather a specific definition with reference to this Convention was definitely required. In other words it was necessary to clarify, for example, who had the duty to notify the discovery of an archaeological object: the master of the vessel or any member of the crew? Portugal proposed the following definition: "person in charge of the discovery or activity". Italy: "person in charge of the activity or who made the discovery". It was decided to solve this issue during the second reading, but, as it is know, no second reading ever took place. Therefore, no definition of "national" was finally inserted in Article 1. Anyway the question was partially solved when drafting Articles 9-12, where the word "national" was transformed in "the national or the master of the vessel".

Article 2 – Objectives and General Principles

1. This Convention aims to ensure and strengthen the protection of underwater cultural heritage.
2. States Parties shall cooperate in the protection of underwater cultural heritage.
3. States Parties shall preserve underwater cultural heritage for the benefit of humanity in conformity with the provisions of this Convention.
4. States Parties shall, individually or jointly as appropriate, take all appropriate measures in conformity with this Convention and with international law that are necessary to protect underwater cultural heritage, using for this purpose

[39] See WP 57, Non-paper by the United States (7 July 2001).

[40] See WP 34 and Non-paper by Spain (22 June 2001).

the best practicable means at their disposal and in accordance with their capabilities.

5. The preservation *in situ* of underwater cultural heritage shall be considered as the first option before allowing or engaging in any activities directed at this heritage.
6. Recovered underwater cultural heritage shall be deposited, conserved and managed in a manner that ensures its long-term preservation.
7. Underwater cultural heritage shall not be commercially exploited.
8. Consistent with State practice and international law, including the United Nations Convention on the Law of the Sea, nothing in this Convention shall be interpreted as modifying the rules of international law and State practice pertaining to sovereign immunities, nor any State's rights with respect to its State vessels and aircraft.
9. States Parties shall ensure that proper respect is given to all human remains located in maritime waters.
10. Responsible non-intrusive access to observe or document *in situ* underwater cultural heritage shall be encouraged to create public awareness, appreciation, and protection of the heritage except where such access is incompatible with its protection and management.
11. No act or activity undertaken on the basis of this Convention shall constitute grounds for claiming, contending or disputing any claim to national sovereignty or jurisdiction.

[Preparatory documents:

a) Working Papers:
   - WG1 WP35, 6 July 2000 (New Article 3 Incorporating Article X proposed by IUCN)
   - WP 22, 29 March 2001 (Amendment proposed by Australia and seconded by Canada)
   - WP 28, 30 March 2001 (Amendment proposed by Mexico and seconded by Portugal)
   - WP 32, 2 April 2001 (New Article 2)
   - WP 34, 2 April 2001 (Amendment proposed by Finland, Germany, Japan, the Netherlands, Norway, the Russian Federation, Spain, Sweden, the United Kingdom and endorsed by the United States)
   - Non-paper by Spain, 22 June 2001
   - Non-paper by the United States, 1 July 2001
   - WP 52, 3 July 2001 (Proposed by Mexico, Portugal, Colombia, Brazil, Peru, South Africa and Croatia)
   - Non-paper 3, 3 July 2001 (State vessels and aircraft, Single Article proposed by UK)
   - WP 57, 5 July 2001 (Report of the informal sub-group of the warships working group)

b) Drafts:
   - ILA Draft (Art. 3)

- first UNESCO/DOALOS draft (Art. 3)
- second UNESCO draft (Art. 3)
- SNT (Art. 3)

c) Other documents:
- Final Report of the First Meeting of Governmental Experts on the Draft Convention on the Protection of Underwater Cultural Heritage, Paris, 29 June-2 July 1998 (UNESCO doc. CLT-98/CONF.202/7), para. VII
- Final Report of the Second Meeting of Governmental Experts on the Draft Convention on the Protection of Underwater Cultural Heritage , Paris, 19-24 April 1999 (UNESCO doc. CLT-99/CONF.204, Paris, August 1999), para. VIII]

The Article dealing with the general principles enshrined in the Convention has very much changed from the first draft to the final text. While negotiations developed it became evident that some principles had to be clearly enunciated right at the beginning of the Convention.

The ILA draft, as well as the first UNESCO/DOALOS draft, simply declared one principle: that States Parties would take all reasonable measures to preserve underwater cultural heritage for the benefit of humankind. It was not a new principle: in Art. 149 of UNCLOS it was possible to find the same idea albeit with reference only to the Area.

When debating this provision, two new ideas already emerged during the first Meeting of Experts: first, some delegations wanted to include the principle of international co-operation; second, others asked for a stronger language requesting States to take all necessary measures in order to prevent commercial exploitation of underwater cultural heritage. The first idea was effectively enshrined – as a second paragraph – in the second UNESCO draft (but in square brackets) so as to read: "[To that end, States Parties shall take all necessary measures to cooperate, specifically in the event of common interest by reason of the localization of the wreck and the flag State or because of the same cultural, archaeological or historical origin.]".

New principles were considered during the second Meeting of Experts: namely, the non applicability of salvage law and possibility of making reservations to the Convention.

The SNT proposed a more articulated provision. It was drafted on the basis of several suggestions: a non-paper by IUCN (International Union for Conservation of Nature); reflections made in Working Group 3 established during the Third Meeting of Experts according to which some important Rules incorporated in the Annex should also be enunciated as general principles within the main body of the Convention; debates in the previous session. The result was the following:

1. This Convention aims to implement and strengthen the protection of the underwater cultural heritage as provided in UNCLOS.
2. States shall preserve underwater cultural heritage for the benefit of humankind in accordance with the provisions of this Convention.
3. States shall, individually or jointly as appropriate, take all measures consistent with this Convention that are necessary to protect underwater cultural

heritage, using for this purpose the best practicable means at their disposal and in accordance with their capability.
4. States shall cooperate in the protection of the underwater cultural heritage, in particular with all other States with a verifiable link to the heritage concerned.
5. The preservation *in situ* of underwater cultural heritage shall be considered as the first option before engaging in or allowing any activities directed at the heritage.
6. Underwater cultural heritage shall not be commercially exploited.

During the last Meeting of Experts (in particular during the first session) the provision was intensively debated and further changes were made. The wording of some paragraphs was slightly modified; reference to UNCLOS was deleted; upon suggestion by France, the principle of international co-operation was given a more prominent role, by placing it second. Any reference to the "verifiable link" was also deleted: some delegations (the Russian Federation and Spain in particular) would have liked to have a clear definition of this concept, but that would have entailed an endless discussion; ICOMOS suggested deleting only the adjective "verifiable", arguing that in the case of the *Titanic*, for example, many States have a link but it is not verifiable for all of them. In the end, no reference to this concept can be found in Article 2 (also because cooperation is felt to be a duty upon all States and not only reserved to those particularly linked to a specific object discovered), and no general definition of "verifiable link" is incorporated in the Convention.

A proposal by Australia and Canada (*WP 22*) aiming to add the sentence "In determining the measures, States may consider significant environmental, health and safety impact" to para. 3 of the SNT was not accepted. A proposal by the United Kingdom to include in the same paragraph the following: "In the protection and management of underwater cultural heritage, including in applying the Rules, the competent services of the States Parties may take into account the cultural, historical or archaeological significance of particular heritage" was similarly rejected.[41]

Instead an amendment by Mexico and Portugal (*WP 28*) on deposit, conservation and management of the underwater cultural heritage (final para. 6) was approved. The same happened for a proposal by several States (*WP 52*) on responsible and not intrusive access to underwater cultural heritage, which became para. 10. Also a paragraph on sovereign immunity of military vessels and another on respect for human remains were included at the end as a consequence of negotiations on the issue of State vessels. As far as para. 9 is concerned, Uruguay suggested avoiding any reference to military maritime graves in order to ensure respect for any human remains, whether civil or military. The same was stressed by some delegates from African States, with reference, in particular, to the high number of black slaves who had perished while being transported to the Americas. Italy, Germany and the United Kingdom reacted by arguing that military graves deserve particular respect. Their remarks were not retained.

[41] About the problem of "significance", see *supra*, comments to Art. 1.

Para. 11 deserves special attention. There is no trace of this paragraph in the text approved by governmental experts on July 8, 2001, nor was its content even discussed. The issue was raised by a delegate when the final text of the Convention – revised by the Drafting Committee[42] – circulated among States. According to the delegate, this important disclaimer clause – originally included as para. 2 of Article 4 of SNT ("Relationship to law of the sea") – had simply been omitted because all the attention was devoted to the highly contentious first paragraph and the lack of a second reading impeded its being considered in a proper manner. In other words, the disclaimer clause had been forgotten. At this point the Chairman decided that it could be inserted as the new paragraph 11 of Article 2. When the adoption of the Convention was discussed in Commission IV of the UNESCO General Conference, Australia made the following declaration:

> It is the understanding of Australia that in relation to Article 2, para. 11, the phrase "shall constitute grounds for claiming, contending or disputing any claim to national sovereignty or jurisdiction" is intended only to be a reference to territorial disputes.

Called to express his views on this point, the Chairman of the Meeting of Experts, Mr. Lund, totally agreed with Australia and stated:

> Art. 2, 11 was introduced as a text that had been proposed at an earlier meeting and had not received any negative reactions. It was felt necessary by the chair in order to deal with the seabed areas on which there were disputes of jurisdiction between different sovereign States in accordance with the reasons that had been given by the sponsor of the proposal at the time it was presented to the Meeting of Governmental Experts. It should of course be interpreted in this limited fashion.[43]

During their statement in Commission IV the United States also made comments on para. 11:

> Article 2(11), which was added by a dubious procedure after the debate had concluded in July, [...] must be read in a manner that does not preclude a challenge to a State's excessive maritime claims based on the provisions of the Convention.[44]

---

[42] A drafting Committee was established during the second session of the Fourth Meeting of Experts. It met during the last days of the negotiations and even after the closure of official negotiations, due to lack of time to finalise the revision of the entire text of the Convention. It goes without saying that the Drafting Committee at this point had no competence in changing any substantial provision of the Convention, but only in making necessary changes in the drafting of the text. When the Drafting Committee finished its work, the new final text of the Convention was circulated among all the delegates and some comments on the final wording were expressed by States.

[43] Quoted by O'Keefe, *supra* note 25, at 56.

[44] The statement of the United States in Commission IV of the General Conference is reprinted under the title *U.S. Concerns Regarding UNESCO Convention on Underwater Heritage*, in (2002) *AJIL* 468.

Article 3 – Relationship between this Convention and the United Nations Convention on the Law of the Sea

Nothing in this Convention shall prejudice the rights, jurisdiction and duties of States under international law, including the United Nations Convention on the Law of the Sea. This Convention shall be interpreted and applied in the context of and in a manner consistent with international law, including the United Nations Convention on the Law of the Sea.

[Preparatory documents:

a) Working papers and comments by States:
   - General remarks by Mr. Hans W. Longva, Director General, Department of Legal Affairs, Royal Norwegian Ministry of Foreign Affairs, 19 April 1999
   - Commentaire de la délégation française sur le projet de Convention sur la protection du patrimoine culturel subaquatique (UNESCO doc. CLT-96/CONF.202/5Rev2), 7 mars 2000
   - Remarks presented by the Government of Italy, April 2000
   - Comments of the United States of America on Selected Articles being considered in Working Group 1, 4 July 2000
   - WG1 WP33, 6 July 2000 (Amendment to Article 2 bis, proposed by Venezuela)
   - Non-paper by delegation of Poland, July 2000

b) Drafts:
   - Second UNESCO draft (Art. 2 bis)
   - SNT (Art. 4)

c) Other documents:
   - Preliminary Study on the Advisability of Preparing an International Instrument for the Protection of the Underwater Cultural Heritage, Annex, Paris, 4 October 1995 (UNESCO doc. 28C/39)
   - Report by the Director-General on the finding of the Meeting of Experts concerning the preparation of an international instrument for the protection of the underwater cultural heritage, Paris, 14 May 1997 (UNESCO doc 151 EX/10 Add.)
   - Final Report of the First Meeting of Governmental Experts on the Draft Convention on the Protection of Underwater Cultural Heritage, Paris, 29 June-2 July 1998 (UNESCO doc. CLT-98/CONF.202/7), paras. 49-50
   - United Nations, General Assembly, Resolution on the Ocean and the Law of the Sea, U.N. doc. A/RES/53/32, 6 January 1999
   - Final Report of the Second Meeting of Governmental Experts on the Draft Convention on the Protection of Underwater Cultural Heritage , Paris, 19-24 April 1999 (UNESCO doc. CLT-99/CONF.204, Paris, August 1999), para. VII
   - United Nations, General Assembly, Resolution on the Ocean and the Law of the Sea, U.N. doc. A/RES/54/31, 18 January 2000

- Summary of Observations by States on the Draft Convention on the Protection of Underwater Cultural Heritage, Paris, April 2000 (UNESCO doc. CLT-2000/CONF.201/3)
- Draft Resolution submitted by Russian Federation and the United Kingdom (and endorsed by the United States), General Conference, 26 October 2001 (UNESCO doc. 31 C/COM.IV/DIR.5)]

A short and apparently neutral provision like Article 3 does hide what is probably the most controversial issue underpinning all the Convention, that is to say its relationship with the UNCLOS. One has to wait for the second UNESCO draft (1999) to see the problem reflected in a specific article within the Convention, but the problem was a ghost present as early as the very beginning of the negotiations (maybe even before). Defining the relationship between the two conventions inevitably meant defining the nature of the UNESCO Convention. Was it an appendix to the UNCLOS or an autonomous instrument developing international law? Was it a legal instrument dealing primarily with the law of the sea or instead a more comprehensive agreement dealing with cultural heritage law, law of the sea, archaeological standards, etc.?

Since the publication by the UNESCO Secretariat of the preliminary study on the advisability of preparing a convention, several comments put forward by States explicitly took a position on the issue of the relationship of the future convention with UNCLOS. Germany, Italy, the United Kingdom and France all took the view – even if with different emphasis – that the delicate balance achieved by the UNCLOS should not be altered. For Germany "the Convention on Law of the Sea represents a universal and fundamental agreement and this achievement cannot be jeopardized"; for Italy "the balance achieved, through the Convention on the Law of the Sea, between the principle of the freedom of the sea and opposing tendencies, should be kept"; the United Kingdom "would be wary of upsetting the jurisdictional package in the United Nations Convention on the Law of the Sea"; France "stresses that the outcome of the deliberations should be consistent with the provisions of the United Nations Convention on the Law of the Sea and create neither maritime zones nor special rights that run counter to those provided for in that text".[45]

The concern of consistency between the two instruments was raised also in another international forum. Under the pressure of the Russian Federation that indicated the UNESCO draft Convention as an attempt, among others, to revise some provisions of the UNCLOS, the General Assembly of the United Nations, in its annual resolution on oceans and the law of the sea, made a reference to the ongoing negotiations within UNESCO and "stress[ed] the importance of ensuring

---

45 *Preliminary Study on the Advisability of Preparing an International Instrument for the Protection of the Underwater Cultural Heritage, Annex*, Paris, 4 October 1995 (UNESCO doc. 28C/39). Germany reiterated its position in commenting the report on the finding of the 1996 Meeting of Experts (see *Report by the Director-General on the Finding of the Meeting of Experts concerning the Preparation of an International Instrument for the Protection of the Underwater Cultural Heritage*, Paris, 14 May 1997 (UNESCO doc. 151 EX/10 Add.).

that the instrument to be elaborated is in full conformity with the relevant provisions of the Convention".[46]

In 1999, at the second Meeting of Experts, the question was debated. Norway intervened to clearly state that "a possible new Convention should be designated in the same way as the 1995 Agreement on straddling fish stocks and highly migratory fish stock,[47] *i.e.* as an agreement for the implementation of the relevant provisions of the UNCLOS". In this view Norway suggested introducing a new Article 2 *bis* into the draft, based on Article 4 of the Straddling Stocks Agreement, reading as follows:

> Nothing in this Agreement shall prejudice the rights, jurisdiction and duties of States under the Convention. [This Agreement shall be interpreted and applied in the context of and in a manner consistent with the Convention].

This Article was indeed inserted in the 1999 draft. It was also proposed to rename the draft as "Agreement on the implementation..." instead of "Convention", in order to stress the idea that the UNESCO legal instrument should be limited to giving implementation to the relevant provision of UNCLOS, but this proposal was not accepted. Norway gave such strong emphasis to the model of the Straddling Stocks Agreement that Italy reacted stating that Norwegian proposals could usefully be considered when a negotiation on the "*straddling* underwater cultural heritage" is opened!

At the third Meeting, Working Group 1, established to deal with Article 1-7, had no time to debate in depth Article 2 *bis*. Anyway, the topic was not forgotten and several delegations made written comments where the issue of the relationship with UNCLOS was also mentioned. The United States considered Article 2 *bis* appropriate but remarked that, to have a sense, no jurisdictional provisions contrary to the UNCLOS had to be inserted in the Convention. Poland agreed on the need to ensure a "strict consistency" between the two Conventions, but at the same time took the view that UNCLOS only lays down general principles in the field of underwater archaeology and it leaves the possibility to adopt a specific and detailed convention on this issue.

Italy, showing significant evolution since 1995, stresses that the UNCLOS presents a legal vacuum (there are no rules for archaeological objects located on the continental shelf) which can seriously affect the underwater cultural heritage. Moreover provisions such as Art. 303, para. 3, of the UNCLOS are dangerous in so far they seem to encourage the looting of the underwater cultural heritage. But on

---

[46] United Nations, General Assembly, Resolution on the Ocean and the Law of the Sea, U.N. doc. A/RES/53/32, 6 January 1999, para. 20. A similar wording was used by the General Assembly in 2000 (United Nations, General Assembly, Resolution on the Ocean and the Law of the Sea, U.N. doc. A/RES/54/31, 18 January 2000, para. 30).

[47] United Nations Agreement for the Implementation of the Provisions of the United Nations Convention on the Law of the Sea of 10 December 1982 relating to the Conservation and Management of Straddling Fish Stocks and Highly Migratory Fish Stocks, New York, 4 August 1995 (U.N. doc. A/CONF.164/37 (1995)).

the whole, according to Italy, the spirit of UNCLOS is that underwater cultural heritage must be protected and, what is more important, Art. 303, para. 4 itself "allows for the drafting of a more specific treaty regime which can ensure a better protection [...]. It would be meaningless to simply repeat the provisions of the UNCLOS, including their shortcomings, without adding any improvements. To leave the regime as it is would lead to an unacceptable consequence: namely, the risk of leaving a great part of the marine cultural heritage without protection".

France was less open to changes: "La France estime que la convention en discussion doit se situer dans le cadre plus général du droit de la mer positif tel que codifié par la Convention des Nations Unies sur le droit de la mer de 1982. Ce projet ne sera acceptable qu'a condition de ne porter atteinte à aucune disposition de la Convention de Montego Bay. En revanche, dans le respect du cadre général ci-dessus défini, toutes les solutions pratiques et juridiques sont envisageables. [...] Nul besoin [...] de modifier l'équilibre des pouvoirs et des compétences difficilement mis sur pied par la Convention de 1982".

In a spirit of compromise, the SNT elaborated a new Article 4 (old Article 2 *bis*):

1. Nothing in this Convention nor any act performed on the basis of this Convention shall prejudice the rights, the present or future claims or legal views of any State relating to the law of the sea.
2. No act or activities undertaken on the basis of this Convention shall constitute grounds for claiming, contending or disputing any claim to national sovereignty or jurisdiction.[48]

Any explicit reference to UNCLOS was deleted and replaced by a general reference to the law of the sea; also the word "jurisdiction" disappeared. These amendments changed the approach: by refusing to borrow the provision from the 1995 Straddling Stocks Agreement, it was implicitly affirmed that the relationship between the UNESCO Convention and the UNCLOS was different from the link between the 1995 Agreement and the UNCLOS.[49]

At the last Meeting of Experts, when the debate was opened on Article 4, a real clash took place. After finding a compromise (although it was a not universally acceptable one) on the core provisions of the Convention – such as salvage law, military vessels and jurisdiction – Article 4 still needed to be agreed upon. It was the last issue to be closed and it was not until midnight of 7 July 2002 that governmental experts found a solution (more because of the pressure of time than for a widespread *consensus* on it).

Norway expressed its opposition to Article 4 as drafted in the SNT. So did Greece, but for opposite reasons: Greece felt that the UNESCO Convention could not avoid an explicit reference to the UNCLOS in order to guarantee some rights

---

[48] As far as the second paragraph is concerned, see *supra*.

[49] Here it will just be pointed out that, notwithstanding the label of "implementing Agreement", the 1995 Straddling Fish Stocks Agreement does change and supplement the UNCLOS regime in some relevant provisions.

ensured by the 1982 Convention. While some States remarked that the old Article 2 *bis* represented a problem for States not Parties to UNCLOS (Turkey, Canada), Argentina proposed a sort of exchange: most States would have accepted the old Article 2 *bis* and Norway would have accepted the overall text of the Convention in a spirit of *consensus*. In effect many States, and not only those clearly in favour of a strong disclaimer provision, such as the United Kingdom, the United States, Germany, the Russian Federation, Sweden and Japan, but also States that would have preferred a less strict relationship between the two Conventions, such as Italy, felt inclined to accept Article 2 *bis* as a compromise, but Norway refused: at that time the jurisdictional question had not yet been solved and, as drafted at that moment, Art. 10 was not acceptable for Norway.

Argentina suggested another compromise: "prejudice" would be considered with reference to "international law, including UNCLOS"; the same for the "interpretation". In such a way the link between the UNESCO Convention and UNCLOS would be less direct: all international law, and UNCLOS as an element of it, would have to be taken into account. For the United States and the Netherlands this proposal was ambiguous; for Germany the UNESCO Convention will develop international law and therefore it would be absurd to insert a reference to international law in a disclaimer provision. Norway clearly expressed the view that the UNESCO Convention must only be implemented and interpreted with reference to UNCLOS and no other international instruments. At this point Italy recalled what the Vienna Convention on the Law of the Treaties says on this point: its Art. 31 allows for the interpretation of a convention "in its context". Here the context was also, but not only, UNCLOS: it had to be considered a "source of inspiration" for the UNESCO Convention but also other issues, dealt with in other international instruments (such as those related to the cultural heritage), were at stake.

Argentina still proposed three different versions:

a) "This Convention shall be interpreted and applied *in the context of and in a manner consistent with* international law, including UNCLOS";
b) "This Convention shall be interpreted and applied *in full conformity and in a manner consistent with* international law, including UNCLOS"
c) "This Convention shall be interpreted and applied *in the context of and in a manner consistent with* UNCLOS *and other relevant international instruments*"

For lack of time the Chairman called for a decision: the plenary preferred the first version with the opposition of Norway and the United States. Then the negotiations on the whole Convention were declared closed.

But the fate of Article 3 was not closed. In Commission IV for Culture of the General Conference, on 26 October 2001, the Russian Federation and the United Kingdom, with the endorsement of the United States, proposed a new amendment to the draft approved by the governmental experts. Among various articles affected by this proposal, also Article 3 appeared. It was suggested to delete "international law, including". The aim was to come back to the old Norwegian idea and to establish a direct and exclusive link between the UNESCO Convention and UNCLOS. The amendment was defeated by 77 votes to 8 with 21 abstentions.

The relationship between the two instruments was one of the main topics raised in the final declarations (before and on vote) made by States. While some States said that they regarded the new Convention as in full conformity with UNCLOS (Argentina,[50] Japan,[51] Ireland,[52] Italy[53]), other completely disagreed and justified their negative vote or abstention just on the unsatisfactory relationship established between the two Conventions (the Netherlands,[54] France,[55] Norway,[56] the Russian Federation,[57] the United Kingdom[58] and the United States[59]).

---

[50] "Valoramos, por otra parte, las multiples referencias en el proyecto a la conformidad de la futura Convención con el derecho internacional del mar, incluido el derecho que codifica la Convención de las Naciones Unidas de 1982".

[51] "As we all know, the focal issue was the relationship between the United Nations Convention on the Law of the Sea and this Convention. While mindful of the need to maintain conformity between the two, Japan participated in the concerted efforts to reach a consensus. Fully convinced of the need to provide for a new international legal framework for the protection of underwater cultural heritage, Japan voted the draft Convention as in its view such need for conformity has been met. We would like to take this opportunity to confirm that, as provided for in Article 3, this Convention shall be interpreted and applied in the context of and in a manner consistent with international law, including the United Nations Convention on the Law of the Sea. It is essential, we believe, that this grand rule be faithfully maintained so that those States, which still find it difficult to join in support of the Convention at this time, will be able to accept it in the future".

[52] "In our view the proposed Convention as now presented to this Conference can provide an effective mechanism for securing protection of underwater cultural heritage without conflicting with the United Nations Convention on the Law of the Sea of 1982 (to which Ireland is Party) or otherwise adversely affecting legitimate rights and interests".

[53] "[...] We share the opinion of Mr. Lund – the Chairman of the Meeting of governmental experts – that this Convention is an important step forward in international law, fully compatible with UNCLOS".

[54] "The Netherlands has the strong conviction that a convention on underwater cultural heritage should explicitly be seen in the relation to the United Nations Convention on the Law of the Sea, UNCLOS. For us, it is extremely important that the careful balance between rights and obligations of coastal States and flag States, as foreseen in UNCLOS, will not be disturbed or infringed upon by other international instruments on specific issues, like underwater cultural heritage. Unfortunately, there is some strain between the text we have at hand and UNCLOS, especially with regard to the provisions on jurisdiction".

[55] "[...] [C]e projet comporte de nombreuses dispositions utiles et positives. Mais, comme vous le savez, la France est en désaccord avec le projet sur deux points précis: le statut des navires d'Etat et les droits de juridiction, dont nous considérons qu'ils sont incompatibles avec les dispositions de la Convention sur le droit de la mer".

[56] "[...] [T]he Convention unfortunately also includes parts, which jeopardise the fine balance of jurisdiction achieved through the carefully drafted UN Convention on the law of the Sea (UNCLOS). This applies in particular to provisions relating to the exclusive economic zone and the continental shelf. Norway is committed to maintaining the fine balance of the UNCLOS regime. Efforts to further strengthen the protection of underwater cultural heritage should be promoted within this framework. This would ensure broad international agreement and support, and thus the efficiency such measures deserve. Norway regrets that the efforts to develop such a text have been unsuccessful. On this basis,

Article 4 – Relationship to Law of Salvage and Law of Finds

Any activity relating to underwater cultural heritage to which this Convention applies shall not be subject to the law of salvage or law of finds, unless it:
a) is authorised by the competent authorities, and
b) is in full conformity with this Convention, and
c) ensures that any recovery of the underwater cultural heritage achieves its maximum protection.

[Preparatory documents:
a) Working papers and comments by States:
- Information paper submitted by the United States of America "Uses and interests in underwater cultural heritage that are compatible with the Convention" (as presented orally at the Meeting of Governmental Experts, Paris, 29 June-2 July 1998)
- Comments of the United States of America on UNESCO Draft Convention on the Protection of the Underwater Cultural Heritage (April 1999)
- Remarks presented by the Government of Italy (April 2000)
- WP 13, 27 March 2001 (Amendment proposed by Italy and Greece)
- WP 42, 4 April 2001 (Small Working Group on Article 5 mandated by Chairman)

b) Drafts:
- ILA draft (Art. 4)
- first UNESCO/DOALOS draft (Art. 12, para.2)
- SNT (Art. 5)

c) Other documents:
- Feasibility Study for the Drafting of a New Instrument for the Protection of the Underwater Cultural Heritage, Paris, 23 March 1995 (UNESCO doc. 146 EX/27), paras. 15-17, 29-34
- Report of the Meeting of Experts for the Draft Convention on the

---

cont.
Norway is not in a position to support the Convention on the protection of underwater cultural heritage".

57 "[. . .] [F]or principal reasons, a number of provisions of the Convention are not acceptable for the Russian Federation. For example, Article 10 may be interpreted as exceeding the scope of rights and jurisdiction of a coastal State in adjacent seas as set forth by the UN Convention on the Law of the Sea 1982. It may be interpreted as providing a coastal State with the right to take, at its own discretion, unilateral measures not excluding force under the pretext of the protection of the underwater cultural heritage. We are unable to agree with it".

58 "The United Kingdom considers that the current text erodes the fundamental principles of customary international law, codified in UNCLOS, of Sovereign Immunity which is retained by a State's warships and vessels and aircraft used for non commercial service limit until expressly abandoned by that State. The text purports to alter the fine balance between the equal, but conflicting, rights of Coastal and Flag States, carefully negotiated in UNCLOS, in a way that is unacceptable to the United Kingdom".

59 "[. . .] [W]e regret that we cannot accept this text because of objections to several key provisions relating to jurisdiction, the reporting scheme, warships, and the relationship of the Convention to UNCLOS".

Protection of Underwater Cultural Heritage, Paris, 22-24 May 1996 (UNESCO doc. CLT-96/CONF.605/6), paras. 45-52
- Final Report of the First Meeting of Governmental Experts on the Draft Convention on the Protection of Underwater Cultural Heritage, Paris, 29 June-2 July 1998, (UNESCO doc. CLT-98/CONF.202/7), para. 30-33, 51
- Letter by Rosalie Balking (Director, Legal and External Relations, IMO) to Mr. Carsten Lund, 3 April 2001]

What role the salvage law and the law of finds had to be given within the Convention was a very difficult question. The main problem was that those principles are commonly applied also with respect to underwater cultural heritage in some countries of common law, where they are even considered very old principles of general international law. On the contrary, they are completely unknown in countries of civil law that therefore deny any status of international principles, while considering them mere concepts of domestic law. In their legal systems, salvage is nothing more than a form of assistance, provided only to ships in peril. Consequently, when a ship has sunk it is no longer subject to the rule of salvage and when a certain time elapses or the owner is unknown the wreck becomes the property of the State. It is even inconceivable in such legal systems that an archaeological or historical object can became the property of a private person by law. These very different legal approaches to the problem, as well as the difficulty in dealing with elements of private law in a public international law convention, made the question of salvage law a serious potential obstacle to the adoption of the UNESCO Convention. This proved not to be the case: the debate was intense but a constructive compromise was eventually reached and adopted by *consensus*. Salvage law was therefore, among the thorny issues at stake, the first to be settled, thus contributing to the illusion that *consensus* was likely to be reached on the overall text of the Convention.

The ILA draft Convention took a clear position by preventing the applicability of salvage law to the underwater cultural heritage (Art. 4).

In the feasibility study made by UNESCO the starting point was the analysis of Art. 303, para. 3 of the UNCLOS, which states: "Nothing in this article affects the rights of identifiable owners, the law of salvage or other rules of admiralty, or law and practices with respect to cultural exchanges". Such a provision seems to allow the commercial exploitation of historic shipwrecks. Besides, it was also recalled that the question of the applicability of salvage law to ancient relicts was also considered by IMO when drafting the 1989 International Convention on Salvage:[60] it was decided not to include provisions on the underwater cultural heritage within that Convention, but to allow States Parties to make a specific reservation at the time of ratification in order not to apply the Convention to maritime cultural property.[61]

---

[60] *International Convention on Salvage* (London, 28 April 1989), IMO doc. LEG/CONF.7/27 (May 2, 1989); reprinted in (1989) *IJECL* 300.

[61] Art. 30, para. 1 d).

At the 1996 Meeting of Experts different positions were expressed: commercial value could be an incentive for excavation and protection; only private companies have the huge amount of funds necessary for the recovery of ancient treasures; archaeologists could monitor the work of salvors; the concept of being financially rewarded would be fundamentally antithetical to archaeological and scientific research, etc.. The IMO expert said that only 8 out of 20 States Parties to the International Salvage Convention had made a reservation excluding its applicability to historic wrecks.[62]

As a result of this initial debate, the first UNESCO/DOALOS draft did not include Art. 4 of the ILA draft. A less strict provision was preferred. It is Art. 12, para. 2, which read as follows: "States Parties shall provide for the non-application of any internal law of regulation having the effect of providing commercial incentives or any other reward for the excavation and removal of underwater cultural heritage". During the first Meeting of Governmental Experts most delegations agreed with this provision. The position of the United States must be mentioned here, which expressed its preference for the so-called "multiple use principle", according to which all users of underwater cultural heritage must be addressed by the Convention. Therefore also the private sector must be allowed to recover underwater cultural heritage, perhaps in partnership with the public sector, respecting the professional scientific standards of the ICOMOS Charter.[63] In other words, the United States took the view that commercial companies can give a positive contribution with funding of excavations, conservation and educational programs. While allowing a commercial use of underwater cultural heritage, the United States at the same time declared "[it did not] support the application of the law of salvage to underwater cultural heritage because it provides commercial incentives to recover such resources. This often conflicts with the basic principles of marine archaeology". The United States returned to the issue of salvage law when commenting the second UNESCO draft: here it declared that it was "still reflecting on the question on whether the Convention should contain a provision that bars the application of the laws of salvage and finds with regard to underwater cultural heritage". Its proposal was the following: to prevent the application of the law of salvage and finds in the Convention, but to give the possibility to States Parties that want to preserve its continued application to do so by a reservation at the moment of ratification. To explain the sometimes ambiguous United States' position on this issue it can be useful to remember that its delegation was the only one where salvors were represented. It is likely that the salvors' community had made a strong lobby in order not to have a total ban of salvage law in the Convention.[64]

---

[62] This can be explained by the fact that for most civil law countries salvage law does not apply to historic wrecks and making a reservation might suggest that it does apply, which could be seen as useless or even contrary to their legal system.

[63] On the ICOMOS Charter, see *infra*, commentary on Art. 33.

[64] See, for example, the letter by senator Jesse Helms to the Secretary of State Madeleine Albright of June 27, 2000, published at <www.imacdigest.com/helmsltr.html> ("American maritime salvors believe (and, I believe, justifiably so) that this Convention will pose a formidable threat to America's maritime

A clear opposition to the applicability of the law of salvage and finds was made by Italy. In its remarks presented in April 2000, Italy denied any international status to these principles of admiralty law. By making explicit reference to the rules applied by some decisions delivered by American courts in the case of the *Titanic*,[65] that could be applied also elsewhere, Italy declared that "[it] cannot accept that any private individual or company can automatically acquire property rights in an object which is a part of the Mediterranean cultural heritage and dispose of it as a private owner. The objects must not serve commercial gain but shall be preserved for the general public purpose of the enhancement of human knowledge. Neither can Italy accept that a foreign judge can declare a prohibited area in the Mediterranean where archaeological research cannot be made by the relevant Italian public authorities". Here Italy stressed an important point: even if sometimes in the past civil law countries had felt it unnecessary to take a clear stand against the applicability of salvage law with reference to underwater cultural heritage, now it was time to say it explicitly in order to prevent courts of countries where salvage law is currently

---

cont.

salvage industry – and, also, to U.S. admiralty jurisprudence, which [...] has strong roots in the United States Constitution"); letter by Pat Clyne, director of the Historic Shipwreck Salvage Policy Council, to Robert Blumberg, of the Department of State and Chief of the U.S. delegation to UNESCO (without date; presumably spring 2001), published at <www.imacdigest.com/hsspc.html> ("The United States delegation should prepare and propose an entire counterproposal draft [to the SNT] that more accurately reflects the hard won gains of the last years of negotiations. [...] The wisdom of the founders that private enterprise with limited government regulation was for the greater public good has been shown by the rediscovery of far more lost ships and their histories with private labor and capital than by exclusively relying on government and academic funding ever could. Thus, the language in the draft convention must be reworked to more adequately reflect the positive role that commercial salvors play in preserving history"); letter by Taffi Fisher Abt, president of Mel Fisher Center, Inc., to George Bush, President of the United States (without date; presumably spring 2001), published at <www.imacdigest.com/bush.htm> ("If there is no profit motive for the industry who attempts to locate and then salvage and conserve the artefacts, I can inform you that this country would be 38,000 artifacts shorter [...]. Shorter on knowledge and education. Shorter on ambition and the American Dream"); letter by James Sinclair, archaeologist Searex Inc., to Robert Blumberg and the U.S. delegation to UNESCO, (without date; presumably spring 2001), published at <www.imacdigest.com/delegate.html> ("If we eliminate all chance of commercial involvement as the Single Negotiating Text does, we will have eliminated a whole host of avenues by which this resource might have been saved. The truth is that commercial interest is not going to disappear. It has been and will continue to be a driving force behind some of the most creative and innovative work of our time (in all areas of endeavour): however, the effect of this document will be, in all likelihood, to make criminals out of many people who otherwise would have and might have made real and lasting contribution to the underwater cultural heritage"); letter by Michele Wells, president of the Sea One International Ltd., to Colin Powell, Secretary of State, (without date; presumably spring 2001), published at <www.imacdigest.com/powell.html> ("[The] UNESCO Treaty Proposal [...] is a dangerous and volatile "nose of the camel" strategy aimed not at "protecting and preserving" alleged "non renewable historic artefacts" – as proclaimed – but a sweeping and abhorrent attempt to annihilate any private sector marine exploration and development and to destroy the future of all privately generated underwater exploration, intervention technology and recovery world wide").

65 *R.M.S. Titanic, Inc. v. Haver*, 171 F.3d 943 (4th Cir., March 24, 1999), reprinted in (1999) *ILM* 796; *R.M.S. Titanic, Inc. v. The Wrecked and Abandoned Vessel*, 9 F. Supp. 2d 624 (E.D.Va., June 23, 1998).

applied from recognising salvage rights over wrecks located in international waters, on the continental shelf or in territorial waters of States refusing salvage law.[66]

In the SNT a new Article (Art. 5) was inserted on the issue of salvage law and it stated:

> Underwater cultural heritage to which this Convention applies shall not be subject to the law of salvage or law of finds unless it is in full conformity with this convention.

With comparison to the ILA draft, the prohibition was not limited to the law of salvage but also to the law of finds, but a door was left open to their applicability under a specific condition.

At the fourth Meeting of Experts Italy and Greece proposed an amendment (*WP 13*) aimed at deleting the last sentence and ensuring a total ban on the law of salvage and finds. During the debate most delegations agreed with this proposal (Portugal, Peru, Iran, France, Mexico, Egypt, Tunisia, ICOMOS). Ireland, the United Kingdom and the United States disagreed: they held that, subject to the respect of the Rules of the Annex, salvors can contribute to the protection of the underwater cultural heritage. At this point the Chairman gave a mandate to a small Working Group to find a compromise. It produced the text (*WP 42*) that was subsequently adopted by the plenary. According to the compromise reached, the salvage law and the law of finds are banned unless three cumulative conditions are met: the activity subject to these laws is authorised by the competent authorities, it is carried out in full conformity with the Convention and the maximum protection of the object recovered is ensured. It must be stressed that this provision is to be read together with other provisions of the Convention which clearly state that the commercial exploitation of the underwater cultural heritage is forbidden.[67]

Not every delegation totally agreed with the new language of the final Article 4. Spain, for example, pointed out some interpretative problems of the provision, such as the identification of "competent authorities". Argentina still considered salvage as incompatible with a protective regime for underwater cultural heritage. Portugal too was contrary. But in a spirit of compromise and conscious that, according the solution found, salvors are no longer totally free to do what they want, the plenary approved the proposal.

Before the final approval of Article 4 a sort of incident happened. The Chairman read to the plenary a letter received by IMO where it was stated that a proposal aiming at excluding salvage law in the UNESCO Convention "would have the effect of overlapping, and potentially clashing, with the scope of application of an IMO Convention, namely, the International Convention on Salvage, 1989. [...][T]he explicit exclusion of salvage law [...] would override the optional right contained in the Salvage

---

66 That proved to be the case with the *Titanic* (located in international waters) and the *Lusitania* (located approximately 12 miles from the Ireland coasts). On this point, see O'Keefe, *supra* note 25, at 62.

67 Para. 8 of the preamble; Art. 2, para. 7; Rule 2.

Convention".[68] Some tension followed this reading, as some delegations, in particular Italy, strongly reacted to such an unexpected last-minute change in the position already taken by IMO. Indeed the IMO position was quite difficult to explain. IMO had been invited by UNESCO to attend the Meetings as an observer and the invitation had been accepted at the beginning of negotiations, but no such a position had ever been expressed before by IMO, when debating the ILA draft that already excluded the application of salvage law.[69] As a consequence, the delegates decided not to take into account the IMO position as expressed in the letter to the Chairman.

Article 5 – Activities Incidentally Affecting Underwater Cultural Heritage

Each State Party shall use the best practicable means at its disposal to prevent or mitigate any adverse effects that might arise from activities under its jurisdiction incidentally affecting underwater cultural heritage.

[Preparatory documents:
a) Working Papers and comments by States:
- WG1 WP37, 6 July 2000 (proposal for the wording of Article X, proposed by the Netherlands)
- WG1 WP38, 6 July 2000 (proposal by the Belgian Delegation)
- Comments by the United States on SNT (unofficial)

b) Drafts:
- second UNESCO draft (Art. X)
- SNT (Art. 6)]

The issue of "activities incidentally affecting underwater cultural heritage" has already been dealt with when commenting the Preamble and definitions.

It was only in the 1999 draft that a new Article (Art. X) aimed at regulating such activities was introduced in square brackets. It read as follows:

1. Each State Party shall take reasonable measures to ensure that activities are avoided that adversely affect known underwater cultural heritage in its internal waters, archipelagic waters, territorial sea, exclusive economic zone or on its continental shelf.
2. Where a State Party designates as requiring special protection underwater

---

[68] The optional right referred to is that provided for in Art. 30, para. 1d) (see *supra*), that is to say the reservation aimed at excluding the application of salvage law to historic wrecks. IUCN informed that as of 5 April 2001, 15 States Parties out of 32 have expressed such a reservation.

[69] "The IMO observer explained that the Salvage Convention is a private law Convention and its objectives are very different from those of this draft, which deals with international public law. The Salvage Convention should not, therefore, apply to historic wrecks. [...] The majority of States also declared that any State, whether or not it made a reservation, would be entitled not to apply the Salvage Convention to historic wrecks" (*Final Report of the First Meeting of Governmental Experts on the Draft Convention on the Underwater Cultural Heritage*, Paris, 29 June-2 July 1998, UNESCO doc. CLT-98/CONF.202/7, para. 51).

cultural heritage in its internal waters, archipelagic waters, territorial sea, exclusive economic zone or on its continental shelf, it shall take all necessary measures to ensure that activities do not adversely affect such underwater cultural heritage.

3. Where UNESCO designates as requiring special protection underwater cultural heritage in the Area, each State Party shall take all necessary measures to ensure that vessels flying its flag do not undertake activities that adversely affect such underwater cultural heritage.

As it can be noted this provision made a distinction on the basis of the location of the underwater cultural heritage and introduced a quite obscure concept of "special protection".

During the third Meeting of Experts, the Netherlands and Belgium proposed two amendments to simplify the provision. In the proposal by the Netherlands only activities exercised in areas under the jurisdiction of the States Parties were considered and a duty for States Parties to assess the impact of such activities and take the necessary measures to mitigate the effects was envisaged. The Belgian Proposal was similar and introduced an idea of proportionality between measures to be taken and the degree of seriousness of possible adverse effects.

The SNT reduced Article X (renumbered Art. 6) to two paragraphs:

1. Each State Party shall use the best practical means at its disposal to prevent any adverse effects that may arise from activities incidentally affecting underwater cultural heritage in its inland waters, internal waters, archipelagic waters, territorial sea, exclusive economic zone or on its continental shelf.
2. Where a State Party designates as requiring special protection underwater cultural heritage in its internal waters, archipelagic waters and territorial sea, or on its continental shelf, it shall take all necessary measures to ensure that activities do not adversely affect such underwater cultural heritage.

Commenting this Article in an unofficial document, the United States complained of the potential of such a provision to be a "back-door expansion of coastal State to infringe on UNCLOS freedom of third Parties [...]. To the extent that it is confined to existing LOS competencies, it isn't necessary".

During the debate it was unanimously decided to delete para. 2. As far as para.1 is concerned, Greece remarked that the contiguous zone had been forgotten and Sweden suggested deleting "inland waters". A practical proposal by the United Kingdom – to replace the list of maritime areas by the expression "activities under its jurisdiction" – was generally accepted.

Article 6 – Bilateral, Regional and Other Multilateral Agreements

1. States Parties are encouraged to enter into bilateral, regional and other multilateral agreements or develop existing agreements, for the preservation of underwater cultural heritage. All such agreements shall be in full conformity with the provisions of this Convention and shall not dilute its universal

character. States may, in such agreements, adopt rules and regulations which would ensure better protection of underwater cultural heritage than those adopted in this Convention.

2. The Parties to such bilateral, regional or other multilateral agreements may invite States with a verifiable link, especially a cultural, historical or archaeological link, to the heritage concerned to join such agreements.
3. This Convention shall not alter the rights and obligations of States Parties regarding the protection of sunken vessels, arising from other bilateral, regional or multilateral agreements concluded before its adoption, and, in particular, those that are in conformity with the purposes of this Convention.

[Preparatory documents:

a) Working papers and comments by States:
   - Commentaire de la délégation française sur le projet de Convention sur la protection du patrimoine culturel subaquatique (UNESCO doc. CLT-96/CONF.202/5Rev2), 7 mars 2000
   - Remarks presented by the Government of Italy, April 2000
   - Comments of the United States of America on Selected Articles being considered in Working Group One, Paris, 4 July 2000
   - WG1 WP20, 5 July 2000 (Amendment to Article 2ter proposed by Argentina)
   - WG1 WP21, 5 July 2000 (Amendment to Article 2ter proposed by Republic of Korea)
   - WG1 WP24, 5 July 2000 (Amendment to Article 2ter proposed by Japan)
   - WG1 WP25, 5 July 2000 (Amendment to Article 2ter proposed by India)
   - WG1 WP31, 6 July 2000 (Amendment to Article 2 proposed by Egypt)
   - WG1 WP32, 6 July 2000 (Amendment to Article 2 proposed by Venezuela)
   - WP 26, 29 March 2001 (proposal by Italy and Tunisia)
   - WP 53, 3 July 2001 (proposal by Finland and Sweden)
b) Drafts:
   - second UNESCO draft (Art. 3 ter)
   - SNT (Art. 7)
c) Other documents:
   - Final Report of the Second Meeting of Governmental Experts on the Draft Convention on the Protection of Underwater Cultural Heritage, Paris, 19-24 April 1999 (UNESCO doc. CLT-99/CONF.204, Paris, August 1999), para. 35
   - Summary of Observations by States on the Draft Convention on the Protection of Underwater Cultural Heritage, Paris, April 2000 (UNESCO doc. CLT-2000/CONF.201/3 and UNESCO doc. CLT-2000/CONF.201/3 Add. 2)]

The 2001 UNESCO Convention is the first universal legal instrument on the protection of underwater cultural heritage. Its possible coming into force does not prevent States Parties from signing other agreements on this topic nor will it have any effect on agreements already in force.[70] The only condition to the drafting of further agreements is that they do not dilute the regime of protection established by the UNESCO Convention. Article 6 deals with this matter. It is only apparently an "easy" provision: negotiations on Art. 6 proved to be quite lively.

In the second UNESCO draft a new Art. 2 *ter* was devoted for the first time to regional agreements:

> States may enter into regional or bilateral agreements, or develop existing agreements for the preservation of common underwater cultural heritage. For this purpose, they may adopt rules and regulations which may be more stringent than those adopted at global level. [These agreements will be open to States of cultural origin and States of historical and archaeological origin.]

Several States put forward comments on this provision. The United States, France, Japan, Sweden and the United Kingdom would have liked a supplementary sentence ensuring consistency between regional agreements and UNCLOS. Italy was in favour of a solution in line with the 1995 Straddling Fish Stocks Agreement: all States having a real interest in the heritage concerned may become party to the regional agreement, but only those States which are party to the regional agreement shall have the right to engage in activities relating to the heritage. Tunisia felt it was unnecessary for regional agreements to be mentioned in the Convention because their conclusion is not mandatory.

During the third Meeting of Experts Working Group 1 considered also the question of regional agreements. A problem arose in particular: did States outside the region but having a cultural, historical or archaeological link with the heritage in question have to be invited to participate in a regional agreement or did the regional agreement have to

---

[70] A small number of bilateral agreements on specific wrecks already exist: *Agreement between The Netherlands and Australia Concerning Old Dutch Shipwrecks*, The Hague, 6 November 1972 (Australian Treaty Series, 1972, No. 18); *Exchange of Notes between South Africa and the United Kingdom Concerning the Regulation of the Terms of Settlement of the Salvaging of the Wreck of HMS Birkenhead*, Pretoria, 22 September 1989 (in United Kingdom Treaty Series, 1990, No. 3; South Africa Government Gazette No. 12117 of 6 October 1989, notice No. 2150; reprinted in (1990) *IJECL* 405); *Agreement Between the Government of the United States of America and the Government of the French republic Concerning the Wreck of the CSS Alabama*, Paris, 3 October 1989 (in *Journal Officiel de la République Française* du 23 décembre 1989, p. 15.996; reprinted in (1989) *RGDIP* 975 and in U.N., *Law of the Sea Bulletin*, 1992, p. 26); *Memorandum of Understanding between the Government of Great Britain and Canada pertaining to the Shipwrecks HMS Erebus and HMS Terror*, 5 and 8 August 1997; *Agreement between the Government of the United States of America and the Government of the French Republic regarding the wreck of La Belle*, Washington, 31 March 2003 (not yet published). To these agreements related to specific wrecks, another agreement must be added; it is a general agreement of maritime delimitation but including specific provisions on wrecks lying on the continental shelf: *Treaty concerning Sovereignty and Maritime Boundaries in the Area between the two Countries, including the Area known as Torres Straits, and Related Matters*, Sidney, 18 December 1978 (reprinted in (1979) *ILM* 291). Finally the *Agreement between the Republic of Finland, the Republic of Estonia and the Kingdom of Sweden Regarding the M/S Estonia*, Tallinn, 23 February 1995, with additional protocol of 26 April 1996 (in *Suomen Säädökokoelman Sopimussarija*, 1995, No. 49; reprinted in (2000) *Nordic Journal of International Law* 330) can be mentioned: at the moment the *Estonia* does not fall within the definition of "underwater cultural heritage", since it sunk in 1994, but with the passing of time it will be the case.

be open to any interested State? Several proposals were put forward. Those of the Republic of Korea (*WG1 WP21*), Japan (*WG1 WP24*), and Egypt (*WG1 WP31*) were in favour of the second hypothesis, while Argentina preferred the first one.

The SNT modified the text of the Article (renumbered 6) as follows:

1. States Parties may enter into regional, partial or bilateral agreements, for the preservation of underwater cultural heritage. All such agreements shall be compatible with the provisions of this Convention and shall not dilute the universal character of the Convention. States may, in such agreements, adopt rules and regulations which would ensure better protection of underwater cultural heritage than those adopted at global level.
2. The Parties to such bilateral, partial or regional agreements may invite States with a verifiable link to the heritage concerned to join such agreement.

As far as the first paragraph is concerned, the Chairman – supported by Iran – suggested deleting the first sentence. Italy expressed a different opinion, arguing that it was fundamental in order not to give immediately the idea that regional agreements are to be feared: they are rather to be encouraged. The United Kingdom would have liked to add the requisite of consistency of regional agreements with international law, but Italy pointed out that this goes without saying, as it is not to be presumed that States conclude a regional agreement just to violate international law. As a conclusion, "may enter" was changed to "are encouraged to enter" and "compatible [. . .] with this Convention" was modified to "in full conformity with".

As it can be noted, in para. 1 of the provision of the SNT "partial agreements" are considered. In the draft Convention they were defined in Art. 1 as agreements between some States Parties which are not from the same geographical region. Spain, Argentina and Greece strongly reacted arguing that this would have been a totally new category of agreement, unknown in international law. So the expression was eventually deleted.

More difficult was the compromise on the second paragraph. While the Netherlands suggested that States with verifiable link "had" to be invited, Italy and Tunisia proposed that regional agreements could "be open" to other States, without the need of any invitation. To summarise, some "coastal" States (such as Argentina) wanted the States of a geographical area to be free to invite who they preferred to participate in the regional agreement and therefore they pointed out that in international law sovereign States cannot be obliged to enter into an agreement with other States. Traditional "maritime" powers (such as Spain and France) instead thought that, having an historical link with shipwrecks in regional seas far from their coasts, they had the right to participate in agreements concerning those waters. In the end, because no alternative version to para. 2 of the SNT was agreed upon, it was accepted as it stood and therefore it will be up to the coastal States of a regional sea to decide whether to invite any State (and which) to join the agreement. Anyway a duty of co-operation in good faith – included in the Convention[71] – should encourage coastal States to invite States with a verifiable link.

---

[71] Art. 2, para. 2.

The third paragraph is the result of a proposal by Finland and Sweden (*WP 53*). It concerns agreements already in force,[72] which will not be affected by the new global Convention. The last sentence ("in particular those that are in conformity with the purposes of this Convention") does not seem a very good provision in international law. According to Argentina, this proposal could be a violation of the principle of non-retroactivity.

Article 7 – Underwater Cultural Heritage in Internal Waters, Archipelagic Waters and Territorial Sea

1. States Parties, in the exercise of their sovereignty, have the exclusive right to regulate and authorise activities directed at underwater cultural heritage in their internal waters, archipelagic waters and territorial sea.
2. Without prejudice to other international agreements and rules of international law regarding the protection of underwater cultural heritage, States Parties shall require that the Rules be applied to activities directed at underwater cultural heritage in their internal waters, archipelagic waters and territorial sea.
3. Within their archipelagic waters and territorial sea, in the exercise of their sovereignty and in recognition of general practice among States, States Parties, with a view to cooperating on the best methods of protecting State vessels and aircraft, should inform the flag State Party to this Convention and, if applicable, other States with a verifiable link, especially a cultural, historical or archaeological link, with respect to the discovery of such identifiable State vessels and aircraft.

[Preparatory documents:

a) Working Papers and comments by States:
   - Comments of the United States of America on UNESCO Draft Convention on the Protection of the Underwater Cultural Heritage (April 1999)
   - Comments of the United States of America on Selected Articles being considered in Working Group One, Paris, 4 July 2000
   - Comments by the United States on SNT (unofficial)
   - WP 19, 29 March 2001 (Chairman's proposal)
   - WP 34, 2 April 2001 (Amendments proposed by Finland, Germany, Japan, the Netherlands, Norway, the Russian Federation, Spain, Sweden, the United Kingdom and endorsed by the United States)
   - WP 39, 3 April 2001 (Proposal by Finland)
   - Non-paper by Spain, 12 June 2001
   - Unofficial proposal of the United Kingdom, 16 June 2001
   - Non-paper by Spain, 22 June 2001

[72] The proposing States had the case of the *Estonia* in mind (see *supra*, note 70), even if it does not fall into the definition of underwater cultural heritage enshrined by the Convention.

- Non-paper by the United States, 1 July 2001
- Non-paper 3, 3 July 2001(State vessels and aircraft, Single Article proposed by UK)
- WP 41, 4 July 2001 (Amendment to Article 2 redrafted by the Secretariat following discussion on plenary)
- WP 57, 5 July 2001 (Report of the informal sub-group of the warships Working Group)
- WP 58, 5 July 2001 (proposal by the Group of 77)

b) Drafts:
- ILA draft (Art. 6)
- first UNESCO/DOALOS draft (Art. 4)
- second UNESCO draft (Art. 4)
- SNT (Art. 8)

c) Other documents:
- Final Report of the First Meeting of Governmental Experts on the Draft Convention on the Protection of Underwater Cultural Heritage, Paris, 29 June–2 July 1998 (UNESCO doc. CLT-98/CONF.202/7), para. 18
- Final Report of the Second Meeting of Governmental Experts on the Draft Convention on the Protection of Underwater Cultural Heritage , Paris, 19-24 April 1999 (UNESCO doc. CLT-99/CONF.204, Paris, August 1999), para. 28-29
- Summary of Observations by States on the Draft Convention on the Protection of Underwater Cultural Heritage, Paris, April 2000 (UNESCO doc. CLT-2000/CONF.201/3 , UNESCO doc. CLT-2000/CONF.201/3 Add. and UNESCO doc. CLT-2000/CONF.201/3 Add. 2)
- Draft Resolution submitted by the Russian Federation and the United Kingdom (and endorsed by the United States), General Conference, 26 October 2001 (UNESCO doc. 31 C/COM.IV/DIR.5)
- Draft Resolution submitted by France, General Conference, 26 October 2001 (UNESCO doc. 31 C/COM.IV/DIR.4)]

The first two paragraphs of this Art. 7 were not very contentious, as they reflect accepted principles of international law, such as the sovereignty of a State in its internal water, archipelagic waters and territorial sea.

The ILA draft already contained a provision (Art. 6) requiring the application by the coastal State of the ICOMOS Charter in its internal and territorial waters. The first UNESCO/DOALOS draft also included a similar provision (Art. 4), enlarging it to archipelagic waters and stressing the idea that States Parties have an exclusive right to regulate activities directed at underwater cultural heritage in such zones. In the comment to this provision the UNESCO made clear that regulating activities in areas under the sovereignty of States Parties was not the primary goal of the Convention, but that it was useful in order to apply common archaeological standards in all States Parties, as usually States have very different national rules. In the second UNESCO draft two alternatives were left in square brackets: the application of the Rules of the Annex in these areas could be either recommended or mandatory. At the second Meeting of Experts the United States expressed itself in favour of the first solution, in order not to have to modify its internal laws,[73] but it was remarked by other delegates that it would be inconsistent on the part of the same coastal State to advocate the application of the Rule in its exclusive economic zone or continental shelf while rejecting a clear commitment in the maritime areas in which its jurisdiction was not disputed.

The SNT did not bring major changes to the draft. When debating the SNT at the last Meeting of Experts, it was decided to delete reference to inland waters (that is non-marine waters), because a specific Article would be reserved to this topic in the final provisions of the Convention. Any reference to the potential application of the "significance" criterion[74] to the heritage located in internal, archipelagic and territorial waters was also rejected by the majority of delegates. Finally, a mandatory application ("*shall* apply") of the Rules of the Annex was preferred also in these maritime areas.

Much more troublesome was the adoption of para. 3. As it has already been said, at the end of the negotiations it was decided not to have a single article dealing with State and military vessels but to split this topic among the articles concerned. Para. 3 of Art. 7 therefore deals with sunken State vessels located in internal waters, archipelagic waters and territorial sea. The problem was to delineate what are the respective rights and obligations of both the coastal and flag State.

The SNT[75] regulated this issue as follows: on one hand, the coastal States could not recover sunken State vessels unless they had been expressly abandoned by the flag State and without the collaboration of the flag State; on the other hand, the flag State could not recover its vessels without the collaboration of the coastal State.

The SNT was soon forgotten and replaced by a plethora of proposals where the differences in language reflected very different approaches. The Group of 77 (*WP 58*) was strongly against any special regime for warships. It was ready to accept only a disclaimer clause on sovereign status of warship and State vessels and a general principle on respect of human remains. Apart from this position, all the other proposals suggested some sort of obligation upon the State in whose water a foreign State vessel lies. In an amendment sponsored by several delegations (*WP 34*) it was suggested that the coastal State and the flag State "shall consult and coordinate" on the best method of preserving the shipwreck: but it was rejected by almost all the G-77. Spain, with two unofficial proposals, took the position for a prohibition of action by the coastal State without the collaboration of the flag State (unless the vessel is abandoned) (*non-paper of 12 June 2001*), then for a need of consultation of the flag State (the coastal State "will consult") (*non-paper of 22 June 2001*). The United

[73] The United States informed that in their country there are more than a dozen federal laws and more than 56 state and federal territorial laws that already provide government agencies with authorities to manage and protect underwater cultural heritage in inland waters, internal waters, archipelagic waters and territorial sea. A mandatory application of the Rules in these areas would have precluded its ratification of the Convention.

[74] See *supra*.

[75] Here there was still a single article dealing with military vessels (Art. 2).

Kingdom, too, put forward two alternative suggestions: the coastal State "undertake to consult and coordinate with the flag State" (*non-paper of 16 June 2001*); the coastal State "shall inform the flag State [...] with a view to co-operating" (*non-paper 3, 3 July 2001*). For the United States the coastal State "shall endeavour to consult and coordinate with the flag State" (*non-paper of 1 July 2001*).

The debate grew more and more lively. Argentina and most G-77 countries rejected any idea of duty upon the coastal State with respect to third States in its territorial sea, as it is sovereign. Therefore no verbal expressions like "will" or "shall" were considered acceptable; Egypt declared that only such expressions as "are encouraged" or "may"[76] could be approved. Canada, pointing out that coastal States are already obliged to apply the Rules in their sovereign areas,[77] suggested the verb "should". But the problem was not only the auxiliary verb: what should the coastal State do? Merely inform the flag State or – and that would entail a much larger duty – consult it? (*WP 57*) The non-abundant practice of States developed up to date[78] was reminded to support both the first and the second argument. Some States called for a spirit of co-operation which should inspire the entire Convention. Italy suggested simply using the verb "inform" without any auxiliary before it. Egypt, Germany, Portugal and at the end also Spain and Argentina accepted it with a view to reach the *consensus*. But English-speaking countries – Canada, the United Kingdom, the United States – strongly disagreed because, as they pointed out, it would not correspond to good legal English style. It would become a descriptive sentence without any legal sense and therefore not suitable for an international convention. At this point the Chairman suggested the formula "should inform", that was even less burdensome for coastal States. France, the United Kingdom and Spain declared themselves ready to accept, even if only for the sake of *consensus*. It was 11 p.m. of July 7 and negotiations had to be closed in a short time: the parties were unable to find a better and generally acceptable alternative. As a consequence, the solution codified in the Convention leaves to the coastal State even more powers than those it actually enjoys by practice: it is not even obliged to inform the flag State that it will recover a sunken foreign military vessel in its territorial waters.[79]

At the General Conference in October 2001 the United Kingdom and the Russian Federation (besides the United States), on one hand, and France, on the other, proposed two amendments.[80] Also Art. 7, para. 3 was involved, in that all the proposing States asked to replace the words "should inform" with "shall consult". The United Kingdom and the Russian Federation also suggested adding a reference to the internal waters and a final sentence: "Such State vessels and aircraft shall not

[76] The United Kingdom pointed out that "may" was completely useless: it is evident that in its territorial sea a sovereign State can do what it wants.

[77] France also remarked that the sovereignty of the coastal State in its territorial sea is already limited by UNCLOS: it is the case of innocent passage (Art. 17).

[78] *Alabama, Birkenhead, Erebus and Terror, La Belle.*

[79] Up to date, in all the cases mentioned above there has been a specific agreement between the coastal State and the flag State: much more than simple information or consultation.

[80] France subsequently withdrew its amendment.

be recovered without the collaboration of the flag State, unless the vessels and aircraft have been expressly abandoned in accordance with the laws of that State". The amendment was rejected by a majority vote.[81]

Article 8 – Underwater Cultural Heritage in the Contiguous Zone

> Without prejudice to and in addition to Articles 9 and 10, and in accordance with Article 303 paragraph 2 of the United Nations Convention on the Law of the Sea, States Parties may regulate and authorise activities directed at underwater cultural heritage within their contiguous zone. In so doing, they shall require that the Rules be applied.

[Preparatory documents:

a) Comments by States:
   - Turkey's views on Article 5 of the Draft Convention on the Protection of the Underwater Cultural Heritage (without date)

b) Drafts:
   - second UNESCO draft (Art. 4 bis)
   - SNT (Art. 9)

c) Other documents:
   - Final Report of the First Meeting of Governmental Experts on the Draft Convention on the Protection of Underwater Cultural Heritage, Paris, 29 June-2 July 1998 (UNESCO doc. CLT-98/CONF.202/7), para. 18
   - Final Report of the Second Meeting of Governmental Experts on the Draft Convention on the Protection of Underwater Cultural Heritage, Paris, 19-24 April 1999 (UNESCO doc. CLT-99/CONF.204, Paris, August 1999), para. 30
   - Summary of Observations by States on the Draft Convention on the Protection of Underwater Cultural Heritage, Paris, April 2000 (UNESCO doc. CLT-2000/CONF.201/3)

An Article devoted to the contiguous zone did not appear in the UNESCO draft until 1999. In the first Meeting of Experts a delegate remarked this loophole in the draft and suggested inserting the contiguous zone within Art. 4 on territorial sea. The issue was again debated at the second Meeting and it was decided to draft a new article on the contiguous zone, which reads as follows:

> States Parties may [in applying Article 303(2) of the United Nations Convention on the Law of the Sea] regulate and authorize [in accordance with Article 303(2) of the United Nations Convention on the Law of the Sea]

[81] See the declaration forwarded to the General Conference by a representative of the Group of 77: "Rouvrir la discussion pour continuer à rechercher un *consensus* qui n'a pu être obtenu en dépit de tous les efforts consentis signifierait renoncer à ce rapprochement et mettre en péril l'équilibre mentionné [...] [I]l existe par ailleurs de nombreux précédents à l'UNESCO de Conventions qui ont été adoptées à la majorité simple. [...] Le Groupe des 77 n'acceptera pas d'amendements au Projet de convention approuvé à la dernière réunion de juillet et est disposé à le voter tel qu'il figure dans le documents 31C/24".

> [activities directed at] underwater cultural heritage within their contiguous zone. In doing so, States Parties [shall] [should] require compliance, at a minimum, with the Rules of the Annex.

This provision gave rise to a strong reaction on the part of Turkey. In a comment of the draft, Turkey wrote:

> Contiguous zone might cause serious problems in areas where the coasts are opposite to each other and no delimitation by an agreement of the maritime areas exists between the concerned coastal States, i.e. a claim to a contiguous zone for the purpose of underwater archaeological objects in an area outside the territorial sea but over the continental shelf of another State where that coastal State has *ipso facto* and *ab initio* rights on the continental shelf. This sort of case would inevitably lead to a conflict between the competencies of the two coastal States especially in narrow and enclosed or semi-enclosed seas. For, in this case, an object within the contiguous zone of one State would at the same time be located on the continental shelf of another State. [...] during the negotiations of Article 303 at the UNCLOS [...] underwater archaeological objects were artificially linked to the contiguous zone. [...] Turkey wants to underline that to declare a contiguous zone for the purpose of controlling the traffic of underwater cultural heritage that lies on or under its continental shelf, not only falls contrary to State practice and to customary rules of international law in this field, but also means to reduce the area of jurisdiction and to confine the coastal State powers. [...] It would also mean and lead to a complete change of the traditional character and also the jurisdiction related to this concept.

The reference is clearly to dispute with Greece over maritime boundaries in the area where Greek islands face the Turkish coasts.

Apart from the particular position of Turkey,[82] the square brackets showed which were the main problems regarding this article: the relationship with the similar provision in UNCLOS (Art. 303, para.2) and the choice between making the Rules of the Annex mandatory or only recommended in this maritime area.

The SNT avoided any reference to UNCLOS, while obliging States Parties to apply the Annex "taking into account the cultural significance of the heritage". Most of delegations (Japan, the Netherlands, Peru, Greece, Spain and others) asked for the reintroduction of a reference to UNCLOS. Italy pointed out the ambiguity of Art. 303, para. 2, which deals only with the removal and not with the possible destruction of an ancient artefact, and therefore asked to borrow from UNCLOS not only the specific content of this paragraph but also the spirit of the entire Article, that is to say the need for the protection of the underwater cultural heritage. Tunisia

[82] Also the positions of Canada and Australia can be mentioned: they proposed to include the contiguous zone in the article dealing with the exclusive economic zone and the continental shelf because the contiguous zone is indeed part of these other areas. But France was strongly in favour of an article specifically dealing with the contiguous zone and at the end it was retained.

was contrary to any reference to UNCLOS because its provisions on the contiguous zone would be already overcome by modern domestic legislations. In the end the reference was retained.

In the final version of the Convention, a sentence was added at the beginning of the provision, making reference to Articles dealing with the exclusive economic zone and the continental shelf. Greece, in its statement on the vote during Commission IV on Culture (29 October 2001, 31st Session of the General Conference) declared that the drafting of Article 8 was one of the reasons which had lead Greece to abstain:

> Greece fails to understand the appearance in article 8 ("underwater cultural heritage in the contiguous zone") of the reference to articles 9 and 10 concerning protection of UCH on the continental shelf and in the exclusive economic zone (EEZ). [...] the introduction of the aforementioned system of consultations in the protective scheme adopted for the contiguous zone is unfortunate. The reference in article 8 to articles 9 and 10 should be deleted as it diminishes the rights, which the coastal State already enjoys in this area under article 303(2) of the LOS Convention.

Article 9 – Reporting and Notification in the Exclusive Economic Zone and on the Continental Shelf

1. All States Parties have a responsibility to protect underwater cultural heritage in the exclusive economic zone and on the continental shelf in conformity with this Convention.
   Accordingly:
   (a) a State Party shall require that when its national, or a vessel flying its flag, discovers or intends to engage in activities directed at underwater cultural heritage located in its exclusive economic zone or on its continental shelf, the national or the master of the vessel shall report such discovery or activity to it;
   (b) in the exclusive economic zone or on the continental shelf of another State Party:
      (i) States Parties shall require the national or the master of the vessel to report such discovery or activity to them and to that other State Party;
      (ii) alternatively, a State Party shall require the national or master of the vessel to report such discovery or activity to it and shall ensure the rapid and effective transmission of such reports to all other States Parties.
2. On depositing its instrument of ratification, acceptance, approval or accession, a State Party shall declare the manner in which reports will be transmitted under paragraph 1 (b) of this Article.
3. A State Party shall notify the Director-General of discoveries or activities reported to it under paragraph 1 of this Article.
4. The Director-General shall promptly make available to all States Parties any information notified to him under paragraph 3 of this Article.

5. Any State Party may declare to the State Party in whose exclusive economic zone or on whose continental shelf the underwater cultural heritage is located its interest in being consulted on how to ensure the effective protection of that underwater cultural heritage. Such declaration shall be based on a verifiable link, especially a cultural, historical or archaeological link, with the underwater cultural heritage.

[Preparatory documents:

a) Working papers and comments by States:
   - Position de la Chine relative au Projet de Convention sur la Protection du Patrimoine Culturel Subaquatique (without date)
   - Turkey's views on Article 5 of the Draft Convention on the Protection of the Underwater Cultural Heritage (without date)
   - Proposal submitted by the delegation of the Russian Federation, 1998
   - Comments of the United States of America on UNESCO Draft Convention on the Protection of the Underwater Cultural Heritage (April 1999)
   - Remarks presented by the Government of Italy, April 2000
   - Comments of the United States of America on Selected Articles being considered in Working Group One, 4 July 2000
   - Non-paper by the delegation of Poland, July 2000
   - Anonymous non-paper (without date)
   - WG1 WP14, 5 July 2000 (Japanese comments on the proposal by the United Kingdom – Article XX (CLT-2000/CONF.201/3 Synoptic Report, Annex, p. 22)
   - WG1 WP15, 5 July 2000 (Amendments proposed by Malta)
   - WG1 NP1, 5 July 2000 (Non-paper proposed by three delegations as possible basis for consensus)
   - WG1 NP3, 6 July 2000 (tentative proposal of Chairman of Working Group 1)
   - WG1 WP17, 4 July 2000 (proposal by Hungary)
   - WG1 WP19, 5 July 2000 (Proposal by the USA on Article 5)
   - WP 2, 27 March 2001 (Amendments proposed by Norway)
   - WP 8, 28 March 2001 (Proposal by Italy, seconded by Tunisia)
   - WP 14, 29 March 2001 (Proposal by Australia, Argentina, Canada)
   - WP 15, 29 March 2001 (Proposal sponsored by Germany, Norway and the United Kingdom, text elaborated by the United States)
   - WP 16, 29 March 2001 (Proposed amendment by Greece and Ireland)
   - WP 24, 29 March 2001(Proposed Amendment by Japan and seconded by Peru)
   - WP 40, 4 April 2001 (Amendment proposed by 10 States: Argentina, Australia, Brazil, Canada, Colombia, Egypt, Ireland, Mexico, Poland, South-Africa, Tunisia, Uruguay)
   - Chairman's draft ("May paper"), 28 May 2001; Chairman's draft ("May paper") Cor.3, 29 June 2001; WP 54, 4 July 2001 (Chairman's draft – Third re-draft of "May paper"); WP 54 rev3, 6 July 2001

- Non-paper by the United States, 1 July 2001
- Non-paper 6, 3 July 2001(Non-paper presented by the United Kingdom – Third redraft of "May Paper"); Non-paper 6 rev., 3 July 2001; Non-paper 6 rev.2, 4 July 2001
- WP 51, 3 July 2001 (Working Paper by Norway and the Russian Federation and endorsed by the United States)
- Unofficial Norway proposal, 4 July 2001
- Non-paper 8, 6 July 2001; Non-paper 8 rev, 6 July 2001

b) Drafts:
- ILA draft (Art. 5)
- first UNESCO/DOALOS draft (Art. 5)
- second UNESCO draft (Art. 5 Option 1; Art. 5 Option 2; Art. 5 Option 3)
- SNT

c) Other documents:
- Feasibility Study for the Drafting of a New Instrument for the Protection of the Underwater Cultural Heritage, Paris, 23 March 1995 (UNESCO doc. 146 EX/27), paras. 22-28
- Preliminary Study on the Advisability of Preparing an International Instrument for the Protection of the Underwater Cultural Heritage, Paris, 4 October 1995 (UNESCO doc. 29C/39), paras. 23-29
- Report of the Meeting of Experts for the Draft Convention on the Protection of Underwater Cultural Heritage, Paris, 22–24 May 1996 (UNESCO doc. CLT-96/CONF.605/6), paras. 27-39
- Report by the Director-General on the Finding of the Meeting of Experts concerning the Preparation of an International Instrument for the Protection of the Underwater Cultural Heritage, Paris, 14 May 1997 (UNESCO doc. 151 EX/10 Add.)
- Final Report of the First Meeting of Governmental Experts on the Draft Convention on the Protection of Underwater Cultural Heritage, Paris, 29 June–2 July 1998 (UNESCO doc. CLT-98/CONF.202/7), para. X
- Final Report of the Second Meeting of Governmental Experts on the Draft Convention on the Protection of Underwater Cultural Heritage, Paris, 19-24 April 1999 (UNESCO doc. CLT-99/CONF.204, Paris, August 1999), para. 31-34
- Summary of Observations by States on the Draft Convention on the Protection of Underwater Cultural Heritage, Paris, April 2000 (UNESCO doc. CLT-2000/CONF.201/3; UNESCO doc. CLT-2000/CONF.201/3Add.; UNESCO doc. CLT-2000/CONF.201/3Add. 2)
- Draft Resolution submitted by the Russian Federation and the United Kingdom (and endorsed by the United States), General Conference, 26 October 2001 (UNESCO doc. 31 C/COM.IV/DIR.5)
- Draft Resolution submitted by France, General Conference, 26 October 2001 (UNESCO doc. 31 C/COM.IV/DIR.4)]

It suffices to consider the huge amount of preparatory work to realize how complex the question of jurisdiction was.[83] Articles 9 and 10 represent the key provisions of the Convention, whose main goal was indeed to create a regime of protection for underwater cultural heritage located in the exclusive economic zone and on the continental shelf of States. This proved to be an incredibly difficult task for various reasons: the ghost of creeping jurisdiction, the fear of violating the untouchable "constitution of the oceans" (*i.e.* UNCLOS), the potential for a limitation of the freedom of the high seas (in particular the freedom of navigation), among others. Endless negotiations, innumerable informal working groups (at any hour, even on Sunday), linguistic hypocrisy,[84] charges of "cultural nationalism"[85] were some of the ingredients which led to the result codified in the Convention.

The origin of Articles 9 and 10 was a very easy provision in the ILA draft: States Parties were allowed to create a "cultural heritage zone", co-extensive with their continental shelf (Art. 1 and 5). In the feasibility study for a new convention, UNESCO took into account the suggestion made by ILA, also considering that some States already exercise their jurisdiction over underwater cultural heritage located on their continental shelf (Australia, China, Ireland, Morocco, Spain, Jamaica, Cape Verde, Iran, Malaysia, Portugal and Bangladesh). At the same time, UNESCO felt that not all States were ready to accept a new marine zone where the jurisdiction of the coastal State could be exercised. This proved to be true during the 1996 Meeting of Experts: the use of a completely new concept, not codified by UNCLOS – some experts felt – could jeopardise the success of the future Convention. Alternative forms of control over underwater cultural heritage on the continental shelf were mentioned: national jurisdiction over nationals (individuals, ships and aircraft) and port State jurisdiction. Commenting the results of this Meeting of Experts, Germany, Greece, Italy, the Netherlands, the Republic of Korea, the United Kingdom and Tunisia refused the establishment of a new marine zone, even though most of them recognised the need to improve the existing regime. Only Spain supported the idea, but limited it to 100 n.m. from the coast.

Taking into account these comments, the first UNESCO/DOALOS draft did not reflect the ILA draft on this point. Its Art. 5 was built on the following principles: obligation of notification to the coastal State of any discovery of underwater cultural

---

[83] Due to such abundance of preparatory works, it will be impossible here to give account of every proposal, as well as to describe in detail all the negotiations regarding the question of jurisdiction. A summary will be provided, trying to give emphasis to the most interesting and significant proposals.

[84] Nowhere in these key provisions of the Convention can the expression "coastal State" be found. The much more complicated expression "State in whose exclusive economic zone or on whose continental shelf the underwater cultural heritage is located" was preferred: a mere aesthetic device in order to avoid the use of a word which could evoke the ghost of creeping jurisdiction. Unfortunately, the result is a more complex reading of an already complex legal text.

[85] When discussing whether the coastal State should be given a special role in protecting the underwater cultural heritage on its continental shelf, Norway angrily remarked that like-minded countries meant to recognise to all States the same duties but not the same rights and this amounted to a sort of "cultural nationalism" (Debate of April 4, 2001).

heritage made on the continental shelf and in the exclusive economic zone;[86] right of the coastal State to regulate and authorise any activities directed at underwater cultural heritage in these areas; possibility to deny the authorization if the activity interfere with the exploitation of natural resources.

At the first Meeting of Experts some delegations regarded this provision as a good compromise, while for others it amounted to a new maritime zone, even though it was not so called, and therefore it was considered unacceptable. Further comments were made by States. Some of them were surprisingly open to new and progressive solutions, if compared to positions taken by these States in the subsequent negotiations. This is the case of the Russian Federation that at this stage proposed the duty to report the discovery to the flag State, the coastal State, the State having a verifiable link and the UNESCO; moreover it would have been impossible to remove an archaeological object without consultation and agreement among all the above-mentioned States, with the flag State having a primary responsibility. China and Poland too supported the extension of the responsibility of the coastal State to the underwater cultural heritage within its exclusive economic zone. For Italy the coastal State has a direct and preferential link with the object and therefore it should be entitled to be informed, to regulate and to authorise all activities in these zones; but also other States having a verifiable link should be able to participate in the protection of the underwater cultural heritage in question. Turkey, while strongly contrary to any contiguous zone, supported the jurisdiction of the coastal State over historical objects on its continental shelf.

The second UNESCO draft presents three different options on jurisdiction. Option 1 (duty to report any discovery to the coastal State; competence of the coastal State to regulate activities) reflected the position of the experts in favour of the jurisdiction of coastal States: Canada, Australia, Italy, Malta, the Philippines, Poland, Tunisia. Option 2 (general need to protect underwater cultural heritage to be taken into account by any State Party) contained the views of the experts opposed to this hypothesis: France, the United Kingdom, Norway, the Netherlands and the United States. According to the latter UNESCO had substantially given up its initial orientation not to propose a new maritime area, because the first option had to be understood as a totally new competence for the coastal State. This was considered, notwithstanding declarations by UNESCO, contrary to the UNCLOS because "Article 5 substantially changes the balance of interests set forth in the Law of the Sea Convention". Option 3 (duty to notify discoveries to the coastal State; exchange of information among States; consultations) was presented by the Chairman of the Working Group, Mr. Gonzalez (Argentina), and tried to achieve a compromise between these two views.

---

[86] The question arose whether it was necessary to speak also of the exclusive economic zone or if it was enough to mention the continental shelf. Italy would have preferred the second option, considering that usually the underwater cultural heritage lies on the seabed included in the present delimitation of the continental shelf (200 n.m. or the continental margin). Spain disagreed, expressing the view that there can be the case where a State has a very small continental shelf but a 200 n.m. exclusive economic zone. The Convention mentions both maritime areas.

At the third Meeting of Experts, Working Group 1, chaired by Mr. Scovazzi (Italy), was entrusted with the question of jurisdiction. In a tentative proposal (*WG1 NP3*) the Chairman suggested a scheme divided into three parts: notification, consultations and provisional measures (prompt notification of discoveries to the coastal State, that has a special responsibility in protecting underwater cultural heritage on its continental shelf, and to the Director-General of UNESCO; consultations among the co-ordinating State,[87] the notifying State and the interested States; possibility up to the co-ordinating States to adopt provisional measures). With the exception of provisional measures, this scheme was followed as a model until the end of negotiations. Indeed the final Article 9 deals with "reporting and notification".

In Working Group 1 another interesting proposal was put forward by three anonymous delegations (*WG1 NP1, 5 July 2000*). It was based on the scheme of reporting and consultation, like the Chairman's proposal, but added two important elements: that the States entitled to participate in the consultations were those with a "verifiable link" with the underwater cultural heritage concerned and that the coastal State had to act not in its own interest but on behalf of all States Parties.

In comparison with the outcome of the third Meeting of Experts, Art. 10 of the SNT was considered disappointing by some: the coastal State *may require* the finder to report a discovery to it; a report will also be made to the flag State. At the fourth Meeting of Experts the SNT never really constituted the basis for discussions. A bigger role was played by the result of Working Group 1 at the third Meeting and by a very high number of new proposals put forward by several delegations, some of them allied to show a common approach and to gain in authority.

As far as notification and reporting is concerned, three different alternative models emerged:

a) a notification by the finder directly to the coastal State and to the flag States (sponsored by Argentina, *WP 14*);
b) a notification by the finder to the flag State; from the flag State to UNESCO and, upon request, to the coastal State; from UNESCO to all States Parties (sponsored by the United States, *WP15*);
c) a notification from the flag State to the coastal State and to UNESCO (sponsored by Italy, *WP 8*).[88]

Like-minded countries (Argentina, Canada, Greece, Italy, Tunisia, Egypt and others) took the view that it was necessary to recognise a particular role to the coastal State, because it was in the best position to ensure the protection of an object on its continental shelf. They agreed not to use the words "special responsibility",[89]

---

[87] Usually the coastal State, unless it invites another State to act as a co-ordinator.

[88] The possibility that, subject to agreement between the coastal State and the flag State, the first State could send observers to observe activities directed at underwater cultural heritage on its continental shelf (proposal by the United States, *WP 15*; idea taken for the 1995 Straddling Fish Stocks Agreement) was regarded with interest by some delegations. But in the end it was not retained: it appeared too complicated to implement.

[89] It had been used in the WG1 NP3 by the Chairman of the Working Group 1 during the third Meeting.

which could justify a fear of creeping jurisdiction, but they could not allow such a "critical" role not to be reflected in the text. They also pointed out that relying entirely upon the flag State would be dangerous: no guarantees of effective protection of underwater cultural heritage would come from this solution because of the widespread phenomenon of the "flags of convenience". Opposite positions were expressed by other delegations (the United States, the United Kingdom, Germany, Norway): any new competence of the coastal State, not considered in UNCLOS, would amount to creeping jurisdiction; the risk of infringing upon the freedom of navigation (even if it was not clear how this could happen[90]) was to be avoided, etc. The question of "to whom" notification had to be made – directly or indirectly to the coastal State – became the core problem and was transformed into a symbolic issue: for some a direct notification was natural and presented no legal obstacles, for others the rights of the coastal State to be directly notified of a discovery or an activity was unacceptable and amounted to an infringement of international law.

Between the first and the second sessions of the fourth Meeting new proposals were put forward – in particular that of the Chairman, the "May paper", upon which many other were built – and new suggestions were added, with a variety of slightly different wordings, each one reflecting a slightly different approach to the matter. The proposal of simultaneous notification to the coastal State and to the flag State[91] retained some attention, but finally the proposal by the United States (*NP 8* and revisions) – subsequently rejected by the United States itself – gained support: the basic idea of the proposal was that, by a declaration at the moment of ratification, a State Party may decide for simultaneous notification to the coastal State and to the flag State or, alternatively, for notification only to the flag State that "will ensure the rapid and effective transmission of such reports to all other States Parties" (and therefore not only to the coastal State).

The problem was that the wording of the United States' proposal was ambiguous and the second alternative could be read in a completely different way. Indeed, Art. 9, para. 1 (b) (ii) of the final text (which comes directly from United States' proposal) states:

> alternatively, a State Party shall require the national or master of the vessel to report such discovery or activity to it and shall ensure the rapid and effective transmission of such reports to all other States Parties.

Because of the lack of appropriate possessive adjectives, the expression "State Party" can be interpreted as the coastal State. The consequence of this reading would be the need for a direct notification by nationals of any States to the coastal State – a potential interpretation rejected by the States authors of the proposal, but welcomed

---

90 Commenting with humour this position, an Italian delegate said that, according to the statements of some other States, it appeared that protecting the underwater cultural heritage was the most dangerous activity taking place in the sea. It was thus better to prohibit it altogether under the famous precautionary principle!

91 But some delegates rightly note that the notification had to be made to the national State of the master of the vessel and not to the flag State.

by others that read in this "constructive ambiguity" the key to allowing the approval of the provision.

France, the United Kingdom, and the Russian Federation (supported by the United States[92]) proposed two amendments at the General Conference. They aimed at removing any ambiguity by using the following words:

(b) *When the discovery or activity is located* in the exclusive economic zone or on the continental shelf of another State Party:
  (i) *a State Party* shall require *its* national or the master of *a* vessel *flying its flag* to report such discovery or activity to *it* and to that other State Party;
  (ii) alternatively, a State Party shall require *its* national or master of *a* vessel *flying its flag* to report such discovery or activity to it and shall ensure the rapid and effective transmission of such reports to all other State Parties.[93]

In such a version it is clear that in the second hypothesis the notification is made to the flag State, which later will forward the information to all other States Parties. Even if the amendment[94] was defeated by a great majority, it seems that the interpretation emerging from it is to be preferred for Art. 9, para. 1 (b) (ii), in conformity with the preparatory works.[95] Indeed, it is evident that, in the intention of the authors of the draft provision, "State Party" was not to be read as "coastal State", but as "flag State".

A final reflection can be made. The final version of the provision emerges from a proposal – that of the United States – which considerably diluted those previously put forward and debated. Realising what a "dangerous" interpretation this proposal could allow, their authors withdrew their support, but by that time it was impossible to come back to a scheme where the coastal State would have enjoyed more substantive powers. The symbolic battle had been largely won by those fearing a new form of creeping jurisdiction but – paradoxically – without their approval.[96] Their success did not contribute to reaching *consensus* over the entire Convention.

Article 10 – Protection of Underwater Cultural Heritage in the Exclusive Economic Zone and on the Continental Shelf

1. No authorisation shall be granted for an activity directed at underwater cultural heritage located in the exclusive economic zone or on the continental shelf except in conformity with the provisions of this Article.
2. A State Party in whose exclusive economic zone or on whose continental shelf

---

92 In the statement in Commission IV of the General Conference the United States declared that "Article 9(1)(b)(ii) can only be read as an obligation on flag States in regard to its own nationals and flag vessels" (reprinted in (2000) *AJIL* 470).

93 In italics the new wording.

94 The one by France, as already said (see *supra* note 80), had been withdrawn.

95 Art. 32 of the Vienna Convention on the Law of Treaties.

96 Besides the United States contrary to the solution approved were also Germany, Norway, the Netherlands and France.

underwater cultural heritage is located has the right to prohibit or authorise any activity directed at such heritage to prevent interference with its sovereign rights or jurisdiction as provided for by international law including the United Nations Convention on the Law of the Sea.

3. Where there is a discovery of underwater cultural heritage or it is intended that activity shall be directed at underwater cultural heritage in a State Party's exclusive economic zone or on its continental shelf, that State Party shall:
   (a) consult all other States Parties which have declared an interest under Article 9 paragraph 5 on how best to protect the underwater cultural heritage;
   (b) co-ordinate such consultations as "Coordinating State", unless it expressly declares that it does not wish to do so, in which case the States Parties which have declared an interest under Article 9 paragraph 5 shall appoint a Coordinating State.
4. Without prejudice to the duty of all States Parties to protect underwater cultural heritage by way of all practicable measures taken in accordance with international law to prevent immediate danger to the underwater cultural heritage, including looting, the Coordinating State may take all practicable measures and/or issue any necessary authorisations in conformity with this Convention, and, if necessary, prior to consultations, to prevent any immediate danger to the underwater cultural heritage whether arising from human activities or any other cause including looting. In taking such measures assistance may be requested from other States Parties.
5. The Coordinating State:
   (a) shall implement measures of protection which have been agreed by the consulting States, which include the Coordinating State, unless the consulting States, which include the Coordinating State, agree that another State Party shall implement those measures;
   (b) shall issue all necessary authorisations for such agreed measures in conformity with the Rules, unless the consulting States, which include the Coordinating State, agree that another State Party shall issue those authorisations;
   (c) may conduct any necessary preliminary research on the underwater cultural heritage and shall issue all necessary authorisations therefor, and shall promptly inform the Director-General of the results, who in turn will make such information promptly available to other States Parties.
6. In coordinating consultations, taking measures, conducting preliminary research and/or issuing authorisations pursuant to this Article, the Coordinating State shall act on behalf of the States Parties as a whole and not in its own interest. Any such action shall not in itself constitute a basis for the assertion of any preferential or jurisdictional rights not provided for in international law, including the United Nations Convention on the Law of the Sea.
7. Subject to the provisions of paragraphs 2 and 4 of this Article, no activity directed at State vessels and aircraft shall be conducted without the agreement of the flag State and the collaboration of the Coordinating State.

[Preparatory documents:
a) Working papers and comments by States:
- [see Article 9]
- WP 34, 2 April 2001 (Amendments proposed by Finland, Germany, Japan, the Netherlands, Norway, the Russian Federation, Spain, Sweden, the United Kingdom and endorsed by the United States)
- Non-paper by Spain, 12 June 2001
- Unofficial proposal of the United Kingdom, 16 June 2001
- Non-paper by Spain, 22 June 2001
- Non-paper by the United States, 1 July 2001
- Non-paper 3, 3 July 2001(State vessels and aircraft, Single Article proposed by UK)
- WP 41, 4 July 2001 (Amendment to Article 2 redrafted by the Secretariat following discussion on plenary)
- WP 57, 5 July 2001 (Report of the informal sub-group of the warships Working Group)

b) Drafts:
- [see Article 9]

c) Other documents:
- [see Article 9]]

Article 10 was negotiated as a package together with Article 9. As it has already been said, it was at the third Meeting of Experts that an orientation took shape, in order to draft a scheme in two parts: "notification and report" on one hand and "protection" on the other. Article 10 deals with the latter. It is to be read together with the last paragraph of Art. 9, which – it has been noted[97] – is strangely placed.

When it became clear that the protection scheme could be envisaged in the form of consultations, delegates tried to solve the following problems: what did the consultations aim at? Who could participate in consultations? Who – if anyone – could lead them, as co-ordinating State? What powers would the co-ordinating State obtain? How should the principle of non-interference with natural resources of the continental shelf be tackled? Could a competence to order provisional measures be envisaged and who could enjoy it? Did warships located on the continental shelf need a special regime? To answer all these questions was not any easier than drafting the notification scheme under Art. 9.

The SNT (Art. 11) proposed a regime of protection of underwater cultural heritage located on the continental shelf almost exclusively based on the concept enshrined in Art. 77 of UNCLOS, as regards the natural resources of the continental shelf. This provision grants the coastal States an exclusive and sovereign right over the exploration and exploitation of the natural resources of its continental shelf, with the consequence that the coastal State can intervene to prevent any interference with the exercise of such rights and therefore (SNT) also to regulate activities directed at underwater cultural heritage which "inevitably affect" those rights. Such a solution

[97] O'Keefe, *supra* note 25, at 86.

was criticized at the fourth Meeting of Experts on two grounds. On one hand some delegations (Spain and the United States) contested that activities directed at underwater cultural heritage *inevitably* interfere with natural resources. Therefore no special role must be attributed to the coastal State. On the other hand other delegates (Italy, Argentina, Australia, and Peru) pointed out that such a solution was not only insufficient but it could represent a bad message. The objective of the Convention was not that of avoiding interference with the natural resources of the coastal State on its continental shelf, but to ensure an effective protection of the underwater cultural heritage. A regime of protection could not entirely rely upon a hypothesis of interference on natural resources. First, because such interference, as rightly pointed out by some delegations, is just a hypothesis and not always true. Second, because even if all archaeological and historical objects were embedded in natural resources, the message would be that the protection of the underwater cultural heritage is itself not a primary and autonomous objective, but that it comes second, after the protection of natural resources: a shipwreck can only be protected insomuch as natural resources – under the jurisdiction of the coastal State – cover it.

It was decided that the concept of "interference" should be retained, but inserted in a much more complex article dealing with the protection of the underwater cultural heritage on the continental shelf. This was not the end of the discussions, because different perspectives took shape in several drafts of this paragraph (finally para. 2): "exclusive" or "not exclusive" right of the coastal State to avoid interference? Should such a right also be granted when an activity "may" interfere or only when it "interferes"? Was there a need for a reference to UNCLOS and international law in order to limit this right or not? Longstanding debates led to the compromise enshrined in the text, where the coastal State has the "right" (not exclusive) to "prohibit and authorize" any activity to "prevent interference", according to "international law including UNCLOS". The United States and the Netherlands refused to accept the words "prevent interference".[98]

As far as the concept of "consultations" is concerned, lively discussions were necessary to clarify that they were not aimed at reaching an agreement on how to deal with the underwater cultural heritage concerned but directly at protecting it. In other words, they must not be intended as a further time-consuming step before a decision is made on how to protect an item. Italy gave a practical example of matters to be dealt with during consultations: the problem of the destination of the wreck, how to protect it effectively, who the owner is, etc. (that is to say, substantial issues).

Who had to be entitled to participate in consultations was another thorny point. Some felt that anyone interested had the right to be consulted. It was preferred to limit this right to those States with a verifiable link. But then a clarification of what the "verifiable link" is was asked by Spain and Greece. Archaeological, historical

[98] In their statement in Commission IV of the General Conference the United States declared that "Article 10(2) can serve only to restate the rights that states already have, as provided in the UNCLOS Parts V and VI, over the protection of natural resources; it cannot be read to create new rights over such resources" (reprinted in (2000) *AJIL* 470).

and cultural links were mentioned but as an open list. This was considered dangerous by Spain which feared that also a commercial link could be invoked. The Chairman gave the example of an artefact found near a cable or an installation: in this case it would be appropriate to consult the State to whom such a cable or installation belongs.

What was the role of the coastal State in the consultations? This problem recalled the one of notification. Two different philosophies clashed: on one hand like-minded countries thought that the coastal State must play a central role and therefore co-ordinate consultations, unless it decides not to do so; on the other hand, other States (Norway, the United States, the United Kingdom) considered that all States which declared an interest could participate, rights being equal, in consultations and that any special role attributed to the coastal State would run counter to UNCLOS. In the end, even Spain and Germany, which had initially been contrary, accepted the idea of the coastal State as the co-ordinating State. Anyway the Convention makes it clear[99] that there is no automatic identification between coastal State and co-ordinating State because any other consulting State can be appointed as co-ordinator, if the coastal State so wishes.

The powers of the co-ordinating State, too, were controversial. Some delegations wanted any measure to protect the underwater cultural heritage concerned to be decided by the consulting States by unanimous vote. That amounted to *de facto* preventing the coastal State from taking any action on its continental shelf and to denying any special role for it. In the end a more favourable solution for the coastal State was accepted.

The issue of provisional measures was perceived as linked to the one which has just been examined. The proposal of provisional measures had originally been put forward by Italy which considered it one of the most important issues to be dealt with by the Convention. The underpinning idea was that, pending the working of the complex mechanism of protection of the underwater cultural heritage, some powers had to be recognised to the coastal State in the case of immediate danger for a specific artefact located in its continental shelf, in order, for example, to prevent the looting of ancient treasures found in a shipwreck. According to Italy, this word – looting – had to explicitly appear within the Convention because it represents the biggest danger for the underwater cultural heritage. But the Italian proposal met with considerable obstacles at least at the beginning. Even like-minded States, such as Argentina and Australia, regarded it with suspicion, arguing that provisional measures would have the bad tendency to become definitive. Moreover it was likely that provisional measures would create disputes among States: lawyers – not the underwater cultural heritage – would take advantage of such situations! It goes without saying that many delegations strongly criticized the proposal because, as a further competency recognised to the coastal State, they represented a real form of creeping jurisdiction. Their name was initially changed, so as to mask their substance, and they became "practicable measures". Italy did not like this change very much, as by "provisional

[99] Art. 10, para. 3 b).

measures" it meant police and enforcement measures. But, as Japan pointed out, no such explicit language would have been acceptable and it was better to hide those enforcement powers under a much more neutral word. Italy accepted the expression "practicable measures" because the idea of urgency linked to provisional measures is still present under the wording "immediate danger".

It remained to be solved *who* could adopt those measures: for the United States all the States having declared an interest; for Norway all the States in consultation with the flag State; for most States (Sweden, the United Kingdom, the Netherlands, Spain) any State. Canada and Argentina suggested a compromise which was finally accepted: the co-ordinating State can take practicable measures to prevent danger, if necessary prior to consultations, but without prejudice to the same competence of all States Parties.

Less controversial, but however not unanimously accepted, was para. 1 – the so-called "golden rule" – according to which no activity is authorized on the continental shelf unless in conformity with the Convention. The same goes for para. 6. It enshrines two important principles. The first – which, as already pointed out,[100] was first put forward at the Third Meeting of Experts by three unnamed delegations (*WG1 NP1*) – clarifies that the co-ordinating State has to act on the behalf of all States Parties. The second is a disclaimer clause, in order to make sure that no action taken by the co-ordinating State can constitute a basis for assertion of any preferential or jurisdictional right not provided for in international law. Both the sentences are to be interpreted as precise guaranties for those who fear that the UNESCO Convention can give rise to new forms of creeping jurisdiction and violations of existing international law.

Para. 7 deals with State and military vessels. Although at least apparently the protection of such kinds of vessels located on the continental shelf of a State should present fewer problems in comparison with the territorial sea, negotiations on this point proved to be quite difficult. The outcome of an informal subgroup on warships created during the last days was the following proposal (*WP 57*):

> The flag State of the State vessel and aircraft located in the exclusive economic zone or on the continental shelf of another State Party will participate in consultations provided for in paragraph A5. No State Party shall undertake or authorize activities directed at State vessels and aircraft in the exclusive economic zone or on the continental shelf of a State Party without the [consent] [agreement] of the flag State.

Tunisia asked for the agreement not only of the flag State but also of the coastal State. Spain disagreed, together with the Russian Federation, France and the United States. It argued that the continental shelf is not a sovereign area of the coastal State and with respect to State vessels it is the flag State that has the primary role. At least Spain could accept an agreement between the co-ordinating State and the flag States. It seemed a compromise to Italy.

---

[100] See *supra* comment to Art. 9, when dealing with *WG1 NP1*.

The United States proposed a new paragraph, reading as follows:

> Without prejudice to coastal State sovereign rights and jurisdiction under international law as set forth in UNCLOS, no activity directed at State vessels and aircraft shall be conducted without the consent of the flag State.

Argentina then suggested the text finally adopted, enshrining the Spanish compromise but also making reference to paras. 2 and 4 of Art. 10 (originally suggested by Egypt). The United States and the United Kingdom strongly disagreed because in para. 4 the co-ordinating State is allowed to take unilateral actions.

The United Kingdom and the Russian Federation proposed the following amendment to Art. 10 at the General Conference, without success:

2. A State Party in whose exclusive economic zone or on whose continental shelf underwater cultural heritage is located has the right to prohibit or authorise any activity directed at such heritage *when necessary* to prevent interference with its sovereign rights or jurisdiction as provided for by international law including the United Nations Convention on the Law of the Sea.
4. Without prejudice to the duty of all States Parties to protect underwater cultural heritage by way of all practicable measures taken in accordance with international law to prevent immediate danger to the underwater cultural heritage, including looting, the Coordinating State may take all practicable measures and/or issue any necessary authorizations in conformity with this Convention and, if necessary prior to consultations, to prevent any immediate danger to the underwater cultural heritage, *from activities directed at underwater cultural heritage*, including looting, *or from natural causes unrelated to human activities*. In taking such measures, assistance may be requested from other States Parties, *but in any event prompt assistance shall be requested from the State Party that is the flag State of the vessel engaged in such activities.*
7. *Notwithstanding* the provisions of paragraphs 2 and 4 of this Article, no activity directed at State vessels and aircraft shall be conducted without the agreement of the flag State.[101]

At the moment of vote in the General Conference many States in their statements made reference to the solution given to the jurisdictional issue to justify their negative vote or abstention. Greece abstained also because in Art. 9 and 10 the coastal State is "only" given a co-ordinating role; Greece likewise considered unsatisfactory the paragraph concerning State vessels and the lack of any definition of "cultural, historical and archaeological link". Norway, the Russian Federation, the United Kingdom and the United States made declarations regretting the solution given to the jurisdictional issue, considered a violation of UNCLOS.

[101] In italics words added.

Article 11 – Reporting and Notification in the Area

1. States Parties have a responsibility to protect underwater cultural heritage in the Area in conformity with this Convention and Article 149 of the United Nations Convention on the Law of the Sea. Accordingly when a national, or a vessel flying the flag of a State Party, discovers or intends to engage in activities directed at underwater cultural heritage located in the Area, that State Party shall require its national, or the master of the vessel, to report such discovery or activity to it.
2. States Parties shall notify the Director-General and the Secretary-General of the International Seabed Authority of such discoveries or activities reported to them.
3. The Director-General shall promptly make available to all States Parties any such information supplied by States Parties.
4. Any State Party may declare to the Director-General its interest in being consulted on how to ensure the effective protection of that underwater cultural heritage. Such declaration shall be based on a verifiable link with that underwater cultural heritage, particular regard being paid to the preferential rights of States of cultural, historical or archaeological origin.

[Preparatory documents:

a) Working Papers and comments by States:
   - Comments of the United States of America on UNESCO Draft Convention on the Protection of the Underwater Cultural Heritage (April 1999)
   - Comments of the United States of America on Selected Articles being considered in Working Group One, 4 July 2000
   - WP 56, 5 July 2001 (draft article proposed by the United Kingdom and Canada)
   - Article 12 (unofficial draft article by Spain)

b) Drafts:
   - first UNESCO/DOALOS draft (Art. 14)
   - second UNESCO draft (Art.7 Option 3; Art. 7bis)
   - ILA (Art.12)

c) Other documents:
   - Report of the Meeting of Experts for the Draft Convention on the Protection of Underwater Cultural Heritage, Paris, 22–24 May 1996 (UNESCO doc. CLT-96/CONF.605/6), paras.43
   - Final Report of the First Meeting of Governmental Experts on the Draft Convention on the Protection of Underwater Cultural Heritage, Paris, 29 June–2 July 1998 (UNESCO doc. CLT-98/CONF.202/7), para. XVIII
   - Final Report of the Second Meeting of Governmental Experts on the Draft Convention on the Protection of Underwater Cultural Heritage , Paris, 19-24 April 1999 (UNESCO doc. CLT-99/CONF.204, Paris, August 1999), para. 38
   - Summary of Observations by States on the Draft Convention on the Protection of Underwater Cultural Heritage, Paris, April 2000 (UNESCO

doc. CLT-2000/CONF.201/3; UNESCO doc. CLT-2000/CONF.201/3Add.; UNESCO doc. CLT-2000/CONF.201/3Add. 2)]

In the UNCLOS there is a specific provision on archaeological and historical objects in the Area (Art. 149):

> All objects of an archaeological and historical nature found in the Area shall be preserved or disposed of for the benefit of mankind as a whole, particular regard being paid to the preferential rights of the State or country of origin, or the State of cultural origin, or the State of historical and archaeological origin.

While the ILA draft did not consider a provision on the underwater cultural heritage found in the Area, the first UNESCO/DOALOS devoted one article (Art. 14) to this issue. Some experts at the Meeting of 1996 had indeed taken the view that archaeological objects located in this zone should be declared the cultural heritage of mankind and administered by an international organization like UNESCO. Art. 14 did not enshrine the first of the two suggestions. It provided for a duty to notify any discovery to the Area to the International Sea-Bed Authority (hereinafter: ISA) that would have subsequently forwarded the information to UNESCO. At the First Meeting of Governmental Experts the role of the ISA was questioned by some delegates (although at the time the ISA was drafting the Mining Code where archaeological objects are considered); others judged positively the collaboration between ISA and UNESCO. In the second UNESCO draft Art. 14, renumbered 7 *bis*, was unchanged. But Art. 7 of Option 3 was inserted: here it was made clear that it is the flag State that must notify the discovery and the recipient of this notification was UNESCO, which would subsequently forward it to the ISA. In their comments to this draft several States (Australia, Canada, Japan, the United States) expressed themselves in favour of UNESCO as the proper organization because the ISA has no specific competences in the field of underwater archaeology.

The SNT changed the provision as follows:

> Any discovery of underwater cultural heritage in the Area shall be reported by the finder to the Director-General of the United Nations Educational, Scientific and Cultural Organization.

At the last Meeting of Experts it was not considered a good basis for negotiations. This draft article concerning the Area was logically negotiated after Art. 9 and 10. At this point two alternatives were put forward. The first – an informal proposal by Spain – was a short article providing for: notification of discoveries or planned activities in the Area to the flag State that will inform UNESCO and ISA; authorization by the flag State of activities in the Area on the basis of the Rules of the Annex; particular regard to be paid to preferential rights. The second proposal – by the United Kingdom and Canada (*WP 56*) – was modelled upon the scheme approved with reference to the continental shelf (notification and protection), with the Director-General of UNESCO replacing the role of the coastal State. It was this second proposal, with an additional reference to preferential rights already considered by Art. 149 UNCLOS, that was finally approved.

It seems that the solution finally adopted is fully compatible with the Mining Code, adopted in 2000 by the International Seabed Authority.[102] Two provisions of the Mining Code deal with underwater cultural heritage, namely Regulations 8 and 34, which read respectively as follows:

> A prospector shall immediately notify the Secretary-General in writing of any finding in the Area of an object of an archaeological or historical nature and its location. The Secretary-General shall transmit such information to the Director-General of the United Nations Educational, Scientific and Cultural Organization.
>
> The contractor shall immediately notify the Secretary-General in writing of any finding in the exploration area of an object of an archaeological or historical nature and its location. The Secretary-General shall transmit such information to the Director-General of the United Nations Educational, Scientific and Cultural Organization. Following the finding of any such object of an archaeological or historical nature in the exploration area, the contractor shall take all reasonable measures to avoid disturbing such object.

Article 12 – Protection of Underwater Cultural Heritage in the Area

1. No authorisation shall be granted for any activity directed at underwater cultural heritage located in the Area except in conformity with the provisions of this Article.
2. The Director-General shall invite all States Parties which have declared an interest under Article 11 paragraph 4 to consult on how best to protect the underwater cultural heritage, and to appoint a State Party to coordinate such consultations as the "Coordinating State". The Director-General shall also invite the International Seabed Authority to participate in such consultations.
3. All States Parties may take all practicable measures in conformity with this Convention, if necessary prior to consultations, to prevent any immediate danger to the underwater cultural heritage, whether arising from human activity or any other cause including looting.
4. The Coordinating State shall:
   (a) implement measures of protection which have been agreed by the consulting States, which include the Coordinating State, unless the consulting States, which include the Coordinating State, agree that another State Party shall implement those measures; and
   (b) issue all necessary authorisations for such agreed measures, in conformity with this Convention, unless the consulting States, which include the Coordinating State, agree that another State Party shall issue those authorisations.
5. The Coordinating State may conduct any necessary preliminary research on the underwater cultural heritage and shall issue all necessary authorisations

[102] ISBA/6/A/18, 13 July 2000.

therefor, and shall promptly inform the Director-General of the results, who in turn shall make such information available to other States Parties.

6. In coordinating consultations, taking measures, conducting preliminary research, and/or issuing authorisations pursuant to this Article, the Coordinating State shall act for the benefit of humanity as a whole, on behalf of all States Parties. Particular regard shall be paid to the preferential rights of States of cultural, historical or archaeological origin of the heritage concerned.
7. No State Party shall undertake or authorise activities directed at State vessels and aircraft in the Area without the consent of the flag State.

[Preparatory documents:

a) Working papers:
   - [see Art. 12]
   - WP 34, 2 April 2001 (Amendments proposed by Finland, Germany, Japan, the Netherlands, Norway, the Russian Federation, Spain, Sweden, the United Kingdom and endorsed by the United States
   - Non-paper 3, 3 July 2001(State vessels and aircraft, Single Article proposed by UK)
   - WP 57, 5 July 2001 (Report of the informal sub-group of the warships Working Group)

b) Drafts:
   - [see Art. 11]

c) Other documents:
   - [see Art. 11]]

Art. 12 was negotiated as a package together with Art. 11. Therefore it does not deserve further comments, with the exception of para. 7 concerning State vessels. It is the unchanged version of the proposal made by a special sub group on warships (*WP 57*). It did not create particular problems.

Article 13 – Sovereign immunity

Warships and other government ships or military aircraft with sovereign immunity, operated for non-commercial purposes, undertaking their normal mode of operations, and not engaged in activities directed at underwater cultural heritage, shall not be obliged to report discoveries of underwater cultural heritage under Articles 9, 10, 11, and 12 of this Convention. However States Parties shall ensure, by the adoption of appropriate measures not impairing the operations or operational capabilities of their warships or other government ships or military aircraft with sovereign immunity operated for non-commercial purposes, that they comply, as far as is reasonable and practicable, with Articles 9, 10, 11, and 12 of this Convention.

[Preparatory documents:

a) Working papers:

- Non-paper 3, 3 July 2001 (State vessels and aircraft – Single Article, proposed by UK)

b) Other documents:
- Draft Resolution submitted by the Russian Federation and the United Kingdom (and endorsed by the United States), General Conference, 26 October 2001 (UNESCO doc. 31 C/COM.IV/DIR.5)]

This provision came out at the very end of the negotiations. It was proposed – initially as a part of a single article on warships, subsequently as a provision inserted in articles dealing with jurisdiction and eventually drafted as a single article by the Drafting Committee – by the United Kingdom (*Non-paper 3, 3 July 2002*) with the support of Sweden. However, as it was remarked during the discussion, it concerns a case where the warship is not the shipwreck discovered but the finder. Such a hypothesis had never been considered before. The United Kingdom justified this proposal arguing that to comply with provisions on jurisdiction (notification, reporting, consultations etc.) State vessels would reveal information that the State prefers to keep secret or that must remain secret for reasons of security (*i.e.* the position of the vessel, details of the operation in which the vessel is engaged etc.).

When presented at the plenary, Argentina, Finland, Greece and Italy strongly reacted. In particular the latter regretted that such a new and important exception to the general jurisdiction regime – painstakingly constructed over years of negotiations – only came up at the very end when time was running short and it was no longer possible to debate it in depth. The main criticism directed at the English proposal was not the idea itself, in that it was conceivable that important reasons of security prevent warships from entirely applying Art. 9 and the following. The problem was that in the original proposal all State vessels and aircraft derogated from the general regime and – given the very broad definition of State vessels agreed upon – the risk was that an excessively high number of vessels (as finders) would be free not to apply the Convention. In other words, as Colombia pointed out, the exception would have been greater that the rule. Argentina and Italy proposed limiting the provision only to warship. Greece remarked that a private commercial company looking for sunken treasures could also operate on a warship. In the end quite a complex compromise was reached, according to which warships and other governmental ships are involved, but only if three cumulative conditions are respected (they do not operate for commercial purposes, they undertake their normal mode of operations and they are not engaged in activities directed at underwater cultural heritage[103]).

At the general Conference, the United Kingdom and the Russian Federation tried

[103] It is not unusual that underwater archaeological research is made with military vessels. It is the case of the most worldwide famous underwater explorer, Robert Ballard: it was when on board the research vessel *Knorr* – offered by the U.S. Navy – that he discovered *Titanic*. Several other searches conducted by Ballard in the Mediterranean Sea in 1997-1999 were made possible by the use of a nuclear submarine – the *NR-1* – again placed at the disposal of the research team by the U.S. Navy. Capable of searching vast regions of the ocean bottom for long periods of time, *NR-1* uses long-range sonar that can detect shipwrecks at a much greater distance than sonars previously used by oceanographers. It was also equipped with a remotely operated arm that was used to recover archaeological objects.

to add also "naval auxiliaries" to the list of vessels covered by this Article, but the amendment did not pass.

Article 14 – Control of Entry into the Territory, Dealing and Possession

States Parties shall take measures to prevent the entry into their territory, the dealing in, or the possession of, underwater cultural heritage illicitly exported and/or recovered, where recovery was contrary to this Convention.162162

[Preparatory documents:

a) Working papers:
   - WP 50, 3 July 2001 (Amendment proposed by the United Kingdom and seconded by Germany)

b) Drafts:
   - SNT

c) Other documents:
   - Final Report of the Third Meeting of Governmental Experts on the Draft Convention on the Protection of Underwater Cultural Heritage, Paris, 3-7 July 2000, Annex 2 Working Group 2 (UNESCO doc. CLT-2000/CONF.201/8 rev., Paris, 5 July 2000)]

Article 14 appeared for the first time (with the title "Import of underwater cultural heritage") in the Report of Chairman of Working Group 2 at the third Meeting of Governmental Experts. This Working Group, chaired by Ms. Ginbrere (the Netherlands) was created to negotiate on Art. 8 to 13 and 15 to 18 of the draft. It was further elaborated in the SNT to read:

1. A state Party shall make it an offence to import into its territory underwater cultural heritage which has not been excavated in accordance with the Convention.
2. To facilitate the import into the coastal State of underwater cultural heritage excavated on its continental shelf, the competent authorities of that State may issue an import permit for the underwater cultural heritage subject to observance of the Rules of the Annex.

This was a rather confused provision, which also left room for arguments about a potential competence of the European Union,[104] which was eventually denied by the European Union itself.[105]

The United Kingdom was for the deletion of this Article and the matter to be dealt with in the provision on sanctions. Italy felt that the second paragraph was

[104] But this problem arose only within the Community meeting, organised alongside the multilateral negotiations.

[105] Informal opinion by M. Vitsentzatos (Legal Service, Council of the European Union), Brussels, 3 April 2001.

useless. The Chairman, Lund, wished to avoid a useless repetition of other UNESCO conventions dealing with the illicit movement of cultural objects. The final compromise was a simplified version of an Irish proposal. It encompasses not only the import, but also the dealing in and possession of underwater cultural heritage illegally excavated.

Article 15 – Non-use of Areas under the Jurisdiction of States Parties

> States Parties shall take measures to prohibit the use of their territory, including their maritime ports, as well as artificial islands, installations and structures under their exclusive jurisdiction or control, in support of any activity directed at underwater cultural heritage which is not in conformity with this Convention.

[Preparatory documents:
a) Working Paper and comments by States:
- WG1 NP1, 5 July 2000 (Non-paper proposed by three delegations for discussion as a possible basis for consensus)
- Comments of the United States of America on UNESCO Draft Convention on the Protection of the Underwater Cultural Heritage (April 1999)

b) Drafts:
- ILA draft (Art. 7)
- first UNESCO/DOALOS draft (Art. 6)
- second UNESCO draft (Art. 6 Option 1; Art. 6 Option 2)
- SNT (Art. 14)

c) Other documents:
- Feasibility Study for the Drafting of a New Instrument for the Protection of the Underwater Cultural Heritage, Paris, 23 March 1995 (UNESCO doc. 146 EX/27), paras. 26
- Report of the Meeting of Experts for the Draft Convention on the Protection of Underwater Cultural Heritage, Paris, 22–24 May 1996 (UNESCO doc. CLT-96/CONF.605/6), paras. 34
- Final Report of the First Meeting of Governmental Experts on the Draft Convention on the Protection of Underwater Cultural Heritage, Paris, 29 June–2 July 1998 (UNESCO doc. CLT-98/CONF.202/7), para. XI
- Final Report of the Second Meeting of Governmental Experts on the Draft Convention on the Protection of Underwater Cultural Heritage , Paris, 19-24 April 1999 (UNESCO doc. CLT-99/CONF.204, Paris, August 1999), para. 36
- Summary of Observations by States on the Draft Convention on the Protection of Underwater Cultural Heritage, Paris, April 2000 (UNESCO doc. CLT-2000/CONF.201/3; UNESCO doc. CLT-2000/CONF.201/3 Add.)]

Article 15 enshrines the so-called "port State jurisdiction", which, together with the "national jurisdiction" and "flag State jurisdiction", was strongly relied upon by all those States contrary to the coastal State jurisdiction. According to them the Convention should not be based on a geographical form of jurisdiction: the respect of the Rules of the Annex should be ensured by States by controlling their nationals, their vessels, their ports.

The ILA draft dealt with the concept of "port State jurisdiction", but that was complementary with the coastal States jurisdiction upon the "cultural heritage zone". The UNESCO feasibility study considered all these different forms of jurisdiction, all of which seemed admissible in international law. At the Meeting of Experts of 1996, when it became clear that the idea of a cultural heritage zone was too revolutionary to be accepted by all States, alternative basis of jurisdiction were considered. Accordingly, the first UNESCO/DOALOS draft included Art. 6, reading as follows:

1. All States Parties shall take measures to prohibit use of their territory, including their maritime ports and off-shore terminals, or other areas under their jurisdiction or control in support of any activity directed at underwater cultural heritage and inconsistent with the Rules of the Annex.
2. This provision shall apply to any such activity beyond that State's territorial sea but not within an area over which another State exercises control [in accordance with customary international law as reflected in the United Nations Convention on the Law of the Sea] unless requested by that State.

At the first Meeting of Experts some expressed reservation concerning this provision voicing doubts as to its conformity with other conventions on port access. In the second UNESCO draft the second paragraph was deleted in Option 1, because other provisions on coastal State control over the exclusive economic zone and continental shelf were inserted, while it was left unchanged in Option 2. In commenting this draft, Japan considered Art. 6 in Option 1 to be contrary to UNCLOS.[106] The SNT retained Art.6 of Option 1, which was just slightly changed during the last Meeting, in order to include reference to artificial islands, installations and structures.

Article 16 – Measures Relating to Nationals and Vessels

States Parties shall take all practicable measures to ensure that their nationals and vessels flying their flag do not engage in any activity directed at underwater cultural heritage in a manner not in conformity with this Convention.

[Preparatory documents:

a) Working Papers:
   - Comments of the United States of America on UNESCO Draft Convention on the Protection of the Underwater Cultural Heritage (April 1999)
   - WG1 NP1, 5 July 2000 (Non-paper proposed by three delegations for discussion as a possible basis for consensus)
   - WP2, 27 March 2001 (Amendment proposed by Norway)

[106] No explanation of this position by Japan was provided in the UNESCO doc. CLT-2000/CONF.201/3 (Summary of Observations by States on the Draft Convention on the Protection of Underwater Cultural Heritage, Paris, April 2000).

d) Drafts:
   - ILA draft (Art. 8)
   - first UNESCO/DOALOS draft (Art. 7)
   - second UNESCO draft (Art. 7 Option 1; Art. 7 Option 2; Art. 6 Option 3)
   - SNT (Art. 15)

e) Other documents:
   - Feasibility Study for the Drafting of a New Instrument for the Protection of the Underwater Cultural Heritage, Paris, 23 March 1995 (UNESCO doc. 146 EX/27), paras. 26
   - Report of the Meeting of Experts for the Draft Convention on the Protection of Underwater Cultural Heritage, Paris, 22–24 May 1996 (UNESCO doc. CLT-96/CONF.605/6), paras. 34
   - Final Report of the First Meeting of Governmental Experts on the Draft Convention on the Protection of Underwater Cultural Heritage, Paris, 29 June–2 July 1998 (UNESCO doc. CLT-98/CONF.202/7), para. XII
   - Final Report of the Second Meeting of Governmental Experts on the Draft Convention on the Protection of Underwater Cultural Heritage, Paris, 19-24 April 1999 (UNESCO doc. CLT-99/CONF.204, Paris, August 1999), para. 37
   - Summary of Observations by States on the Draft Convention on the Protection of Underwater Cultural Heritage, Paris, April 2000 (UNESCO doc. CLT-2000/CONF.201/3; UNESCO doc. CLT-2000/CONF.201/3 Add.)]

National jurisdiction and flag State jurisdiction are the concepts underlying this provision. Art. 8 of the ILA draft was further elaborated in the first UNESCO/DOALOS draft, where a second paragraph concerning measures that the flag State can adopt to prevent illegal activities in the high sea or on the continental shelf of other States Parties – borrowed from the 1995 Straddling Fish Stocks Agreement – was added:

1. A State Party shall take such measures as may be necessary to ensure that its nationals and vessels flying its flag do not engage in any activity affecting underwater cultural heritage in a manner inconsistent with the principles of the Charter.
2. Measures to be taken by a State Party in respect of its nationals and vessels flying its flag shall include, among others, the establishment of regulations:
   (a) to prohibit activities affecting underwater cultural heritage in areas where no State Party exercises its jurisdiction under Article 5 otherwise than in accordance with the terms and conditions of a permit or authorization granted in compliance with the provision of the Charter
   (b) to ensure that they do not engage in activities affecting underwater cultural heritage within the exclusive economic zone or continental shelf of a State Party which exercises its jurisdiction under Article 5, in a manner contrary to the laws and regulations of the State.

At the 1998 Meeting of Experts some delegates pointed out that these two forms of jurisdiction, if taken alone, could not grant an effective protection of the underwater cultural heritage: control over nationals would be very difficult to apply in practice; flags of convenience show that an efficient control by the flag State is not always possible; no control at all could be exercised over vessels flying the flag of non States Parties. Japan considered the provision contrary to the UNCLOS.[107]

The second UNESCO draft before, and the SNT after, did not change this provision very much. At the last Meeting of Experts Norway put forward a very long and comprehensive proposal on national and flag State jurisdiction (*WP 2*). In the Norwegian approach this articulated and detailed proposal should replace the entire jurisdictional regime based on coastal State control as elaborated during negotiations up to that moment. Norway – whose aim was clearly to avoid any power for the coastal State – suggested a complex system of control by the States Parties over their nationals and vessels, based also on inquiries, judicial proceedings and sanctions; a remarkable international co-operation in the field of police would be built up, so that each State Party could rely upon the assistance of others. This Norwegian proposal was rejected as too complex. Negotiations were developing towards the complex scheme of notification/protection explained above and the Norwegian proposal was a radical change in a different direction. In the end, the first paragraph of Art. 15 of the SNT was adopted with minor linguistic changes, while the second paragraph (control over activities in the high sea or on the continental shelf of other States Parties) was deleted.

Article 17 – Sanctions

1. Each State Party shall impose sanctions for violations of measures it has taken to implement this Convention.
2. Sanctions applicable in respect of violations shall be adequate in severity to be effective in securing compliance with this Convention and to discourage violations wherever they occur and shall deprive offenders of the benefit occurring from their illegal activities.
3. States Parties shall cooperate to ensure enforcement of sanctions imposed under this Article.

[Preparatory documents:

a) Working Papers:
    - Comments of the United States of America on UNESCO Draft Convention on the Protection of the Underwater Cultural Heritage (April 1999)
    - WP2, 27 March 2001 (Amendment proposed by Norway)
b) Drafts:
    - ILA draft (Art. 11)
    - first UNESCO/DOALOS draft (Art. 10)
    - second UNESCO draft (Art.10)
    - SNT (Art. 16)

[107] No explanation of this position by Japan was provided (*ibidem*).

c) Other documents:
- Final Report of the First Meeting of Governmental Experts on the Draft Convention on the Protection of Underwater Cultural Heritage, Paris, 29 June–2 July 1998 (UNESCO doc. CLT-98/CONF.202/7), para. XIV
- Final Report of the Third Meeting of Governmental Experts on the Draft Convention on the Protection of Underwater Cultural Heritage, Paris, 3-7 July 2000, Annex II, Working Group 2 (UNESCO doc. CLT-2000/CONF.201/8 rev., Paris, 5 July 2000)
- Summary of Observations by States on the Draft Convention on the Protection of Underwater Cultural Heritage, Paris, April 2000 (UNESCO doc. CLT-2000/CONF.201/3)]

The ILA draft included a provision establishing penal sanctions for importation of underwater cultural heritage illegally excavated and international co-operation in their enforcement. The first UNESCO/DOALOS draft enlarged the concept of sanctions, including also administrative sanctions. During the 1998 Meeting of Experts some delegates asked for the inclusion of civil sanctions too; the United States considered that the co-operation in the field of extradition, mentioned in the second paragraph, could raise many difficulties. Accordingly, the second UNESCO draft added the civil sanctions in square brackets and deleted the list of possible forms of co-operation among States. The SNT also put into square brackets the criminal and administrative measures.

The issue was fully considered only at the last Meeting. Italy was not completely satisfied with the draft. It asked for a provision indicating the severity of the sanction. Then France proposed the following:

> Each State Party undertakes to define and implement the sanctions it shall impose on all conducts contrary to the present Convention such that those sanctions be sufficiently dissuasive in accordance with the domestic legislation.

The plenary preferred a provision – which became para. 2 of Art. 17 – taken from the Norwegian proposal on national and flag State jurisdiction (*WP 2*). Para. 1 of the SNT was approved without any indication of the type of sanctions. Para. 2 was adopted with few linguistic changes.

Article 18 – Seizure and Disposition of Underwater Cultural Heritage

1. Each State Party shall take measures providing for the seizure of underwater cultural heritage in its territory that has been recovered in a manner not in conformity with this Convention.
2. Each State Party shall record, protect and take all reasonable measures to stabilise underwater cultural heritage seized under this Convention.
3. Each State Party shall notify any seizure of underwater cultural heritage that it has made under this Convention to the Director-General and to any other State with a verifiable link, especially a cultural, historical or archaeological link, to the heritage concerned.

4. A State Party which has seized underwater cultural heritage shall ensure that its disposition be for the public benefit, taking into account the need for conservation and research; the need for re-assembly of a dispersed collection; the need for public access, exhibition and education; and the interests of any State with a verifiable link, especially a cultural, historical or archaeological link, to the heritage concerned.

[Preparatory documents:
a) Working Papers:
  - Comments of the United States of America on UNESCO Draft Convention on the Protection of the Underwater Cultural Heritage (April 1999)
b) Drafts:
  - ILA draft (Art. 10)
  - first UNESCO/DOALOS draft (Art. 9 and 12)
  - second UNESCO draft (Art. 9 and 12)
  - SNT (Art. 17)
c) Other documents:
  - Final Report of the First Meeting of Governmental Experts on the Draft Convention on the Protection of Underwater Cultural Heritage, Paris, 29 June–2 July 1998 (UNESCO doc. CLT-98/CONF.202/7), para. XIV and 29-31
  - Summary of Observations by States on the Draft Convention on the Protection of Underwater Cultural Heritage, Paris, April 2000 (UNESCO doc. CLT-2000/CONF.201/3)
  - Final Report of the Third Meeting of Governmental Experts on the Draft Convention on the Protection of Underwater Cultural Heritage, Paris, 3–7 July 2000, Annex II, Working Group 2 (UNESCO doc. CLT-2000/CONF.201/8 rev., Paris, 5 July 2000)]

Like the ILA draft, also the first UNESCO/DOALOS draft included a provision on the seizure of the underwater cultural heritage. Moreover it added an article on its ultimate disposition for the public benefit. Art. 9 reads as follows:

1. Subject to Article 8, each State Party shall provide for the seizure of underwater cultural heritage excavated or retrieved in a manner not in conformity with the operative provisions of the Charter, which is brought to its territory, either directly or indirectly.
2. A State Party shall seize underwater cultural heritage known to have been excavated or retrieved from the exclusive economic zone or the continental shelf of another State Party exercising control of those areas in accordance with Article 5 paragraphs 2 to 5 above only after the request or with the consent of that State.

Art. 12 dealt with the disposition of the underwater cultural heritage for the public benefit:

1. A State Party which has seized underwater cultural heritage shall decide on its ultimate disposition for the public benefit taking into account the needs for

conservation and research, including the need for reassembly of a dispersed collection, as well as public access, exhibition and education, and the interests of those States which have expressed a national heritage interest in it.

2. States Parties shall provide for the non-application of any internal law or regulation having the effect of providing commercial incentives for the excavation and removal of underwater cultural heritage.

According to the comment provided by UNESCO to this provision, para. 1 was based on Art. 149 UNCLOS (preservation of the underwater cultural heritage for the benefit of humankind), avoiding its ambiguous wording.

At the first Meeting of Experts Art. 9 was considered satisfactory while Art. 12 was confusing (no indication of the location of the underwater cultural heritage concerned; public benefit which does not coincide with benefit of mankind, etc.). In the second draft, Art. 9, para. 2 was put into square brackets. In Art. 12, para. 1, a final phrase was added coming back to the "ambiguous" language of Art. 149 UNCLOS: "pursuant the preferential rights as State of origin, State of cultural origin, or State of historical and archaeological origin". Para. 2 was considered to be deleted because it was included among the general principles.

At the third Meeting the two provisions were merged and changed and subsequently almost identically inserted into the SNT. Art. 17 of the SNT was then debated at the last Meeting of Experts where it was decided only to delete a redundant sentence of the first paragraph and to entirely adopt it.

However a remark made by the Italian delegation deserves some attention. It concerns para. 4. Italy pointed out that – as it was – it could be contrary to the provisions of the 1970 UNESCO Convention on the Means of Prohibiting and Preventing the Illicit Import, Export and Transfer of Ownership of Cultural Property. If a looter exports an illegally excavated object into another State Party, according to Art. 18 this State Party must seize it and dispose of it for the public benefit. The Convention does not say – as it would be right – that the object must be returned to the State where it was originally located. Italy also argued that the provision was potentially conflicting with the scheme of protection elaborated in Art. 9-10 of the Convention: in the case of a statue of State A located on the continental shelf of State B and illegally exported to State C, there should be consultations among A, B and C, under the coordination of B. Therefore Italy suggested adding at the beginning of para. 4 the following: "Without prejudice of the States having a verifiable link".[108] The Chairman was contrary to this suggestion and the proposal was dropped. The text remained unchanged.

Article 19 – Cooperation and Information-sharing

1. States Parties shall cooperate and assist each other in the protection and management of underwater cultural heritage under this Convention, includ-

[108] According to Art. 149 of UNCLOS, States having a verifiable link with the heritage concerned, have preferential rights – not simple interests, as mentioned in Art. 18, para. 4 of the UNESCO Convention.

ing, where practicable, collaborating in the investigation, excavation, documentation, conservation, study and presentation of such heritage.

2. To the extent compatible with the purposes of this Convention, each State Party undertakes to share information with other States Parties concerning underwater cultural heritage, including discovery of heritage, location of heritage, heritage excavated or recovered contrary to this Convention or otherwise in violation of international law, pertinent scientific methodology and technology, and legal developments relating to heritage.
3. Information shared between States Parties, or between UNESCO and States Parties, regarding the discovery or location of underwater cultural heritage shall, to the extent compatible with their national legislation, be kept confidential and reserved to competent authorities of States Parties as long as the disclosure of such information might endanger or otherwise put at risk the preservation of such underwater cultural heritage.
4. Each State Party shall take all practicable measures to disseminate information, including where feasible through appropriate international databases, about underwater cultural heritage excavated or recovered contrary to this Convention or otherwise in violation of international law.

[Preparatory documents:

a) Comments by States:
   - Comments by the United States on SNT (unofficial)

b) Drafts:
   - ILA draft (Art. 13)
   - first UNESCO/DOALOS draft (Art. 13)
   - second UNESCO draft (Art. 13)
   - SNT (Art. 18)

c) Other documents:
   - Final Report of the First Meeting of Governmental Experts on the Draft Convention on the Protection of Underwater Cultural Heritage, Paris, 29 June–2 July 1998 (UNESCO doc. CLT-98/CONF.202/7), para. XVII
   - Summary of Observations by States on the Draft Convention on the Protection of Underwater Cultural Heritage, Paris, April 2000 (UNESCO doc. CLT-2000/CONF.201/3 Add. 2)
   - Final Report of the Third Meeting of Governmental Experts on the Draft Convention on the Protection of Underwater Cultural Heritage, Paris, 3–7 July 2000, Annex II, Working Group 2 (UNESCO doc. CLT-2000/CONF.201/8 rev., Paris, 5 July 2000)]

Art. 13 of the first UNESCO/DOALOS draft reflects the idea that an archaeological or historical object is not an object of interest for a single State. It is essential that information relating to it is widely shared by all Parties. Art. 13 was entirely based on Art. 13 of the ILA draft, with the sole exception of a reference to a "national heritage interest" replacing the "patrimonial interest". During the first Meeting of Experts ICOMOS as well as many States stressed that collaboration should not be optional but mandatory and made independent from the location of the heritage. Others pointed out that an obligation to share information as regards underwater cultural heritage located in the territorial sea could be a source of conflict. The second UNESCO draft did not change the provision. In commenting it, Poland argued that the particular position of the State of origin had to be emphasized, while the Philippines raised the problem of confidentiality in the sense that sometimes transparent information-sharing can place an artefact at risk of looting.

At the Third Meeting of Experts some substantial changes were made. The duty of co-operation, independently of the existence of a national interest, was made clearer. A new paragraph was added to take into account the possible need for confidentiality. The SNT embodied these suggestions and the text was adopted without major amendments. The United States expressed the view that the consultation scheme finally enshrined in Art. 9 and 10 (declaration of interest by those with verifiable link and consultations) should be placed within this provision. During the debate Sweden and Finland pointed out that in their national constitutions the duty to give information is a key principle and therefore para. 3 on confidentiality could create some problems. Anyway in the SNT, as well as in the final text, consistency with national legislation is taken into account.

Article 20 – Public Awareness

Each State Party shall take all practicable measures to raise public awareness regarding the value and significance of underwater cultural heritage and the importance of protecting it under this Convention.

[Preparatory documents:

a) Comments by States:
   - Comments of the United States of America on UNESCO Draft Convention on the Protection of the Underwater Cultural Heritage (April 1999)

b) Drafts:
   - ILA draft (Art. 14)
   - first UNESCO/DOALOS draft (Art. 15)
   - second UNESCO draft (Art. 15)
   - SNT (Art. 19)

c) Other documents:
   - Final Report of the First Meeting of Governmental Experts on the Draft Convention on the Protection of Underwater Cultural Heritage, Paris, 29 June–2 July 1998, UNESCO doc. CLT-98/CONF.202/7, para. 41 and 44
   - Summary of Observations by States on the Draft Convention on the Protection of Underwater Cultural Heritage, Paris, April 2000 (UNESCO doc. CLT-2000/CONF.201/3 Add. 2)
   - Final Report of the Third Meeting of Governmental Experts on the Draft Convention on the Protection of Underwater Cultural Heritage, Paris, 3–7 July 2000, Annex II, Working Group 2 (UNESCO doc. CLT-2000/CONF.201/8 rev., Paris, 5 July 2000)]

Art. 20 – which up to the very end was under the title "Education" – was considered an important provision because education is felt to be the best mean of combating vandals and looters. The provision did not pose many problems. At the first Meeting of Experts the request was made to render the role of the public more apparent, but the second draft repeated the same wording. The United States pointed out that the drafting of the provision could create problems for federal countries, because education is often a competence of federated states. On suggestion by the Philippines at the Third Meeting of Experts the importance of protecting heritage was inserted as one of the main aims to be reached through education (replacing awareness of the threat to heritage posed by violations of the Convention) and in this form it was finally adopted at the last Meeting.

Article 21 – Training in Underwater Archaeology

> States Parties shall cooperate in the provision of training in underwater archaeology, in techniques for the conservation of underwater cultural heritage and, on agreed terms, in the transfer of technology relating to underwater cultural heritage.

[Preparatory documents:

a) Working Papers:
   - Comments of the United States of America on UNESCO Draft Convention on the Protection of the Underwater Cultural Heritage (April 1999)

b) Drafts:
   - first UNESCO/DOALOS draft (Art. 16)
   - second UNESCO draft (Art. 16)
   - SNT (Art. 20)

c) Other documents:
   - Final Report of the First Meeting of Governmental Experts on the Draft Convention on the Protection of Underwater Cultural Heritage, Paris, 29 June–2 July 1998, UNESCO doc. CLT-98/CONF.202/7, para. XIV and 42 and 43
   - Summary of Observations by States on the Draft Convention on the Protection of Underwater Cultural Heritage, Paris, April 2000 (UNESCO doc. CLT-2000/CONF.201/3)
   - Final Report of the Third Meeting of Governmental Experts on the Draft Convention on the Protection of Underwater Cultural Heritage, Paris, 3–7 July 2000, Annex II, Working Group 2 (UNESCO doc. CLT-2000/CONF.201/8 rev., Paris, 5 July 2000)]

In the ILA draft there was no provision on training, but it was felt necessary by UNESCO that drafted Art. 16 as follows:

> State Parties shall take measures to further research in accordance with the operative provision of the Charter by providing training in underwater archaeological investigation and excavation methods and in techniques for the

conservation of underwater cultural heritage, or by encouraging the competent bodies or organisations to do so.

Since the first Meeting of Experts it was felt that the idea of international co-operation and transfer of technology should be incorporated: this was a sensitive point for developing countries that lack resources and know-how to implement the duty to provide training. Indeed in the second draft a second paragraph on the transfer of technology was inserted. Commenting the whole provision the United States felt that the provision was too broad for a federal State like the United States: competent bodies and organs – not States – should be encouraged to provide training. At the Third Meeting also the idea of co-operation among States on this sensitive issue was added. At the last Meeting, discussions opened on the transfer of technologies and it was decided to add that it will be made "on agreed terms", so as to take into account complex issues such as trade, patents and finance, which could not be dealt with by the UNESCO Convention.

Article 22 – Competent Authorities

1. In order to ensure the proper implementation of this Convention, States Parties shall establish competent authorities or improve the existing ones where appropriate, with the aim of providing for the establishment, maintenance and updating of an inventory of underwater cultural heritage, the effective protection, conservation, presentation and management of underwater cultural heritage, as well as research and education.
2. States Parties shall communicate to the Director-General the names and addresses of their competent authorities relating to underwater cultural heritage.

[Preparatory documents:

a) Working Papers:
   - Comments of the United States of America on UNESCO Draft Convention on the Protection of the Underwater Cultural Heritage (April 1999)

b) Drafts:
   - first UNESCO/DOALOS draft (Art. 18)
   - second UNESCO draft (Art. 18)
   - SNT (Art. 21)

c) Other documents:
   - Summary of Observations by States on the Draft Convention on the Protection of Underwater Cultural Heritage, Paris, April 2000 (UNESCO doc. CLT-2000/CONF.201/3)
   - Final Report of the Third Meeting of Governmental Experts on the Draft Convention on the Protection of Underwater Cultural Heritage, Paris, 3–7 July 2000, Annex II, Working Group 2 (UNESCO doc. CLT-2000/CONF.201/8 rev., Paris, 5 July 2000)]

The original Art. 18 of the first UNESCO/DOALOS draft, under the title

"National Services", was composed of three paragraphs. The first was about the establishment of competent national services. The second aimed at encouraging co-operation between salvors, divers and local historians. The third provided for the establishment of internal procedures for resolving disputes regarding the violation of the Charter. Because of the new approaches which were emerging during negotiations with respect to salvage law and to the settlement of disputes, it was decided to delete the second and third paragraphs. The SNT further elaborated the first paragraph, which was debated at the last Meeting. Here the Netherlands suggested making reference to the establishment of a national inventory of the underwater cultural heritage. Belgium proposed replacing "national services" by "competent authorities" and communicating the list to UNESCO.

Article 23 – Meetings of States Parties

1. The Director-General shall convene a Meeting of States Parties within one year of the entry into force of this Convention and thereafter at least once every two years. At the request of a majority of States Parties, the Director-General shall convene an Extraordinary Meeting of States Parties.
2. The Meeting of States Parties shall decide on its functions and responsibilities.
3. The Meeting of States Parties shall adopt its own Rules of Procedure.
4. The Meeting of States Parties may establish a Scientific and Technical Advisory Body composed of experts nominated by the States Parties with due regard to the principle of equitable geographical distribution and the desirability of a gender balance.
5. The Scientific and Technical Advisory Body shall appropriately assist the Meeting of States Parties in questions of a scientific or technical nature regarding the implementation of the Rules.

Article 24 – Secretariat for this Convention

1. The Director-General shall be responsible for the functions of the Secretariat for this Convention.
2. The duties of the Secretariat shall include:
   a) organizing Meetings of States Parties as provided for in Article 23 paragraph 1; and
   b) assisting States Parties in implementing the decisions of the Meetings of States Parties.

[Preparatory documents:

a) Working Papers:
   - Comments of the United States of America on UNESCO Draft Convention on the Protection of the Underwater Cultural Heritage (April 1999)

b) Drafts:
   - first UNESCO/DOALOS draft (Art. 17)
   - second UNESCO draft (Art. 17)

- SNT (Art. 22 and 23 alternative; Art. 22-23 Chairman's proposal; Art. 24)

c) Other documents:
   - Summary of Observations by States on the Draft Convention on the Protection of Underwater Cultural Heritage, Paris, April 2000 (UNESCO doc. CLT-2000/CONF.201/3)
   - Final Report of the Third Meeting of Governmental Experts on the Draft Convention on the Protection of Underwater Cultural Heritage, Paris, 3–7 July 2000, Annex II, Working Group 2 (UNESCO doc. CLT-2000/CONF.201/8 rev., Paris, 5 July 2000)]

The institutional issues are commented together here because they were negotiated as a whole.

The first UNESCO/DOALOS draft, as well as the second draft, did not really present an institutional framework for the Convention. Art. 17 was titled "Assistance of UNESCO"; based on a similar provision of other UNESCO Conventions, it considered the possibility for States Parties to call upon the UNESCO for technical assistance or in connection with any other problem arising out of the application of the Convention; UNESCO was also allowed to conduct research and studies on relevant matters. Spain asked for UNESCO to inform States Parties on activities directed at underwater cultural heritage and to help in finding out verifiable links. Egypt and the United States felt unsatisfied with this Provision because UNESCO is considered as a Party to the Convention while this is open only to States.

The SNT radically changed Art. 17. It was transformed into Art. 24 ("Secretariat to the Convention") and two other articles were added, respectively about the "Meeting of States Parties" (Art. 22) and a "Scientific and Technical Advisory Body" (Art. 23). Two alternative texts were provided for Art. 22 and 23. The first was more detailed, with a long list of the functions of the Meeting of the States Parties. After an intensive debate at the fourth Meeting the second alternative – proposed by the Chairman – was preferred but with a relevant amendment. Most States wondered whether the Scientific and Technical Committee was really necessary and, at Italy's suggestion, it was decided to add two paragraphs in Art. 23: the Meeting of States Parties will decide whether to establish it. At the request of some delegations it was made clear that this technical committee will have an advisory – and not an executive – role. Norway asked for a guarantee of equitable geographical and gender balance among their members. ICOMOS stressed the importance that the members of the committee, even if nominated by States, are experts in underwater archaeology and not politicians: they will have a key role in evaluating reports received by UNESCO.

Art. 24 of the SNT, concerning the Secretariat of the Convention, was adopted without changes.

Article 25 – Peaceful Settlement of Disputes

1. Any dispute between two or more States Parties concerning the interpretation

or application of this Convention shall be subject to negotiations in good faith or other peaceful means of settlement of their own choice.

2. If those negotiations do not settle the dispute within a reasonable period of time, it may be submitted to UNESCO for mediation, by agreement between the States Parties concerned.
3. If mediation is not undertaken or if there is no settlement by mediation, the provisions relating to the settlement of disputes set out in Part XV of the United Nations Convention on the Law of the Sea apply *mutatis mutandis* to any dispute between States Parties to this Convention concerning the interpretation or application of this Convention, whether or not they are also Parties to the United Nations Convention on the Law of the Sea.
4. Any procedure chosen by a State Party to this Convention and to the United Nations Convention on the Law of the Sea pursuant to Article 287 of the latter shall apply to the settlement of disputes under this Article, unless that State Party, when ratifying, accepting, approving or acceding to this Convention, or at any time thereafter, chooses another procedure pursuant to Article 287 for the purpose of the settlement of disputes arising out of this Convention.
5. A State Party to this Convention which is not a Party to the United Nations Convention on the Law of the Sea, when ratifying, accepting, approving or acceding to this Convention or at any time thereafter shall be free to choose, by means of a written declaration, one or more of the means set out in Article 287 paragraph 1 of the United Nations Convention on the Law of the Sea for the purpose of settlement of disputes under this Article. Article 287 shall apply to such a declaration, as well as to any dispute to which such State is party, which is not covered by a declaration in force. For the purpose of conciliation and arbitration, in accordance with Annexes V and VII of the United Nations Convention on the Law of the Sea, such State shall be entitled to nominate conciliators and arbitrators to be included in the lists referred to in Annex V Article 2 and Annex VII Article 2 for the settlement of disputes arising out of this Convention.

[Preparatory documents:

a) Working Papers:
   - Comments of the United States of America on UNESCO Draft Convention on the Protection of the Underwater Cultural Heritage (April 1999)
   - WP6, 28 March 2001 (Proposed amendment by Egypt, Germany, Italy and Tunisia to the Informal Draft Negotiating Text)
   - WP44, 4 April 2001 (Proposed amendment by Venezuela, Turkey and Thailand to the Informal Draft Negotiating Text)
   - WP49, 3 July 2001 (Amendment proposed by Norway, supported by Germany and Italy)

b) Drafts:
   - ILA draft (Art. 16)
   - first UNESCO/DOALOS draft (Art. 19)

- second UNESCO draft (Art. 19)
- SNT (Art. 25)

c) Other documents:
- Summary of Observations by States on the Draft Convention on the Protection of Underwater Cultural Heritage, Paris, April 2000 (UNESCO doc. CLT-2000/CONF.201/3, UNESCO doc. CLT-2000/CONF.201/3 Add.2)]

Art. 16 of the ILA draft dealt with both an internal and an international procedure for dispute settlement. The latter was split into three stages: negotiations before, then arbitration; if States were unable to agree on arbitration, the International Court of Justice would have been competent to settle the dispute on demand by one of States concerned. The first UNESCO/DOALOS draft provision on dispute settlement considered only international disputes (internal disputes were dealt with in Art. 18 "National Service"); the draft was the same as the one proposed by the ILA. The text remained unchanged also in the second draft. Several comments were received by UNESCO. France, Sweden, Tunisia and the United Kingdom proposed that provisions relating to the settlement of disputes set out in Part XV of UNCLOS should apply; Egypt suggested a reference to Art. 33 of the Charter of the United Nations; for the United States the compulsory dispute settlement was unnecessary and inappropriate for this Convention; Spain was in favour of arbitration and proposed a very complex and detailed arbitration procedure. Finally, Norway suggested a provision modelled upon Art. 30 of the 1995 Straddling Stocks Agreement, which makes reference to Part. XV of UNCLOS; according to Norway's proposal, also regional agreements should use the same disputes resolution system.

The question was negotiated only at the last Meeting of Experts. The SNT suggested the following steps: negotiations, mediation by UNESCO, arbitration and, alternatively or subsequently, decision by the International Court of Justice. Venezuela, Turkey and Thailand (*WP 44*), as not Party to UNCLOS, suggested settlement by peaceful means listed in Art. 33 of the U.N. Charter. Germany, Egypt, Italy and Tunisia felt that, in cases where the mediation does not settle the dispute, Part XV of UNCLOS should apply. Subsequently Italy and Germany supported Norway in the proposal already previously presented, which, with minor changes, was adopted as the final text (with the deletion of the part relating to regional agreements). Italy felt that, due to the "constructive ambiguity" of many provisions, there was the need for a "strong" dispute settlement mechanism. Paras. 4 and 5 are taken from the 1995 Agreement, which has been ratified also by States like the United States and Canada that are not Parties to UNCLOS.

The Norwegian proposal also contained an Art. 25 *bis* dealing with provisional measures, which could be prescribed by the court or tribunal chosen under Art. 25 in order to prevent damage to the underwater cultural heritage concerned (the model was Art. 290-292 of UNCLOS). Argentina, Egypt and Belgium were contrary to this hypothesis and the provision was deleted.

Turkey and Venezuela justified their negative vote to the Convention, both at the Meeting of Experts and at the General Conference, on the system of settlement of disputes chosen: not being Parties to UNCLOS, they considered it unacceptable.

Article 26 – Ratification, Acceptance, Approval or Accession

1. This Convention shall be subject to ratification, acceptance or approval by Member States of UNESCO.
2. This Convention shall be subject to accession:
   a) by States that are not members of UNESCO but are members of the United Nations or of a specialised agency within the United Nations system or of the International Atomic Energy Agency, as well as by States Parties to the Statute of the International Court of Justice and any other State invited to accede to this Convention by the General Conference of UNESCO;
   b) by territories which enjoy full internal self-government, recognised as such by the United Nations, but have not attained full independence in accordance with General Assembly resolution 1514 (XV) and which have competence over the matters governed by this Convention, including the competence to enter into treaties in respect of those matters.
3. The instruments of ratification, acceptance, approval or accession shall be deposited with the Director-General.

[Preparatory documents:
a) Working papers:
   - WP 43, 5 April 2001 and WP 43rev., 5 July 2001 (Amendment proposed by Egypt, Yemen, the United Arab Emirates and Algeria)
b) Drafts:
   - ILA draft (Art. 18 and 21)
   - first UNESCO/DOALOS draft (Art. 20)
   - second UNESCO draft (Art. 20)
   - SNT (Art. 27)]

According to the ILA draft, not only Member States of UNESCO but also non Members – to which an entire Article was devoted (Art. 21) – could become Party to the Convention. Art. 20 of the first UNESCO/DOALOS draft considered ratification open also to both Member and non-Member States.

At the last Meeting of Experts a group of Arab States proposed an amendment whose main aim was to allow Palestine to become Party to the Convention. It was based on the precedent of UNCLOS (Art. 305, para.1, e)). Israel argued that other UNESCO Conventions were open only to Member States of UNESCO, but eventually the plenary approved the proposal put forward by the Arab States.[109]

Article 27 – Entry into Force

This Convention shall enter into force three months after the date of the deposit of the twentieth instrument referred to in Article 26, but solely with

[109] Belgium, as the State holding the presidency of the European Union, made a declaration of approval of the amendment, on behalf of the European Union and its Member States.

respect to the twenty States or territories that have so deposited their instruments. It shall enter into force for each other State or territory three months after the date on which that State or territory has deposited its instrument.

[Preparatory documents:
a) Working papers:
- WP 43, 5 April 2001 and WP 43rev., 5 July 2001 (Amendment proposed by Egypt, Yemen, the United Arab Emirates and Algeria)

b) Drafts:
- ILA draft (Art. 22)
- first UNESCO/DOALOS draft (Art. 20)
- second UNESCO draft (Art. 20)
- SNT (Art. 27)]

The only problem posed by this Article was the decision about the number of ratifications necessary for the Convention to enter into force. The ILA draft proposed ten ratifications, while the first UNESCO/DOALOS draft only five.[110] The SNT came back to the idea of ten ratifications and the same was proposed by some Arab States (*WP 43*). At the 2001 Meeting of Experts Germany, supported by the United Kingdom, the Netherlands, Norway and Sweden, felt that ten ratifications were not enough: a comparison between the UNESCO Convention and the 1995 Straddling Fish Stocks Agreement was suggested and, as their importance was considered equal, the same number of ratifications (thirty) was required. Italy and Argentina disagreed. The former argued that there is no link between the importance of a convention and the number of ratifications needed for coming into force: it is a political decision based on whether States want the convention to enter into force sooner or later on in time. Argentina expressed the view that no comparison could be made between the UNESCO Convention and the 1995 Agreement or UNCLOS, which are much more complex legal instruments. The urgency for the international community to have a convention on the underwater cultural heritage had to be considered and therefore fifteen or twenty ratifications would have been the best solution. ICOMOS made a practical consideration: as the implementation of this Convention will not be easy, it is useful that a few States start to enforce it among themselves, so as to test on a minor scale its future global implementation. At the end of this discussion the Chairman suggested the number of twenty and it was approved.

Article 28 – Declaration as to Inland Waters

When ratifying, accepting, approving or acceding to this Convention or at any time thereafter, any State or territory may declare that the Rules shall apply to inland waters not of a maritime character.

---

[110] The model was the 1954 UNESCO Convention on the Protection of Cultural Property in the Event of Armed Conflict and the UNIDROIT Convention. Both required the deposit of 5 instruments of ratification to enter into force.

[Preparatory documents:
a) Drafts:
- ILA draft (Art. 8, para.3)

b) Other documents:
- Summary of Observations by States on the Draft Convention on the Protection of Underwater Cultural Heritage, Paris, April 2000 (UNESCO doc. CLT-2000/CONF.201/3, UNESCO doc. CLT-2000/CONF.201/3 Add.)]

The origins of this provision are to be found in the SNT. In the first UNESCO/DOALOS draft, the Article concerning the scope of application of the Convention (Art. 2) did not clarify the geographical scope and Art. 4 only mentioned the internal waters, archipelagic waters and territorial sea. In the second draft, in Art. 2, it could be read in square brackets that "The Convention applies to underwater cultural heritage found at sea". Some States – not only landlocked States, like Hungary, but also coastal States such as France, Argentina and Venezuela – felt that this was an unduly narrow scope of the Convention: it should apply also to inland waters. But during the discussion there was no agreement on this point: while the inclusion of inland waters could be agreed upon by many States, some felt that the implementation of the Rules of the Annex could not be made mandatory and that States Parties should be left free to decide how to protect the underwater cultural heritage found in their inland waters. Therefore the SNT, accepting the proposal by Argentina, enshrines in Art. 8, para. 3 the possibility for a State Party to make a declaration at the time of ratification regarding this issue. At the last meeting two questions were debated. First, some confusion arose as to the exact meaning of "inland waters" with Kenya also questioning whether Lake Victoria should be considered inland or maritime waters. Second, Italy considered that obviously Art. 8, para. 3, cannot be considered as a reservation because it enlarges the scope of application of the Convention (while usually a reservation restricts it);[111] for Spain it was instead an interpretative declaration. Mexico, supported by Argentina and Spain, suggested replacing this Article in the final provisions of the Convention and this solution was approved.

Article 29 – Limitations to Geographical Scope

> At the time of ratifying, accepting, approving or acceding to this Convention, a State or territory may make a declaration to the depositary that this Convention shall not be applicable to specific parts of its territory, inland waters, internal waters, archipelagic waters or territorial sea, and shall identify therein the reasons for such declaration. Such State shall, to the extent practicable and as quickly as possible, promote conditions under which this Convention will apply to the areas specified in its declaration, and to that end shall also withdraw its declaration in whole or in part as soon as that has been achieved.

[111] For Italy, Art. 29 is clearly a reservation, the only one admitted by the treaty.

[Preparatory documents:
a) Working Papers:
- WP 48, 2 July 2001 (Amendment proposed by Canada and the United States of America)
- WP 48rev., 3 July 2001 (Amendment proposed by Canada supported by Ireland and endorsed by United States of America)

b) Drafts:
- SNT (Art. 26)]

This provision replaces the so-called "federal clause" and it represents a valuable compromise reached after a longstanding debate.

It was Canada that first called for a federal clause to be inserted into the Convention. Under its federal system, some areas of its territorial sea and internal waters are within provincial jurisdiction. This is the reason why Canada is not Party to UNCLOS even though it supports most of its provisions and this problem was likely to be the same with respect to the UNESCO Convention, which deals also with internal waters and territorial sea. To answer the Canadian request, the SNT inserted a new Art. 26 titled "Federal State clause" and entirely based on Art. 34 of the UNESCO World Heritage Convention. In summary, according to this provision, federal States simply had the obligation to inform their individual units of the provisions of the Convention, with the recommendation to ratify it.

Art. 26 met with the strong opposition of some unitary States. As pointed out by Italy, according to the Vienna Convention when a State ratifies an international treaty it engages all its territory. At the international level engagements are taken by sovereign States and they do not change according to domestic constitutional arrangements. The share of competence between the federation and the federated units is a mere internal problem. According to Italy Art. 26 was *de facto* a reservation, incompatible with the object and the purpose of the Convention. An example was given to support this argument: while it was decided to ban salvage law, a federal State would have still been able to apply it on its continental shelf and, even worse, the high seas and the continental shelf of other States, as it was merely in the obligation of recommending to its federated states to ratify the Convention. Other States, such as Spain, France and the Russian Federation, supported Italy. If federal States were not able to bind themselves for the whole of their territory, as other States do, they must be replaced in the negotiations by their federated entities. The United States made an alternative proposal: a declaration at the time of ratification by which a State could decide that in its internal waters, archipelagic waters and territorial sea the Convention will be applied according to the domestic legislation. This was considered by some delegations even worse than Art. 26, in that international law would have to be adapted to domestic legislation rather than the opposite.

Canada was genuinely engaged in this Convention and it even belonged to those like-minded countries that looked for an effective regime of protection of underwater cultural heritage. Therefore it was really interested in finding a compromise which would make it possible for it to ratify the Convention. Together with the United States Canada suggested the following provision (*WP 48*):

> At the time of ratifying, accepting, approving or acceding to this Convention, a State may declare that the Convention shall not be applicable to specific parts of its territory, internal waters or territorial sea. This declaration may be withdrawn in whole or in part at any time.

It was subsequently improved with the support of Ireland (*WP 48rev.*):

> At the time of ratifying, accepting, approving or acceding to this Convention, a State may declare that the Convention shall not be applicable to specific parts of its territory, internal waters or territorial sea, and shall identify the reasons for such declaration. Such State shall, to the extent practicable, and as quickly as possible, promote conditions under which the Convention will apply to the areas specified in its declaration and to that end, may withdraw its declaration in whole or in part at any time.

This was considered a good compromise in that it did not concern only federal States, but any State; the declaration must be justified; and it did not concern the continental shelf and the exclusive economic zone. A further change was made in order to guarantee a rapid withdrawal of the declaration.

At the beginning it was proposed to insert this provision into the Article on ratification. Spain disagreed because in any international treaty a reservation has never been placed within the provision on ratification and it suggested putting it in the Article on reservations. Finally an autonomous Article was preferred (under a new title), placed before the one on reservations.

Article 30 – Reservations

> With the exception of Article 29, no reservations may be made to this Convention.

[Preparatory documents:

a) Comments by States:
   - Comments of the United States of America on UNESCO Draft Convention on the Protection of the Underwater Cultural Heritage (April 1999)

b) Drafts:
   - ILA draft (Art. 20)
   - first UNESCO/DOALOS draft (Art. 21)
   - second UNESCO draft (ART. 21)
   - SNT (Art. 28)]

The ILA draft allowed States Parties to make reservations. Not so the UNESCO drafts. At the last Meeting of Experts Turkey, the United States and the Russian Federation – which objected on different substantive provisions of the draft – called for the admissibility of reservations. Italy, supported by several delegations (Greece, Egypt, France, Belgium, Spain) argued that any reservation to this Convention – which was mainly negotiated as a package – could seriously jeopardise the regime of protection of underwater cultural heritage (that was particularly true for a possible reservation concerning the applicability of salvage law). As the so-called federal clause was a reservation, the solution was to ban any reservation with the exception of Art. 29. It was finally so agreed.

Article 31 – Amendments

1. A State Party may, by written communication addressed to the Director-General, propose amendments to this Convention. The Director-General shall circulate such communication to all States Parties. If, within six months from the date of the circulation of the communication, not less than one half of the States Parties reply favourably to the request, the Director-General shall present such proposal to the next Meeting of States Parties for discussion and possible adoption.
2. Amendments shall be adopted by a two-thirds majority of States Parties present and voting.
3. Once adopted, amendments to this Convention shall be subject to ratification, acceptance, approval or accession by the States Parties.
4. Amendments shall enter into force, but solely with respect to the States Parties that have ratified, accepted, approved or acceded to them, three months after the deposit of the instruments referred to in paragraph 3 of this Article by two-thirds of the States Parties. Thereafter, for each State or territory that ratifies, accepts, approves or accedes to it, the amendment shall enter into force three months after the date of deposit by that State Party of its instrument of ratification, acceptance, approval or accession.
5. A State or territory which becomes party to this Convention after the entry into force of amendments in conformity with paragraph 4 of this Article shall, failing an expression of different intention by that State or territory, be considered:
   a) as party to this Convention as so amended; and
   b) as party to the unamended Convention in relation to any State Party not bound by the amendment.

[Preparatory documents:

a) Comments by States:
   - Comments of the United States of America on UNESCO Draft Convention on the Protection of the Underwater Cultural Heritage (April 1999)

b) Drafts:
   - ILA draft (Art. 15)
   - first UNESCO/DOALOS draft (Art. 22)
   - second UNESCO draft (Art. 22)
   - SNT (Art. 29)

c) Other documents
   - Final Report of the Third Meeting of Governmental Experts on the Draft Convention on the Protection of Underwater Cultural Heritage, Paris, 3-7

July 2000, Annex III, Working Group 3 (UNESCO doc. CLT-2000/CONF.201/10, Paris, 5 July 2000)]

The ILA draft established a specific provision for the revision of the ICOMOS Charter, subject to specific objections by States Parties. In the first UNESCO/DOALOS draft instead a long Article on amendment of the whole Convention was inserted. In the second UNESCO draft a specific paragraph was devoted to the amendments of the Charter, which could be proposed by ICOMOS and adopted according to a less complex procedure. This was deleted in the SNT, which took into account the new institutional arrangements included in the Convention. Some States contested the quorum of two thirds of States Parties to adopt amendments and suggested an adoption by *consensus*, as is the case in the 1995 Straddling Fish Stocks Agreement. Others made opposite criticisms: it was felt quite strange that, while the simple majority is sufficient to adopt the whole Convention, a qualified majority is needed to adopt amendments. Italy and Argentina refused any comparison with the 1995 Agreement as this was to be considered a treaty independent from UNCLOS. Moreover *consensus* would have meant a sort of power of veto for each State Party. Finally the majority of two thirds was retained.

Article 32 – Denunciation

1. A State Party may, by written notification addressed to the Director-General, denounce this Convention.
2. The denunciation shall take effect twelve months after the date of receipt of the notification, unless the notification specifies a later date.
3. The denunciation shall not in any way affect the duty of any State Party to fulfil any obligation embodied in this Convention to which it would be subject under international law independently of this Convention.

This is a standard provision which did not raise any problem.

Article 33 – The Rules

The Rules annexed to this Convention form an integral part of it and, unless expressly provided otherwise, a reference to this Convention includes a reference to the Rules.

[Preparatory documents:
a) Working Papers:
 - WP 20, 29 March 2001

b) Drafts:
 - first UNESCO/DOALOS draft (Art. 24)
 - second UNESCO draft (Art. 24)
 - SNT (Art. 31)

c) Other documents:
 - Preliminary Study on the Advisability of Preparing an International

Instrument for the Protection of the Underwater Cultural Heritage, Paris, 4 October 1995 (UNESCO doc. 29C/39), paras. 36-38

- Feasibility Study for the Drafting of a New Instrument for the Protection of the Underwater Cultural Heritage, Paris, 23 March 1995 (UNESCO doc. 146 EX/27), paras. 35-37
- Report of the Meeting of Experts for the Draft Convention on the Protection of Underwater Cultural Heritage, Paris, 22–24 May 1996 (UNESCO doc. CLT-96/CONF.605/6), paras. 57-66
- Final Report of the Third Meeting of Governmental Experts on the Draft Convention on the Protection of Underwater Cultural Heritage, Paris, 3–7 July 2000, Annex III, Working Group 3 (UNESCO doc. CLT-2000/ CONF.201/10, Paris, 5 July 2000)]

The ILA draft incorporated by reference the ICOMOS International Charter on the Protection and Management of Underwater Cultural Heritage, adopted in Sofia in 1996. The Charter set out standards for the proper handling of the underwater cultural heritage. Since the Preliminary Study on the Advisability of Preparing an International Convention UNESCO had taken into account the solution adopted by the ILA draft. At the Meeting of Experts of 1996 some argued that the ICOMOS Charter was a good basis but not all the principles had the appropriate normative shape of obligations between States and that some principles were rather in terms that would work between individuals, groups or governmental bodies. Besides that, two alternatives were considered: to incorporate the ICOMOS principles into the body of the Convention or to present them as an Annex to the Convention, allowing modification of these principles as archaeological practices evolved. Another problem raised was whether those standards should be binding or not for States.

Art. 24 of the first UNESCO/DOALOS draft considered the Charter as an Annex to the Convention and, at the same time, an integral part of it. The amendment procedure for the Annex would be simplified with comparison to the rest of the Convention. The second Meeting of Experts decided that it was more appropriate to take the general standards of the Charter, rather than its complete text, and formulate a set of Rules which could be annexed to the Convention. A Working Group was established to produce a draft Annex.

At the Third Meeting of Experts an *ad hoc* Working Group 3 – chaired by Mr. Kirwan (Ireland) – was created in order to negotiate the Rules. The Group decided by *consensus* that the Annex should form an integral part of the Convention. Art. 31 of the SNT enshrined this principle which was unanimously adopted by the plenary at the Fourth Meeting. As a consequence, the term "Convention" means the Convention *and* its Annex and the Annex will be amended according to the same procedure established for the rest of the Convention.

The proposal by the Chairman (*WP 20*) to apply the Rules of the Annex to underwater cultural heritage with regard to the cultural significance of the heritage was rejected.[112]

---

[112] See *supra*, comment on Art. 1.

Article 34 – Registration with the United Nations

> In conformity with Article 102 of the Charter of the United Nations, this Convention shall be registered with the Secretariat of the United Nations at the request of the Director-General.

Article 35 – Authoritative Texts

> This Convention has been drawn up in Arabic, Chinese, English, French, Russian and Spanish, the six texts being equally authoritative.

These are standard provisions for conventions negotiated within the U.N. or its specialised agencies.

Some remarks can be done about the different linguistic versions.

First of all, the good work done by the Drafting Committee (chaired by Mr. Dorion, Canada) in a short time[113] and with a very complex text must be acknowledged. Nevertheless, some discrepancies remain between the linguistic versions of the Convention. The discrepancies between the English and the French texts are analysed here. The most evident one is in Art. 28: while in the English text this provision is correctly titled "Declaration as to *inland* waters", the French text is "Déclaration relative aux eaux *continentales*". The expression "eaux continentales" is not legally correct, as the right word is instead "eaux *internes*". This adjective is used in French also with reference to inland waters, that is to say waters of non-maritime character.

A second example of problematic translation can be found in paras. 6 and 7 of Art. 1, dealing with definitions. In English the expressions "activities directed at underwater cultural heritage" and "activities incidentally affecting underwater cultural heritage" are used. They are translated in French into "*intervention* sur le patrimoine culturel subaquatique" and "*intervention* ayant une incidence fortuite sur le patrimoine culturel subaquatique". Not only does "intervention" not seem to be the proper equivalent for "activity",[114] but Article 5 in the French version is titled "*Activités* ayant une incidence fortuite sur le patrimoine culturel subaquatique", which is therefore inconsistent with the wording used in the definition.

---

[113] Due to lack of time during the negotiations, the Drafting Committee, with the support of the UNESCO Secretariat, was not able to finalise the revision of the whole text before the end of the negotiations. Therefore, the plenary of governmental experts voted on July 7, 2001 on the text of the Convention as it resulted from the first reading (only the Annex was adopted on second reading). Then the Chairman of the plenary, Mr. Lund, asked the meeting for a mandate for the Secretariat, the Chairman and the Chairman of the Drafting Committee to finalise the Convention from a formal point of view (the other chairmen of geographical groups being informed all the time of the questions raised by the Drafting Committee). The Drafting Committee met in its plenary form from 19 to 20 July 2001 to make its recommendations to the Chairman, eventually accepted. Formal changes were therefore brought to the final text of the Convention, which was sent to the General Conference for adoption.

[114] This seems to be particularly true with reference to activities incidentally affecting underwater cultural heritage: they are not a form of "intervention" upon the archaeological object, as the French term rather suggests.

Another relevant problem – of which the Drafting Committee itself was fully aware – was the French translation of the English terms "law of salvage" and "law of finds". As already pointed out,[115] these are very well known principles in common law countries, while they are completely unfamiliar in civil law countries. That is why it was almost impossible to find the proper translation in French: the concept itself does not exist in French.[116] During the negotiations the expression "*droit de l'assistance et du sauvetage*" and "*droit des trésors* " were used. The Drafting Committee remarked that such translations were quite unsatisfactory and consulted an expert on the matter. His opinion was followed and so the final French version is "*droit de l'assistance et droit des trésors*". However in a UNESCO communication concerning the final results of the Drafting Committee it can be read: "Cependant, le Comité de rédaction a estimé important de spécifier que cette expression trouve ses origines dans le droit commun des pays anglo-saxon et n'a pas d'équivalent exact dans d'autres systèmes juridiques. Cette remarque est importante pour la traduction de ces notions en d'autres langues et pour la bonne interprétation de cette Convention qui en découlerait".

Finally, a last question can be raised. It has already been said that Art. 9, para. 1, (b) (ii) on notification of the discovery of an object on the continental shelf was ambiguously drafted and it leaves room for very different interpretations to the ones the original drafters intended.[117] Since most debates, proposals, materials etc. were made in English, this provision, like most of the others, was originally drafted in English. It is thus obvious that, even if it was evident that the provision was ambiguously drafted, the French translation could not but literally follow the original English. As a consequence, also in the French version, the possessive adjectives are omitted and an interpretation favourable to the coastal State is therefore allowed (but not in good faith).

---

[115] See *supra*, comments on Art. 4.

[116] The UNCLOS dealt with the same problem in Art. 303, para. 3. The English expression "law of salvage and other rules of admiralty" was translated into "droit de récupérer des épaves et autres règles du droit maritime".

[117] See *supra*, comment on Art. 9.

ANNEX
RULES CONCERNING ACTIVITIES DIRECTED AT UNDERWATER CULTURAL HERITAGE[118]

[Preparatory documents:[119]

a) Drafts:
   - second UNESCO draft
   - SNT

b) Other documents:
   - Summary of Observations by States on the Draft Convention on the Protection of Underwater Cultural Heritage, Paris, April 2000 (UNESCO doc. CLT-2000/CONF.201/3; UNESCO doc. CLT-2000/CONF.201/3 Add. and UNESCO doc. CLT-2000/CONF.201/3 Add. 2)
   - Final Report of the Third Meeting of Governmental Experts on the Draft Convention on the Protection of Underwater Cultural Heritage, Paris, 3–7 July 2000, Annex III, Working Group 3 (UNESCO doc. CLT-2000/CONF.201/10, Paris, 5 July 2000)]

I. General Principles

Rule 1. The protection of underwater cultural heritage through *in situ* preservation shall be considered as the first option. Accordingly, activities directed at underwater cultural heritage shall be authorised in a manner consistent with the protection of that heritage, and subject to that requirement may be authorised for the purpose of making a significant contribution to protection or knowledge or enhancement of underwater cultural heritage.

Rule 1 is one among the few (together with Rules 2, 7 and 34) that was not adopted by *consensus* within Working Group 3 of the Third Meeting of Experts and therefore needed further consideration and adoption at the Fourth Meeting. The main issue was that some States felt that it is not always possible to preserve an object *in situ*. However, while according to the draft it "*should be* considered as the first option", in the final text adopted it "*shall be* considered as the first option", as suggested by the SNT.

Rule 2. The commercial exploitation of underwater cultural heritage for trade or speculation or its irretrievable dispersal is fundamentally incompatible with the

[118] As mentioned above, at the second Meeting of Experts it was decided not to annexe the ICOMOS Charter – as it was – to the Convention, but to use its principles as a reference, to re-draft them in a manner appropriate to an international instrument binding on States and to include such Rules in an Annex which is part of the Convention. Therefore it is only from the second UNESCO draft onwards that the draft rules were annexed to the Convention.

[119] The preparatory documents are the same for all the rules and therefore indicated only once at the beginning of the commentary. If a specific Working Paper was produced with reference to a rule, it is indicated when commenting that rule.

protection and proper management of underwater cultural heritage. Underwater cultural heritage shall not be traded, sold, bought or bartered as commercial goods.

This Rule cannot be interpreted as preventing:

a) the provision of professional archaeological services or necessary services incidental thereto whose nature and purpose are in full conformity with this Convention and are subject to the authorisation of the competent authorities;
b) the deposition of underwater cultural heritage, recovered in the course of a research project in conformity with this Convention, provided such deposition does not prejudice the scientific or cultural interest or integrity of the recovered material or result in its irretrievable dispersal; is in accordance with the provisions of Rules 33 and 34; and is subject to the authorisation of the competent authorities.

[Further preparatory documents:

- WP 3, 27 March 2001 (amendment presented by the United Kingdom to Annex, Rule2)
- WP 12, 28 March 2001 (Amendment proposed by Ireland and seconded by the United Kingdom)]

This Rule was one of the most controversial of the entire Annex and required intensive debate. In the second UNESCO draft it was much shorter and reads:

> The commercial exploitation of underwater cultural heritage for trade or speculation [, other than in the provision of services] or its irretrievable dispersal is fundamentally incompatible with the protection and proper management of the underwater cultural heritage. Underwater cultural heritage shall [should] not be traded, sold, bought and bartered as items of commercial value.

At the Third Meeting many delegates pointed out that it should be made clear that professional archaeological services consistent with the Convention were not being referred to in this Rule. The last sentence met with considerable opposition by some States. The United States, for example, expressed the view that only the sale of objects recovered not in accordance with the Convention should be forbidden.

The SNT enshrined not only the idea of professional archaeological services, but also of the deposition of underwater cultural heritage to a body which sponsored the project, as situations not prevented by the Rule in question.

At the Fourth Meeting the United Kingdom put forward a proposal in order to allow competent authorities of States Parties to pay a reward for recoveries made in accordance with the Annex (*WP 3*). This could have become a way to ensure that salvage law could still be applied as compatible with the Convention. Such a proposal was strongly rejected by several States (Portugal, Italy, Greece, Nigeria, Argentina, Spain), which pointed out that it could result in a dangerous incentive for treasure hunters. This was exactly the opposite of the purpose of this Convention. The United States – which felt that commercial activities should not be considered incompatible with the Convention – suggested introducing a paragraph: "Nothing in this Rule can prevent a State Party from authorising the exchange, transfer, acquisition and disposal of underwater cultural heritage in accordance with professional museum standards". All but the United Kingdom disagreed with this proposal; Spain pointed out that it could be interpreted as an authorization by UNESCO to sell artefacts and it could encourage the export of objects from developing countries to museums of developed States.

A new proposal by Ireland and supported by the United Kingdom (*WP 12*) was considered a good compromise and adopted with few amendments.

> **Rule 3.** Activities directed at underwater cultural heritage shall not adversely affect the underwater cultural heritage more than is necessary for the objectives of the project.

This Rule, so drafted in the second UNESCO draft, did not meet with any opposition.

> **Rule 4.** Activities directed at underwater cultural heritage must use non-destructive techniques and survey methods in preference to recovery of objects. If excavation or recovery is necessary for the purpose of scientific studies or for the ultimate protection of the underwater cultural heritage, the methods and techniques used must be as non-destructive as possible and contribute to the preservation of the remains.

Rule 4 was substantially agreed upon in the Third Meeting. In the Fourth Meeting it was just decided to delete a reference to the use of sampling in the first sentence.

> **Rule 5.** Activities directed at underwater cultural heritage shall avoid the unnecessary disturbance of human remains or venerated sites.

Rule 5 echoes Art. 2, para. 9, of the Convention. As it has been noted,[120] while the Article is a general principle addressed to States, Rule 5 is "an injunction to those who carry out activities directed at underwater cultural heritage". While in Art. 1 of the Convention no reference to spiritual sites was included – notwithstanding the proposal by Australia – here "venerated sites" are mentioned. New Zealand called for the duty to obtain the explicit authorization of a cultural or indigenous group when it is necessary to remove human remains or disturb holy sites, but this was not retained.

No amendments were made to the draft Rule 5 and therefore the final version is the same as in the second UNESCO draft.

> **Rule 6.** Activities directed at underwater cultural heritage shall be strictly regulated to ensure proper recording of cultural, historical and archaeological information.

No amendments were put forward concerning this Rule, which was unanimously adopted at the Third Meeting.

---

[120] O'Keefe, *supra* note 25, at 162.

> **Rule 7.** Public access to *in situ* underwater cultural heritage shall be promoted, except where such access is incompatible with protection and management.

The original draft of Rule 7 was quite different:

> Public access to conduct activities relating to underwater cultural heritage that are non-intrusive (such as photography) should, where practicable, be encouraged.

At the Third Meeting it was changed as follows:

> Public access to conduct activities relating to underwater cultural heritage and to its archaeological context that are non-intrusive and are consistent with its conservation should, where practicable, be encouraged.

Reference to the archaeological context had been requested by Italy and Greece. These States also were of the view that Rule 7 should provide for authorization requirements regarding activities relating to underwater cultural heritage, because also photographing can represent some risks for underwater object. At the Fourth Meeting the United States strongly reacted against this proposal: in its opinion, if an activity does not interfere with underwater cultural heritage, then no authorization is necessary. Ireland, Australia and the Netherlands agreed with the United States. Italy suggested a compromise: to add at the end of the paragraph "under appropriate control of the competent authorities on condition that these activities are non-intrusive to this heritage and are consistent with its conservation". Norway argued that such strict control over all types of activity was too burdensome to enforce along its 2,000 km coastline. The United States could accept only a principle encouraging public access, without any conditions. The ICOMOS suggested a new formula which was eventually unanimously accepted.

> **Rule 8.** International cooperation in the conduct of activities directed at underwater cultural heritage shall be encouraged in order to further the effective exchange or use of archaeologists and other relevant professionals.

Rule 8 was originally Rule 36 in the second UNESCO draft. A footnote indicated that it had to be decided whether this principle should be enshrined in the body of the Convention or remain within the Annex. A provision on international co-operation was eventually inserted into the text of the Convention (Art. 19), but despite this at the Third Meeting it was agreed that Rule 36 should be kept in the Annex but placed among the general principles. It became Rule 8.

II. Project Design

> **Rule 9.** Prior to any activity directed at underwater cultural heritage, a project design for the activity shall be developed and submitted to the competent authorities for authorisation and appropriate peer review.

This Rule was accepted as originally drafted.

Rule 10. The project design shall include:

a) an evaluation of previous or preliminary studies;
b) the project statement and objectives;
c) the methodology to be used and the techniques to be employed;
d) the anticipated funding;
e) an expected timetable for completion of the project;
f) the composition of the team and the qualifications, responsibilities and experience of each team member;
g) plans for post-fieldwork analysis and other activities;
h) a conservation programme for artefacts and the site in close cooperation with the competent authorities;
i) a site management and maintenance policy for the whole duration of the project;
j) a documentation programme;
k) a safety policy;
l) an environmental policy;
m) arrangements for collaboration with museums and other institutions, in particular scientific institutions;
n) report preparation;
o) deposition of archives, including underwater cultural heritage removed; and
p) a programme for publication.

Letters a) and b) of the original draft read as follows: "a) proposals for, or results of, all preliminary work as appropriate; b) the objective of the project". The new language was suggested by the Netherlands, Portugal and ICOMOS. Upon proposal by Australia letter l) on the environmental policy was added to the original draft.

Rule 11. Activities directed at underwater cultural heritage shall be carried out in accordance with the project design approved by the competent authorities.

No changes were made to this Rule during negotiations.

Rule 12. Where unexpected discoveries are made or circumstances change, the project design shall be reviewed and amended with the approval of the competent authorities.

No changes were made to this Rule during negotiations.

Rule 13. In cases of urgency or chance discoveries, activities directed at the underwater cultural heritage, including conservation measures or activities for a period of short duration, in particular site stabilisation, may be authorized in the absence of a project design in order to protect the underwater cultural heritage.

Only minor wording changes were made to this Rule in comparison with the original version. It can be mentioned that in the SNT a new Rule had been inserted before this, reading as follows: "In the case of a preliminary survey, activities directed at underwater cultural heritage for a period of short duration may be authorized in the absence of a project design". At the Fourth Meeting of Experts *consensus* was reached to delete this provision.

III. Preliminary Work

Rule 14. The preliminary work referred to in Rule 10 (a) shall include an assessment that evaluates the significance and vulnerability of the underwater cultural heritage and the surrounding natural environment to damage by the proposed project, and the potential to obtain data that would meet the project objectives.

With respect to the original draft, only the adjective "scientific" before "significance" has been deleted. The rest is unchanged.

Rule 15. The assessment shall also encompass background studies of available historical and archaeological evidence, the archaeological and environmental characteristics of the site, and the consequences of any potential intrusion for the long-term stability of the underwater cultural heritage affected by the activities.

No changes were made to this Rule during negotiations.

IV. Project Objective, Methodology and Techniques

Rule 16. The methodology shall comply with the project objectives and the techniques employed shall be as non-intrusive as possible.

Rule 16 was adopted without any changes.

V. Funding

Rule 17. Except in cases of emergency to protect underwater cultural heritage, an adequate funding base shall be assured in advance of any activity, sufficient to complete all stages of the project design, including conservation, documentation and curation of recovered artefacts, and report preparation and dissemination.

In the original draft, the first clause was in square brackets and the option was left open between "shall/should" in the second line. At the Third Meeting it was decided to accept the words in square brackets and to make the granting of funds mandatory.

Rule 18. The project design shall exhibit demonstrated ability, such as securing a bond, to fund the project through to completion.

No changes were made to this Rule during negotiations.

Rule 19. The project design shall include a contingency plan that will ensure conservation of underwater cultural heritage and supporting documentation in the event of any interruption of anticipated funding.

Rule 19 was adopted without any changes.

In the original draft a further paragraph was included as Rule 19: "Project funding shall [should] not require the sale, acquisition or barter of underwater cultural heritage". It disappeared in the SNT and the final text.

VI. Project Duration – Timetable

Rule 20. An adequate timetable shall be developed to assure in advance of any activity directed at underwater cultural heritage the completion of all stages of the project design, including conservation, documentation and curation of recovered underwater cultural heritage, as well as report preparation and dissemination.

Rule 20 was adopted without any changes.

Rule 21. The project design shall include a contingency plan that will ensure conservation of underwater cultural heritage and supporting documentation in the event of any interruption in or termination of the project.

Rule 21 was unanimously adopted as drafted in the original version.

VII. Competence and Qualifications

Rule 22. Activities directed at underwater cultural heritage shall only be undertaken under the direction and control of, and in the regular presence of, a qualified underwater archaeologist with scientific competence appropriate to the project.

The original draft left the choice between "the control/the presence". At the Third Meeting both options were accepted.

Rule 23. All persons on the project team shall be qualified and have demonstrated competence appropriate to their project roles.

No changes were made to this Rule.

VIII. Conservation and Site Management

Rule 24. The conservation programme shall provide for the treatment of the archaeological remains during the activities directed at underwater cultural heritage, during transit and in the long term. Conservation shall be carried out in accordance with current professional standards.

Rule 25. The site management programme shall provide for the protection and management *in situ* of underwater cultural heritage, in the course of and upon termination of fieldwork. The programme shall include public information, reasonable provision for site stabilisation, monitoring, and protection against interference.

IX. Documentation

Rule 26. The documentation programme shall set out thorough documentation including a progress report of activities directed at underwater cultural heritage, in accordance with current professional standards of archaeological documentation.

Rule 27. Documentation shall include, at a minimum, a comprehensive record of the site, including the provenance of underwater cultural heritage moved or removed in the course of the activities directed at underwater cultural heritage, field notes, plans, drawings, sections, and photographs or recording in other media.

X. Safety

Rule 28. A safety policy shall be prepared that is adequate to ensure the safety and health of the project team and third parties and that is in conformity with any applicable statutory and professional requirements.

All the three chapters (VIII, IX and X) were adopted by *consensus* without any amendment to the original draft.

XI. Environment

Rule 29. An environmental policy shall be prepared that is adequate to ensure that the seabed and marine life are not unduly disturbed.

This chapter and Rule 29 are the consequence of the insertion of letter l) in Rule 10, upon request by Australia.

XII. Reporting

Rule 30. Interim and final reports shall be made available according to the timetable set out in the project design, and deposited in relevant public records.

No changes were made to the original draft.

Rule 31. Reports shall include:
a) an account of the objectives;
b) an account of the methods and techniques employed;
c) an account of the results achieved;
d) basic graphic and photographic documentation on all phases of the activity;
e) recommendations concerning conservation and curation of the site and of any underwater cultural heritage removed; and
f) recommendations for future activities.

Letter d) was in square brackets in the original draft and placed as letter f). At the Third Meeting of Experts, the Working Group 3 decided to retain the text and to replace it.

XIII. Curation of Project Archives

Rule 32. Arrangements for curation of the project archives shall be agreed to before any activity commences, and shall be set out in the project design.

This Rule was adopted without any amendment, but it was replaced as originally it was the second Rule of this chapter on curation of project archives.

Rule 33. The project archives, including any underwater cultural heritage removed and a copy of all supporting documentation shall, as far as possible, be kept together and intact as a collection in a manner that is available for professional and public access as well as for the curation of the archives. This should be done as rapidly as possible and in any case not later than 10 years from the completion of the project, in so far as may be compatible with conservation of the underwater cultural heritage.

The original draft read as follows:

The project archives, including any underwater cultural heritage removed and a copy of all supporting documentation, should [shall], as far as possible, be kept together and intact as a collection in a manner that can [be available] provide for scientific and public access as well as for the curation of the archives [within at least five years of the completion of the archaeological fieldwork].

At the Third Meeting of Experts the Chairman of Working Group 3 suggested retaining "shall" and changing the last sentence as follows: "as rapidly as possible and not later than 10 years; in so far as may be compatible with [intellectual property rights and] conservation of underwater cultural heritage". Redrafting the Rule, the SNT deleted the reference to intellectual property rights, but this change was not specifically approved by the plenary during the Fourth Meeting.

Rule 34. The project archives shall be managed according to international professional standards, and subject to the authorisation of the competent authorities.

[Further preparatory documents:
- WP 11, 20 March 2001 (Amendment of Annex, proposed by Ireland and seconded by Canada)]

In the original draft this Rule read as follows:

The project archive shall be prepared according to current professional standards.

At the Third Meeting of Experts some delegations were of the opinion that this text should be replaced by a text which would provide for the application of internationally accepted professional standards and would permit deaccessioning consistent with such standards. The United States and the United Kingdom proposed the following text:

The project archive shall be prepared according to current international accepted professional standards, such as the International Council of Museums Code of Ethics, and may permit deaccessioning consistent with those standards.

The SNT drafted a new text:

De-accessioning of elements of the project archive may be allowed by competent authorities of a State Party, provided that it takes place in full conformity with internationally recognised museum standards, and that it is not used, directly or indirectly, as a means of project funding except as may be allowed under Rule 2.

Nothing in this Rule shall impose any obligation on States Parties to permit de-accessioning contrary to their domestic legislation or practice.

Finally a shorter Rule was agreed upon by delegates at the Fourth Meeting.

XIV. Dissemination

Rule 35. Projects shall provide for public education and popular presentation of their results where appropriate.

At the Fourth Meeting Australia expressed the view to replace " shall " by " may ". This was not accepted, but Australia was successful in calling for "where appropriate" at the end of the sentence.

Rule 36. A final synthesis of a project shall be:

a) made public as soon as possible, having regard to the complexity of the project and the confidential or sensitive nature of the information; and
b) deposited in relevant public records.

The reference to the confidentiality and sensitive nature of the information – not present in the original draft – was introduced by an amendment of the Chairman of Working Group 3 at the Third Meeting of Experts and subsequently accepted.

Chapter 5

THE CRUCIAL COMPROMISE ON SALVAGE LAW AND THE LAW OF FINDS

*Guido Carducci**

One of the major achievements of the UNESCO *Convention on the protection of the underwater cultural heritage* (the "Convention"), adopted on 2 November 2001, is in our view the crucial compromise reached concerning salvage law and the law of finds in the field of underwater cultural heritage ("UCH"). This regime, embodied in Article 4 of the Convention, deserves to be analysed under several points of view.

1. The Regime Adopted and its Importance

One of the most crucial issues of the whole negotiations was the status, if any, to recognize in relation to UCH to two traditional maritime institutions: the law of salvage and the law of finds. While these institutions have traditionally been applied to "ordinary" objects, essentially vessels at peril as concerns the law of salvage, and sunken and abandoned vessels as concerns law of finds, their application to UCH does not go without saying.

That was clear since the beginning of the negotiations. Even before, the ILA Draft

---

* Chief, International Standards Section, Cultural Heritage Division, UNESCO. The opinions expressed in this article are not necessarily those of UNESCO and do not commit the Organization.

The Author, French Ph.D (*Docteur en droit*, University Paris II), Italian Ph.D (*Dottore di Ricerca*), Diploma, The Hague Academy of International Law (1991), Member of the ILA International Committee on Cultural Heritage Law, and of the SFDI (*Société française pour le droit international*), was Member of the Italian Delegation at the UNESCO Meetings of Experts for the elaboration of the Draft Convention (then adopted by the General Conference on 2 November 2001).

This brief article reproduces part of a more extensive study on the whole Convention: Carducci, *The Expanding Protection of the Underwater Cultural Heritage: the New UNESCO Convention Versus Existing International Law*, in Camarda & Scovazzi (eds.). *The Protection of the Underwater Cultural Heritage, Legal Aspects*, Milano, 2002, p. 135–216. A shorter article introductory to the UNESCO Convention, as a "current development" in international law, has been published in the *AJIL*, 2002.

Roberta Garabello and Tullio Scovazzi (eds.), The Protection of the Underwater Cultural Heritage, 193–206.

(1994) had excluded the application of the law of salvage to UCH.[1] At a much later stage an Italian and Greek proposal excluded the law of salvage and the law of finds from the scope of application of the Convention on UCH.[2] The majority of Delegations, which expressed their views on the issue, accepted the proposal.[3] Actually, also in domestic practice we find similar solutions. For instance, in France the Decree of 26 December 1961 on "épaves maritimes" had already excluded the law of finds,[4] and even more clearly the Law of 1 December 1989 on cultural maritime goods ("*biens culturels maritimes*") has excluded law of finds and also law of salvage. The salvor has to leave *in situ* the UCH and can operate only after having obtained an administrative authorization and, last but not least, he does not "*automatically*" have a "*right*" to payment.[5] In the United States, for abandoned shipwrecks the *Abandoned Shipwreck Act* of 1987 (ASA) excludes both the law of salvage and the law of finds,[6] and this mainly because, as for any UCH, also for these shipwrecks "the function of the ship has changed (from a means of transport to a time capsule)".[7]

However, on the request of the maritime powers an informal discussion was reopened with mainly the Italian and Greek Delegations, which resulted in the compromise solution finally adopted: any activity relating to UCH to which the Convention applies shall not be subject to the law of salvage or law of finds, unless it: a) is authorized by the competent authorities, and b) is in full conformity with the Convention, and c) ensures that any recovery of the UCH achieves its maximum protection. It is clear that these conditions are cumulative, so that only where the three conditions are met salvage law or law of finds may apply to UCH under the Convention.

---

1 Art. 4.

2 Working Paper 13.

3 Nevertheless, outside the UNESCO negotiations, if a strong criticism has been addressed to the exclusion of salvage by the ILA Draft and early UNESCO Draft, up to considering that this exclusion of "cultural" salvage evinces "a strong, and perhaps even irrational, antipathy towards international maritime law and the admiralty courts that administer it" (Bederman, *The UNESCO Draft Convention on Underwater Cultural Heritage: A Critique and Counter-Proposal*, in (1999) *JMLC* 331, at 332-334), it may be assumed this criticism to be even stronger on this proposal, though felt useful by the majority of the Delegations, which excluded law of salvage *and* law of finds on UCH.

For a different view, in favour of the exclusion of salvage for UCH, see Society for Historical Archaeology, *Statement of Principles on the Revised UNESCO Draft Convention*; Varmer, *The Case Against the " Salvage " of the Cultural Heritage*, in (1999) *JMLC* 279; Elia, *US Protection of Underwater Cultural Heritage beyond Territorial Sea: Problems and Prospects*, in (2000) *IJNA* 43, at 51; Verlaan, *Marine Archaeology : a Troyan (Sea) Horse ?*, in (1989) *Ocean Yearbook* 231.

4 For the finder of a "épave" of an archaeological, historical and artistic character, *Décret n.61-1547 du 26 décembre 1961 fixant le regime des épaves maritimes* (Art. 24).

5 *Loi n.89-874 du 1er Décembre 1989 relative aux biens culturels maritimes.* If the owner of the UCH is not found, title goes to the State not to the finder (Art. 2). Payment to the salvor *may* be given and determined in its amount by the competent administrative authority (Art. 6). Any operation on, or removal of, UCH requires a previous administrative authorization. It is worth noticing that these provisions and their importance for the protection of UCH extend also to UCH located up to 24 miles (Art. 12).

6 *Abandoned Shipwreck Act* of 1987, Section 7.

7 Time capsule that can tell much about our past: Giesecke, *The Abandoned Shipwreck Act through the Eyes of its Drafter*, in (1999) *JMLC* 167, at 171.

Several degrees of importance concern this regime. First of all, the importance of simply existing while for quite a while the issue of salvage and the law of finds appeared to be an emerging deal-breaker for the whole negotiations. Secondly, the importance of achieving a real "consensus" oriented regime beyond the objective diversities of legal traditions, in (private) comparative law, and of current policies on the protection of UCH. Thirdly, the importance of being acceptable to the majority of States[8] and, at the same time, of achieving a threshold for the protection of UCH which is well beyond UNCLOS. The latter reserved the applicability of the law of salvage and other rules of admiralty (Art. 303, 3). Though this reserve is usually interpreted as not overriding the duty to protect UCH and co-operate for this purpose set out in paragraph 1 of the same Article,[9] this reserve risks to be interpreted in a more extreme way and, especially, it sets no precondition at all in view of the protection of UCH during and after the salvage operations.

Under the new Convention, three conditions have to be met and all the three converge in setting these requirements before, during and after the salvage operations.[10] It should also be observed that these conditions specific to salvage (and law of finds) do not prevent *ex se* activities directed at the recovery of UCH from the seabed where such an exception to the *in situ* preservation principle is deemed necessary by the competent authorities and these activities are in conformity with the Convention and its Annex (especially with Rules 1-6).

Once the regime adopted has been presented in its importance, it deserves to be better explained and appreciated in the light of several questions raised by practice and the regimes of salvage and of the law of finds in comparative law.

2. The Genesis of the Regime: (Private) Comparative Law Difficulties and Beyond

As a complete exclusion of law of salvage and law of finds was alleged to raise serious difficulty to some maritime powers, sometimes even of a constitutional law level, and to endanger their possibility to join the Convention, on their request an informal meeting mainly with Italian and Greek Delegates was held in a spirit of co-operation and understanding.

Finding a common language on salvage law and the law of finds among the States represented within UNESCO was not an easy task. Seeking uniformity at an international level would prove a failure.

Concerning customary law, though it is since centuries recognized the duty, moral but progressively also legal, to save a person in peril,[11] beyond a few

[8] At least to those represented within UNESCO.

[9] See also Brice, *Maritime Law of Salvage*, (3 ed.), London 1999, p. 261 n. 4-22.

[10] And among the three conditions, the last two (b), which implies also full conformity with the Annex, and (c) are the most effective for this purpose.

[11] For instance, "L'assistance en mer a été de tout temps l'une des obligations humanitaires que des marins dignes de ce nom ont toujours eu à coeur de respecter. Une fois de plus on constate que la coutume a frayé les voies au droit positif": de Ferron, *Le droit international de la mer*, II, Genève, 1958, p. 131 n. 82.

general principles, no precise and complete international customary regime of salvage appears, especially for UCH. Also, beyond the appearance of uniformity, Gidel had since long observed that "*l'application du principe ne laisse pas de présenter des difficultés*".[12] However, interestingly enough, American courts usually consider salvage law as belonging to *ius gentium*, international customary law of the general maritime law, while British courts consider it simply part of domestic law.[13]

Concerning treaty-law, the existence of the three conventions of Brussels (1910 and its 1967 Protocol, 1938[14]) and London (1989) helped only partially to find a common language. Actually, they are neither universally ratified nor specifically directed to salvage applied to UCH. This is true also for the important 1989 Convention which sets rules on the main aspects of ordinary and commercial salvage operations,[15] as their performance and the rights of salvor in case of useful result.[16] Although it may apply also to UCH unless a reservation against is made,[17] it would be quite excessive to pretend that the content of the Convention derogates from traditional needs of "commercial" salvage[18] to substantially satisfy specific concerns linked with "cultural" salvage of UCH. If these concerns have ever been satisfied, even partially, is more the result of a valuable case law, which progressively required salvors to respect *at least some* archaeological standards during their activities.[19]

Difficulty to find common language was also due to a diversity of legal traditions. Legal comparison is a precondition for an effective international negotiation on legal issues, mutual understanding and research for an acceptable and potentially uniform solution. First of all, even within the Common Law tradition several aspects of salvage law differ to quite an extent.[20] Secondly, salvage law in the tradition of common law countries is an institution of a rather large scope which covers in Civil Law countries *several* and *different* traditional *notions* and *regimes*: not less than three in Italian law (*soccorso* divided into *assistenza* and *salvataggio,* and *ricupero*[21]), mainly two in French law (*secours en mer* divided into *assistance aux navires* and

---

12 Gidel, *Le droit international public de la mer. Le temps de paix*, T.I, 1932, p. 369.

13 See Brice, *supra* note 9, at 33, and the explanations proposed, mainly of an historical nature.

14 The 1938 Convention never entered into force.

15 Articles 6 and 7.

16 Articles 12, 13 and 14.

17 Art. 30, 1, d).

18 With one major exception: concern of pollution may not be considered traditional in commercial salvage but is certainly one of the main inspirations of the 1989 Convention. See Art. 1, d, Art. 8, 1, b and 2, b; Art. 9 and Art. 11.

19 Also an author, Bederman, *supra* note 3, at 345, who appreciates, as we do, these progressive requirements in case-law (in the United States), recognizes that "This is not to say, of course, that commercial salvors have been held to exactly the same technical standards as adopted by nautical archaeologists". On these case law developments see Fletcher-Tomenius, O'Keefe & Williams, *Salvor in Possession: Friend or Foe to Marine Archaeology?*, in (2000) *IJCP* 263, at 285-299.

20 See the several differences between American and English salvage law presented in Brice, *supra* note 9.

21 See Articles 489-509 of the Italian *Codice della navigazione*, and D'Ovidio, Pescatore & Tullio, *Diritto della navigazione*, (9 ed.), Milano, 2000, p. 649–682.

sauvetage des épaves[22]) and mainly three in Spanish Law (*asistencia*, *salvamento*, *auxilio*[23]).

Under the influence of the common law "salvage" model some of these various traditional notions and regimes have been unified by the Brussels (1910) and the London (1989) Conventions. Such a unification is nevertheless true: 1) only to the extent of the substantial scope of application of the Conventions. The scope *ratione loci* of the 1989 Convention is remarkably wide as the latter applies *regardless* the traditional distinction between domestic and international cases; 2) only in the States Parties that belong to the civil law tradition[24] or to other legal traditions but share nevertheless a variety of notions and regimes on "salvage"; 3) only in those countries which maintain the one notion and one regime system also under domestic legislation enacted *after* the implementation of the convention, which is not always the case in this field where several distinctions within the broad understanding of "salvage" are well-rooted from a doctrinal and/or legislative standpoint.[25]

The variety of civil law notions and regimes opposed to "salvage" law explains also the potential *multifunctional* language of the latter in civil law frameworks: face to a uniform "salvage" English terminology the French texts refer to "assistance" but also to "droit de récupérer des épaves", according to the main objective of salvage in the two Conventions concerned, respectively, London on Salvage (1989) and UNCLOS (1982).[26]

Faced to these difficulties at international and comparative law level, and to more practical constraints as time limitations, we personally suggested that, in order to avoid the emerging dead-lock for the whole Convention of extreme "yes" or "no" answers to this crucial issue of acceptance of reject of salvage and law of finds within the Convention, a mid-way and "consensus" solution could only be sought *outside* the legal *regime* of the two institutions[27] and focusing just on some crucial *conditions* concerning their *effects* for their applicability under the Convention. The proposal was accepted by the other few Delegates sharing this

---

22 See Reuter, *La notion d'assistance en mer*, Paris, 1975, p. 47; du Pontavice, *Les épaves maritimes aériennes et spatiales en droit français*, Thèse pour le Doctorat, Paris, 1961, p. 167 n. 236; De Juglart & Villenau, *Répertoire méthodique et pratique de l'assistance en mer*, Paris, 1962; Ripert, *Droit maritime*, T.3, Paris, 1953, n. 2152 p. 121; Rodière, *Droit maritime. Le navire*, Paris, 1980, n. 102 p. 131; Rodière & du Pontavice, *Droit maritime*, 12 Ed., Paris, 1997, p. 446 n. 450-1.

23 See Arroyo's comment on Supreme Court (judgment 27 November 1993) and the distinctions under Spanish Law among (expressed in French language) *assistance*, *aide* and *sauvetage maritime* ((1995) *Droit Maritime Français* 775). See also Matilla Alegre, *Internacionalidad del Derecho marítimo y jurisdicción international*, Bilbao, 1999, p. 203.

24 Limiting to the traditional opposition between Civil Law – Common Law traditions would be too restrictive, in a universal context as UNESCO or other negotiations within the UN system.

25 See for instance the case of Italian domestic law in relation to the 1910 Brussels Convention and its criticism by Berlingieri, *Assistenza e salvataggio nella navigazione marittima, interna ed aerea, ricupero e ritrovamento*, in (1967–1968) *Il diritto marittimo* 54. See also the case of French domestic legislation (1916), Ripert, *supra* note 22, n. 2154 at 123.

26 Art. 303, 3.

27 Which therefore remained ruled by the national applicable law and, if applicable, by the 1989 Convention concerning salvage.

task,[28] the "compromise" solution was then elaborated by determining the number and the content of these conditions, and later, most importantly, accepted with *no amendments* by the plenary.

This genesis of Article 4 explains why the latter focuses simply on these three conditions[29] and provides neither definitions of salvage law and law of finds, nor their regime in terms of conditions and legal effects. These definitions and regimes are to be found under the domestic law applicable and, to some extent, international law concerning salvage. From a comparative law standpoint, generally salvage law sets peril at sea as condition and its effects are not related to ownership, but to title to recover salvage remuneration, while law of finds requires abandonment of the vessel and provides ownership on it.[30]

3. Ownership, the Convention and Some Doubts on "Spontaneous" Salvage Applied *Ex Se* on UCH

Technically speaking, the Convention does not deal with ownership of UCH. The importance of law of finds for the protection of UCH required nevertheless negotiators to deal with this issue linked to ownership. Especially, the Convention does not "rule" on the law of finds. The latter is, as well as ownership, and remains under the Convention, ruled by the domestic legislation applicable. Only its application to UCH is excluded if its nature and effects are incompatible with the conditions set by the Convention.

If the law of finds provides a title to the finder over the object previously abandoned, and salvage law does not, the latter can nevertheless have an impact on ownership. Usually the salvor has simply an exclusive possessory right on the salvaged property but, once the latter is brought within the jurisdiction of a court in admiralty to enforce its maritime lien, the court can, as stated by the United States Court of Appeals (4th Circuit) in the famous *Titanic* case, execute the salvor's lien "and sell the property, or if the sale of the property would prove insufficient to compensate the salvor (RMST) fairly, the court can award title in the property to the salvor (RMST)".[31] This latter possibility appears reasonable in relation to "ordinary" salved objects but rather questionable if it where to be applied as such to UCH. Then the salvor would end up with having title and the main prerogatives of the finder without the condition of a previous abandonment by the owner.

This questionable character increases where the applicability of salvage to UCH and outside "ordinary" vessels and objects in peril tends to be spatially generalized

---

[28] Were present Delegates from Italy, Greece, Canada, United Kingdom, United States, Australia. Within this small informal (open-ended) group, convened on the invitation of Chairman C. Lund, a useful and genuine search for "consensus" has been possible.

[29] To which a fourth and implicit one is to be added: (strong) presumption against abandonment of property in the law of finds framework (see *infra*).

[30] See generally Brice, *supra* note 9, at 1, 280.

[31] *R.M.S.Titanic Inc. v. Haver*, 171 F.3d 943, 966 (4th Cir., March 24, 1999).

because salvage law is felt, as in American practice, to be a part of *ius gentium* with the resulting statement that the solutions mentioned, among which awarding title to the salvor, belong to "shared maritime principles" applied basically all over the world.[32] One thing is the desirable uniformity of regimes on the high seas,[33] a different thing, definitely less desirable, is to generalize national solutions and/or regimes as being part of customary international law and to then presume them in principle identical all over the world, and even applicable to UCH in spite of the specificity of its nature and needs of protection. On the contrary, the differences mentioned before within the Common Law tradition and, even more, between the latter and several Civil Law systems prove that salvage law belongs mainly to *domestic law* and varies among national legal orders.[34] In any case, it is even more up to each national legislator the assessment on the *opportunity if*, and *to which extent*, of a submission of UCH to solutions and regimes, only to some extent similar in comparative law, conceived for "ordinary" objects and traditional "commercial" salvage.

More generally speaking, the salvor's maritime lien on the salvaged object until full payment[35] may prove incompatible with the need of scientific and public access to, and protection of, UCH. Furthermore, even without going as far as the prerogatives of title granted to the salvor, compensation to salvors might reveal sometimes too expensive for the owner or the State of origin of a UCH. Given that even in the ordinary "commercial" conception of salvage the owner has the right to prohibit any "spontaneous" salvage operation on its ownership and if the prohibition is disregarded no payment is due to the salvor,[36] it would appear a reasonable compromise that because of the specificity of UCH the right to prohibit "spontaneous" salvage should not only be certainly granted to the identified owner, as already stated in domestic legislation,[37] but also that the State of cultural, historic and or archaeological origin, though not necessarily "owner" properly speaking, be consulted by the salvor prior to any intended salvage service on the usefulness of the latter, particularly recovery of UCH, and on the affordable amount for compensation. In a way, "spontaneous" salvage should shift to, *if anything* on UCH, to "contractual" salvage where the salvor's intervention is previously asked and agreed between the parties.

Coming back to the Convention, its condition of a previous authorization by the

32 *Ibidem*, p. 966–7.

33 For instance, in the terms of U.S. Court of Appeal (4th Cir.), 24 March 1999, "The need for courts of admiralty to apply the law similarly is fundamentally important to international commerce and to the policies supporting order on the high seas". *Ibidem*, p. 967.

34 For different views and "universal" statements, see for instance Sweeney, *An Overview of Commercial Salvage Principles in the Context of Marine Archaeology*, in (1999) *JMLC* 185, at 188 "The general maritime law of salvage is very ancient and also uniform throughout the maritime world".

35 Or until a satisfactory security for his claim has been duly tendered or provided, as admitted by the 1989 Salvage Convention (Art. 20, 2).

36 See 1989 London Convention, Art. 19. In domestic law, see for instance Art. 491, 1, of the Italian *Codice della navigazione*.

37 See for instance *Loi n. 89-874 du 1er Décembre 1989 relative aux biens culturels maritimes* (Art. 9).

competent authorities (Art. 4) supports such a shift of perspective, at least to the extent that under the local (administrative) law the authorization implies agreement (in the "contractual" sense) from the authorities on the salvage operation.

It should also be observed that faced with a "contractual" salvage, even the 1989 Salvage Convention can be *contracted out*[38] and does *not* apply any more and, with it, its assumption that its regime for "commercial" or "ordinary" salvage applies in principle also to UCH.

4. The Condition of "Peril": Should Salvage Law Apply to UCH?

This is a key-point of the debate as the essential condition for salvage is the existence of a maritime peril.[39] The salvor operates in order to avoid the main and traditional peril at sea which is sinking. Though, an authoritative opinion submitted that immobilisation of property on the seabed is a sufficient "danger".[40] Differently, another authoritative opinion had reserved the regime of the Italian institution closest to salvage (*soccorso*) to situations where the ship was not able to get rid of the peril by its own resources.[41] Then salvage law seems to be excluded once the ship has sunk as not only the resources of the ship but also, if any, further assistance have proved insufficient and the peril has taken its toll.

In a Civil Law jurisdiction as for instance under traditional Italian Law, outside the 1989 Convention, with reference to a shipwreck it would be considered that since the peril was not arrested and took its toll by sinking the vessel, it would be a matter not of salvage law (*soccorso* divided into *assistenza* or *salvataggio*) but of a different institution: *ricupero*.[42] And for the same reason, that the existence of peril is the precondition of both "assistance" and "salvage" under the 1910 Convention but *not* the precondition of *ricupero*, the latter should not have been considered subject to the Convention.[43]

Differently, American case law appears favourable to a wide notion of salvage including sunken ships and their cargoes, applicable also to UCH but not without some uncertainties. In the Columbus-America case, this wider notion was confirmed in 1992 and salvage law was presented as "historically" applied "when ships and their cargo have been recovered from the bottom of the sea".[44] Law of salvage was applied concerning the S.S. Central America sunk in 1857, but the same United States Court of Appeals (4th Circuit) stated in 1995 that "in a typical salvage case" assistance is given to a vessel "that has become disabled, but has not

[38] With an important exception (*unlikely* to concern directly salvage of UCH) concerning the duties to prevent or minimize damage to the environment (Art. 6).

[39] This condition is traditionally required. See for instance *Klein v. Unidentified Wrecked and Abandoned Sailing Vessel*, 758 F.2d 1511, 1515 (11th Cir., April 29, 1985).

[40] Brice, *supra* note 9, at 305.

[41] Berlingieri, *supra* note 25, at 105.

[42] See D'Ovidio, Pescatore, & Tullio, *supra* note 21, at 653 n. 476.

[43] See Berlingieri, *supra* note 25, at 295.

[44] *Columbus-America Discovery Group v. Atlantic Mutual Insurance Company*, 974 F.2d 450 (4th Cir., August 26, 1992).

yet sunk".[45] The "historical" application of salvage seems not to confirm a "typical salvage case". Anyway, the same case shows the importance of careful handling of the respective factual preconditions of the two institutions: the district court had found an abandonment of property, applied the law of finds and awarded the entire treasure to the salvor, while the court of appeal denied such an abandonment and applied salvage law.[46]

If we then turn to international conventions seeking certainties and uniformity because they focus exclusively on one regime (but on two notions: assistance and salvage under the 1910 Convention) or even on one notion ("salvage") and one regime (1989 Salvage Convention) then our expectations are frustrated as unfortunately neither the former nor the latter provide a precise definition of "peril".[47] The case law has proved flexible on "peril" but it appears not to provide certainties on its existence once the vessel has sunk.[48] Concerning the 1989 London Convention it is important to observe that if its regime on salvage may apply to UCH[49] that does not imply *ex se* the irrebutable presumption that UCH is *by definition* in peril. On the contrary, the existence of a "danger" has to be proved for the existence of a "salvage operation" and for the application of the Convention in general,[50] *not* particularly on UCH, and the "nature and degree of danger" have to be proved and taken into account, not for the Convention to apply to UCH, but simply to fix the reward.[51]

In any case, the opposite solution would also be extreme and unacceptable: to set the irrebutable presumption that UCH is never in peril. However, it appears a justified presumption, definitely not irrebutable, that UCH is not *ex se* in marine peril in the traditional sense of "ordinary" salvage. So that if, at least in the United States practice, so far "shipwrecks are often characterized as being in marine peril under the general maritime law, and thus do qualify for salvage",[52] for the future a *more restrictive* and *specific* notion of "marine peril" for UCH appears desirable and more in line with the compromise solution adopted within UNESCO. Only exceptionally may UCH be considered in peril because of human or natural external elements,[53] as for instance if UCH were lying under a frequent maritime way in shallow waters.[54] Then, the next issue is the burden of the proof of such peril for UCH: general principles of law put the burden on salvors, concerning peril for the specific UCH concerned, as claimant and beneficiary from salvage law if declared applicable, and this also under the 1989 Convention which may apply to UCH.

---

45 *Columbus-America Discovery Group v. Atlantic Mutual Insurance Company*, 56 F.3d 556, 570 (4th Cir. June 14, 1995).

46 See decision quoted *supra* note 44, p. 467.

47 They simply envisage peril as element to fix salvage remuneration.

48 See Vincenzini, *International Salvage Law*, London, 1992, p. 56–60.

49 In case of no reservation under Art. 30, 1, d).

50 Art. 1, a).

51 These two elements are criteria among several others taken into account to fix the reward (Art. 13, 1, d).

52 Bederman, *supra* note 3, at 348.

53 See also Varmer, *supra* note 3, at 280, who recalls that the lack of oxygen slows substantially down the deterioration rate for shipwrecks covered by the seabed.

54 It may occur in a harbour but not exclusively.

Further arguments make the extension to UCH of salvage conceived for "ordinary" vessels or objects questionable.

First of all, since the principle of *in situ* preservation has been adopted by the ICOMOS Charter (1996), given a binding character by the Convention and even before adopted in domestic legislation,[55] at least as a principle the *in situ* preservation denies completely the idea the UCH is irrebutably presumed in "peril" and also establishes the principle that UCH left *in situ* is presumed *not* to be in peril, at least according to the rather high preservation threshold set by the Annex. Under the Convention, as already under domestic legislation,[56] only the competent authorities may decide, and not the "spontaneous" salvor on his/her *own* initiative,[57] if a specific UCH is exceptionally in peril and its protection deserves removal or other activities. It is also incompatible with the *in situ* preservation under the Convention the pressure put on the salvor to remove at least some parts of UCH to bring within the judicial district in order to benefit from the exercise of constructive *in rem* jurisdiction over wrecks located also in the high seas as in the *Titanic* case.[58] This pressure is frequent as the maritime lien under English and American salvage law entitles salvor to proceed *in rem* and to arrest the salved property, to which a possessory lien is added if the salvor is in possession,[59] and the maritime lien is perfected and enforceable *in rem*[60] where part of the wreck is brought into the admiralty court jurisdiction, which is usually an easier and more effective solution than the *a personam* action against the owner,[61] often a foreign owner with the consequent complications.[62]

---

55 For instance, see *Loi n. 89-874 du 1er Décembre 1989 relative aux biens culturels maritimes* (Art. 3, 1).

56 See for instance under French Law, *Loi n. 89-874 du 1er Décembre 1989 relative aux biens culturels maritimes* (Art. 3, 1 and Art. 7,2).

57 It should not be lost of sight that in order to benefit from a claim for a salvage award one of the conditions is that the salvor has operated on the basis of a *voluntary* act, where he rendered assistance under no official or legal duty to render it. See also *Klein v. Unidentified Wrecked and Abandoned Sailing Vessel*, 758 F.2d 1511, 1515 (11th Cir., April 29, 1985), *Zych v. Unidentified Wrecked & Abandoned Vessel*, 19 F.3d 1136, 1141 (7th Cir., March 21, 1994) and *R.M.S. Titanic Inc. v. Haver*, 171 F.3d 943, 963 (4th Cir., March 24, 1999). The general idea, as clearly stated in the latter case, is "The law of salvage presumes that the owner desires the salvage service" (*ibidem*, p. 943).

If this presumption is normal in "commercial" salvage, it becomes rather questionable for salvage applied to UCH and even unacceptable under the *in situ* preservation principle. Under the Convention the competent authorities will decide if salvage, or more generally recovery of UCH, is "desirable".

Also under the 1989 Salvage Convention, the *normal* case is " spontaneous " salvage (Art. 1, a) and not the "contractual" salvage or the "obligatory" (to *persons* in danger, Art. 10) salvage.

58 *R.M.S. Titanic, Inc. v. The Wrecked and Abandoned Vessel believed to be the R.M.S. Titanic*, 9 F. Supp. 2d 624, 632 (E.D.Va, June 23, 1998).

59 For these general effects of maritime lien and confirmation of this basic principle of the possessory lien in both legal systems, although with a scant authority in English Law, see Brice, *supra* note 9, at 126 (2-13), 207 (2-301) and 143 (2-78).

60 With reference to previous case law, *R.M.S. Titanic, Inc. v. The Wrecked and Abandoned Vessel believed to be the R.M.S. Titanic*, 9 F. Supp. 2d 624, 633 (E.D.Va, June 23, 1998).

61 Action open to the salvor. See also 171 F.3d 963.

62 By definition we are considering situations of an international character. The latter may concern *inter alia* the nationality or domicile or residence of the owner, each of them having a relevance variable according to the forum where action is effectively brought. From a US law point of view, on the

Secondly, even before the formal adoption of the *in situ* preservation by the ICOMOS Charter and the Convention, if it is true that salvage law grants possession of the object "for the purpose of saving it from destruction, damage, or loss",[63] in relation to UCH which has sunk since a long time, for instance at least a century under the Convention,[64] such events may be assumed to have already occurred – and then "peril" is not actual anymore.[65] Should they have exceptionally not yet occurred they are quite unlikely to occur after such a long time *and* also at the moment of salvage. The absence of peril is sometimes argued and when rejected the ground is not always clear and satisfactory.[66]

5. The Condition of Abandonment: Should Law of finds apply on UCH and on Warships?

The Convention went a long way from an old Draft, which declared the future Convention applicable only to abandoned UCH. As finally adopted, the Convention not only applies to UCH *irrespectively* the possibility of a previous abandonment, but also does not mention expressly that the application of the law of finds requires a previous abandonment of ownership. If time was not generous enough to allow elaboration also of this requirement as an explicit fourth condition in Article 4, this requirement is nevertheless to be considered a fourth implied condition specific to the law of finds.[67] It reflects common practice where a previous abandonment of ownership is required and never presumed.[68]

---

cont.

justification of *quasi in rem* actions as an exception to their decline since *Shaffer* by the Supreme Court (1977), see Lowenfeld, *International Litigation and Arbitration*, West, 1993, p. 230, 242 ; Scoles & Hay, *Conflict of Laws*, 2nd Ed., West, 1992 (94), p. 234–260.

63 See decision quoted *supra* note 44, p. 460.

64 In order the Convention to apply.

65 Or is still present but in a lower degree. But then up to which lower, and then minimum, degree of peril the condition of peril should still *not artificially* be met?

66 For instance, in *Treasure Salvors v. Unidentified Wrecked and Abandoned Sailing Vessel*, 569 F.2d 330, 337 (5th Cir., March 13, 1978), the government argued that no marine peril existed and that the district court erred in applying the law of salvage. However, the Court of Appeal rejected the argument.

On one side, marine peril includes more than the threat of storm, fire or piracy to a vessel in navigation. The statement is clear and rather acceptable *ex se* but the example provided from another case where the anchors and chains were lost does not seem to affect substantially the case of the sunken vessel (*Nuestra Señora de Atocha*) since 1622 although the Court underlines that " There is no dispute that the *Atocha* was lost ".

On the other side, the Court observes that even after discovery of the vessel's location it is still in peril of being lost through the actions of the elements. The remark depends actually from several factors (depth, potential currents at sea-bed level, condition and shape of the sea-bed etc.) and lacks substance to be presented as a general statement.

67 While the three explicit conditions address to both law of salvage and law of finds.

68 See for instance, the decision quoted *supra* note 44 (*Columbus-America Discovery Group v. Atlantic Mutual Insurance Company*): "Such an abandonment must be proved by clear and convincing evidence, though, such as an owner's express declaration abandoning title" (p. 464).

If the principle itself appears certain, the real issue is more the "*degree*" *of certainty* of abandonment and therefore the *forms* and/or the *acts* accepted to prove such a previous abandonment. Not surprisingly, practice shows several degrees.[69] In our view this issue should be taken seriously and solved through a *strong presumption against* such an abandonment of ownership by the owner. Though strong, this presumption is simply rebuttable and not conclusive. Actually, this presumption aims to protect the rights of the owner under the Convention as *mutatis mutandis* already UNCLOS protects the rights of identifiable owners.[70] In favour of this strong presumption is also the majority view, before the modification resulting in the present provision, that excluded completely the law of finds to UCH and, with it, the threat it represents for the rights of the owner, and this exclusion was *regardless* the "degree" of a possible abandonment.

In domestic practice, we also find similar needs against an "easy" abandonment, as the one underlying the United States *Abandoned Shipwreck Act* of 1987 (ASA),[71] where the terms of "deserted" and "relinquished" used by Congress have been regarded as a "terms-of-art, a congressional recognition" of a strong presumption against abandonment.[72]

While the strong presumption we suggest would address generally any UCH under the Convention, and *a fortiori* to public vessels which became UCH, concerning warships and military vessels the issue of a previous abandonment for the applicability of law of finds is of a particular importance for, and seen particularly restrictively by, several States. Keeping in mind the necessary distinction between jurisdictional issues and ownership issues on warships, States practice on warships and military vessels express this particularly restrictive notion of abandonment. For instance, in the recent *La Galga* and *Juno* cases, two Spanish vessels which sank in 1750 and 1802 respectively off the coast of Virginia, the 4th Circuit Court stated that Spain had abandoned neither vessel.[73] The Court also noted that under Treaty Law[74] as well as under general principles of international comity the United States as *Amicus Curiae* defended Spain's ownership and stressed that by supporting Spain it sought "to insure that its sunken vessels and lost crew are treated as sovereign ships and honoured graves, and are not subject to exploration, or exploitation, by private

---

[69] For instance, in *Fairport International Exploration Inc. v. The Shipwrecked Vessel*, the lapse of time alone was not deemed to establish abandonment (177 F.3d 491, 499) In the *Columbus-America Discovery Group* case, a narrower view of abandonment, close to a simple presumption because of a long time under water since sinking, was presented by dissenting Circuit Judge Wiedenr (974 F.2d 470, 474). One step further in this direction, which also means one degree lower in the protection of the owner, was provided by an even narrower view expressed by the U.S. Court of Appeals in *Treasure Salvors v. Unidentified Wrecked and Abandoned Sailing Vessel* quoted *supra* note 66, p. 337.

[70] Art. 303, 3.

[71] The Act provides no definition of abandonment neither in Section 3 nor in Sections 6 and 7.

[72] See Bederman, *supra* note 3, at 336.

[73] On June 21, 2000. On the contrary, the district court (*Sea Hunt v. Unidentified Shipwrecked Vessel*, 47 F. Supp. 678) had erroneously interpreted the Treaty of Peace (between France, Great Britain, Spain) of Paris (1763) as to express abandonment of the *La Galga* by Spain.

[74] Applicable was the 1902 Treaty of Friendship and General Relations.

parties seeking treasures of the sea".[75] Though with some uncertainties,[76] this practice is rather consistent and the question is whether it has or not achieved a customary stage. For instance, if any custom is to be seen in the United States on no abandonment of warships unless by an explicit act, it was said, it is one "of very recent origin".[77] The abandonment or transfer of title to sunken warships subject exclusively to the law of the flag State was considered a "rule of international law" recognized by the United States.[78]

State practice is confirmed also by the *Alabama* case. Though the *Alabama* had sunk in 1864 and was found in 1984 in the French territorial waters, ownership was not considered to be lost or abandoned. France did not claim title that the applicable French law would have granted to the (French) State if the owner of the shipwreck were unknown or impossible to be found.[79]

The Convention shares the concerns both on protection of warships, which are considered UCH and protected as such,[80] even partially exempted of report and notification duties,[81] and on respect to be given to their lost crews.[82] Respect of military graves is also a common concern.[83] However, it should be emphasized that the Convention does not set any explicit condition of abandonment for any UCH, and even less an explicit and more restrictive condition on abandonment concerning military vessels and/or State vessels as opposed to "ordinary" vessels.

Actually, the proposal which came the closest to such a more restrictive condition was made by the United Kingdom, followed by the Russian Federation, at the very end of negotiations:[84] State vessels and aircraft shall not be recovered without the collaboration of the flag State, unless they have been expressly abandoned in accordance with the laws of that State. The General Conference rejected this proposal. At any rate, its destination would have been Article 7, 3 concerning only

---

75 See Brief for the United States as *Amicus Curiae* and the decisions relating to *La Galga* and *Juno*, in (2000) *AJIL* 678.

76 For instance, the district Court in *Sea Hunt v. Unidentified Shipwrecked Vessel*, does not seem to vary the conditions of abandonment according to the "ordinary" or "warship" nature of the wrecks: "Regardless of whether or not *Juno* and *La Galga* are considered to be warships, they are subject to a rule of express abandonment" (47 F. Supp. 678, 691).

77 Bederman, *supra* note 3, at 337, note 33.

78 See the *Statement by the President of the United States on the U.S. Policy for the Protection of Sunken Warships* (The White House, 19 January 2001).

79 See *Chronique* of Quenedec, in (1990) *Annuaire français de droit international* 747.

80 Obviously, one thing is the insertion of Warships among "State vessels and aircraft" (Art. 1, 8), and a different thing is that the Warship concerned will be considered as UCH and protected by the Convention: that occurs only if the Warship concerned meets the conditions and the 100 years time requirement set by Art. 1, a).

81 See Art. 13.

82 More precisely, such a respect is to be given to all human remains, regardless the military or not military nature of the UCH concerned (Art. 2, 9).

83 See also the Agreement between the Government of the United Kingdom of Great Britain and Northern Ireland and the Government of the Republic of South Africa concerning the regulation of the terms of settlement of the salvaging of the Wreck of *HMS Birkenhead* (September 1989).

84 The idea had already been submitted in other forms also during the negotiations, as in the "non paper" (3 July 2001) on State vessels and aircraft (proposed by UK).

UCH in internal waters, archipelagic waters and territorial sea.[85] The clear reference to abandonment appears nevertheless far-reaching in view not only of recovery *ex se*, or related to other provisions concerning activities directed at the same States vessels and aircraft,[86] but also of a wider concern linked to the law of finds.[87] Had the provision been adopted in Article 4, it would have been extended to all maritime zones.[88]

It should also be noted that the Convention sets no particular condition on salvage law as applied to warships. Nevertheless, neither the 1910 Brussels Convention[89] nor the 1989 London Convention[90] apply to warships, *contrarily* to the 1967 Protocol which replaced the pertaining provision of the 1910 Convention and made the latter applicable to warships.[91]

---

85 Internal waters is inserted in the proposal (31 C/COM.IV/DR.5, reproduced *infra*, in the documents section) but not in the present Art. 7, 3. The latter is not coherent with the title, as well as with paragraphs 1 and 2, of Art. 7.

86 See Art. 10, 7 and Art. 12, 7.

87 Once title is recognized, by the law of finds, to the finder, the main freedom and following act are usually to decide on the removal, in part or for the whole, of the UCH.

88 And in Article 4 this provision could have been drafted as a fourth condition specific to State vessels and aircraft, while the three adopted conditions apply to any UCH.

89 Art. 14.

90 Art. 4, unless the State Party decides to apply the Convention.

91 Art. 1 of the 1967 Protocol, replacing Art. 14 of the Brussels Convention.

DOCUMENTS

A) MULTILATERAL TREATIES

1. United Nations Convention on the Law of the Sea (Montego Bay, 10 December 1982)

Article 149

Archaeological and Historical Objects
All objects of an archaeological and historical nature found in the Area shall be preserved or disposed of for the benefit of mankind as a whole, particular regard being paid to the preferential rights of the State or country of origin, or the State of cultural origin, or the State of historical and archaeological origin.

Article 303

Archaeological and Historical Objects Found at Sea
1. States have the duty to protect objects of an archaeological and historical nature found at sea and shall cooperate for this purpose.
2. In order to control traffic in such objects, the coastal State may, in applying article 33, presume that their removal from the seabed in the zone referred to in that article without its approval would result in an infringement within its territory or territorial sea of the laws and regulations referred to in that article.
3. Nothing in this article affects the rights of identifiable owners, the law of salvage or other rules of admiralty, or laws and practices with respect to cultural exchanges.

Roberta Garabello and Tullio Scovazzi (eds.), The Protection of the Underwater Cultural Heritage, 207–292.

4. This article is without prejudice to other international agreements and rules of international law regarding the protection of objects of an archaeological and historical nature.

2. United Nations Conference on the Law of the Sea. Informal Proposal by Cape Verde, Greece, Italy, Malta, Portugal, Tunisia and Yugoslavia of 27 March 1980: UN Doc. A/Conf.62/C.2/Informal Meeting/43/Rev. 3

The coastal State may exercise jurisdiction, while respecting the rights of identifiable owners over any object of an archaeological and historical nature on or under its continental shelf for the purpose of research, recovery and protection. However, particular regard shall be paid to the preferential rights of the State or country of origin, or the State of cultural origin, or the State of historical and archaeological origin in case of sale or any other disposal, resulting in the removal of such object out of the coastal State.

3. United Nations Convention on the Law of the Sea – Declarations made by Cape Verde, the Netherlands, Malaysia, Portugal and Bangladesh

Declaration made by Cape Verde on 10 August 1987 on Ratification of the UNCLOS

The republic of Cape Verde declares, without prejudice to article 303 of the United National Convention on the Law of the Sea, that any objects of an archaeological and historical nature found within the maritime areas over which it exerts sovereignty or jurisdiction shall not be removed without its prior notification and consent.

Declaration made by the Netherlands on 26 June 1996 on Ratification of the UNCLOS

Jurisdiction over objects of an archaeological and historical nature found at sea is limited to articles 149 and 303 of the Convention. The Kingdom of the Netherlands does however consider that there may be a need to further develop, in international co-operation, the international law on the protection of the underwater cultural heritage.

Declaration made by Malaysia on 14 October 1996 on ratification of the UNCLOS

[...] The Malaysian Government declares, without prejudice to article 303 of the Convention on the Law of the Sea, that any objects of an archaeological and historical nature found within the maritime areas over which it exerts sovereignty or jurisdiction shall not be removed, without its prior notification and consent.

Declaration made by Portugal on 3 November 1997 on Ratification of the UNCLOS

Portugal declares, without prejudice to the provisions of Article 303 of the United Nations Convention on the Law of the Sea and to the application of other legal instruments of international law regarding the protection of the underwater archaeological heritage, [that] any objects of a historical or archaeological nature found in the maritime zones under its sovereignty or jurisdiction may be removed only after prior notice to and subject to the consent of the competent Portuguese authorities.

Declaration made by Bangladesh on 27 July 2001 on ratification of the UNCLOS

[...] The Bangladesh Government declares, without prejudice to article 303 of the Convention on the Law of the Sea, that any objects of an archaeological and historical nature found within the maritime areas over which it exercises sovereignty or jurisdiction shall not be removed, without its prior notification and consent.

4. International Convention on Salvage (London, 28 April 1989)

Article 30

Reservations

1. Any State may, at the time of signature, ratification, acceptance, approval or accession, reserve the right not to apply the provisions of this Convention:
   (a) when the salvage operation takes place in inland waters and all vessels involved are of inland navigation;
   (b) when the salvage operations take place in inland waters and no vessel is involved;
   (c) when all interested parties are nationals of that State;
   (d) when the property involved is maritime cultural property of prehistoric, archaeological or historic interest and is situated on the sea-bed.
2. Reservations made at the time of signature are subject to confirmation upon ratification, acceptance or approval.
3. Any State which has made a reservation to this Convention may withdraw it at any time by means of a notification addressed to the Secretary-General. Such withdrawal shall take effect on the date the notification is received. If the notification states that the withdrawal of a reservation is to take effect on a date specified therein, and such date is later than the date the notification is received by the Secretary-General, the withdrawal shall take effect on such later date.

5. Convention on the Protection of the Underwater Cultural Heritage (UNESCO, Paris, 2 November 2001)

The General Conference of the United Nations Educational, Scientific and Cultural Organization, meeting in Paris from 15 October to 3 November 2001, at its 31st session,

Acknowledging the importance of underwater cultural heritage as an integral part of the cultural heritage of humanity and a particularly important element in the history of peoples, nations, and their relations with each other concerning their common heritage,

Realizing the importance of protecting and preserving the underwater cultural heritage and that responsibility therefor rests with all States,

Noting growing public interest in and public appreciation of underwater cultural heritage,

Convinced of the importance of research, information and education to the protection and preservation of underwater cultural heritage,

Convinced of the public's right to enjoy the educational and recreational benefits of responsible non-intrusive access to *in situ* underwater cultural heritage, and of the value of public education to contribute to awareness, appreciation and protection of that heritage,

Aware of the fact that underwater cultural heritage is threatened by unauthorized activities directed at it, and of the need for stronger measures to prevent such activities,

Conscious of the need to respond appropriately to the possible negative impact on underwater cultural heritage of legitimate activities that may incidentally affect it,

Deeply concerned by the increasing commercial exploitation of underwater cultural heritage, and in particular by certain activities aimed at the sale, acquisition or barter of underwater cultural heritage,

Aware of the availability of advanced technology that enhances discovery of and access to underwater cultural heritage,

Believing that cooperation among States, international organizations, scientific institutions, professional organizations, archaeologists, divers, other interested parties and the public at large is essential for the protection of underwater cultural heritage,

Considering that survey, excavation and protection of underwater cultural heritage necessitate the availability and application of special scientific methods and the use of suitable techniques and equipment as well as a high degree of professional specialization, all of which indicate a need for uniform governing criteria,

Realizing the need to codify and progressively develop rules relating to the protection and preservation of underwater cultural heritage in conformity with international law and practice, including the UNESCO Convention on the Means of Prohibiting and Preventing the Illicit Import, Export and Transfer of Ownership of Cultural Property of 14 November 1970, the UNESCO Convention for the Protection of the World Cultural and Natural Heritage of 16 November 1972 and the United Nations Convention on the Law of the Sea of 10 December 1982,

Committed to improving the effectiveness of measures at international, regional and national levels for the preservation *in situ* or, if necessary for scientific or protective purposes, the careful recovery of underwater cultural heritage,

Having decided at its twenty-ninth session that this question should be made the subject of an international convention,

Adopts this second day of November 2001 this Convention.

Article 1 – Definitions

For the purposes of this Convention:

1. (a) "Underwater cultural heritage" means all traces of human existence having a cultural, historical or archaeological character which have been partially or totally under water, periodically or continuously, for at least 100 years such as:
   (i) sites, structures, buildings, artefacts and human remains, together with their archaeological and natural context;
   (ii) vessels, aircraft, other vehicles or any part thereof, their cargo or other contents, together with their archaeological and natural context; and
   (iii) objects of prehistoric character.

   (b) Pipelines and cables placed on the seabed shall not be considered as underwater cultural heritage.

   (c) Installations other than pipelines and cables, placed on the seabed and still in use, shall not be considered as underwater cultural heritage.
2. (a) "States Parties" means States which have consented to be bound by this Convention and for which this Convention is in force.

   (b) This Convention applies mutatis mutandis to those territories referred to in Article 26, paragraph 2(b), which become Parties to this Convention in accordance with the conditions set out in that paragraph, and to that extent "States Parties" refers to those territories.
3. "UNESCO" means the United Nations Educational, Scientific and Cultural Organization.
4. "Director-General" means the Director-General of UNESCO.
5. "Area" means the seabed and ocean floor and subsoil thereof, beyond the limits of national jurisdiction.
6. "Activities directed at underwater cultural heritage" means activities having underwater cultural heritage as their primary object and which may, directly or indirectly, physically disturb or otherwise damage underwater cultural heritage.
7. "Activities incidentally affecting underwater cultural heritage" means activities which, despite not having underwater cultural heritage as their primary object or one of their objects, may physically disturb or otherwise damage underwater cultural heritage.
8. "State vessels and aircraft" means warships, and other vessels or aircraft that were owned or operated by a State and used, at the time of sinking, only for government non-commercial purposes, that are identified as such and that meet the definition of underwater cultural heritage.
9. "Rules" means the Rules concerning activities directed at underwater cultural heritage, as referred to in Article 33 of this Convention.

Article 2 – Objectives and General Principles

1. This Convention aims to ensure and strengthen the protection of underwater cultural heritage.
2. States Parties shall cooperate in the protection of underwater cultural heritage.
3. States Parties shall preserve underwater cultural heritage for the benefit of humanity in conformity with the provisions of this Convention.
4. States Parties shall, individually or jointly as appropriate, take all appropriate measures in conformity with this Convention and with international law that are necessary to protect underwater cultural heritage, using for this purpose the best practicable means at their disposal and in accordance with their capabilities.
5. The preservation *in situ* of underwater cultural heritage shall be considered as the first option before allowing or engaging in any activities directed at this heritage.
6. Recovered underwater cultural heritage shall be deposited, conserved and managed in a manner that ensures its long-term preservation.
7. Underwater cultural heritage shall not be commercially exploited.
8. Consistent with State practice and international law, including the United Nations Convention on the Law of the Sea, nothing in this Convention shall be interpreted as modifying the rules of international law and State practice pertaining to sovereign immunities, nor any State's rights with respect to its State vessels and aircraft.
9. States Parties shall ensure that proper respect is given to all human remains located in maritime waters.
10. Responsible non-intrusive access to observe or document *in situ* underwater cultural heritage shall be encouraged to create public awareness, appreciation, and protection of the heritage except where such access is incompatible with its protection and management.
11. No act or activity undertaken on the basis of this Convention shall constitute grounds for claiming, contending or disputing any claim to national sovereignty or jurisdiction.

Article 3 – Relationship between this Convention and the United Nations Convention on the Law of the Sea

Nothing in this Convention shall prejudice the rights, jurisdiction and duties of States under international law, including the United Nations Convention on the Law of the Sea. This Convention shall be interpreted and applied in the context of and in a manner consistent with international law, including the United Nations Convention on the Law of the Sea.

Article 4 – Relationship to Law of Salvage and Law of Finds

Any activity relating to underwater cultural heritage to which this Convention applies shall not be subject to the law of salvage or law of finds, unless it:

(a) is authorized by the competent authorities, and
(b) is in full conformity with this Convention, and
(c) ensures that any recovery of the underwater cultural heritage achieves its maximum protection.

Article 5 – Activities Incidentally Affecting Underwater Cultural Heritage

Each State Party shall use the best practicable means at its disposal to prevent or mitigate any adverse effects that might arise from activities under its jurisdiction incidentally affecting underwater cultural heritage.

Article 6 – Bilateral, Regional or Other Multilateral Agreements

1. States Parties are encouraged to enter into bilateral, regional or other multilateral agreements or develop existing agreements, for the preservation of underwater cultural heritage. All such agreements shall be in full conformity with the provisions of this Convention and shall not dilute its universal character. States may, in such agreements, adopt rules and regulations which would ensure better protection of underwater cultural heritage than those adopted in this Convention.
2. The Parties to such bilateral, regional or other multilateral agreements may invite States with a verifiable link, especially a cultural, historical or archaeological link, to the underwater cultural heritage concerned to join such agreements.
3. This Convention shall not alter the rights and obligations of States Parties regarding the protection of sunken vessels, arising from other bilateral, regional or other multilateral agreements concluded before its adoption, and, in particular, those that are in conformity with the purposes of this Convention.

Article 7 – Underwater Cultural Heritage in Internal Waters, Archipelagic Waters and Territorial Sea

1. States Parties, in the exercise of their sovereignty, have the exclusive right to regulate and authorize activities directed at underwater cultural heritage in their internal waters, archipelagic waters and territorial sea.
2. Without prejudice to other international agreements and rules of international law regarding the protection of underwater cultural heritage, States Parties shall require that the Rules be applied to activities directed at underwater cultural heritage in their internal waters, archipelagic waters and territorial sea.
3. Within their archipelagic waters and territorial sea, in the exercise of their sovereignty and in recognition of general practice among States, States Parties, with a view to cooperating on the best methods of protecting State vessels and aircraft, should inform the flag State Party to this Convention and, if applicable, other States with a verifiable link, especially a cultural, historical or archaeological link, with respect to the discovery of such identifiable State vessels and aircraft.

Article 8 – Underwater Cultural Heritage in the Contiguous Zone

Without prejudice to and in addition to Articles 9 and 10, and in accordance with Article 303, paragraph 2, of the United Nations Convention on the Law of the Sea, States Parties may regulate and authorize activities directed at underwater cultural heritage within their contiguous zone. In so doing, they shall require that the Rules be applied.

Article 9 – Reporting and Notification in the Exclusive Economic Zone and on the Continental Shelf

1. All States Parties have a responsibility to protect underwater cultural heritage in the exclusive economic zone and on the continental shelf in conformity with this Convention.
   Accordingly:
   a) a State Party shall require that when its national, or a vessel flying its flag, discovers or intends to engage in activities directed at underwater cultural heritage located in its exclusive economic zone or on its continental shelf, the national or the master of the vessel shall report such discovery or activity to it;
   b) in the exclusive economic zone or on the continental shelf of another State Party:
      (i) States Parties shall require the national or the master of the vessel to report such discovery or activity to them and to that other State Party;
      (ii) alternatively, a State Party shall require the national or master of the vessel to report such discovery or activity to it and shall ensure the rapid and effective transmission of such reports to all other States Parties.
2. On depositing its instrument of ratification, acceptance, approval or accession, a State Party shall declare the manner in which reports will be transmitted under paragraph 1(b) of this Article.
3. A State Party shall notify the Director-General of discoveries or activities reported to it under paragraph 1 of this Article.
4. The Director-General shall promptly make available to all States Parties any information notified to him under paragraph 3 of this Article.
5. Any State Party may declare to the State Party in whose exclusive economic zone or on whose continental shelf the underwater cultural heritage is located its interest in being consulted on how to ensure the effective protection of that underwater cultural heritage. Such declaration shall be based on a verifiable link, especially a cultural, historical or archaeological link, to the underwater cultural heritage concerned.

Article 10 – Protection of Underwater Cultural Heritage in the Exclusive Economic Zone and on the Continental Shelf

1. No authorization shall be granted for an activity directed at underwater cultural heritage located in the exclusive economic zone or on the continental shelf except in conformity with the provisions of this Article.

2. A State Party in whose exclusive economic zone or on whose continental shelf underwater cultural heritage is located has the right to prohibit or authorize any activity directed at such heritage to prevent interference with its sovereign rights or jurisdiction as provided for by international law including the United Nations Convention on the Law of the Sea.
3. Where there is a discovery of underwater cultural heritage or it is intended that activity shall be directed at underwater cultural heritage in a State Party's exclusive economic zone or on its continental shelf, that State Party shall:
   (a) consult all other States Parties which have declared an interest under Article 9, paragraph 5, on how best to protect the underwater cultural heritage;
   (b) coordinate such consultations as "Coordinating State", unless it expressly declares that it does not wish to do so, in which case the States Parties which have declared an interest under Article 9, paragraph 5, shall appoint a Coordinating State.
4. Without prejudice to the duty of all States Parties to protect underwater cultural heritage by way of all practicable measures taken in accordance with international law to prevent immediate danger to the underwater cultural heritage, including looting, the Coordinating State may take all practicable measures, and/or issue any necessary authorizations in conformity with this Convention and, if necessary prior to consultations, to prevent any immediate danger to the underwater cultural heritage, whether arising from human activities or any other cause, including looting. In taking such measures assistance may be requested from other States Parties.
5. The Coordinating State:
   (a) shall implement measures of protection which have been agreed by the consulting States, which include the Coordinating State, unless the consulting States, which include the Coordinating State, agree that another State Party shall implement those measures;
   (b) shall issue all necessary authorizations for such agreed measures in conformity with the Rules, unless the consulting States, which include the Coordinating State, agree that another State Party shall issue those authorizations;
   (c) may conduct any necessary preliminary research on the underwater cultural heritage and shall issue all necessary authorizations therefor, and shall promptly inform the Director-General of the results, who in turn will make such information promptly available to other States Parties.
6. In coordinating consultations, taking measures, conducting preliminary research and/or issuing authorizations pursuant to this Article, the Coordinating State shall act on behalf of the States Parties as a whole and not in its own interest. Any such action shall not in itself constitute a basis for the assertion of any preferential or jurisdictional rights not provided for in international law, including the United Nations Convention on the Law of the Sea.
7. Subject to the provisions of paragraphs 2 and 4 of this Article, no activity directed at State vessels and aircraft shall be conducted without the agreement of the flag State and the collaboration of the Coordinating State.

Article 11 – Reporting and Notification in the Area

1. States Parties have a responsibility to protect underwater cultural heritage in the Area in conformity with this Convention and Article 149 of the United Nations Convention on the Law of the Sea. Accordingly when a national, or a vessel flying the flag of a State Party, discovers or intends to engage in activities directed at underwater cultural heritage located in the Area, that State Party shall require its national, or the master of the vessel, to report such discovery or activity to it.
2. States Parties shall notify the Director-General and the Secretary-General of the International Seabed Authority of such discoveries or activities reported to them.
3. The Director-General shall promptly make available to all States Parties any such information supplied by States Parties.
4. Any State Party may declare to the Director-General its interest in being consulted on how to ensure the effective protection of that underwater cultural heritage. Such declaration shall be based on a verifiable link to the underwater cultural heritage concerned, particular regard being paid to the preferential rights of States of cultural, historical or archaeological origin.

Article 12 – Protection of Underwater Cultural Heritage in the Area

1. No authorization shall be granted for any activity directed at underwater cultural heritage located in the Area except in conformity with the provisions of this Article.
2. The Director-General shall invite all States Parties which have declared an interest under Article 11, paragraph 4, to consult on how best to protect the underwater cultural heritage, and to appoint a State Party to coordinate such consultations as the "Coordinating State". The Director-General shall also invite the International Seabed Authority to participate in such consultations.
3. All States Parties may take all practicable measures in conformity with this Convention, if necessary prior to consultations, to prevent any immediate danger to the underwater cultural heritage, whether arising from human activity or any other cause including looting.
4. The Coordinating State shall:
   (a) implement measures of protection which have been agreed by the consulting States, which include the Coordinating State, unless the consulting States, which include the Coordinating State, agree that another State Party shall implement those measures; and
   (b) issue all necessary authorizations for such agreed measures, in conformity with this Convention, unless the consulting States, which include the Coordinating State, agree that another State Party shall issue those authorizations.
5. The Coordinating State may conduct any necessary preliminary research on the underwater cultural heritage and shall issue all necessary authorizations therefor, and shall promptly inform the Director-General of the results, who in turn shall make such information available to other States Parties.
6. In coordinating consultations, taking measures, conducting preliminary research, and/or issuing authorizations pursuant to this Article, the Coordinating State

shall act for the benefit of humanity as a whole, on behalf of all States Parties. Particular regard shall be paid to the preferential rights of States of cultural, historical or archaeological origin in respect of the underwater cultural heritage concerned.

7. No State Party shall undertake or authorize activities directed at State vessels and aircraft in the Area without the consent of the flag State.

Article 13 – Sovereign Immunity

Warships and other government ships or military aircraft with sovereign immunity, operated for non-commercial purposes, undertaking their normal mode of operations, and not engaged in activities directed at underwater cultural heritage, shall not be obliged to report discoveries of underwater cultural heritage under Articles 9, 10, 11 and 12 of this Convention. However States Parties shall ensure, by the adoption of appropriate measures not impairing the operations or operational capabilities of their warships or other government ships or military aircraft with sovereign immunity operated for non-commercial purposes, that they comply, as far as is reasonable and practicable, with Articles 9, 10, 11 and 12 of this Convention.

Article 14 – Control of Entry into the Territory, Dealing and Possession

States Parties shall take measures to prevent the entry into their territory, the dealing in, or the possession of, underwater cultural heritage illicitly exported and/or recovered, where recovery was contrary to this Convention.

Article 15 – Non-use of Areas under the Jurisdiction of States Parties

States Parties shall take measures to prohibit the use of their territory, including their maritime ports, as well as artificial islands, installations and structures under their exclusive jurisdiction or control, in support of any activity directed at underwater cultural heritage which is not in conformity with this Convention.

Article 16 – Measures Relating to Nationals and Vessels

States Parties shall take all practicable measures to ensure that their nationals and vessels flying their flag do not engage in any activity directed at underwater cultural heritage in a manner not in conformity with this Convention.

Article 17 – Sanctions

1. Each State Party shall impose sanctions for violations of measures it has taken to implement this Convention.
2. Sanctions applicable in respect of violations shall be adequate in severity to be effective in securing compliance with this Convention and to discourage violations

wherever they occur and shall deprive offenders of the benefit deriving from their illegal activities.

3. States Parties shall cooperate to ensure enforcement of sanctions imposed under this Article.

Article 18 – Seizure and Disposition of Underwater Cultural Heritage

1. Each State Party shall take measures providing for the seizure of underwater cultural heritage in its territory that has been recovered in a manner not in conformity with this Convention.
2. Each State Party shall record, protect and take all reasonable measures to stabilize underwater cultural heritage seized under this Convention.
3. Each State Party shall notify the Director-General and any other State with a verifiable link, especially a cultural, historical or archaeological link, to the underwater cultural heritage concerned of any seizure of underwater cultural heritage that it has made under this Convention.
4. A State Party which has seized underwater cultural heritage shall ensure that its disposition be for the public benefit, taking into account the need for conservation and research; the need for reassembly of a dispersed collection; the need for public access, exhibition and education; and the interests of any State with a verifiable link, especially a cultural, historical or archaeological link, in respect of the underwater cultural heritage concerned.

Article 19 – Cooperation and Information-sharing

1. States Parties shall cooperate and assist each other in the protection and management of underwater cultural heritage under this Convention, including, where practicable, collaborating in the investigation, excavation, documentation, conservation, study and presentation of such heritage.
2. To the extent compatible with the purposes of this Convention, each State Party undertakes to share information with other States Parties concerning underwater cultural heritage, including discovery of heritage, location of heritage, heritage excavated or recovered contrary to this Convention or otherwise in violation of international law, pertinent scientific methodology and technology, and legal developments relating to such heritage.
3. Information shared between States Parties, or between UNESCO and States Parties, regarding the discovery or location of underwater cultural heritage shall, to the extent compatible with their national legislation, be kept confidential and reserved to competent authorities of States Parties as long as the disclosure of such information might endanger or otherwise put at risk the preservation of such underwater cultural heritage.
4. Each State Party shall take all practicable measures to disseminate information, including where feasible through appropriate international databases, about underwater cultural heritage excavated or recovered contrary to this Convention or otherwise in violation of international law.

Article 20 – Public Awareness

Each State Party shall take all practicable measures to raise public awareness regarding the value and significance of underwater cultural heritage and the importance of protecting it under this Convention.

Article 21 – Training in Underwater Archaeology

States Parties shall cooperate in the provision of training in underwater archaeology, in techniques for the conservation of underwater cultural heritage and, on agreed terms, in the transfer of technology relating to underwater cultural heritage.

Article 22 – Competent Authorities

1. In order to ensure the proper implementation of this Convention, States Parties shall establish competent authorities or reinforce the existing ones where appropriate, with the aim of providing for the establishment, maintenance and updating of an inventory of underwater cultural heritage, the effective protection, conservation, presentation and management of underwater cultural heritage, as well as research and education.
2. States Parties shall communicate to the Director-General the names and addresses of their competent authorities relating to underwater cultural heritage.

Article 23 – Meetings of States Parties

1. The Director-General shall convene a Meeting of States Parties within one year of the entry into force of this Convention and thereafter at least once every two years. At the request of a majority of States Parties, the Director-General shall convene an Extraordinary Meeting of States Parties.
2. The Meeting of States Parties shall decide on its functions and responsibilities.
3. The Meeting of States Parties shall adopt its own Rules of Procedure.
4. The Meeting of States Parties may establish a Scientific and Technical Advisory Body composed of experts nominated by the States Parties with due regard to the principle of equitable geographical distribution and the desirability of a gender balance.
5. The Scientific and Technical Advisory Body shall appropriately assist the Meeting of States Parties in questions of a scientific or technical nature regarding the implementation of the Rules.

Article 24 – Secretariat for this Convention

1. The Director-General shall be responsible for the functions of the Secretariat for this Convention.
2. The duties of the Secretariat shall include:
   (a) organizing Meetings of States Parties as provided for in Article 23, paragraph 1; and

(b) assisting States Parties in implementing the decisions of the Meetings of States Parties.

Article 25 – Peaceful Settlement of Disputes

1. Any dispute between two or more States Parties concerning the interpretation or application of this Convention shall be subject to negotiations in good faith or other peaceful means of settlement of their own choice.
2. If those negotiations do not settle the dispute within a reasonable period of time, it may be submitted to UNESCO for mediation, by agreement between the States Parties concerned.
3. If mediation is not undertaken or if there is no settlement by mediation, the provisions relating to the settlement of disputes set out in Part XV of the United Nations Convention on the Law of the Sea apply *mutatis mutandis* to any dispute between States Parties to this Convention concerning the interpretation or application of this Convention, whether or not they are also Parties to the United Nations Convention on the Law of the Sea.
4. Any procedure chosen by a State Party to this Convention and to the United Nations Convention on the Law of the Sea pursuant to Article 287 of the latter shall apply to the settlement of disputes under this Article, unless that State Party, when ratifying, accepting, approving or acceding to this Convention, or at any time thereafter, chooses another procedure pursuant to Article 287 for the purpose of the settlement of disputes arising out of this Convention.
5. A State Party to this Convention which is not a Party to the United Nations Convention on the Law of the Sea, when ratifying, accepting, approving or acceding to this Convention or at any time thereafter shall be free to choose, by means of a written declaration, one or more of the means set out in Article 287, paragraph 1, of the United Nations Convention on the Law of the Sea for the purpose of settlement of disputes under this Article. Article 287 shall apply to such a declaration, as well as to any dispute to which such State is party, which is not covered by a declaration in force. For the purpose of conciliation and arbitration, in accordance with Annexes V and VII of the United Nations Convention on the Law of the Sea, such State shall be entitled to nominate conciliators and arbitrators to be included in the lists referred to in Annex V, Article 2, and Annex VII, Article 2, for the settlement of disputes arising out of this Convention.

Article 26 – Ratification, Acceptance, Approval or Accession

1. This Convention shall be subject to ratification, acceptance or approval by Member States of UNESCO.
2. This Convention shall be subject to accession:
   (a) by States that are not members of UNESCO but are members of the United Nations or of a specialized agency within the United Nations system or of the International Atomic Energy Agency, as well as by States Parties to the

Statute of the International Court of Justice and any other State invited to accede to this Convention by the General Conference of UNESCO;

(b) by territories which enjoy full internal self-government, recognized as such by the United Nations, but have not attained full independence in accordance with General Assembly resolution 1514 (XV) and which have competence over the matters governed by this Convention, including the competence to enter into treaties in respect of those matters.

3. The instruments of ratification, acceptance, approval or accession shall be deposited with the Director-General.

Article 27 – Entry Into Force

This Convention shall enter into force three months after the date of the deposit of the twentieth instrument referred to in Article 26, but solely with respect to the twenty States or territories that have so deposited their instruments. It shall enter into force for each other State or territory three months after the date on which that State or territory has deposited its instrument.

Article 28 – Declaration as to Inland Waters

When ratifying, accepting, approving or acceding to this Convention or at any time thereafter, any State or territory may declare that the Rules shall apply to inland waters not of a maritime character.

Article 29 – Limitations to Geographical Scope

At the time of ratifying, accepting, approving or acceding to this Convention, a State or territory may make a declaration to the depositary that this Convention shall not be applicable to specific parts of its territory, internal waters, archipelagic waters or territorial sea, and shall identify therein the reasons for such declaration. Such State shall, to the extent practicable and as quickly as possible, promote conditions under which this Convention will apply to the areas specified in its declaration, and to that end shall also withdraw its declaration in whole or in part as soon as that has been achieved.

Article 30 – Reservations

With the exception of Article 29, no reservations may be made to this Convention.

Article 31 – Amendments

1. A State Party may, by written communication addressed to the Director-General, propose amendments to this Convention. The Director-General shall circulate such communication to all States Parties. If, within six months from the date of the circulation of the communication, not less than one half of the States Parties reply favourably to the request, the Director-General shall present

such proposal to the next Meeting of States Parties for discussion and possible adoption.
2. Amendments shall be adopted by a two-thirds majority of States Parties present and voting.
3. Once adopted, amendments to this Convention shall be subject to ratification, acceptance, approval or accession by the States Parties.
4. Amendments shall enter into force, but solely with respect to the States Parties that have ratified, accepted, approved or acceded to them, three months after the deposit of the instruments referred to in paragraph 3 of this Article by two thirds of the States Parties. Thereafter, for each State or territory that ratifies, accepts, approves or accedes to it, the amendment shall enter into force three months after the date of deposit by that Party of its instrument of ratification, acceptance, approval or accession.
5. A State or territory which becomes a Party to this Convention after the entry into force of amendments in conformity with paragraph 4 of this Article shall, failing an expression of different intention by that State or territory, be considered:
   (a) as a Party to this Convention as so amended; and
   (b) as a Party to the unamended Convention in relation to any State Party not bound by the amendment.

Article 32 – Denunciation

1. A State Party may, by written notification addressed to the Director-General, denounce this Convention.
2. The denunciation shall take effect twelve months after the date of receipt of the notification, unless the notification specifies a later date.
3. The denunciation shall not in any way affect the duty of any State Party to fulfil any obligation embodied in this Convention to which it would be subject under international law independently of this Convention.

Article 33 – The Rules

The Rules annexed to this Convention form an integral part of it and, unless expressly provided otherwise, a reference to this Convention includes a reference to the Rules.

Article 34 – Registration with the United Nations

In conformity with Article 102 of the Charter of the United Nations, this Convention shall be registered with the Secretariat of the United Nations at the request of the Director-General.

Article 35 – Authoritative Texts

This Convention has been drawn up in Arabic, Chinese, English, French, Russian and Spanish, the six texts being equally authoritative.

ANNEX
RULES CONCERNING ACTIVITIES DIRECTED AT UNDERWATER CULTURAL HERITAGE

I. General Principles

Rule 1. The protection of underwater cultural heritage through *in situ* preservation shall be considered as the first option. Accordingly, activities directed at underwater cultural heritage shall be authorized in a manner consistent with the protection of that heritage, and subject to that requirement may be authorized for the purpose of making a significant contribution to protection or knowledge or enhancement of underwater cultural heritage.

Rule 2. The commercial exploitation of underwater cultural heritage for trade or speculation or its irretrievable dispersal is fundamentally incompatible with the protection and proper management of underwater cultural heritage. Underwater cultural heritage shall not be traded, sold, bought or bartered as commercial goods.

This Rule cannot be interpreted as preventing:

(a) the provision of professional archaeological services or necessary services incidental thereto whose nature and purpose are in full conformity with this Convention and are subject to the authorization of the competent authorities;
(b) the deposition of underwater cultural heritage, recovered in the course of a research project in conformity with this Convention, provided such deposition does not prejudice the scientific or cultural interest or integrity of the recovered material or result in its irretrievable dispersal; is in accordance with the provisions of Rules 33 and 34; and is subject to the authorization of the competent authorities.

Rule 3. Activities directed at underwater cultural heritage shall not adversely affect the underwater cultural heritage more than is necessary for the objectives of the project.

Rule 4. Activities directed at underwater cultural heritage must use non-destructive techniques and survey methods in preference to recovery of objects. If excavation or recovery is necessary for the purpose of scientific studies or for the ultimate protection of the underwater cultural heritage, the methods and techniques used must be as non-destructive as possible and contribute to the preservation of the remains.

Rule 5. Activities directed at underwater cultural heritage shall avoid the unnecessary disturbance of human remains or venerated sites.

Rule 6. Activities directed at underwater cultural heritage shall be strictly regulated to ensure proper recording of cultural, historical and archaeological information.

Rule 7. Public access to *in situ* underwater cultural heritage shall be promoted, except where such access is incompatible with protection and management.

Rule 8. International cooperation in the conduct of activities directed at underwater cultural heritage shall be encouraged in order to further the effective exchange or use of archaeologists and other relevant professionals.

II. Project Design

Rule 9. Prior to any activity directed at underwater cultural heritage, a project design for the activity shall be developed and submitted to the competent authorities for authorization and appropriate peer review.

Rule 10. The project design shall include:

(a) an evaluation of previous or preliminary studies;
(b) the project statement and objectives;
(c) the methodology to be used and the techniques to be employed;
(d) the anticipated funding;
(e) an expected timetable for completion of the project;
(f) the composition of the team and the qualifications, responsibilities and experience of each team member;
(g) plans for post-fieldwork analysis and other activities;
(h) a conservation programme for artefacts and the site in close cooperation with the competent authorities;
(i) a site management and maintenance policy for the whole duration of the project;
(j) a documentation programme;
(k) a safety policy;
(l) an environmental policy;
(m) arrangements for collaboration with museums and other institutions, in particular scientific institutions;
(n) report preparation;
(o) deposition of archives, including underwater cultural heritage removed; and
(p) a programme for publication.

Rule 11. Activities directed at underwater cultural heritage shall be carried out in accordance with the project design approved by the competent authorities.

Rule 12. Where unexpected discoveries are made or circumstances change, the project design shall be reviewed and amended with the approval of the competent authorities.

Rule 13. In cases of urgency or chance discoveries, activities directed at the underwater cultural heritage, including conservation measures or activities for a period of short duration, in particular site stabilization, may be authorized in the absence of a project design in order to protect the underwater cultural heritage.

III. Preliminary Work

Rule 14. The preliminary work referred to in Rule 10 (a) shall include an assessment that evaluates the significance and vulnerability of the underwater cultural heritage and the surrounding natural environment to damage by the proposed project, and the potential to obtain data that would meet the project objectives.

Rule 15. The assessment shall also include background studies of available historical and archaeological evidence, the archaeological and environmental characteristics of the site, and the consequences of any potential intrusion for the long-term stability of the underwater cultural heritage affected by the activities.

IV. Project Objective, Methodology and Techniques

Rule 16. The methodology shall comply with the project objectives, and the techniques employed shall be as non-intrusive as possible.

V. Funding

Rule 17. Except in cases of emergency to protect underwater cultural heritage, an adequate funding base shall be assured in advance of any activity, sufficient to complete all stages of the project design, including conservation, documentation and curation of recovered artefacts, and report preparation and dissemination.

Rule 18. The project design shall demonstrate an ability, such as by securing a bond, to fund the project through to completion.

Rule 19. The project design shall include a contingency plan that will ensure conservation of underwater cultural heritage and supporting documentation in the event of any interruption of anticipated funding.

VI. Project Duration – Timetable

Rule 20. An adequate timetable shall be developed to assure in advance of any activity directed at underwater cultural heritage the completion of all stages of the project design, including conservation, documentation and curation of recovered underwater cultural heritage, as well as report preparation and dissemination.

Rule 21. The project design shall include a contingency plan that will ensure conservation of underwater cultural heritage and supporting documentation in the event of any interruption or termination of the project.

VII. Competence and Qualifications

Rule 22. Activities directed at underwater cultural heritage shall only be undertaken under the direction and control of, and in the regular presence of, a qualified underwater archaeologist with scientific competence appropriate to the project.

Rule 23. All persons on the project team shall be qualified and have demonstrated competence appropriate to their roles in the project.

VIII. Conservation and Site Management

Rule 24. The conservation programme shall provide for the treatment of the archaeological remains during the activities directed at underwater cultural heritage, during transit and in the long term. Conservation shall be carried out in accordance with current professional standards.

Rule 25. The site management programme shall provide for the protection and management *in situ* of underwater cultural heritage, in the course of and upon termination of fieldwork. The programme shall include public information, reasonable provision for site stabilization, monitoring, and protection against interference.

IX. Documentation

Rule 26. The documentation programme shall set out thorough documentation including a progress report of activities directed at underwater cultural heritage, in accordance with current professional standards of archaeological documentation.

Rule 27. Documentation shall include, at a minimum, a comprehensive record of the site, including the provenance of underwater cultural heritage moved or removed in the course of the activities directed at underwater cultural heritage, field notes, plans, drawings, sections, and photographs or recording in other media.

X. Safety

Rule 28. A safety policy shall be prepared that is adequate to ensure the safety and health of the project team and third parties and that is in conformity with any applicable statutory and professional requirements.

XI. Environment

Rule 29. An environmental policy shall be prepared that is adequate to ensure that the seabed and marine life are not unduly disturbed.

XII. Reporting

Rule 30. Interim and final reports shall be made available according to the timetable set out in the project design, and deposited in relevant public records.

Rule 31. Reports shall include:

(a) an account of the objectives;
(b) an account of the methods and techniques employed;
(c) an account of the results achieved;
(d) basic graphic and photographic documentation on all phases of the activity;
(e) recommendations concerning conservation and curation of the site and of any underwater cultural heritage removed; and

(f) recommendations for future activities.

XIII. Curation of Project Archives

Rule 32. Arrangements for curation of the project archives shall be agreed to before any activity commences, and shall be set out in the project design.

Rule 33. The project archives, including any underwater cultural heritage removed and a copy of all supporting documentation shall, as far as possible, be kept together and intact as a collection in a manner that is available for professional and public access as well as for the curation of the archives. This should be done as rapidly as possible and in any case not later than ten years from the completion of the project, in so far as may be compatible with conservation of the underwater cultural heritage.

Rule 34. The project archives shall be managed according to international professional standards, and subject to the authorization of the competent authorities.

XIV. Dissemination

Rule 35. Projects shall provide for public education and popular presentation of the project results where appropriate.

Rule 36. A final synthesis of a project shall be:

(a) made public as soon as possible, having regard to the complexity of the project and the confidential or sensitive nature of the information; and
(b) deposited in relevant public records.

The foregoing is the authentic text of the Convention duly adopted by the General Conference of the United Nations Educational, Scientific and Cultural Organization during its thirty-first session, which was held in Paris and declared closed the third day of November 2001.

IN WITNESS WHEREOF we have appended our signatures this 6th day of November 2001.

The President of the General Conference *The Director-General*

Done in Paris this 6th day of November 2001 in two authentic copies bearing the signature of the President of the thirty-first session of the General Conference and of the Director-General of the United Nations Educational, Scientific and Cultural Organization, which shall be deposited in the archives of the United Nations Educational, Scientific and Cultural Organization and certified true copies of which shall be delivered to all the States and territories referred to in Article 26 as well as to the United Nations.

B) DOCUMENTS RELATING TO THE UNESCO CONVENTION

6. INTERNATIONAL LAW ASSOCIATION – DRAFT CONVENTION ON THE PROTECTION OF THE UNDERWATER CULTURAL HERITAGE (BUENOS AIRES, 20 AUGUST 1994)

Preamble

States party to the present Convention,

Acknowledging the importance of the underwater cultural heritage as an integral part of the cultural heritage of humanity and a particularly important element in the history of peoples, nations, and their relations with each other concerning their shared heritage;

Noting growing public interest in the underwater cultural heritage;

Perceiving that growing threats to the underwater cultural heritage include increasing construction activity, advanced technology that enhances identification of and access to wreck, exploitation of marine resources, and commercialization of efforts to recover underwater cultural heritage;

Determining that the underwater cultural heritage may be threatened by irresponsible activity and that therefore cooperation among States, salvors, divers, their organizations, marine archaeologists, museums and other scientific institutions is essential for the protection of the underwater cultural heritage;

Considering that exploration, excavation, and protection of the underwater cultural heritage necessitates the application of special scientific methods and the use of suitable techniques and equipment as well as a high degree of professional specialization, all of which indicates a need for uniform governing criteria;

Recognizing that the underwater cultural heritage belongs to the common heritage of humanity, and that therefore responsibility for protecting it rests not only with the State or States most directly concerned with a particular activity affecting the heritage or having an historical or cultural link with it, but with all States and other subjects of international law;

Bearing in mind the need for more stringent supervision to prevent any clandestine excavation which, by destroying the environment surrounding underwater cultural heritage, would cause irremediable loss of its historical or scientific significance;

Realizing the need to codify and progressively develop the law in conformity with international rules and practice, including provisions in the 1982 United Nations Convention on the Law of the Sea;

Convinced that information and multidisciplinary education about the underwater cultural heritage, its historical significance, serious threats to it, and the need for responsible diving, deep-water exploration and other activity affecting the underwater cultural heritage, will enable the public to appreciate the importance of the underwater cultural heritage to humanity and the need to preserve it; and

Committed to improving the effectiveness of measures at international and national levels for the preservation in place or, if necessary for scientific or protective purposes, the careful removal of the heritage that may be found beyond the territorial sea;

Have agreed as follows:

Article 1: Definitions

For the purposes of this Convention:

1. "Underwater cultural heritage" means all underwater traces of human existence including:
   a. sites, structures, buildings, artifacts and human remains, together with their archaeological and natural contexts; and
   b. wreck such as a vessel, aircraft, other vehicle or any part thereof, its cargo or other contents, together with its archaeological and natural context.
2. Underwater cultural heritage shall be deemed to have been "abandoned":
   a. whenever technology would make exploration for research or recovery feasible but exploration for research or recovery has not been pursued by the owner of the heritage within 25 years after discovery of the technology; or
   b. whenever no technology would reasonably permit exploration for research or recovery and at least 50 years have elapsed since the last assertion of interest by the owner in the underwater cultural heritage.
3. "Cultural heritage zone" means all the area beyond the territorial sea of the State up to the outer limit of its continental shelf as defined in accordance with relevant rules and principles of international law.
4. "Charter" means the "Charter for the Protection and Management of the Underwater Cultural Heritage" prepared by the International Council for Monuments and Sites (ICOMOS) and annexed to this Convention.

Article 2: Scope of the Convention

1. This Convention applies to underwater cultural heritage which has been lost or abandoned and is submerged underwater for at least 100 years. Any State Party may, however, protect underwater cultural heritage which has been submerged underwater for less than 100 years.
2. This Convention does not apply to any warship, military aircraft, naval auxiliary, or other vessels or aircraft owned or operated by a State and used for the time being only on government non-commercial service, or their contents.

Article 3: General Principle

States Party shall take all reasonable measures to preserve underwater cultural heritage for the benefit of humankind.

Article 4: Non-Applicability of Salvage Law

Underwater cultural heritage to which this Convention applies shall not be subject to the law of salvage.

Article 5: Cultural Heritage Zone

1. A State party to this Convention may establish a cultural heritage zone and notify other States party of its action. Within this zone, the State Party shall have jurisdiction over activities affecting the underwater cultural heritage.
2. A State Party shall take measures to ensure that activities within its zone affecting the underwater cultural heritage comply at a minimum with the provisions of the Charter.

Article 6: Internal and Territorial Waters

States Party shall transmit a copy of the Charter to all relevant authorities within their jurisdiction, requiring them to take appropriate measures to apply the Charter, at a minimum, to activity within their internal and territorial waters.

Article 7: Prohibition of the Use of Territory in Support of Activities Violating the Charter

No State Party shall allow its territory or any other areas over which it exercises jurisdiction to be used in support of any activity affecting underwater cultural heritage and inconsistent with the criteria of the Charter. This provision shall apply to any such activity beyond that State's territorial sea but not within a territorial sea or cultural heritage zone of another State Party.

Article 8: Prohibition of Certain Activities by Nationals and Ships

Each State Party shall undertake to prohibit its nationals and ships of its flags from activities affecting underwater cultural heritage in respect of any area which is not within a cultural heritage zone or territorial sea of another State Party. The prohibition shall not apply to activities affecting the underwater cultural heritage that comply with the Charter.

Article 9: Permits

A State Party to this Convention may provide for the issuance of permits allowing entry into its territory of underwater cultural heritage excavated or retrieved after the effective date of this Convention so long as the State has determined that the excavation and retrieval activities have complied or will comply with the Charter.

Article 10: Seizure of Heritage

1. Subject to Article 9, on the request of any Party or on its own initiative, each State Party, in accordance with its constitutional procedures, shall seize any underwater cultural heritage brought within its territory, directly or indirectly, after having been excavated or retrieved in a manner not conforming with the Charter.
2. A State shall seize underwater cultural heritage known to have been excavated or retrieved from a cultural heritage zone or territorial sea of another State Party only after obtaining the consent of that State.

Article 11: Penal Sanctions

1. Each State party undertakes to impose penal sanctions for importation of underwater cultural heritage which is subject to seizure under Article 10.
2. Each State party agrees to cooperate with other Parties in the enforcement of these sanctions. Such cooperation, consistent with national procedures, shall include but not be limited to, production and transmission of documents, making witnesses available, service of process and extradition.

Article 12: Notification Requirements and Treatment of Seized Heritage

1. Each State party undertakes to notify the State or States of origin, if known, of its seizure of underwater cultural heritage under this Convention.
2. Each State Party undertakes to record, protect and take all reasonable measures to conserve underwater cultural heritage seized under this Convention.
3. Each Party undertakes, wherever possible, to keep underwater cultural heritage seized under this Convention on display or otherwise ensure the fullest reasonable access to it for the benefit of the public.

Article 13: Collaboration and Information-Sharing

1. Whenever a State has expressed a patrimonial interest in particular underwater cultural heritage to another State Party, the latter shall consider collaborating in the investigation, excavation, documentation, conservation, study and cultural promotion of the heritage.
2. To the extent compatible with the purposes of this Convention, each State Party undertakes to share information with other States Party concerning underwater cultural heritage, such as but not limited to, discovery of heritage, location of heritage, heritage excavated or retrieved contrary to the Charter or otherwise in violation of international law, pertinent scientific methodology and technology, and legal developments relating to heritage.
3. Whenever feasible, each State Party shall use appropriate international databases to disseminate information about underwater cultural heritage excavated or retrieved contrary to the Charter or otherwise in violation of international law.

Article 14: Education

Each State Party shall endeavor by educational means to create and develop in the public mind a realization of the value of the underwater cultural heritage as well as the threat to this heritage posed by violations of this Convention and non-compliance with the Charter.

Article 15: Revision of the Charter

Revisions in the Charter by the International Council for Monuments and Sites shall be deemed to be revisions in the annexed Charter, binding on States Party except for those State Parties that notify their non-acceptance to the Director-General of the United Nations Educational, Scientific and Cultural Organization within six months after the effective date of a revision. UNESCO shall inform the States Party of such revisions prior to the effective date of the revision.

Article 16: Dispute Resolution

1. States, on becoming Parties to this Convention, undertake to establish an internal procedure or procedures for resolving disputes concerning whether an activity resulting in excavation or retrieval of the underwater cultural heritage did or did not comply with the Charter.
2. Any dispute between two or more States Party concerning the interpretation or application of the present Convention that is not settled by negotiation shall, at the request of one of them, be submitted to arbitration. If, within six months from the date of the request for arbitration, the States Party are unable to agree on the organization of the arbitration, any one of those States Party may refer the dispute to the International Court of Justice, or a special chamber thereof, by a request in conformity with the Statute of the Court.

Article 17: Official Languages

This Convention is drawn up in Arabic, Chinese, English, French, Russian and Spanish, the six texts being equally authoritative.

Article 18: Ratification or Acceptance

1. This Convention shall be subject to ratification or acceptance by States Members of the United Nations Educational, Scientific and Cultural Organization, in accordance with their respective constitutional procedures.
2. The instruments of ratification or acceptance shall be deposited with the Director-General of the United Nations Educational, Scientific and Cultural Organization.

Article 19: Applicability to Territorial Units

1. If a State Party has two or more territorial units in which different systems of law are applicable in relation to the matters dealt with in this Convention, it may, at the time of ratification, acceptance, approval or accession, declare that this Convention is to extend to all its territorial units or only to one or more of them, and may substitute its declaration by another declaration at any time.
2. These declarations are to be notified to the depository and are to state expressly the territorial units to which the Convention extends.

Article 20: Reservations, Understandings and Declarations

1. The Director-General of the United Nations Educational, Scientific and Cultural Organization shall receive and circulate to all States Party the text of reservations, understandings and declarations made by States at the time of ratification or accession.
2. A reservation incompatible with the objects and purposes of the present Convention shall not be permitted.
3. Reservations may be withdrawn at any time by notification to that effect addressed to the Director-General of the United Nations Educational, Scientific and Cultural Organization, who shall then inform all States. Such notification shall take effect on the date on which it is received by the Director-General of the United Nations Educational, Scientific and Cultural Organization.

Article 21: Accession by Nonmember States

1. This Convention shall be open to accession by all States not Members of the United Nations Educational, Scientific and Cultural Organization.
2. Accession shall be effected by the deposit of an instrument of accession with the Director-General of the United Nations Educational, Scientific and Cultural Organization.

Article 22: Entry into Force

This Convention shall enter into force three months after the date of the deposit of the tenth instrument of ratification, acceptance or accession, but only with respect to those States which have deposited their respective instruments of ratification, acceptance or accession on or before that date. It shall enter into force with respect to any other State three months after the deposit of its instruments of ratification, acceptance or accession.

Article 23: Denunciations

1. Each State Party to this Convention may denounce the Convention.
2. The denunciation shall be notified by an instrument in writing, deposited with the

Director-General of the United Nations Educational, Scientific and Cultural Organization.

3. The denunciation shall take effect six months after notification.

The foregoing is the authentic text of the Convention duly adopted by the General Conference of the United Nations Education, Scientific and Cultural Organization during its . . . session, which was held in . . . and declared closed on the . . . day of . . ..

IN FAITH WHEREOF, we have appended our signatures this . . . day of . . ..

The President of the General Conference

The Director-General

7. Amendment to the Draft UNESCO Convention Proposed by Russia and United Kingdom and sponsored by the USA

UNESCO
General Conference
31st session
Commission IV

31 C/COM.IV/DR.5
(COM.IV)
26 October 2001
Original: English

Item **8.4** of the agenda

DRAFT RESOLUTION
submitted by RUSSIAN FEDERATION and UNITED KINGDOM

DRAFT CONVENTION ON THE PROTECTION
OF THE UNDERWATER CULTURAL HERITAGE

The authors inform the General Conference that this draft resolution is endorsed by the United States of America

Article 3: delete "international law, including"

Article 9(1) (new wording):

"(b) When the discovery or activity is located in the exclusive economic zone or on the continental shelf of another State Party:
 (i) a State Party shall require its national or the master of a vessel flying its flag to report such discovery or activity to it and to that other State Party;
 (ii) alternatively, a State Party shall require its national or the master of a vessel flying its flag to report such discovery or activity to it and shall ensure the rapid and effective transmission of such reports to all other States Parties."

Article 10(2):

- add "when necessary" after "directed at such heritage";
- change "international law including" to "international law as set forth in".

Article 10(4) (new wording):

"Without prejudice to the duty of all States Parties to protect underwater cultural heritage by way of all practicable measures taken in accordance with international law to prevent immediate danger to the underwater cultural heritage, including looting, the Coordinating State may take all practicable measures and/or issue any necessary authorizations in conformity with this Convention and, if necessary prior to consultations, to prevent any immediate danger to the underwater cultural heritage, from activities directed at underwater cultural heritage, including looting, or from natural causes unrelated to human activities. In taking such measures, assistance may be requested from other States Parties, but in any event prompt assistance shall be requested from the State Party that is the flag State of the vessel engaged in such activities".

Article 7(3):

Within their internal waters, archipelagic waters and territorial sea, in the exercise of their sovereignty and in recognition of general practice among States, States Parties, with a view to cooperating on the best methods of protecting State vessels and aircraft, shall consult ~~should inform~~ the flag State Party to this Convention and, if applicable, other States with a verifiable link, especially a cultural, historical or archaeological link, with respect to the discovery of such identifiable State vessels and aircraft. Such State vessels and aircraft shall not be recovered without the collaboration of the flag State, unless the vessels and aircraft have been expressly abandoned in accordance with the laws of that State.

Article 10(7):

Notwithstanding ~~Subject to~~ the provisions of paragraphs 2 and 4 of this Article, no activity directed at State vessels and aircraft shall be conducted without the agreement of the flag State ~~and the collaboration of the Coordinating State~~.

Article 13:

Warships, naval auxiliaries and other government ships or military aircraft with sovereign immunity, operated for non-commercial purposes, undertaking their normal mode of operations, and not engaged in activities directed at underwater cultural heritage, shall not be obliged to report discoveries of underwater cultural heritage under Articles 9, 10, 11 and 12 of this Convention. However, States Parties shall ensure, by the adoption of appropriate measures not impairing the operations or operational capabilities of their warships, naval auxiliaries or other government ships or military aircraft with sovereign immunity operated for non-commercial purposes, that such ships and aircraft ~~they~~ comply, as far as is reasonable and practicable, with Article 9, 10, 11 and 12 of this Convention.

[Note: These proposals have been put forward by the above delegations as improvements to the text in an effort to broaden support for the Convention; however, not every delegation views each of these proposals as essential.]

8. STATEMENTS:

a) Remarks Presented by the Government of Italy (July 2000)

DRAFT CONVENTION ON THE PROTECTION OF THE UNDERWATER CULTURAL HERITAGE

Third Meeting of Governmental Experts
UNESCO headquarters, Paris, 3-7 July 2000

1. As a centre and crossroad of several civilisations, the cultural heritage of Italy is particularly rich. Objects of an archaeological and historical nature are also often found in the Mediterranean waters adjacent to the Italian peninsula. While this heritage spiritually belongs to mankind as a whole, Italy, and the other Mediterranean countries linked with the objects in question, are more directly interested in its preservation. This is the reason why Italy attaches a great importance to the draft Convention on the protection of the underwater cultural heritage which is presently being negotiated within the framework of UNESCO.

2. Two provisions of the 1982 United Nation Convention on the Law of the Sea (UNCLOS) deal with archaeological and historical objects. Under Art. 149, if these objects are found in the seabed beyond the limits of national jurisdiction (the Area), they "shall be preserved or disposed of for the benefit of mankind as a whole, particular regard being paid to the preferential rights of the State or country of origin, or the State of cultural origin, or the State of historical and archaeological origin". Under Art. 303, para. 2, in order to control traffic in such objects, the coastal State may presume that their removal from the seabed in the 24-mile contiguous zone without its approval would result in an infringement within its territory or territorial sea of its laws and regulations.

3. A question may be asked in this respect. What rules apply to archaeological and historical objects which are found on the continental shelf, that is on the seabed located between the 24 miles from the coast and the Area? There is no clear response in the UNCLOS. This legal vacuum greatly affects the protection of cultural heritage.

4. Nevertheless, it is within the spirit of UNCLOS that the cultural heritage must be protected, wherever in the sea it is located. According to Art. 303, para. 1, "States have the duty to protect objects of an archaeological and historical nature found at sea and shall co-operate for this purpose". This general obligation binds every Party and applies to all such objects, wherever they are found. Very important for the present negotiation is para. 4 of the same Art. 303: "This article [i.e. Art. 303] is without prejudice to other international agreements and rules of international law regarding the protection of objects of an archaeological and historical nature". This is an interesting point: the UNCLOS allows for the drafting of more specific treaty

regimes which can ensure a better protection of the underwater cultural heritage. In other words, the UNCLOS itself fully encourages the future filling of the gaps that it has left open, which are particularly evident in the case of the cultural heritage found on the continental shelf. This opportunity should not be lost by the States participating in the present UNESCO negotiations. It would be meaningless to simply repeat the provisions of the UNCLOS, including their shortcomings, without adding any improvements.

5. To leave the regime as it is now would lead to an unacceptable consequence: namely, the risk of leaving a great part of the marine cultural heritage without protection. The problems posed by flags of convenience should also be taken into consideration. Availing himself of an abstract application of the principle of freedom of the sea, any person on board any ship or submarine could explore the continental shelf adjacent to another State, bring the archaeological and historical objects to the surface, become their owner under a domestic legislation, import the objects into his national country, and sell them on the private market. Is this a proper use of the cultural heritage? Is there any guarantee that the objects are disposed of for the public benefit rather than for a private commercial gain? Can a coastal State which has a direct cultural link with the objects in question accept such an increasing pillage of its history? In the case of Italy the answer is negative.

6. The establishment of an effective protection regime for objects located on the continental shelf or within the exclusive economic zone cannot be seen as an encroachment on the freedom of the sea; nor is it the creation of another jurisdictional zone. It is difficult to see how clear rules and entitlements on the underwater cultural heritage could affect, for example, navigation in the superjacent waters. While generally committed to the principle of freedom of the sea, Italy believes that the sea is free only for uses which are not injurious to the legitimate interests of any nation and the international community as a whole. The concept of freedom of the sea is today to be understood not in an abstract way, but in the context of the present range of marine activities and in relation to the other potentially conflicting uses and interests. Also the idea that the coastal State can exercise rights on the mineral resources of its continental shelf could have seemed, when it was proposed, an encroachment on the freedom of the high seas. Presumed encroachments on the freedom of the high seas can be easily found also in the recent 1995 Straddling and Highly Migratory Fish Stocks Agreement. They were considered a necessary tool to promote the conservation and sound management of living marine resources and, as such, were found reasonable and acceptable by the great majority of States. Similarly effective solutions need now to be agreed upon also as regards the underwater cultural heritage. Why should there remain a freedom-of-fishing-type regime for objects of an archaeological and historical nature? Do they need less protection than fish? This is the core of our present UNESCO negotiation: a "first come, first served" regime is to be definitely banned.

7. The coastal State is a country directly concerned with the protection of the underwater cultural heritage found on its continental shelf. This is even more evident

where the coastal State has a direct and preferential link with the objects in question, being the State of origin, or the State of cultural origin, or the State of historical and archaeological origin. The coastal State should be entitled to be informed of, to regulate and to authorize all activities relating to underwater cultural heritage found on its continental shelf (or in its exclusive economic zone). This is the best way to promote the preservation of the heritage and to ensure the disposal of it for the public benefit. Rights of this kind are neither specifically allowed, nor prohibited by UNCLOS. It is the filling of an UNCLOS gap, as permitted by UNCLOS itself.

8. Of course, States other than the coastal State can also have an interest in archaeological and historical objects. The special position of the States of cultural, historical or archaeological origin could be taken into consideration not only in the Area (as already provided for by Art. 149), but also in the case of objects found on the continental shelf of another State. The merits of the States whose nationals have lawfully and openly made substantial efforts in the research and location of objects could also be taken into account. An obligation of all the States directly concerned to co-operate in, and negotiate the finding of, reasonable solutions should in this respect be envisaged. Italy, bearing the example of the Mediterranean Sea in mind (but the same applies to other regional seas as well), proposed that more stringent rules may be adopted at the regional level under agreements open to the participation of States of cultural, historical and archaeological origin. These agreements are directed at the preservation of a common cultural heritage. Again, all these are consequences arising from the main point: that a "first come, first served" (or a "freedom-of-fishing-type") regime is to be clearly banned. Why – to give a purely hypothetical example – should a citizen of a country which has no link whatsoever with a specific heritage be able to survey with submarines the continental shelf of other States and use remotely-powered vehicles to remove any objects he chooses, without any notice to the States concerned?

9. In the light of what is said above, Italy believes that a sound regime can be negotiated for the protection of the underwater cultural heritage. Aiming at this objective Italy is participating in the present UNESCO negotiations with a constructive spirit. It is ready to examine and discuss any proposals made by other States. It believes that, despite the differences in their positions, all the other States participating in the negotiation substantially agree on the basic assumption that a "freedom-of-fishing-type" regime is not the acceptable solution.

b) Remarks Prior to Vote during Debates in Commission IV on Culture (29 October 2001, 31st Session of the General Conference, UNESCO)

Argentina

La Argentina participó en el proceso de elaboración del proyecto de Convención sobre el patrimonio cultural subacuático, proceso iniciado hacia 1996 que consumió mas de diez encuentros formales u oficiosos de expertos gubernamentales. A lo largo del mismo, pudimos comprobar como paulatinamente se logró encontrar respuestas a inquietudes inicialmente planteadas respecto de la mejor manera de asegurar la protección de los bienes culturales situados bajo el agua.

Creemos que el producto de esta intensa y extensa labor responde a las intenciones que inspiraron su elaboración. Quisiéramos destacar los siguientes aspectos del mismo.

En primer lugar, y como sostuviera el señor Bouchenaki en su presentación inicial, la futura Convención cubrirá un vacio importante en la arquitectura normativa de la UNESCO para la protección del patrimonio mundial. Coincidimos con los otros países de América Latina y el Caribe en que este vacio nos resulta inquietante, dado que nos priva de un instrumento internacional que nos permita, primero, conocer actos de pillaje del patrimonio cultural situado frente a nuestras costas, y luego, poder prevenirlos o evitarlos, en cooperacion con otros Estados interesados, la UNESCO y las organizaciones no gubernamentales competentes. Hemos podido constatar que ésta es una necesidad compartida por nuestros colegas de la demás regiones geograficas – en especial, Africa, Asia, la región árabe y el Pacífico.

Valoramos, por otra parte, las múltiples referencias en el proyecto a la conformidad de la futura Convención con el derecho internacional del mar, incluido el derecho que codifica la Convención de las Naciones Unidas de 1982.

En el mismo sentido, apreciamos que el proyecto logra construir un esquema eficaz de cooperación entre Estados, que se superpone y supera a la lógica reduccionista de confrontación de derechos y obligaciones – lógica en la que el único prejudicado es el patrimonio cultural.

Finalmente, nos satisface comprobar la visión que evidencia el proyecto al prever la formación de capacidades y la transferencia de tecnología. Ello es importante para que países como el nuestro puedan asociarse activamente al mecanismo de protección internacional que contempla la Convención.

Por lo motivos señalados, nuestro país presta su conformidad al proyecto de Convención incluido en el parrafo 13 del documento 31C/24. Pensamos que su adopción por la UNESCO y en Paris, una reconocida capital de la cultura y del patrimonio, constituira un auspicioso símbolo para su futuro.

Canada

Canada supports fully the adoption of the draft Convention on the Protection of the Underwater Cultural Heritage during the course of this General Conference. We have all worked very hard to reach a text that the largest number of countries can support. We have delicately balanced positions that, in some cases, were diametrically opposed at the start of our Experts Group deliberations. All participants have moved toward a common position. It is Canada's hope that all, sooner or later, will be able to ratify this Convention.

Let me take just a few minutes to touch on the themes that, for Canada, are of particular importance in this Convention.

First, the activity regulated by the Convention:

Our work has resulted in a text that is focussed on "activities directed at" underwater cultural heritage. The oceans represent an enormous portion of the earth's surface and a daunting challenge for any Convention of this type. By focussing on "activities directed at" underwater heritage, we take aim at what concerns us most: targeted activities that may disturb or destroy our common heritage.

Secondly, the roles of different States Parties in respect of the heritage.

Canada has continuously maintained that the protection of underwater cultural heritage is the responsibility of all States. For us, flag State jurisdiction is an important norm that also implies important duties. Coastal States, in turn, have significant responsibilities that complement their rights under international law regarding their territorial seas, exclusive economic zones and continental shelves. The draft Convention represents an appropriate balance of these rights and responsibilities, as well as those of States having a "verifiable link".

Thirdly, the control of activities directed at underwater cultural heritage:

Canada is very pleased that "activities directed at" underwater cultural heritage cannot take place until they have been authorized under this Convention. Together, we have set out a clear regime that requires the reporting of finds, the prior authorization of any targeted activity and the mandatory application of an effective set of rules to such activity.

Canada is looking forward to seeing the fruits of our collective labour result in a new UNESCO Convention that – together with a spirit of international cooperation and understanding – will take us a long way toward our common objective of protecting the world's underwater cultural heritage.

Japan

We would like first to commend the untiring efforts by Mr. Lund, Chairman of the experts meetings, the Member States, the Secretariat and all the parties concerned to finalize the Draft Convention on the Protection of the Underwater Cultural Heritage.

We faced various difficulties in the course of your negotiations, but with great patience and cooperation we have been able to come up with a final draft Convention. There is no denying the fact that, as a result of compromising efforts to absorb different views and positions to the extent possible, we had to sacrifice clarity from time to time. This ambiguity, however, was the good facilitator to reconcile some conflicting views and should be called as "constructive ambiguity".

As we all know, the focal issue was the relationship between the United Nations Convention on the Law of the Sea and this convention. While mindful of the need to maintain conformity between the two, Japan participated in the concerted efforts to reach a consensus.

Fully convinced of the need to provide for a new international legal framework for the protection of underwater cultural heritage, Japan voted the draft Convention as in its view such need for conformity has been met.

We would like to take this opportunity to confirm that, as provided for in Article 3, this Convention shall be interpreted and applied in the context of and in a manner consistent with international law, including the United Nations Convention on the Law of the Sea.

It is essential, we believe, that this grand rule be faithfully maintained so that those States, which still find it difficult to join in support of the Convention at this time, will be able to accept it in the future.

It is our hope that with the implementation of this Convention, the precious underwater cultural heritage of mankind will now be effectively protected.

The Netherlands

Let me start by underlining that the Netherlands does value a Convention on Underwater Cultural Heritage very much. At present, sufficient protection for underwater cultural heritage is lacking. A convention on underwater cultural heritage will therefore be a useful and necessary addition to the protection regime for cultural heritage. The Netherlands does not only state this as the legal owner of the ships of the Dutch East India Company, which ships do as a matter of fact fall under the definition of underwater cultural heritage. It states this as well because a Convention on underwater cultural heritage would fit in the main objective of our common policy on cultural heritage, which is to work cooperatively on a lasting physical preservation of this heritage.

However, notwithstanding to what I just said, I have some specific remarks to make.

First of all, a procedural one. The Netherlands finds it unsatisfactory that at the end of the expert meeting last July we all had to vote on a text that wasn't at hand and that couldn't be looked upon in a second reading. And although in a later stadium States had the opportunity to react on the text, unfortunately, there hasn't been a second reading until now. The Netherlands does regret this.

Now concerning the content of the text in front of us. The Netherlands has the strong conviction that a convention on underwater cultural heritage should explicitly be seen in the relation to the United Nations Convention on the Law of the Sea, UNCLOS. For us, it is extremely important that the careful balance between rights and obligations of coastal States and flag States, as foreseen in UNCLOS, will not be disturbed or infringed upon by other international instruments on specific issues, like underwater cultural heritage. Unfortunately, there is some strain between the text we have at hand and UNCLOS, especially with regard to the provisions on jurisdiction. After all, in this draft convention the room to act for the coordinating State (which will mostly be the coastal State) is that far reaching that it cannot be excluded at all that in practice the competences as foreseen in UNCLOS will be exceeded.

Besides that, with regard to specific important elements of the text, like the above mentioned jurisdiction issue, the expert meeting in Paris last July choose for a so-called "constructive ambiguity" approach. It was supposed to be desirable and constructive that this determined ambiguity could give State parties the opportunity to interpret elements of the text on a manner that would be the most suitable for them. However, this is clearly in contradiction of a primary objective of treaties, like the realization of uniformity of law. Besides that, an approach like this harms the common striving for apparent treaty provisions. Considering that the expert meeting choose for this kind of approach to avoid conflicts during the negotiations as much as possible, it is foreseeable that conflicts still will occur at the moment of actual application of the Convention. On the basis of what I just said, it is clear that the provisions of the present draft Convention cannot be considered as forming part of current customary law.

Finally, something about the implementation. At this moment, it is still unclear whether the Netherlands can implement the Convention sufficiently. For several ministries in the Netherlands, this is a matter still under investigation. The Netherlands has the opinion that it is only fair to give a positive signal when it is sufficiently clear that obligations actually can be fulfilled.

c) Statements on Vote during Commission IV on Culture (29 October 2001, 31st Session of the General Conference, UNESCO)

Australia

Australia makes the following declaration of understanding in relation to the Convention.

It is the understanding of Australia that in relation to Article 2, para. 11, the phrase "*shall constitute grounds for claiming, contending or disputing any claim to national sovereignty or jurisdiction*" is intended only to be a reference to territorial disputes.

Finland

My delegation voted for the Convention. While recognizing its shortcomings, my delegation could approve the Draft Convention as a whole. We regret that the convention could not be adopted by consensus despite the last minute efforts to that end.

We are in agreement with the main objectives of the Convention, its substantive approach and the regulatory regime it establishes for the protection of the underwater cultural heritage. In some of its provisions, however, there is admittedly room for clarification and, in some, we would not have had difficulty in adjusting our position with that of those taking a more critical view of the results of the work of the government experts.

In this line, we may put on record a few observations.

Regarding "Reporting and notification in the exclusive economic zone and on the continental shelf", we think that direct reporting *to the flag State* rather than the coastal State of a discovery or an activity intended to be directed at underwater cultural heritage is the best practical way of dealing with the matter. We recognize that this position is intended to be covered by subparagraph 1 (b)(ii) of Article 9 and read it accordingly.

In paragraph 2 of Article 10, we indicated our willingness to go along with several alternative formulations. All of them should have the same *bona fide* interpretation: the coastal measures referred to should be objectively justified to prevent interference with the coastal State's sovereign rights or jurisdiction.

Similarly, the disclaimer in paragraph 11 of Article 2 cannot be read to *authorize* whatever coastal claims there may be presented.

In the preparation of the Convention, my delegation took particular interest in the determination of the status, under the Draft, of State vessels sunken to the bottom of the territorial sea. In our view, measures aimed at their protection, like the protection of any wrecks in the territorial sea, come within coastal sovereignty. This is now confirmed by paragraph 3 of Article 7.

While my delegation approves the provision as it now stands, we could have seen some of its elements modified. For us, there was no problem in including more mandatory language concerning reports to flag States of sunken State vessels and aircraft. We were also willing to include internal (maritime) waters within the scope of the provision; that would have been well in line with the overall goal of international cooperation for the protection of underwater cultural heritage.

France

La France s'est abstenue lors du vote sur le projet de Convention sur le patrimoine culturel subaquatique. Nous regrettons que les conditions n'aient pas été réunies pour nous permettre de nous rallier au consensus. En effet, comme l'a dit le délégué de la Suède, l'universalité est la meilleure garantie d'une application effective et efficace de la Convention.

Nous le regrettons d'autant plus que ce projet comporte de nombreuses dispositions utiles et positives. Mais, comme vous le savez, la France est en désaccord avec le projet sur deux points précis: le statut des navires d'Etat et les droits de juridiction, dont nous considérons qu'ils sont incompatibles avec les dispositions de la Convention sur le droit de la mer.

Je pense que le Secrétariat pourra tirer d'utiles leçons du déroulement et de la conclusion de cette négociation et s'interroger, en particulier, sur la bonne gestion des réunions et du temps nécessaire pour parvenir au consensus, comme vient de le dire le représentant du Royaume-Uni.

Cela dit, je tiens à réaffirmer que l'objectif de préservation du patrimoine subaquatique demeure, pour la France, une priorité. Dans le domaine pratique, nous avons une tradition bien établie de coopération en matière d'archéologie sous-marine, selon des règles saines et équitables, avec de nombreux pays en développement et nous poursuivrons activement cette coopération. Au demeurant, la France n'aura aucune difficulté à mettre en oeuvre, de façon unilatérale, les règles techniques contenues dans l'annexe qui nous paraissent répondre excellentement à l'objectif de protection du patrimoine culturel subaquatique.

Greece

Greece, one of the most archaeologically-rich nations in the world, has a particular interest in protecting its underwater heritage. It therefore attaches great importance to the elaboration of a comprehensive and workable legal regime for the protection of the cultural heritage of the oceans. It should be recalled that back in 1971, it was Greece which proposed the inclusion of "archaeological and historical treasures of the seabed and the ocean floor beyond the limits of national jurisdiction" in the list of topics for discussion at the Sea-Bed Committee, and later on, in 1979, during the negotiations at the Third UN Conference on the Law of the Sea, the protection of archaeological and historical objects found on the continental shelf and the exclusive economic zone. Greece participated actively in the UNESCO negotiations, and in a spirit of compromise, sacrificed positions of importance and accepted, *inter alia,* a qualified exclusion of the law of salvage (cf. article 4) and a qualified prohibition of the commercial exploitation of the underwater cultural heritage (cf. Rule 2 of the Annex).

However, at the last meeting of Governmental Experts at UNESCO in July 2001, when a vote was taking place on the Draft, Greece abstained, the main reason being that due to technical difficulties, it was not possible to have a second reading of the whole text so that it was adopted on the basis of the first reading already made of each of the articles. Thus, very important issues, such as jurisdiction and sovereign immunity of State vessels could not be reviewed or examined in the general context of the draft. For example, Greece fails to understand the appearance in article 8 ("underwater cultural heritage in the contiguous zone") of the reference to articles 9 and 10 concerning protection of UCH on the continental shelf and in the exclusive economic zone (EEZ).

The draft Convention, no doubt, adopts protective measures for cultural remains found in international waters, which would otherwise be unprotected given the limited scope of application of the relevant provisions of the UN Convention on the Law of the Sea (1982). However, the jurisdictional clauses are drafted in such a manner that would not facilitate if not complicate and prevent the enforcement of such measures, at least so far as the continental shelf and the exclusive economic zone are concerned. This lack of precision in the jurisdictional clauses is even more problematic, in the light of the compromise provisions on salvage and commercial exploitation of UCH.

More specifically, Greece's objections focus on four main points.

First, the protection of UCH found on the continental shelf and the exclusive economic zone (article 9 and 10), which is based on a system of consultations with all States Parties, which have declared an interest on the basis of a "verifiable link, especially a cultural, historical or archaeological link" to the UCH concerned. This system leaves to the coastal State only a "coordinating role" on its own continental shelf and does not ensure its right to be notified of discoveries of UCH or intended activities directed at UCH found in the area (see in particular article 9(1)(b)ii). Despite the fact that throughout the negotiations at UNESCO the majority of governmental experts were in favour of extending coastal rights over UCH on the continental shelf, the Draft Convention does not even mention the term "coastal State".

Second, the introduction of the aforementioned system of consultations in the protective scheme adopted for the contiguous zone is unfortunate. The reference in article 8 to articles 9 and 10 *should be deleted* as it diminishes the rights, which the coastal State already enjoys in this area under article 303(2) of the LOS Convention.

Third, the exclusion of warships and other State vessels from the obligation to report discoveries of underwater cultural heritage on the continental shelf and in the EEZ (cf. article 13), may have detrimental effects on UCH, as in practice submarines have already located archaeological remains incidentally. Greece, is also concerned with the requirement in article 7(3), even in a non-obligatory form, to inform the flag

State of identifiable State vessels and aircraft found within the archipelagic waters and the territorial sea. The same applies for article 10(7) requiring the prior agreement of the flag State for any activity directed at State vessels and aircraft found on the continental shelf and in the EEZ. One reason more is that article 2(8) of the Draft reserves not only the rules of international law, but also "State practice pertaining to sovereign immunities". Apart from the poor drafting of this paragraph, it is questionable whether there is consistency in State practice with respect to the legal status of sunken vessels and aircraft.

Fourth, Greece has certain objections with respect to the accommodation of the interests of the "States with a verifiable link, especially a cultural, historical or archaeological link" under the draft. Greece has throughout the negotiations stressed the fact that this is a very vague concept, which is open to different interpretations and controversy. It should at least be made clear that only States parties with an identifiable link can participate in the proposed conventional system, since in article 7(3) there is provision for informing "other States" with such a verifiable link, with respect to the discovery of identifiable State vessels found within the archipelagic waters and the territorial sea.

In the light of the above, Greece regrets that it cannot accept the Draft Convention as it stands and would have to abstain. It does, however, reserve its position for the future.

Norway

Norway voted against the adoption of this Convention.

Norway remains committed to a further strengthening of international co-operation for the protection of underwater cultural heritage. The effective protection of this heritage represents a global challenge, which deserves our very best efforts. Accordingly, Norway has supported the development of a Convention for this purpose and devoted time and resources to contribute to this end.

The Rules provided in the Annex to the Convention represent an important step forward in this respect. They deserve and enjoy our full support.

The Convention itself also provides appropriate principles and measures that serve to bring forward and strengthen international co-operation far this purpose.

However, the Convention unfortunately also includes parts, which jeopardise the fine balance of jurisdiction achieved through the carefully drafted UN Convention on the law of the Sea (UNCLOS). This applies in particular to provisions relating to the exclusive economic zone and the continental shelf.

Norway is committed to maintaining the fine balance of the UNCLOS regime. Efforts to further strengthen the protection of underwater cultural heritage should be promoted within this framework. This would ensure broad international agreement and support, and thus the efficiency such measures deserve. Norway regrets that the efforts to develop such a text have been unsuccessful.

On this basis, Norway is not in a position to support the Convention on the protection of underwater cultural heritage. Norway will furthermore be prevented from participation in any international co-operation based on the Convention in relation to the exclusive economic zone or the continental shelf.

Norway will, however, consider unilateral application of the Rules provided in the Annex to the Convention. Due to the urgent need of improving the protection of underwater cultural heritage, Norway would also encourage other States to consider unilateral application of these Rules.

Finally, Norway considers that the Convention is covered by UNCLOS Article 311 paragraph 3. The Convention on Underwater Cultural Heritage will thus not affect the enjoyment by States Non-Parties to this Convention of their rights or performance of their obligations under UNCLOS. We will look very carefully into whether the provisions of the Convention relating to the exclusive economic zone and the continental shelf are compatible with the effective execution of the object and purpose of the UNCLOS or affect the application of the basic principles embodied therein. We reserve our right to revert to this issue in the appropriate fora.

Russian Federation

The Russian Federation pays a lot of attention to the elaboration of an effective universal mechanism of the protection of the underwater cultural heritage. The work, undertaken under the auspices of UNESCO, has led to very important positive results which, in particular, consist in harmonizing rules on the underwater cultural heritage.

However, for principal reasons, a number of provisions of the Convention are not acceptable for Russia. For example, Article 10 may be interpreted as exceeding the scope of rights and jurisdiction of a coastal State in adjacent seas as set forth by the UN Convention on the Law of the Sea 1982. It may be interpreted as providing a coastal State with the right to take, at its own discretion, unilateral measures not excluding force under the pretext of the protection of the underwater cultural heritage. We are unable to agree with it. In our opinion, ambiguity and vagueness of some Articles of the Convention may create conflict situations.

In addition, the draft limits norms of international customary law related to the inviolability of sunken warships.

The Russian side believe that, in conformity with international law, the Convention will be binding only for its States Parties and, in consequence, will not provide its States Parties with any additional rights related to ship under flags of other States and aircraft registered in other States.

At the same time the Russian side confirms its readiness to continue and develop co-operation for the protection of the underwater cultural heritage based on the UN Convention on the Law of the Sea 1982 and provisions of the UNESCO Convention for the protection of the underwater cultural heritage contained in its Annex, which were reached by consensus.

Sweden

Sweden has abstained from voting on the Convention on underwater cultural heritage.

To this General Conference, a final text was presented. Regrettably this text will not gain support from all States, particularly those that are active in our neighbouring seas. This makes it difficult for Sweden to take part in this novel interpretation on international law.

The consensus goal stumbled over two crucial issues: jurisdiction and State vessel. The legal problem is well known. The United Nations Convention on the Law of the Sea does not regulate in a practical manner how the underwater cultural heritage should be protected. The need for international rules supplementing UNCLOS is obvious. In order for such new rules to be regarded as a legitimate, progressive development of international law and, as a result, to create an effective legal regime, – consensus is crucial.

Our problem rests with the fact that consensus has not been achieved as regards coastal State jurisdiction with respect to underwater cultural heritage located on the continental shelf and exclusive economic zone of the coastal State.

The fact that it has not been possible to reach consensus means that the Convention is not likely to be ratified by all States. This, in turn, will prevent the rules contained in the Convention from achieving customary law status. Hence, we will be left with two legal regimes that are likely to clash with each other. Since the Convention is only valid *inter partes* it will be impossible to implement it against the will of non States Parties.

Sweden regrets the fact that consensus has not been achieved, particularly since consensus, in our view, might have been reached, had we had the chance to work on the text in a more constructive manner.

Finally, let me end on a somewhat more positive note by shedding the light on some important achievements with the Convention.

The provisions of the Annex on "Rules concerning activities directed at underwater cultural heritage" are most welcome. Sweden will apply the majority of rules in the Annex voluntarily and irrespective of whether of not Sweden is a Party to the Convention.

Sweden welcomes that the legal contents of the rules concerning the mandate of the coastal State in its declared contiguous zone is clarified in the Convention and regards this clarification as an indication of customary law.

Sweden has noted with satisfaction that there has been an overwhelming support for the inclusion of provisions to secure that proper respect shall be given to human remains in maritime waters.

Sweden still believes that measures must continue to be taken to protect underwater cultural heritage throughout the world. To this end, Sweden does not exclude adhering to the Convention should it gain a wide acceptance from a majority of States representing all categories of concerned States neighbouring the Baltic Sea. In the meantime, Sweden is prepared to further explore other means of international co-operation at a regional level for the protection of underwater cultural heritage, in particular the Baltic Sea.

Turkey

We have participated to all the preparatory meeting of the experts who drafted the Convention on the protection of the underwater cultural heritage. We did our best in order to contribute to the preparation and universal adoption of the draft Convention. Some of our views were taken into consideration, but some matters which are of vital importance to us were not accepted.

I will briefly state our difficulties. One of them is that 1982 UN Convention is one of the bases for juridical context of the present Draft Convention. Turkey is not a party to 1982 Convention. Therefore, we are not in a position to go along with this reference.

Another difficulty is related to peaceful settlement of disputes. Again in Article 25 there is reference to Article 287 of the 1982 UN Convention. During preparatory meetings we have submitted other alternatives. Although a minority of States agreed with our proposals, the majority did not find them acceptable.

Finally, to overcome difficulties for us and for some other States we wanted to have the right to put reservations. But the experts did not find it acceptable either.

I would like to add that in our mind preparatory work needed more time in order to have a better Convention which would be universally acceptable.

Essentially, for these reasons I state that Turkey will not be able to support this Draft Convention.

United Kingdom

As a nation with a long maritime history, the United Kingdom attaches great importance to the preservation of Underwater Cultural Heritage. There are many historic wrecks lying on the seabed in the waters off our shores and there are wrecks of British origins all over the world. Many or those wrecks contain the remains of British seafarers. We are, therefore, committed to a global Convention for the Protection of Underwater Cultural Heritage and entered these negotiations in a very positive spirit. Much good progress has been made and the UK can support most of the articles in the current draft of the Convention, particularly the provisions in the Annex. It is with great regret, therefore, that the UK was unable to vote in favour of the text before us today. Our reasons will be familiar to those who have taken part in the expert group meeting at which we have tried to explain our concerns.

The discussions about warships and State vessels and aircraft used for non-commercial service have proved contentious. There have been exhaustive attempts to reach consensus between the competing claims or the Sovereign Immunity enjoyed by Flag Slates on the one hand and jurisdictional claims of Coastal States on the other. Unfortunately the differences have not been resolved. The United Kingdom considers that the current text erodes the fundamental principles of customary international law, codified in UNCLOS, of Sovereign Immunity which is retained by a State's warships and vessels and aircraft used for non commercial service until expressly abandoned by that State. The text purports to alter the fine balance between the equal, but conflicting, rights of Coastal and Flag States, carefully negotiated in UNCLOS, in a way that is unacceptable to the United Kingdom.

The procedure for the protection of underwater archaeology adopted in the Annex are those which are already followed by the United Kingdom with regard to the designation of wreck sites within its territorial sea and internal waters. However, the text obliges signatory States to extend the same very high standards of protection to all underwater archaeology over 100 years old. It is estimated that there are probably about 10,000 wreck sites on the seabed under the United Kingdom territorial sea and it would neither be possible nor desirable to extend legal protection to all of them. The United Kingdom believes that it is better to focus its efforts and resources on protecting the most important and unique examples of underwater cultural heritage. It would simply be impossible to enforce the application of the rules in the Annex to every one of the thousands of wreck sites.

We very much regret that the artificial deadline created by this Conference has prevented the Parties to this negotiation from agreeing a text to meet these concerns. In its last meeting in July much progress was made on the difficult issue of jurisdiction and we recognise the enormous efforts made by many delegations to achieve a compromise. We believe that given more time and reflection, a way could have been found to meet our remaining concerns. We note that the United Kingdom is far from alone in having serious reservations about the text, and we believe that it is very regrettable that the Member States of UNESCO are about to approve a Convention which will not he capable of attracting universal support.

United States of America
I wish to thank the Chairman, the Secretariat, and other delegations for their hard work on this Convention. We wish to note that we have been a partner in this work over many years to develop compromise positions that could find broad support. We regret that these suggestions were not accepted and in some instances not considered.

We note and take satisfaction in the substantial progress that has been made in certain areas. In particular, agreement on the Annexed Rules, Preamble and support of non-intrusive responsible public access were substantial achievements.

Nonetheless, we regret that we cannot accept this text because of objections to several key provisions relating to jurisdiction, the reporting scheme, warships, and the relationship of the Convention to UNCLOS.

We do not believe the text is ripe for adoption. We do believe that if we had more time, a broadly ratifiable text could have been arrived at by consensus. And we hope that there will be a future opportunity to build on the progress that we did make in regard to the Rules, the Preamble, Public Access and other provisions. Only a broadly ratifiable text will actually contribute to effective protection of the underwater cultural heritage.

We wish to note for the record that in our view, as a matter of international law and with particular reference to Article 311 (3) of UNCLOS, the Convention's provisions apply only among Parties to it. This is particularly true of the provisions in the article on jurisdiction on the continental shelf and the Exclusive Economic Zone. It is our assumption that other delegations share this understanding.

We ask that these views be incorporated into the formal records of this meeting and of the General Conference.

Venezuela
La delegación de Venezuela solicitó el uso de la palabra para explicar, una vez más, las razones que la apartan de la decisión recién adoptada.

En su oportunidad, durante la segunda parte de la cuarta reunion de expertos gubernamentales celebrada en el mes de julio 2001, y consistente con lo que ha sido nuestra posición tradicional, la delegación de Venezuela fue clara al expresar su inconformidad con el espíritu de uno de los apartados del artículo 25 del proyecto de Convención sobre la Protección del Patrimonio Cultural Subacuático referido a la solución pacífica de controversias. Consideramos a todas luces desconcertante el tratar de imponer a un Estado no parte de la Convención de las Naciones Unidas sobre el Derecho del Mar de 1982, disposiciones de un instrumento jurídico por el cual no nos encontramos obligados por no haberlo suscrito, y en particular, por la decisión de aplicar la Parte XV de la citada Convención del mar que obliga a cualquier Estado, sea o no parte de la Convención citada, a procedimientos conducentes a decisiones obligatorias, por la simple petición de una de las partes.

Además el texto no propicia un espacio para las reservas, tal y como fue mencionado por la delegación de Turquía esta mañana.

Por último, la delegación de Venezuela quisiera manifestar que el voto negativo – por las razones antes aludidas – no significa en manera alguna diferencias fundamentales con respecto a la sustancia del instrumento, posición que fuera expresada en el seno del Grupo de los 77 y del Grupo Latino Americano y del Caribe, cuvo trabajo elogiamos al igual que el del resto de las delegaciones participantes en este arduo proceso de negociaciones.

La delegación de Venezuela quisiera, así mismo, consultar a la presidencia sobre la forma mas apropiada de hacer constar en actas el contenido de la presente declaración, y solicitar, si es posible, la lectura de la misma durante la reunión plenaria de la Conferencia General, o si estima que debe ser la misma delegación de Venezuela la que proceda a la lectura correspondiente.

C) BILATERAL AGREEMENTS

9. Agreement between the Netherlands and Australia concerning old Dutch Shipwrecks (The Hague, 6 November 1972)

THE UNDERSIGNED:

1. MR WIM BLOKZIJL, resident of The Hague, Head of the Inspection Division of the State Property Directorate of the Ministry of Finance, acting on behalf of the State of the Netherlands, hereinafter referred to as 'The Netherlands'.
2. DR LLOYD DOUGLAS THOMSON, M.V.O., Australian Ambassador to the Netherlands, acting on behalf of the Government of the Commonwealth of Australia, hereinafter referred to as 'Australia':

HAVING REGARD TO THE FACT:

A. That vessels that belonged to the Dutch 'VEREENIGDE OOSTINDISCHE COMPAGNIE' known as the V.O.C, hereinafter referred to as 'the V.O.C.', were wrecked on or off the coast of Western Australia;
B. That the Netherlands, by virtue of article 247 of the 1789 Constitution of the Batavian Republic, is the present legal successor to the V.O.C.:

AGREE AS FOLLOWS:

Article 1: The Netherlands, as successor to the property and assets of the V.O.C., transfers all its right, title and interest in and to wrecked vessels of the V.O.C. lying on or off the coast of the State of Western Australia and in and to any articles thereof to Australia which shall accept such right, title and interest.

Article 2: For the purpose of this Agreement, the expression 'articles' means any part of vessels as referred to in article 1, that have become or have been detached or removed therefrom, as well as the fittings, goods and other property, wherever situated, that were installed or carried on those vessels.

Article 3: Australia shall make no claim on the Netherlands for reimbursement of any costs incurred in searching for any of the vessels referred to in article 1 of this Agreement or in recovering any articles from those vessels.

Article 4: Australia recognises that the Netherlands has a continuing interest, particularly for historical and other cultural purposes, in articles recovered from any of the vessels referred to in article 1 of this Agreement.

Accordingly, Australia shall set up a Committee to determine the disposition and subsequent ownership of the recovered articles between the Netherlands, Australia and the State of Western Australia.

Article 5: The Committee referred to in article 4 of this Agreement shall be set up within 90 days after the entry into force of the Agreement and shall compose two persons nominated by the Netherlands and two persons nominated by Australia. These persons shall have the scientific and cultural expertise appropriate for the discharge of their functions.

Article 6: The Committee shall determine the disposition of the recovered articles in accordance with the principles which have been agreed upon by Australia and the Netherlands and are set out in the Arrangement signed by Australia and the Netherlands and attached to this document.

Article 7: Expenditure incurred by the Committee in the performance of its work shall be shared between the two Parties represented on the Committee, the share to be borne by the Netherlands being one third and that by Australia two thirds provided that:

(i) each Party shall bear the costs of travel by the Committee members nominated by it,
(ii) the costs of communications by a party to the Committee shall be borne by the despatching party, and
(iii) the expenses of transportation of articles distributed in accordance with determinations of the Committee shall be borne by the recipients of the articles.

Article 8: If the members of the Committee referred to in article 4 of this Agreement cannot come to an agreement on the disposition of particular articles, Australia and the Netherlands shall appoint an independent consultant to report on the matter in issue and the report shall be referred to the Committee for re-consideration of the matter. The cost of the report shall be shared between the two Parties represented on the Committee, the share to be borne by the Netherlands being one third and that by Australia two thirds.

Article 9: If, on considering the consultant's report on a matter, the members of the Committee cannot come to an agreement on the disposition of the recovered articles, the matter will be referred to the Government of the Kingdom of the Netherlands and the Government of the Commonwealth of Australia, which will settle the matter by negotiation.

Article 10: This Agreement shall enter into force on the date of the signatures of both Parties.

DONE at The Hague this sixth day of November in the year One thousand nine hundred and seventy-two in two originals in the English language.

ARRANGEMENT SETTING OUT THE GUIDING PRINCIPLES FOR THE COMMITTEE TO DETERMINE THE DISPOSITION OF MATERIAL FROM THE SHIPWRECKS OF DUTCH EAST INDIA COMPANY VESSELS OFF THE COAST OF WESTERN AUSTRALIA

THE COMMITTEE

Responsibility

The Committee's responsibility will embrace all material recovered from the wrecks-whether recovered before or after the coming into operation of the Western Australian Museum Act in December 1964 which contains provisions for vesting in the Museum title to the wrecks of the *Batavia*, the *Gilt Dragon*, the *Zuytdorp* and *Zeewijk*.

Conduct of Business

The Committee is small enough to meet if occasion demands but most of its work could be done by correspondence.

GENERAL PRINCIPLES

Representative collections

The cost of recovery (including treatment) is likely to exceed by far the intrinsic or antiquarian sale-value of material recovered. The Government of Western Australia is spending considerable sums on this work ($92,000 in the last financial year) and estimates that the total cost will be $2,000,000 or more. Although a division would not be warranted by consideration of cash value alone, the historic, educational, scientific and international considerations are such as to make the deposition of representative collections in the museums of the Netherlands and Australia most desirable. The remainder of the material would be held in the Western Australian Museum.

Considerations governing the partition of archaeological collections

In modern archaeological practice sites are no longer regarded merely as a source of important individual items, but rather as a body of material whose collective value far outweighs the importance of the individual pieces and in which the relationship of the individual objects within the sample are a major part of its historical value. Accordingly, the sharing of material from an archaeological site is best regarded as the accommodation in several localities of a corporate entity rather than its division into parts.

If the decision is made that the contents of an archaeological site are to be apportioned between two or more institutions, the first principle to be observed is that the total assemblage should be capable of reassembly to allow further statistical and scholarly analysis. It follows, therefore, that unnecessary splitting of a sample of closely similar objects capable of statistical treatment should be avoided and, where samples are accommodated in more than one institution, those institutions should contract not to disperse them further and, moreover, to agree to allow samples to be brought together for analysis and study as required. The second principle is that where unique or rare objects, themselves, form a meaningful assemblage within the whole, this assemblage should not be split or, if split, perfect replicas be made to complete the assemblage. As in the case of the division of statistical samples an agreement should be made between the recipients to reconstitute the original assemblage if it is required for scholarly research.

Treatment of material recovered

The contents of the ancient shipwrecks of the Dutch East India Company include abundant statistical samples such as coins, bricks, objects of pottery, elephant tusks, and so on. There are also many articles which are less abundant but which are duplicated many times over. Many of these are ship fittings such as cannons, anchors, cannon balls etc. There are also other articles which are relatively rare, or even unique, in the deposits (e.g. articles possessed by crew members or passengers, such as barber's instruments, navigational instruments, ornaments etc.). Most articles are fragmentary and in need of immediate chemical conservation and stabilisation in the laboratory as soon as they are recovered. This treatment cannot await distribution.

OPERATING PRINCIPLES

Code of Operation

The Committee will operate by reviewing proposals for distribution made, from time to time, by the Director of the Western Australian Museum; it could decide that the proposed samples be increased or decreased in content in the light of the total material collected and other factors.

General aims

In its deliberations the Committee will have, as its general aim, the purpose of ensuring that representative series of statistical samples and sufficient examples of the rarer objects will be deposited in the museums of the Netherlands and Australia to convey the variety and contents of each wreck to both the public and to scholars while, at the same time, ensuring that major projects of scholarly research will not be impeded by over fragmentation of the collection. Dispersal in this way, among separate repositories will also help to ensure the permanent safety of representative material in the event of the destruction of any one repository.

Statistical samples

Most material so far recovered from the vessels are samples capable of statistical treatment.

A representative collection of the contents of each statistical sample should be made available to a museum of the Netherlands Government and a museum of the Commonwealth Government. Thus, in the case of coin, for example, both the Netherlands and Commonwealth Governments would receive as complete a series as possible representing the mintings and values contained within each of the wrecks. These will provide their museums with ample material of this class of objects for display purposes and sufficient to enable a scholar to make the initial qualitative studies which would possibly lead him to a more detailed statistical treatment of the bulk sample retained in the Western Australian Museum.

Less common or rare objects

In order to ensure that both the Netherlands and Commonwealth Governments acquire, in due course, representative collections of the less common and even unique objects, the following procedure will be adopted. Since the relationships of such objects to the whole sample cannot be known until excavation is complete, the distribution of specimens of this nature cannot be considered during the continuing process of recovery. However, at reasonable intervals (of say two or three years) it should be possible to assemble a representative sample with fair certainty that all duplicates of any rare object present in a particular excavation should have been recovered and their nature taken into consideration during the deliberations of the Committee.

The Hague
6th November, 1972

10. Exchange of notes between South Africa and the United Kingdom concerning the regulation of the term of settlement of the salvaging of the wreck *HMS Birkenhead* (Pretoria, 22 September 1989)

No. 1

Her Majesty's Ambassador at Pretoria
to the Minister of Foreign Affairs of the Republic of South Africa

Pretoria, 22 September 1989

Your Excellency,

I have the honour to refer to recent discussions between our two Governments about the question of the wreck of the *Birkenhead* and to propose a settlement of all outstanding issue in the following terms.

The wreck of the *Birkenhead* shall, as a military grave, continue to be treated at all stages with respect. In particular, the South African Government shall seek to ensure that the salvors treat reverently and refrain from disturbing or bringing to the surface any human remains which may be discovered at the site of the wreck or in its vicinity. British military historians shall have temporary access for research purposes to salvaged artefacts designed for South African museums.

The South African Government shall as far as possible ensure that representative examples of salvaged artefacts identifiable with a particular British regiment or institution are offered without charge to that regiment (or its successor) or to such institution.

The British Government shall not enter into any salvage contract in respect of the *Birkenhead* and shall not object to the South African Government maintaining its existing salvage arrangements in regard to the wreck under the applicable South African legislation.

If any gold coin (apart from the coins considered to have been in private ownership) were to be recovered, such coin (after deduction of the share due to the salvors in accordance with existing salvage arrangement) would be shared equally between our two Governments.

In order to facilitate the implementation of these arrangements, consultation shall be held as necessary between representatives of our two Governments, the salvors and other South African institutions concerned.

This settlement is without prejudice to the respective legal positions of our two Governments.

If the above is acceptable to the Government of the Republic of South Africa, I have the honour to propose that this letter and Your Excellency's reply to that shall constitute an agreement between our two Governments in this matter which shall enter into force on the date of Your Excellency's reply.

I avail myself of this opportunity to renew to Your Excellency the assurance of my highest consideration.

ROBIN RENWICK

No. 2

The Minister of Foreign Affairs of the Republic of South Africa to Her Majesty's Ambassador at Pretoria

Pretoria, 22 September 1989

Your Excellency

I have the honour to acknowledge receipt of Your Excellency's letter of 22 September 1989 which reads as follows:

[As in No. 1]

In reply, I wish to confirm that these proposals are acceptable to the Government of the Republic of South Africa who therefore agree that Your Excellency's letter and this reply shall constitute an agreement between our two Governments, which shall enter into force on the date of this letter.

I avail myself of this opportunity to renew to Your Excellency the assurance of my highest consideration.

R. F. BOTHA

11. Agreement between the Government of the United States of America and the Government of the French Republic concerning the wreck of the *CSS Alabama* (Paris, 3 October 1989)

The Government of the United States of America and the Government of the French Republic,

Recognizing the historical and archaeological importance of the *CSS Alabama*, sunk in battle with *USS Kearsarge* on June 19, 1864, approximately 7 nautical miles off the coast of Cherbourg, France,

Wishing to co-operate to ensure the protection and study of the wreck, situated in French territorial waters,

Have agreed as follows:

Article 1. A Scientific Committee composed of two representatives of each of the two governments and of experts designated by each government is hereby established on a basis of equality.

Article 2. Any measure related to scientific activities or any project concerning the development of the wreck of the *CSS Alabama* shall be reviewed by the Scientific Committee, which shall make its decisions by agreement of the representatives of both governments.

Article 3. The provisions adopted by the French government to establish a zone of protection around the wreck of the *CSS Alabama* shall remain in force for the term of this agreement, unless the Parties decide otherwise. The competent French authorities may amend these provisions, as necessary. Neither Party shall take measures adversely affecting the wreck or its associated artefacts without the agreement of the other Party.

If the conservation of the wreck is compromised, the competent French authorities may take, on their own authority or at the request of United States authorities, the conservation measures necessitated by the situation. In the event of such urgent action is taken by French authorities, they will notify the United States authorities promptly of the full details regarding such action.

Article 4. Proposals adopted by the Scientific Committee will be submitted to the French Minister of Culture, who shall grant the necessary authorizations with due regard for the procedures provided for by French law.

Article 5. The Scientific Committee shall review the execution of the authorized scientific activities and shall follow the corresponding operations as they occur.

Article 6. Each Party will bear the coast of its representatives and its experts.

Article 7. Each Party will be entitled to have at least one observer present at each excavation operation.

Article 8. The Scientific Committee shall agree upon, as necessary, the procedure governing the participation of the Government of the United Kingdom of Great Britain and Northern Ireland in the operations that are undertaken.

Article 9. Such activities as the two Parties may undertake under this arrangement shall be contingent, for each, upon the availability of the necessary funds.

Article 10. This Agreement shall enter into force on the date of signature. It may be terminated by either Party by three months advance written notice to the other Party sent through the diplomatic channel.

Done at Paris, on the 3rd of October 1989, in duplicate in the French and English languages, both texts being equally authentic.

For the Government of the French Republic	For the Government of the United States of America
Jean-Pierre PUISSOCHET	M. Peter BERNHARDT

12. Memorandum of understanding between the Governments of Great Britain and Canada pertaining to the shipwrecks *HMS Erebus* and *HMS Terror* (5, 8 August 1997)

This Memorandum of Understanding between the Government of Great Britain ("Britain") and the Government of Canada ("Canada") pertains to activities surrounding the exploration, recovery and disposition of the *HMS Erebus* and *HMS Terror*, two wrecked ships of Her Majesty's Royal Navy within Canada ("the wrecks") that have been designated by the Minister of Canadian Heritage to be National Historic Sites.

1. The Parties desire to ensure the commemorative integrity of the wrecks through the orderly and scientific exploration, recovery and disposition of the wrecks and their contents. The Parties further intend that proper archaeological research and disclosure shall prevail over interests of financial gain and media coverage.

2. Britain, as owner of the wrecks, hereby assigns custody and control of the wrecks and their contents to the Government of Canada, and acknowledges Canada as its agent for purposes of this Understanding. In so doing, Britain does not waive ownership or sovereign immunity with respect to the wrecks or their contents while they are on the seabed, but accepts that any site investigation, excavation or recovery of either of the wrecks or their contents will be under Canada's control.

3. In exercising custody and control, Canada has the discretion to take any actions with respect to the wrecks and their contents that it considers appropriate. Canada may accordingly deny at any time permission for investigation, excavation or recovery of the wrecks or their contents, and will seek to ensure that any such permission will only be granted to approved organizations or persons in accordance with an approved plan and procedure.

4. Once either of the wrecks has been positively located and identified, Britain will assign to Canada ownership of everything recovered form that wreck and its contents, except that

a) any gold recovered form the wrecks, apart from coins considered to have been in private ownership, will after deduction of any share which may by law be due to any third party be shared equally between Canada and Britain, and
b) any recovered artifacts identified by Britain as being of outstanding significance to the Royal Navy will be offered to Britain for display in an appropriate museum. Britain will assume responsibility for all reasonable costs associated with the recovery, conservation and transportation of such artifacts.

5. Canada will seek to ensure that any recovered contents are dealt with in accordance with applicable Canadian law and with a plan and procedures approved by marine archaeologists of the Government of Canada, and are properly conserved and made available for public display or other museological purposes, education or research. British historians and archaeologists will be given reasonable access for

research purposes to information derived from site investigations, to artifacts raised, and to all reports produced.

6. Canada will seek to ensure that anyone dealing in any way with either of the wrecks and their contents treat reverently, and refrain from disturbing or bringing to the surface, any human remains that are discovered at the sites of the wrecks or in their vicinity. Any human remains that must be removed in order to conduct archaeological work, or that are inadvertently recovered, will be re-interred with proper respect and reverence, and in consultation with Britain.

7. Canada will keep Britain apprised on a regular basis of developments relating to the recovery of the wrecks.

8. In order to facilitate the implementation of, amendments to, or the resolution of any dispute arising under this Understanding, either Party may request consultations to be held between their representatives, including any of their concerned institutions.

9. This Understanding may be amended on the mutual consent of the Parties.

10. This Understanding will take effect when it is signed by both Parties, and will remain in effect until one of the Parties provided thirty days notice in writing of its intention to terminate.

Signed this 5th day of August, 1997

For the Government of Canada:

PHILIPPE KIRSCH
Legal Adviser
Dep. Of Foreign Affairs and
Int. Trade

Signed this 8th day of August, 1997

For the Government of Great Britain:

His Excellency
Sir ANTHONY GOODENOUGH
High Commissioner to Canada

13. AGREEMENT BETWEEN THE GOVERNMENT OF THE UNITED STATES OF AMERICA AND THE GOVERNMENT OF THE FRENCH REPUBLIC REGARDING THE WRECK OF *LA BELLE* (WASHINGTON, 31 MARCH 2003)

The Government of the United States of America and the Government of the French Republic (hereinafter, the "Parties"),

Considering that the vessel *La Belle*, which had been provided to Cavelier de la Salle by the King of France in 1684 to establish a colony at the mouth of the Mississippi River, sank in 1686 in what is now Matagorda Bay, in the State of Texas of the United States of America;

Recognizing that the Texas Historical Commission, an agency of the State of Texas (hereinafter, "the Commission"), located the remains of *La Bell*e in July 1995 and that the State of Texas is currently in possession of the wreck of *La Belle* and its associated artefacts (herein, "the wreck of *La Belle*");

Recognizing also the historical and archaeological importance of the wreck of *La Belle*, the site of the sinking, and the related documentation;

Desiring to preserve and conserve the remains of the wreck of *La Belle*, and excavation records as well as the site of the sinking in order to transmit to future generations the historical evidence of the exploratory mission of Cavelier de la Salle in what is now the Texas;

Considering further that, to this end, cooperation in the field of research, preservation and display of the wreck of *La Belle*, in particular through the organization of exhibitions throughout the world, is necessary and that this can not be possible without a prior agreement on ownership of the wreck of *La Belle*, its use and any other legal issues of this nature;

Have agreed as follows:

Article 1

1. At the time of its sinking, *La Belle* was an auxiliary vessel of the French Navy.

2. The French Republic has not abandoned or transferred title of the wreck of *La Belle* and continues to retain title to the wreck of *La Belle*.

Article 2

1. The French Republic does not desire the return of the wreck of *La Belle* to its territory.

2. The wreck of *La Belle* shall remain in the custody of the commission for a period of ninety-nine years from the date of entry into force of this Agreement, which period shall be automatically renewed unless the Parties agree otherwise.

3. Artifacts may be placed on temporary loan for public exhibition as agreed between the parties to the administrative arrangement referred to in Article 3.

4. Artifacts in the custody of the Commission shall not be subject to seizure.

Article 3

1. The Musée National de la Marine, a public agency under the authority of the French Ministry of Defence, and the Commission shall negotiate and conclude, consistent with this Agreement, an administrative arrangement relating to the curation (including the security, storage, preservation and conservation), research, documentation, and exhibition of the wreck of *La Belle*.

2. The arrangement shall also provide for a regime applicable to publication relating the wreck of *La Belle*.

3. Treatment and burial of human remains from La Salle's exploratory mission to Texas shall be as agreed between the French Ambassador to the United States or his representative and the Commission.

Article 4

All activities and commitments undertaken under this Agreement by the Parties and any administrative arrangement entered into pursuant to this Agreement shall be contingent upon the availability of funds.

Article 5

1. This Agreement shall enter into force on signature and shall be of unlimited duration.

2. The Agreement may be terminated only by mutual agreement of the parties.

Washington, 31 March 2003

For the Government of the French Republic:
Jean-David Levitte
(Ambassador of France to the United States)

For the Government of the United States of America:
Paula Dobriansky
(Under-Secretary of State for Global Affairs)

D) OTHER MATERIALS

14. Recommendation 848 (1978) of the Parliamentary Assembly of the Council of Europe on the underwater cultural heritage

The Assembly,

1. Welcoming the report on the underwater cultural heritage, presented by its Committee on Culture and Education (Doc. 4200);
2. Recognising the historical and cultural significance of this heritage, but aware that positive action is urgently needed on both national and European levels in order to ensure its proper protection;
3. Noting with satisfaction the growing public interest in the underwater heritage, and anxious that this interest be channelled into a better realisation of the potential value of the heritage rather than lead rapidly to its unauthorised destruction;
4. Stressing the essential unity of land and underwater archaeology, and its contribution to a greater understanding of the history and culture of the peoples of Europe;
5. Particularly concerned by the lack of professional experts competent in the field of underwater archaeology, by the small scale of government funding, and by the inadequacies of existing legislation and administrative practice in most member states,
6. Recommends that the Committee of Ministers:

Action at European level

a. draw up a European convention on the underwater cultural heritage, open to all member states of the Council of Europe and also to all non-member states bordering on seas in the European area;
b. negotiate agreement between member states on the declaration of national cultural protection zones up to the 200-mile limit, wherever that limit is in keeping with geographical realities, as a basis for the implementation of the proposed convention;
c. encourage, in co-operation with UNESCO and ICOM, the administration of the application of the convention at regional level, by agreement between states bordering on the same sea or part sea;
d. express its support for the setting up of a European Group for Underwater Archaeology, which, among other things, could prepare and keep up to date a series of European manuals (supplemented where appropriate with visual material) on:
   i. existing legislation and administrative regulations concerning the underwater heritage;
   ii. underwater archaeological techniques;
   iii. basic procedures to be followed on locating finds;
e. bring the report of the Committee on Culture and Education (Doc. 4200) to the

attention of interested expert committees in the Council of Europe, with the following proposals for further action at European level :

i. in the field of culture and education, for encouraging training of technicians and archaeologists in underwater questions for scientific research, and for responsible public education (both inside and outside educational institutions) in the significance of the underwater cultural heritage;

ii. in the field of environmental protection, for co-ordination of action being taken in favour of the natural and cultural underwater heritage;

iii. for inclusion of protection of the underwater cultural heritage where appropriate in any future Council of Europe conventions or agreements;

iv. to the European Youth Centre and European Youth Foundation, for encouraging seminars of young people interested in this field;

Action at National Level

f. urge member governments, on the basis of proposals set out in the Annex to this recommendation :

i. to revise where necessary existing legislation;

ii. to take further action for the underwater cultural heritage, if possible in concertation amongst themselves, in the areas calling for priority attention.

ANNEX

Minimum Legal Requirements

i. There should be no loopholes in the system of protection. The definition of underwater objects and sites should extend up to what is covered by land antiquities legislation.

ii. Protection should cover all objects that have been beneath the water for more than 100 years, but with the possibility of discretionary exclusion of less important objects (or of less important antiquities) once they have been properly studied and recorded, and the inclusion of historically or artistically significant objects of more recent date.

iii. Individual, and apparently isolated, underwater objects should be protected to the same extent as wrecks or sites.

iv. National jurisdiction should be extended up to the full 200mile limit, with an international agreement providing for reciprocal treatment of cultural finds landed in countries other than those in whose cultural zones they were found.

v. Existing salvage and wreck law should not apply to any items protected under ii and iv above.

vi. Reporting of finds to the appropriate authorities should be compulsory.

vii. A single authority should be given primary responsibility for dealing with both land and underwater finds, and determining their significance.

viii. A standard system of fixed finder's monetary rewards should be established, related to each identification of an object or site and not necessarily linked to the commercial value of the find. It should differentiate between an individual object and a site, and be heavily weighted in favour of the latter.

ix. Provision should be made for appropriate enforcement measures.

Priority Areas for Further Action at National Level

i. The establishment of stocks of equipment for underwater research, including mobile laboratories and support vessels.
ii. The training of more technicians and underwater archaeologists and the improvement of career possibilities for those working in this field.
iii. The setting up of centres for the analysis and treatment of underwater material, for research and for training.
iv. The systematic preparation of inventories of underwater sites.
v. The more effective protection and policing of known underwater sites.
vi. Increased financial support for rescue excavations and for the careful scientific excavation of really significant sites.
vii. Encouragement of the responsible presentation of the underwater heritage to the public (in particular by television, by publishers and by museums).
viii. Assistance to the efforts made by local authorities for the display of underwater finds of cultural importance.

15. Recommendation 1486 (2000) of the Parliamentary Assembly of the Council of Europe on maritime and fluvial cultural heritage

1. The Assembly is aware of the historical significance of the sea and inland waterways as routes of cultural transmission and exchange in the development of Europe and its contacts with the rest of the world.
2. In 1978, the Assembly adopted Recommendation 848 on the underwater cultural heritage.
3. However, the Committee of Ministers failed to bring to fruition one of the main proposals, namely the elaboration of a European convention on the protection of the underwater cultural heritage.
4. Nevertheless, certain elements of Recommendation 848 were included in the revised European Convention on the Protection of the Archaeological Heritage (1992).
5. The Assembly observes that recent technological advances in deep-sea diving now render vulnerable many well-preserved wrecks in international waters that were previously inaccessible.
6. Their commercial exploitation is encouraged by the publicity given to spectacular achievements such as the location and recoveries from the Titanic, and the associated success of the recent film.
7. There is also a threat to the maritime and fluvial heritage from irresponsible exploitation of the oceans and commercial and industrial operations in inland waters, on the coasts and in inland waterways.
8. The Assembly recognises that the past twenty years have witnessed the emergence of Europe-wide interest in the maritime and fluvial heritage, and sees the need for co-ordination and co-operation and for the encouragement of networks of experts and non-governmental bodies in such related fields as underwater archaeology, shipping, maritime museums or scientific laboratories.
9. The Assembly observes the varying degrees of success with which defunct maritime and fluvial installations are being converted to alternative uses.
10. The Assembly further observes the increased attraction of traditional maritime and fluvial vessels for interest and for leisure activities.
11. The Assembly notes with approval the Memorandum of Understanding on the mutual recognition of certificates for the safe operation of traditional ships, signed by the maritime authorities of seven European nations on 8 September 2000.
12. The Assembly notes, however, with concern that in some countries vessels of great historic value are at risk of being lost for want of resources for their maintenance.
13. The Assembly therefore recommends that the Committee of Ministers:
    i. encourage European co-operation for the protection of the maritime and fluvial heritage with regard to sunken wrecks and associated objects, the immovable heritage and the documentary record with emphasis on collaboration between the public authorities and interested non-governmental bodies and persons from the commercial, academic, sports voluntary or private sectors;

ii. provide the necessary resources for the European Foundation for Heritage Skills (FEMP) to make a meaningful contribution to this co-operation;
iii. ensure that the cultural dimension is fully incorporated in any European maritime agency set up as proposed in Assembly Resolution 1168 and Recommendation 1387 on future challenges in European maritime science and technology (1998);
iv. associate the Council of Europe with the elaboration by Unesco of an international convention on the underwater cultural heritage and in the preparation at European and international level of any other legal instruments relating to the maritime and fluvial heritage;
v. encourage states to ensure that the underwater cultural heritage is protected from commercial recovery operations from the high seas;
vi. encourage member states to legislate to protect the underwater cultural heritage from commercial and/or unauthorised recovery operations in their internal waters, territorial seas, contiguous zones, continental shelves and exclusive economic zones, and to take such measures as are in their power to thwart such operations by their own nationals or by nationals of other countries seeking to sail under their maritime flags or to use their territory as bases or ports of landing;
vii. encourage regional co-operation on the underwater cultural heritage between countries (whether member states of the Council of Europe or not), bordering on the same sea or part sea, by sharing information or by concluding bilateral or multilateral agreements which may be more stringent than global agreements;
viii. in particular to encourage the conclusion of such agreements as will mitigate the sovereign immunity which states retain over vessels of war and other state-owned vessels wherever they are sunk, with particular regard to the high proportion of such vessels which are of significant historic value and to the high proportion which contain human remains and especially those which are war graves;
ix. encourage local and regional co-operation to protect the maritime and fluvial heritage from commercial developments such as construction, cable or pipe laying, oil and gas prospecting and recovery, mining of coal or minerals, sand or gravel extraction and waste and spoil disposal;
x. encourage the protection of fixed installations of maritime and cultural heritage from destruction by property developers who are interested only in land values;
xi. encourage the control and assistance of the conversion of such installations to useful alternative purposes without undue sacrifice of their essential character;
xii. encourage the conservation of such installations as have heritage value but which are not suitable or attractive for redevelopment, and, where demolition is unavoidable, the preservation of a proper documentary record;
xiii. encourage the restoration and preservation of historic inland waterways

and waterfront locations, as far as possible, for public access and amenity and commercial use;

xiv. encourage support and co-operation in the capturing of the original working character of these installations in maritime and waterways museums in the form of displays of artefacts, pictures and photographs, video- and audio-tapes, literary and graphic documents, electronic retrieval, interactive displays or live (including interactive) presentations;

xv. support and encourage public and private bodies and voluntary associations which preserve historic vessels, or life-size or large scale replicas, in working order;

xvi. encourage the display and use of these vessels for the education and enjoyment of the general public;

xvii. encourage further development of a system of mutual acceptability by the maritime authorities of nation states of standards for the safe operation of traditional vessels in European waters.

16. Statement by the President of the United States of America on U.S. Policy for the protection of sunken warships (19 January 2001)

Thousands of United States Government vessels, aircraft, and spacecraft ("State craft"), as well as similar State craft of foreign nations, lie within, and in waters beyond, the territorial sea and contiguous zone. Because of recent advances in science and technology, many of these sunken Government vessels, aircraft, and spacecraft have become accessible to salvors, treasure hunters and others. The unauthorized disturbance or recovery of their crews and passengers is a growing concern both within the United States and internationally. In addition to deserving treatment as gravesites, these sunken State craft may contain objects of a sensitive national security, archaeological, or historical nature. They often also contain unexploded ordnance that could pose a danger to human health and the marine environment if disturbed, or other substances, including fuel oil and other hazardous liquids, that likewise pose a serious threat to human health and the marine environment if released.

I believe that United States policy should be clearly stated to meet this growing concern.

Pursuant to the property clause of Article IV of the Constitution, the United States retains title indefinitely to its sunken State craft unless title has been abandoned or transferred in the manner Congress authorized or directed. The United States recognizes the rule of international law that title to foreign sunken State craft may be transferred or abandoned only in accordance with the law of the foreign flag state.

Further, the United States recognizes that title to a United States or foreign sunken State craft, wherever located, is not extinguished by passage of time, regardless of when such sunken State craft was lost at sea.

International law encourages nations to preserve objects of maritime heritage wherever located for the benefit of the public.

Those who would engage in unauthorized activities directed at sunken State craft are advised that disturbance or recovery of such craft should not occur without the express permission of the sovereign and should only be conducted in accordance with professional scientific standards and with the utmost respect for any human remains.

The United States will use its authority to protect and preserve sunken State craft of the United States and other nations, whether located in the waters of the United States, a foreign nation or in international waters.

President William J. Clinton

17. Siracusa Declaration on the Submarine Cultural Heritage of the Mediterranean Sea (Siracusa, 10 March 2001), adopted during the international conference "Means for the protection and touristic promotion of the marine cultural heritage in the Mediterranean"

The experts of several countries bordering the Mediterranean Sea,

attending the International Conference "Means for the Protection and Touristic Promotion of the Marine Cultural Heritage in the Mediterranean", held in Palermo and Siracusa, Italy, on 8-10 March 2001,

concerned by the fact that the submarine cultural heritage is threatened by activities of uncontrolled exploration and appropriation not respecting the need for conservation and research, increasing commercialization of the objects discovered, damages resulting from other marine activities,

looking forward to the early conclusion of the negotiations at UNESCO for a Convention on the protection of underwater cultural heritage,

acting in their personal capacity,

adopt the following

SIRACUSA DECLARATION ON THE SUBMARINE CULTURAL HERITAGE OF THE MEDITERRANEAN SEA

I. Objectives

1. The Mediterranean basin is characterized by the traces of ancient civilisations which flourished along its shores and, having developed the first seafaring techniques, established close relationships with each other.
2. The Mediterranean cultural heritage is unique in that it embodies the common historical and cultural roots of many civilizations. It is also an integral part of the cultural heritage of humanity and an important element in the history of peoples and societies.
3. The Mediterranean countries have a special responsibility to ensure that the submarine cultural heritage they share is made known and preserved for the benefit of humankind.

II. Principles

4. Activities directed at the Mediterranean submarine cultural heritage should take place only if full respect of the fundamental principles of scientific archaeology is ensured, as reflected in the 1996 ICOMOS Charter and other relevant instruments.
5. Objects of any kind belonging to the Mediterranean submarine cultural heritage should not be acquired, sold, bartered or exploited for commercial purposes or private benefit.

   Economic use of sites and objects belonging to the Mediterranean submarine cultural heritage should be conducted only under strict public supervision.

6. States should avoid the dispersal and fragmentation of components of archaeological contexts.
7. Without prejudice to the rights of the coastal State, activities directed at the Mediterranean submarine cultural heritage should be carried out ensuring prior information and the possible involvement of countries having a verifiable link with the objects in question.
8. Without prejudice to the rights of the coastal State, consultations on how to ensure the appropriate investigation, effective protection and, if they are not preserved *in situ*, final destination of the objects belonging to the Mediterranean submarine cultural heritage should be held between the countries having a verifiable link with the objects in question.
9. Activities directed at submarine cultural heritage should avoid any damage to the surrounding environment and, when necessary, environmental impact assessment and measures for restoration should be undertaken.

III. Consequences

10. In view of their special responsibility, the Mediterranean countries should cooperate in protecting the submarine cultural heritage from natural and man-made risks. They should study the possibility of adopting a regional convention that enhances cooperation in the investigation and protection of the Mediterranean submarine cultural heritage and sets forth the relevant rights and obligations.
11. Mediterranean countries should promote the conclusion of bilateral or multilateral agreements incorporating the objectives and principles of this Declaration and relating to specific components of the Mediterranean submarine cultural heritage, such as wrecks or single objects.
12. Mediterranean countries should establish submarine protected archaeological sites or parks. They should consider means for the establishment of a list of submarine protected archaeological sites or parks of Mediterranean importance. Appropriate measures should be taken to protect submarine archaeological sites from dangerous activities.
13. The establishment of a network of museums where objects of Mediterranean submarine cultural heritage are conserved and displayed should be encouraged and properly publicized.
14. Mediterranean countries should exchange information on, and cooperate in, the training of marine archaeologists.
15. Mediterranean countries should encourage the cooperation of their competent authorities with local governments, scientific institutions, non-governmental organizations, associations of fishermen, seafarers, divers and other professions in the protection and promotion of submarine cultural heritage.

Siracusa, 10 March 2000.

BIBLIOGRAPHY

Books

Ballard & Archbold, *Lost Liners*, Toronto, 1997, p. 116

—— , *The Discovery of the Titanic*, 2nd ed., Toronto, 1998

Boesten, *Activities Affecting Archaeological and/or Historical Valuable Shipwrecks in International Waters: Public International Law and What it Offers*, The Hague, 2002

Brice, *Maritime Law of Salvage*, 3rd ed., London, 1999

Camarda & Scovazzi (eds.), *The Protection of the Underwater Cultural Heritage. Legal Aspects*, Milano, 2002

Cornu & Fromageau (sous la direction de), *Le patrimoine culturel et la mer. Aspects juridiques et institutionnels*, Tome I et II, Paris, 2002

Dromgoole, *Legal Protection of the Underwater Cultural Heritage: National and International Perspectives*, The Hague/London/Boston, 1999

Dumas, *La plongée sous-marine et le droit*, Paris, 1957

Frigo, *La protezione dei beni culturali nel diritto internazionale*, Milano, 1986

Leanza, *Le nouveau droit international de la mer Méditerranée*, Napoli, 1984

Li Vigni & Tusa (a cura di), *Strumenti per la protezione del patrimonio culturale marino. Aspetti archeologici*, Milano, 2002

McCann & Freed, *Deep Water Archaeology: A Late-Roman Ship from Carthage and an Ancient Trade Route near Skerki Bank off Northwest Sicily*, Ann Arbor, 1994

Migliorino, *Il recupero degli oggetti storici e archeologici sommersi nel diritto internazionale*, Milano, 1984

O'Keefe, *Shipwrecked Heritage: A Commentary on the UNESCO Convention on Underwater Cultural Heritage*, Leicester, 2002

Prott & O'Keefe, *Law and the Cultural Heritage*, vol. I *Discovery and Excavation*, Oxford, 1984

Prott & Srong (eds.), *Background Materials on the Protection of the Underwater Cultural Heritage*, vol. I, Paris, 1999

Prott, Planche, Roca-Hachem (eds.), *Background Materials on the Protection of the Underwater Cultural Heritage*, vol. II, Paris, 2000

Schoenbaum, *Admiralty and Maritime Law*, 2nd ed., St. Paul, 1994

Strati, *The Protection of the Underwater Cultural Heritage: An Emerging Objective of the Contemporary Law of the Sea*, The Hague/London/Boston, 1995

Throckmorton (ed.), *History from the Sea: Shipwrecks and Archaeology. From Homer's Odyssey to the Titanic*, London, 1987

Vedovato & Vlad Borrelli (a cura di), *La tutela del patrimonio archeologico subacqueo*, Roma, 1995

Vincenzini, *International Salvage Law*, London, 1992

Vitzthum & Talmon, *Alles fliesst. Kulturgüterschutz und innere Gewässer im Neuen Seerecht*, Baden-Baden, 1998

ARTICLES

Abbass, *A Marine Archaeologist Looks at Treasure Salvage*, in *JMLC*, 1999, p. 261

Ajello, *La ricerca archeologica nell'evoluzione del diritto del mare*, in Panuccio (ed.), *Ritrovamenti e scoperte di opere d'arte*, Milano, 1989, p. 101

Alexander, *Treasure Salvage beyond the Territorial Sea: An Assessment and Recommendations*, in *JMLC*, 1989, p. 1

Allain, *Maritime Wrecks: Where the Lex Ferenda of Underwater Cultural Heritage Collides with the Lex Lata of the Law of the Sea Convention*, in *VJIL*, 1998, p. 747

Alpern, *CIA's Mission Impossible*, in *Newsweek*, 1975, p. 24

Alves & Castro, *New Portuguese Legislation on Mangement of the Underwater Cultural Heritage*, in *Conservation and Management of Archaeological Sites*, 1999, p. 159

Amorosino, *I beni culturali subacquei: profili giuridici*, in *Rivista giuridica dell'edilizia*, 1995, p. 103.

Arend, *Archaeological and Historical Objects: The International Legal Implications of Unclos III*, in *VJIL*, 1982, p. 777

Attard, *The International Regime for the Protection of Archaeological and Historical Objects found at Sea: A Mediterranean Perspective*, in *Journal of Mediterranean Studies*, 1999, p. 113

Aubry, *Federal and State Shipwreck Management in the U.S.*, in *Cultural Resource Management*, 1992, p. 13

Aznar Gómez, *La rivendicazione spagnola per i galeoni affondati di fronte alle coste degli Stati Uniti d'America: il caso de* La Galga *e della* Juno, in *La Comunità Internazionale*, 2001, p. 251

Ballard, *High-Tech Search for Roman Shipwrecks*, in *National Geographic*, April 1998, n.4, p. 32

Balmond, *L'épave du navire*, in Société Française pour le Droit International, *Le navire en droit international*, Colloque de Toulon, Paris, 1992, p. 69

Bangert, *A New Area of International Law: The Protection of Maritime Cultural Property*, in Yee & Tieya (eds.), *International Law in the Post-Cold War World. Essays in Memory of Li Haopei*, London/New York, 2001, p. 119

Barrowman, *The Recovery of Shipwrecks in International Waters: A Multinational Solution*, in *Michigan Yearbook of International Legal Studies*, 1987, p. 231

Beaucourt, *Le "Secret de l'épave" ou l'étrange évolution du régime de sa propriété*, in *Le Droit Maritime Français*, 1986, p. 451

Becker, *Regulating the Business of Culture: The Abandoned Shipwreck Act – Can Preservationists, Salvors and Divers Sail in Calmer Waters?*, in *DePaul Law Review*, 2001, p. 569

Bederman, *Historic Salvage and the Law of the Sea*, in *The University of Miami Inter-American Law Review*, 1998, p. 99

——, *The Unesco Draft Convention on Underwater Cultural Heritage: A Critique and Counter-Proposal*, in *JMLC*, 1999, p. 331

——, *Rethinking the Legal Status of Sunken Warships*, in *ODIL*, 2000, p. 97

——, *Admiralty Jurisdiction*, in *JMLC*, 2000, p. 189

——, *Maritime Preservation Law: Old Challenges, New Trends*, in *WLSJ*, 2002, p. 163

Berean, *Sea Hunt, Inc. v. The Unidentified Shipwrecked Vessel or Vessels: How the Fourth Circuit Rocked the Road*, in *Brooklyn Law Review*, 2002, p. 1249

Berlingieri, *Assistenza e salvataggio nella navigazione marittima, interna ed aerea – Ricupero e ritrovamento*, in *Il diritto marittimo*, 1967–1968, p. 54

——, *Salvataggio e assistenza marittima in acque interne ed aerea – Ritrovamento di relitti di mare*, in *Il diritto marittimo*, 1968, p. 471

Berns, *A Sovereign's Perspective on Treasure Salvage*, in *JMLC*, 1999, p. 269

Beurier, *Pour un droit international de l'archéologie sous-marine*, in *RGDIP*, 1989, p. 45

Blackman, *Is Maritime Archaeology on Course?*, in *American Journal of Archaeology*, 2000, p. 596

Blake, *The Protection of Turkey's Underwater Cultural Archaeological Heritage. Legislative Measures and Other Approaches*, in *IJCP*, 1994, p. 273

——, *The Protection of the Underwater Cultural Heritage*, in *ICLQ*, 1996, p. 819

——, *On Defining the Cultural Heritage*, in *ICLQ*, 2000, p. 61

Blanco-Bazan, *The IMO Guidelines on Particular Sensitive Sea Areas (PSSAs). Their Possible Application to the Protection of Underwater Cultural Heritage*, in *MP*, 1996, p. 337

Blatt, *SOS (Save Our Ship)! Can the UNESCO 1999 Draft Convention on the Treatment of Underwater Cultural Do Any Better?*, in *Emory International Law Review*, 2000, p. 1581

Booth, *The Collision of Property Rights and Cultural Heritage; the Salvors' and Insurers' Viewpoints*, paper presented at the "International Bar Association Conference 2002", Durban, South Africa, 20-25 October 2002

Boyer, *Is the Titanic in the Right Hands? A Discussion of R.M.S. Titanic, Inc. in Federal District Court and the Fourth Circuit*, in *Widener Journal of Public Law*, 2000, p. 379

Brækhus, *Salvage of Wrecks and Wreckage. Legal Issues arising form the Runde Find*, in *Scandinavian Studies in Law*, 1976, p. 37

Braunstein, *Shipwrecks Lost and Found at Sea: The Abandoned Shipwreck Act of 1987 is still Causing Confusion and Conflict rather than Preserving Historic Shipwrecks*, in *WLSJ*, 2002, p. 301

Brice, *Salvage and the Underwater Cultural Heritage*, in *MP*, 1996, p. 337

Broad, *20,000 Leagues under the Sea*, in *UNESCO Sources*, No. 97, February 1997, p. 14

Brown, *Protection of the Underwater Cultural Heritage. Draft Principles and Guidelines for Implementation of Art. 303 of the United Nations Convention on the Law of the Sea, 1982*, in *MP*, 1996, p. 325

——, *Legal Loopholes ...*, in *UNESCO Sources*, No. 97, February 1997, p. 10

Bryant, *The Archaeological Duty of Care: The Legal, Professional and Cultural Struggle over Salvaging Historic Shipwrecks*, in *Albany Law Review*, 2001, p. 97

Butler, *Admiralty – Salvage Rights – Sovereign Claims on the Outer Continental Shelf Do Not Extend to Abandoned Vessels*, in *Georgia Journal of International and Comparative Law*, 1977, p. 169

Caflisch, *Submarine Antiquities and the International Law of the Sea*, in *Netherlands Yearbook of International Law*, 1983, p. 3

——, *La condition des épaves maritimes en droit international public*, in *Mélanges en l'honneur de Nicolas Valticos*, Paris, 1999, p. 67

Callegari & Vallega, *Coastal Cultural Heritage: A Management Tool*, in *Journal of Cultural Heritage*, 2002, p. 227

Camarda, *Legislazioni nazionali, diritto comunitario e problematiche di "adattamento" in tema di protezione del patrimonio culturale sommerso*, in *Nuove autonomie*, 2001, p. 533

Carducci, *La Convenzione UNESCO sul patrimonio culturale subacqueo*, in *RDI*, 2002, p. 53

——, *New Developments in the Law of the Sea: The UNESCO Convention on the Protection of Underwater Cultural Heritage*, in *AJIL*, 2002, p. 419

Cassidy, *Historic Shipwrecks and Blanket Declaration*, in *Bulletin of the Australian Institute for Maritime Archaeology*, 1991, p. 4

Castagné, *L'archéologie sous-marine et le droit*, in Société Française pour le Droit International, *Actualités du droit de la mer*, Colloque de Montpellier, Paris, 1973, p. 164

Cederlund, *Marine Archaeology in Society and Science*, in *IJNA*, 1995, p. 9

Chun, *Charting through Protection for Historic Shipwrecks found in U.S. Territorial Waters: Sea Hunt, Inc. v. Unidentified, Shipwrecked Vessel or Vessels*, in *Virginia Environmental Law Journal*, 2000, p. 87

Ciciriello, *Il patrimonio culturale subacqueo e l'ordinamento italiano*, in *La Comunità Internazionale*, 1998, p. 72

——, *Il progetto di convenzione UNESCO sul patrimonio culturale subacqueo: una nuova sfida al principio della libertà dei mari?*, in *La Comunità Internazionale*, 2000, p. 611

Clément, *Le concept de* responsabilité collective *de la communauté internationale pour la protection de biens culturels dans les conventions et recommandations de l'UNESCO*, in *Revue belge de droit international*, 1993, p. 534

——, *Current Developments at UNESCO Concerning the Protection of the Underwater Cultural Heritage*, in *MP*, 1996, p. 309

Cohen, *Should Noli Forfendi Apply to Sunken Ships?*, in *Boston University Law Review*, 1993, p. 193

Collins, *The Salvage of Sunken Military Vessels*, in *International Lawyer*, 1976, p. 681

Concannon, *R.M.S. Titanic the Legal Leviathan*, in *Delaware Lawyer*, 1999, p. 25

—— , *The Battle for the R.M.S. Titanic*, in *The Philadelphia Lawyer*, 1999, no. 2

Coolbaugh, *Raiders of the Lost ... Sub? The Potential for Private Claims of Ownership to Military Shipwrecks in International Waters: The Case of Japanese Submarine I-52*, in *Buffalo Law Review*, 2001, p. 929

Cottrell, *The Law of the Sea and International Marine Archaeology: Abandoning Admiralty Law to Protect Historic Shipwrecks*, in *Fordham International Law Journal*, 1994, p. 667

Croome, *The United States' Abandoned Shipwreck Act Goes into Action – A Report*, in *IJNAUE*, 1992, p. 39

Cycon, *Legal and Regulatory Issues in Marine Archaeology*, in *Oceanus*, 1985, p. 78

Cyriax & Wordie, *Centenary of the Sailing of Sir. John Franklin with the* Erebus *and* Terror, in *The Geographical Journal*, 1945, p. 169

Davidde, *Underwater Archaeological Parks: A New Perspective and a Challenge for Conservation – The Italian Panorama*, in *IJNA*, 2002, p. 83

Debenedctis, *"Finders Keepers" Modified. Insurance Companies Due Part of the Treasure from Recovered Shipwreck*, in *American Bar Association Journal*, November 1992, p. 26

Del Bianco, *Underwater Recovery Operation in Offshore Waters: Vying for Rights to Treasure*, in *Boston University International Law Journal*, 1987, p. 153

DeLanis, *Jurisdiction – Continental Shelf – Abandoned Vessel Salvaged from the Surface of the United States Continental Shelf Beyond Territorial Waters Is Not Under Jurisdiction of United States Government*, in *Vanderbilt Journal of Transnational Law*, 1975-76, p. 915

Delgado, *Diving on the Titanic*, in *Archaeology*, January/February 2001, p. 52

Dellino & Endere, *The HMS Shift Shipwreck. The Development of Underwater Heritage Protection in Argentina*, in *Conservation and Archaeological Sites*, 2001, p. 219

Des épaves chargées d'histoire, in *Annuaire du Droit de la Mer*, 1998, p. 552

de Yturriaga Barberán, *Convención sobre la protección del patrimonio cultural subacuático*, in Drnas de Clément (coord.), *Estudios de Derecho Internacional en homenaje al Professor Ernesto J. Rey Caro*, Cordoba, 2003, p. 451

Dicke, *Ricerca archeologica e protezione dei beni culturali*, in Leanza, (a cura di), *Il regime giuridico internazionale del Mare Mediterraneo*, Milano, 1987, p. 355

Dorsey III, *Historic Salvors, Marine Archaeologists and The UNESCO Draft Convention on Underwater Cultural Heritage*, paper presented at the "Houston Marine Insurance Seminar", September 2000

Dromgoole & Gaskell, *Who Has Rights to Historic Wrecks and Wreckage?*, in *IJCP*, 1993, p. 217

—— , *Draft UNESCO Convention on the Protection of the Underwater Cultural Heritage 1998*, in *IJMCL*, 1999, p. 171

Dromgoole, *Protection of Historic Wreck: The UK Approach. Part I: The Present Legal Framework*, in *IJECL*, 1989, p. 26

——, *Protection of Historic Wreck: The UK Approach. Part II: Towards Reform*, in *IJECL*, 1989, p. 95

—— , *Military Remains on and around the Coast of the United Kingdom: Statutory Mechanisms of Protection*, in *IJMCL*, 1996, p. 23

—— , *A Protective Legal Regime for the Underwater Cultural Heritage: The Problem of International Waters*, in *Annuaire de droit maritime et océanique*, 1997, p. 119

—— , *A Note on the Meaning of "Wreck"*, in *IJNAUE*, 1999, p. 319

—— , *2001 UNESCO Convention on the Protection of the Underwater Cultural Heritage*, in *IJMCL*, 2003, p. 59

Elia, *Diving for Diamonds. The Ongoing Saga of the RMS Titanic and Efforts to Protect Shipwrecks and Submerged Sites*, in *Archaeology*, September 2000

—— , *The US Protection of the Underwater Cultural Heritage beyond the Territorial Sea – Problems and Prospects*, in *IJNAUE*, 2000, p. 43

—— , *Titanic in the Courts*, in *Archaeology*, 2001, p. 54

Elkin, *Argentina and the UNESCO Convention on Underwater Cultural Heritage*, paper presented at the "Conference on Historical and Underwater Archaeology", Mobile (Alabama), 8–12 January 2002

Endere, *¿Quien protege el patrimonio arqueológico subacuático en Argentina?*, in *Acta del XII Congreso Nacional de Arqueología*, La Plata, 1997

Eustis III, *The Glomar Explorer Incident: Implications for the Law of Salvage*, in *VJIL*, 1975, p. 177

Firth, *Archaeology Underwater in France*, in *IJECL*, 1992, p. 57

Fisher, *The Abandoned Shipwreck Act: The Role of Private Enterprise*, in *C–VLA JL&A*, 1988, p. 373

Flecker, *The Ethics, Politics, and Realities of Maritime Archaeology in Southeast Asia*, in *IJNA*, 2002, p. 12

Fletcher-Tomenius & Forrest, *Historic Wreck in International Waters: Conflict or Consensus?*, in *MP*, 2000, p. 1

Fletcher-Tomenius, O'Keefe, Williams, *Salvor in Possession: Friend or Foe to Marine Archaeology?*, in *IJCP*, 2000, p. 263

Fletcher-Tomenius & Williams, *The Protection of Wrecks Act 1973: A Breach of Human Rights?*, in *IJMCL*, 1998, p. 623

—— , *The Draft UNESCO/DOALOS Convention on the Protection of Underwater Cultural Heritage and the European Convention on Human Rights*, in *IJNAUE*, 1999, p. 145

—— , *Regulating Recovery of Historic Wreck in UK Waters: When is a Salvor not a Salvor?*, in *Lloyd's Maritime and Commercial Law Quarterly*, 2000, p. 208

Forrest, *State Claims to Shipwrecks in the US. The Brother Jonathan*, in *Lloyd's Maritime and Commercial Law Quarterly*, 1998, p. 509

—— , *New Laws for the Millenium – Archaeology AND Salvage?*, paper presented at the 4th World Archaeological Congress, University of Cape Town, 10–14 January 1999

—— , *A New International Regime for the Protection of Underwater Cultural Heritage*, in *ICLQ*, 2002, p. 511

—— , *Defining "Underwater Cultural Heritage"*, in *IJNA*, 2002, p. 3

—— , *An International Perspective on Sunken State Vessels as Underwater Cultural Heritage*, in *ODIL*, 2003, p. 41

Franco, *Ancient Mediterranean Harbours: A Heritage to Preserve*, in *Ocean and Coastal Management*, 1996, p. 115

Fry, *The Treasure below: Jurisdiction over Salving Operations in International Waters*, in *Columbia Law Review*, 1988, p. 863

Fu, *A Chinese Perspective on the UNESCO Convention on the Protection of the Underwater Cultural Heritage*, in *IJMCL*, 2003, p. 109

Gardner, *Deep Diving, New Underwater Equipment, and their Potentials for the Future of Archaeology*, paper presented at the 4th World Archaeological Congress, University of Cape Town, 10–14 January 1999

Gasser, *Making Sense of the Muddle: Deep Sea Research Takes on the Abandoned Shipwreck Act and the Eleventh Amendment in California v. Deep Sea Research Inc.*, in *The Maritime Lawyer*, 1999, p. 567

Gibson, *Lusitania and the Ownership of the Wreck*, in *IJECL*, 1986, p. 323

—— , *Protection of Military Remains Act of 1986*, in *IJECL*, 1987, p. 182

Giesecke, *Shipwrecks. The Past and the Present*, in *Coastal Management*, 1987, p. 179

—— , *The Abandoned Shipwreck Act: Affirming the Role of the States in Historic Preservation*, in *C –VLA JL&A*, 1988, p. 379

—— , *The Abandoned Shipwreck Act Through the Eyes of its Drafter*, in *JMLC*, 1999, p. 167

Giorgi, *Underwater Archaeology and Historical Objects*, in Dupuy (R.-J) & Vignes (eds.), *A Handbook on the New Law of the Sea*, vol. I, Dordrecht/Boston/ Lancaster, 1991, p. 561

Goy, *L'épave du Titanic et le droit des épaves en haute mer*, in *Annuaire français de droit international*, 1989, p. 752

Green, *Management of Maritime Archaeology under Australian Legislation*, in *Bulletin of Australian Institute for Maritime Archaeology*, 1995, p. 33

Harris J.R., *The Protection of Sunken Warships as Gravesites at Sea*, in *OCLJ*, 2001, p. 75

—— , *Protecting sunken Warships as Objects Entitled to Sovereign Immunity*, in *The University of Miami Inter-American Law Review*, 2002, p. 101

Harris J. M., *Who Owns the Pot of Gold at the End of the Rainbow? A Review of the Impact of Cultural Property on Finders and Salvage Law*, in *Arizona Journal of International & Comparative Law*, 1997, p. 223

Hawkins, *Reconsidering the Maritime Laws of Finds and Salvage: A Free Market Alternative*, in *George Washington Journal of International Law & Economics*, 1996, p. 75

Hayashi, *Archaeological and Historical Objects under the United Nations Convention on the Law of the Sea*, in *MP*, 1996, p. 291

Henderson, *Significant Assessment or Blanket Protection?*, in *IJNA*, 2001, p. 3

Hess, *The Trouble with Treasure: Ethical Dilemmas for the Salvage Attorney*, in *JMLC*, 1999, p. 253

Hewitt, *The Proposed Abandoned Shipwreck Acts of 1987 – Archaeological Preservation and Maritime Law*, in *Suffolk Transnational Law Journal*, 1988–89, p. 381

Hoagland, *Managing the Underwater Cultural Resources of the China Seas: A Comparison of Public Policies in Mainland China and Taiwan*, in *IJMCL*, 1997, p. 265

Horrell, Telepossession *is Nine-Tenth of the Law: The Emerging Industry of Deep Ocean Discovery*, in *Pace Yearbook of International Law*, 1991, p. 309

Hoyle, *Historic and Archaeological Treasures*, in Allen & Hanson (eds.), *New Developments in Marine Science and Technology: Economic, Legal and Political Aspects of Change*, Honolulu, 1999, p. 84

Hutchinson, *Threats to Underwater Cultural Heritage. The Problems of Unprotected Archaeological and Historic Sites, Wrecks and Objects Found at Sea*, in *MP*, 1996, p. 287

Izuel, *Property Owners' Constructive Possession of Treasure Trove: Rethinking the Finders Keepers Rule*, in *UCLA Law Review*, 1991, p. 1659

Jacobsson & Klabbers, *Rest in Peace? New Developments Concerning the Wreck of the M/S Estonia*, in *Nordic Journal of International Law*, 2000, p. 317

Jasinski, *Which Way Now? Maritime Archaeology and Underwater Heritage into the 21st Century*, paper presented at the 4th World Archaeological Congress, University of Cape Town, 10-14 January 1999

Jeffery & Cook, *UNESCO Convention on the Protection of the Underwater Cultural Heritage: Implications for the Federated States of Australia*, paper presented at the conference "*The Protection of Underwater Cultural Heritage*", The University of Queensland, The Centre for Maritime Law, 27 September 2001

Johnson, *For Keeping or for Keeps? An Australian Perspective on Challenges Facing the Development of a Regime for the Protection of Underwater Cultural Heritage*, in *Melbourne Journal of International Law*, 2000, p. 19

—— , *The Draft Convention and the LOSC: Conformity, Compatibility or Conundrum?*, paper presented at the conference "*The Protection of Underwater Cultural Heritage*", The University of Queensland, The Centre for Maritime Law, 27 September 2001

Jones J.E., *Possessory Rights in Abandoned Vessels*, in *VJIL*, 1979-1980, p. 473

Jones P.J., *The United States Supreme Court and Treasure Salvage: Issues Remaining After Brother Jonathan*, in *JMLC*, 1999, p. 205

Kahn, *Sunken Treasures: Conflicts between Historic Preservation Law and the Maritime Law of Finds*, in *Tulane Environmental Law Journal*, 1994, p. 595

Kaoru & Hoagland, *The Value of Historic Shipwrecks: Conflicts and Management*, in *Coastal Management*, 1994, p. 195

Karagiannis, *Une nouvelle zone de juridiction: la zone archéologique maritime*, in *ERM*, 1990, p. 1

Keller, *Salvor-Sovereign Relations: How the State of Illinois Destroyed the Lady Elgin*, in *JMLC*, 1999, p. 245

Kerr, *The International Convention on Salvage 1989 – How it Came to Be*, in *ICLQ*, 1990, p. 530

Kimball, *Jurisdiction: A United States Admiralty Court Can Award and Enforce Salvage Rights in a Shipwreck in International Waters: R.M.S. Titanic, Inc. v. Haver*, in *JMLC*, 1999, p. 691

King, *Admiralty Law: Evolving Legal Treatment of Property Claims to Shipwrecks in International Waters*, in *Harvard International Law Journal*, 1990, p. 313

Klabbers, *Les cimetières marins sont-ils établis comme des régimes objectifs? A propos de l'accord sur l'épave du M/S Estonia*, in *ERM*, 1997, p. 121

Korthals Altes, *Submarine Antiquities and the Law*, in *Annuaire de l'AAA*, 1974, p. 127
——, *Submarine Antiquities: A Legal Labyrinth*, in *Syracuse Journal of International Law and Commerce*, 1976, p. 77
La Motte, *Introductory Note to UNESCO Convention on the Protection of the Underwater Cultural Heritage*, in *ILM*, 2002, p. 37
Larsen, *Ownership of Historic Shipwrecks in US Law*, in *IJMCL*, 1994, p. 31
Le Gurun, *L'épave, bien culturel maritime: une notion à découvrir*, in *Annuaire de Droit Maritime*, 1995, p. 268
Leanza, *La zona archeologica marina e la protezione dei beni culturali subacquei*, in Paone (a cura di), *La protezione internazionale e la circolazione comunitaria dei beni culturali mobili*, Napoli, 1998, p. 91
——, *Zona archeologica marina*, in Francioni, Del Vecchio, De Caterini (a cura di), *Protezione internazionale del patrimonio culturale: interessi nazionali e difesa del patrimonio comune della cultura*, Milano, 2000, p. 41
——, *Le patrimoine culturel sous-marin de la Méditerranée*, in Cataldi (sous la direction de), *La Méditerranée et le droit de la mer à l'aube du 21ème siècle*, Bruxelles, 2002, p. 139
Leslie & Nguyen, *The Treasure of the I-52*, in *Newsweek*, 1995, p. 64
Lin, *Salvage Rights and Intellectual Property: Are Copyright and Trademark Rights Included in the Salvage Rights to the R.M.S. TITANIC?*, in *The Maritime Lawyer*, 1999, p. 483
Long, *The Good Samaritan and Admiralty: A Parable of a Statute Lost at Sea*, in *Buffalo Law Review*, 2000, p. 591
Lorello, *The Abandoned Shipwreck Act of 1987: Navigating Through the Fog*, in *Gonzaga Law Review*, 1999-2000, p. 75
Lund, *Protection of the Under-Water Cultural Heritage*, in Leanza, (a cura di), *Il regime giuridico internazionale del Mare Mediterraneo*, Milano, 1987, p. 351
Maarleveld, *Archaeological Heritage Management – Cultural and Legislative Perspective*, in Maarleveld (ed.), *Archaeological Heritage Management in Dutch Waters: Exploratory Studies*, 1998, p. 23
MacInnis, *Fire on the Ice: Men of the* Erebus *and* Terror, in *Canadian Geographical Journal*, 1978, p. 52
Mainetti, *The 2001 UNESCO Convention on the Protection of the Underwater Cultural Heritage: A Commentary*, paper presented for the course "*The International Law of the Sea*", Graduate Institute of International Studies, Geneva, 2001–02
Mantzouka-Syson, *Underwater Archaeology in Greece: Past, Present and Future*, paper presented at the 4th World Archaeological Congress, University of Cape Town, 10-14 January 1999
Martini, *Ritrovamenti in mare di relitti e di cose di interesse artistico e storico*, in *Il diritto marittimo*, 1964, p. 284
Mather, *Technology and the Search for Shipwrecks*, in *JMLC*, 1999, p. 175
Mayer, *Protection of Historic Shipwreck – Outline of Legal Issues*, ALI-ABA Course of Study Materials, Historic Preservation Law, Vol. II, October 1998
McCormack, *The Titanic Venture: Who Owns the Ocean Deep?*, paper presented at the "Houston Marine Insurance Seminar", September 1999

McQuown, *An Archaeological Argument for the Inapplicability of Admiralty Law in the Disposition of Historic Shipwrecks*, in *William Mitchell Law Review*, 2000, p. 289

McWilliams, *Salvage of Ancient Treasure Ships*, in *Lloyd's Maritime and Commercial Law Quarterly*, 1986, p. 16

Meazell, *Being and Embeddedness: The Abandoned Shipwreck Act's Historical Proxy is All at Sea*, in *Georgia Law Review*, 2000, p. 1743

Meenan, *Cultural Resources Preservation and Underwater Archaeology: Some Notes on the Current Legal Framework and a Model Underwater Antiquities Statute*, in *San Diego Law Review*, 1978, p. 623

Migliorino, *Submarine Antiquities and the Law of the Sea*, in *Marine Policy Reports*, 1982, p. 1

——, *The Recovery of Sunken Warships in International Law*, in Vukas (ed.), *Essays on the New Law of the Sea*, Zagreb, 1985, p. 244

—— , In Situ *Protection of the Underwater Cultural Heritage under International Treaties and National Legislation*, in *IJMCL*, 1995, p. 483

Miller E.M., *A Time for Decision on Submerged Cultural Resources*, in *Oceanus*, 1988, p. 25

Miller R., *Charting the Future of Historic Shipwreck Legislation in California: Application of the English Model in the Salvage of the* Brother Jonathan, in *Hastings International and Comparative Law Review*, 1994, p. 793

Monden & Wils, *Art Objects as Common Heritage of Mankind*, in *Revue belge de droit international*, 1986, p. 327

Morgan, *The New Law of the Sea: Rethinking the Implications for Sovereign Jurisdiction and Freedom of Action*, in *ODIL*, 1996, p. 5

Murphy, *Jurisdiction over Salvage Claims Outside U.S. Territory: RMS Titanic*, in *AJIL*, 2000, p. 125

—— , *Ownership of Sunken Spanish Warships*, in *AJIL*, 2000, p. 678

—— , *U.S. Concerns Regarding UNESCO Convention on Underwater Heritage*, in *AJIL*, 2002, p. 468

Nafziger, *Finding the Titanic: Beginning an International Salvage of Derelict Law of the Sea*, in *C–VLA JL&A*, 1988, p. 339

—— , *Report – The Draft Convention on the Protection of the Underwater Cultural Heritage*, in *ODIL*, 1994, p. 391

__ , *The Buenos Aires Draft Convention on the Protection of the Underwater Cultural Heritage*, in *IJCP*, 1997, p. 119

—— , *The Titanic Revisited*, in *JMLC*, 1999, p. 311

—— , *Historic Salvage Law Revisited*, in *ODIL*, 2000, p. 81

—— , *The Evolving Role of Admiralty Courts in Litigation Related to Historic Wrecks*, in *Harvard International Law Journal*, 2003, p. 251

Nelson, *Guiding the Ocean Search Process: Applying Public Land Experience to the Design of Leasing and Permitting Systems for Ocean Mining and Ocean Shipwrecks*, in *ODIL*, 1989, p. 577

Newton, *Finders Keepers? The* Titanic *and the 1982 Law of the Sea Convention*, in *Hastings International and Comparative Law Review*, 1986–87, p. 159

Nicholson, *Mutiny as to the Bounty: International Law's Failing Preservation Efforts*

Regarding Shipwrecks and their Artifacts Located in International Waters, in *University of Missouri at Kansas City Law Review*, 1997, p. 135

O'Keefe, *The European Convention on the Protection of the Archaeological Heritage – Relevance to Maritime Archaeology*, in *The Bulletin of the Australian Institute for Marine Archaeology*, 1993, p. 27

——, *Protecting the Underwater Cultural Heritage. The International Law Association Draft Convention*, in *MP*, 1996, p. 297

——, *Protection of the Underwater Cultural Heritage: Developments at UNESCO*, in *IJNA*, 1996, p. 169

——, *Finders Keepers*, in *UNESCO Sources*, No. 97, February 1997, p. 11

——, *Second Meeting of Governmental Experts to Consider the Draft Convention on the Protection of Underwater Cultural Heritage*, in *IJCP*, 1999, p. 568

O'Keefe & Prott, *Australian Protection of Historic Shipwrecks*, in *The Australian Year Book of International Law*, 1978, p. 119

O'Shea, *The Evolution of Maritime Historic Preservation Jurisprudence*, in *WLSJ*, 2002, p. 417

Owen, *Some Legal Troubles with Treasure: Jurisdiction and Salvage*, in *JMLC*, 1985, p. 139

——, *The Abandoned Shipwreck Act of 1987: Good-bye to Salvage in the Territorial Sea*, in *JMLC*, 1988, p. 499

Oxman, *The Third United Nations Conference on the Law of the Sea: The Ninth Sessions (1980)*, in *AJIL*, 1981, p. 211

——, *Le régime des navires de guerre dans le cadre de la Convention des Nations Unies sur le Droit de la Mer*, in *Annuaire français de droit international*, 1982, p. 811

——, *Marine Archaeology and the International Law of the Sea*, in *C-VLA JL&A*, 1988, p. 353

Papa, *Tutela e valorizzazione del patrimonio culturale subacqueo nell'ordinamento italiano: aspetti problematici e prospettive future*, in *Rivista giuridica dell'edilizia*, 2002, p. 1033

Pazarci, *Sur la recherche archéologique subaquatique en Méditerranée*, in Leanza (a cura di), *Il regime giuridico internazionale del Mare Mediterraneo*, Milano, 1987, p. 359

Pecoraro, *Nota sulla protezione del patrimonio culturale subacqueo*, in Leanza, (a cura di), *Il regime giuridico internazionale del Mare Mediterraneo*, Milano, 1987, p. 367

——, *Il regime giuridico della ricerca archeologica marina nell'ambito della zee*, in Leanza & Sico (a cura di), *Zona economica esclusiva e mare Mediterraneo*, Napoli, 1989, p. 137

Peltz, *Salvaging Historic Wrecks*, in *TMLJ*, 2000, p. 1

Poltrack, *Recent Development: Sea Hunt, Inc. v. Unidentified Shipwrecked Vessel or Vessels: The United States Court of Appeals for the Fourth Circuit Interprets the Standard for Abandonment under the Abandoned Shipwreck Act of 1987*, in *University of Baltimore Journal of Environmental Law*, 2000, p. 170

Prott, *Legal Principles for Protecting Underwater Cultural Heritage*, in Mostafa, Grimal, Nakashima (eds.), *Underwater Archaeology and Coastal Management. Focus on Alexandria*, UNESCO Publication, Paris, 2000

Prott & O'Keefe, *International Legal Protection of the Underwater Cultural Heritage*, in *Revue belge de droit international*, 1978–79, p. 86

Rau, *Kulturgüterschutz im Meer: eine erste Analyse der neuen UNESCO-Konvention*, in *Zeitschrift für ausländisches öffentliches Rechts und Völkerrecht*, 2001, p. 833

——, *The UNESCO Convention on Underwater Cultural Heritage and the International Law of the Sea*, in *Max Planck Yearbook of United Nations Law*, 2002, p. 387

Rigambert, *Le droit des épaves maritimes de l'antiquité au XXe siècle*, in *Annuaire de droit maritime et océanique*, 1998, p. 371

Roach, *France Concedes United States has Title to CSS Alabama*, in *AJIL*, 1991, p. 381

——, *Sunken Warships and Military Aircraft*, in *MP*, 1996, p. 351

——, *Shipwrecks: Reconciling Salvage and Underwater Archaeology*, in Nordquist & Moore (eds.), *Ocean Policy. New Institutions, Challenges and Opportunities*, The Hague/Boston/London, 1999, p. 305

Robol, *The SS Central America Project: International Law and Individual Freedom*, in *International Legal Practitioner*, December 1991, p. 118

——, *Legal Protection for Underwater Cultural Resources: Can We Do Better?*, in *JMLC*, 1999, p. 303

Romolotti, *Il recupero di navi militari affondate nel diritto internazionale*, in *Rivista Marittima*, 1999, p. 67

Ronzitti, *Stato costiero, archeologia sottomarina e tutela del patrimonio storico sommerso*, in *Il diritto marittimo*, 1984, p. 3

Roucounas, *Sub-Marine Archaeological Research: Some Legal Aspects*, in Leanza (a cura di), *Il regime giuridico internazionale del Mare Mediterraneo*, Milano, 1987, p. 309

Rubin, *Sunken Soviet Submarines and Central Intelligence; Laws of Property and the Agency*, in *AJIL*, 1975, p. 855

Ruffman, Townsend Gault & VanderZwaag, *Legal Jurisdiction Over the Titanic*, in *Lighthouse*, publication of the Canadian Hydrographic Association, Spring 1988, p. 23

Ruiz, *Decisive Times for Underwater Archaeology: Who Owns the Watery Past?*, in *The Art Newspaper*, September 2000

Runyan, *Shipwreck Legislation and the Preservation of Submerged Artefacts*, in *Case Western Reserve Journal of International Law*, 1990, p. 31

Savadogo, *La Convention sur la protection du patrimoine culturel subaquatique (2 novembre 2001)*, in *RGDIP*, 2003, p. 31

Schubert, *La condition juridique des épaves maritimes: problèmes de droit international public*, in *ERM*, 1991, p. 125

Sclafani, *Sea Hunt, Inc. v. Unidentified Shipwrecked Vessels: Defining a Standard of "Abandonment" for the Shipwreck of a Sovereign*, in *TMLJ*, 2001, p. 559

Scovazzi, *Il Melqart di Sciacca 35 anni dopo*, in *RDI*, 1990, p. 915

——, *Liberté de la mer: vers l'affaiblissement d'un principe vénérable?*, in *Annuaire de droit de la mer*, 1998, p. 13

——, *The 2001 UNESCO Convention on the Protection of the Underwater Cultural Heritage*, in *Italian Yearbook of International Law*, 2001, p. 9

—— , *Convention on the Protection of Underwater Cultural Heritage*, in *Environmental Policy and Law*, 2002, p. 152

Scrimo, *Raising the Dead: Improving the Recovery and Management of Historic Shipwrecks*, in *OCLJ*, 2000, p. 271

Shallcross & Giesecke, *Recent Developments in Litigation Concerning the Recovery of Historic Shipwrecks*, in *Syracuse Journal of International Law and Commerce*, 1983, p. 371

Shapreau, *The* Brother Jonathan *Decision: Treasure Salvor's "Actual Possession" of Shipwreck Gives Rise to Federal Jurisdiction for Title Claim*, in *IJCP*, 1998, p. 475

—— , *Settlement Reached in Deep Sea Research, Inc. v. The Brother Jonathan, et al.*, in *IJCP*, 1999, p. 522

—— , *Extention of Express Abandonment Standard for Sovereign Shipwrecks in Sea Hunt, Inc. et al., Raises Troublesome Issues Regarding Protection of Underwater Cultural Property*, in *IJCP*, 2001, p. 276

Shelton, *Recent Developments in International Law Relating to Marine Archaeology*, in Conseil Européen de Droit de l'Environnement, *Technologie et droit international*, Funchal, 1999, p. 61

Shore, *Marine Archaeology and International Law: Background and Some Suggestions*, in *San Diego Law Review*, 1972, p. 668

Shuzhong, *What Kind of Underwater Heritage Convention Do We Need?*, in *IJCP*, 1999, p. 575

Sico, *Osservazioni sull'articolo 59 della Convenzione di Montego Bay*, in Leanza & Sico (a cura di), *Zona economica esclusiva e mare Mediterraneo*, Napoli, 1989, p. 281

—— , *Le norme internazionali e comunitarie concernenti l'illecita rimozione dei beni culturali rinvenuti sul fondo marino*, in Paone (a cura di), *La protezione internazionale e la circolazione comunitaria dei beni culturali mobili*, Napoli, 1998, p. 239

Siegler, *"Finders Keepers" Revised for the High Seas*, in *TMLJ*, 1993, p. 353

Skrk, *The 1987 Law of Yugoslavia on the Coastal Sea and the Continental Shelf*, in *ODIL*, 1989, p. 501

Staniforth, *Underwater Cultural Heritage Management in Australia: A Model in Need of Repair*, paper presented at the 4th World Archaeological Congress, University of Cape Town, 10-14 January 1999

Starkle, *Les épaves de navires en haute mer et le droit international. Le cas du "Mont-Louis"*, in *Revue belge de droit international*, 1984–85, p. 496

Stemm, *The Claims of Spain – Death Knell for Shipwreck Exploration?*, in *UM*, November 2000

—— , *Thoughts on the UNESCO Convention: A Perspective from Inside the Process*, in *UM*, January 2001

—— , *Where Do We Go from Here?*, in *UM*, November-December 2001

—— , *UNESCO Gets Its Feet Wet. An Overview of the UNESCO Convention for the Protection of Underwater Cultural Heritage*, in *Minerva: International Review of Ancient Art and Archaeology*, January 2002

—— , *The New UNESCO Convention: Rules You Need To Know*, in *UM*, January-February 2002

Stemm & Roach, *Shipwrecks in the Deep Freeze*, in *Maritime Heritage Magazine*, April 1998

Stern, *Smart Salvage: Extending Traditional Maritime Law to Include Intellectual Property Rights in Historic Shipwrecks*, in *Fordham Law Review*, 2000, p. 2489

Strati, *Deep Seabed Cultural Property and the Common Heritage of Mankind*, in *ICLQ*, 1991, p. 859

——, *Draft Convention on the Protection of Underwater Cultural Heritage. A Commentary*, UNESCO doc. CLT-99/WS/8, April 1999

Sweeney, *An Overview of Commercial Salvage Principles in the Context of Marine Archaeology*, in *JMLC*, 1999, p. 185

Thompson, *Finders Weepers Losers Keepers: United States of America v. Steinmetz. The Doctrine of State Succession, Maritime Finds, and the Bell of the CSS Alabama*, in *Connecticut Law Review*, 1996, p. 479

Tibbetts, *The Long Voyage of the Lusitania*, in *New York Law School Journal of International and Comparative Law*, 1999, p. 285

Tiberg, *Why Cover the Wreck of a Sunken Ship?*, in *Scandinavian Studies in Law*, 2000, p. 481

Timpany, *Ownership Rights in the Titanic*, in *Case Western Reserve Law Review*, 1986, p. 72

Treves, *La nona sessione della Conferenza sul diritto del mare*, in *RDI*, 1980, p. 432

——, *Stato costiero e archeologia sottomarina*, in *RDI*, 1993, p. 698

Valenzuela, *A salvo de los buscadores de tesoros*, in *El Pais*, 21 febbraio 2001, p. 64

Van Meurs, *Legal Aspects of Marine Archaeological Research*, in *Acta Juridica*, 1986, p. 83

Van Tilburg, *Chinese Maritime History and Nautical Archaeology: Where Have All the Ships Gone?*, in *Bulletin of Australian Institute for Maritime Archaeology*, 1994, p. 25

Varmer, *The Case Against the "Salvage" of the Cultural Heritage*, in *JMLC*, 1999, p. 279

Verlaan, *Marine Archaeology: A Trojan (Sea) Horse?*, in *Ocean Yearbook*, 1989, p. 231

Vierucci, *Le statut juridique des navires de guerre ayant coulé dans des eaux étrangères: le cas des frégates espagnoles* Juno *et* La Galga *retrouvées au large des côtes des États-Unis*, in *RGDIP*, 2001, p. 705

Vitányi, *L'immunité des navires d'Etat*, in *Netherlands International Law Review*, 1963, p. 33

Yormak, *Canadian Treasure: Law and Lore*, in *JMLC*, 1999, p. 229

War and Neutrality – Right to a Captured Vessel – "S.S. Admiral Nakhimov", in *The Japanese Annual of International Law*, 1986, p. 185

War Vessels, in *Digest of United States Practice in International Law*, 1980, p. 999

Weiss, *Maritime Disasters Through the Ages*, in *JMLC*, 2001, p. 215

Werz, *South Africa Shipwrecks and Salvage: The Need for Improved Management*, in *IJNA*, 1993, p. 237

——, *Between the Devil and the Deep Blue Sea. The Development and Future of Maritime Archaeology in South Africa*, paper presented at the 4th World Archaeological Congress, University of Cape Town, 10–14 January 1999

White, *Draft Convention on the Protection of Underwater Cultural Heritage: A Critical Analysis*, paper presented at the conference "*The Protection of Underwater Cultural Heritage*", The University of Queensland, The Centre for Maritime Law, 27 September 2001

——, *Sea Hunt, Inc. v. Unidentified Shipwrecked Vessel or Vessels, 221 F.3d 634*, in *AJIL*, 2001, p. 678

Williams M.V., *A Legal History of Shipwreck in England*, in *Annuaire du droit maritime et océanique*, 1997, p. 71

Williams S., *Underwater Heritage, a Treasure Trove to Protect*, in *UNESCO Sources*, February 1997, p. 7

Zander, *The Antiquities Act. Regulating Salvage of Historic Shipwrecks*, in *Cultural Resource Management*, 1996, n. 7, p. 88

Zander & Varmer, *Closing the Gaps in Domestic and International Law: Achieving Comprehensive Protection of Submerged Cultural Resources*, in *Common Ground*, 1996, p. 60

Zhao, *Recent Developments in the Legal Protection of Historic Shipwrecks in China*, in *ODIL*, 1992, p. 305

POST SCRIPTUM

While this book was in printing the following articles have been published:

Amber, Mastone & Russel, *The UNESCO Convention: The US Professional Archaeological Community's Response*, paper presented at the 5th World Archaeological Congress, Catholic University of America, Washington D.C., 21–26 June 2003

Aznar Gómez, *La Convención sobre Protección del Patrimonio Cultural Subacuático, de 2 de noviembre de 2001*, in *Anuario Español de Derecho Internacional*, 2002, p. 475

Beukes, *Underwater Cultural Heritage: Archaeological Preservation or Salvage?*, in *South African Yearbook of International Law*, 2001, p. 62

Forrest, *Salvage Law and the Wreck of the Titanic*, in *Lloyd's Maritime & Commercial Law Quarterly*, 2000, p. 1

Forrest, *The UCH Convention and the Illicit Traffic in Cultural Heritage*, paper presented at the 5th World Archaeological Congress, Catholic University of America, Washington D.C., 21–26 June 2003

Forrest, *Has the Application of Salvage Law to Underwater Cultural Heritage Become a Thing of the Past?*, in *JMLC*, 2003, p. 309

Forrest & Gribble, *The Illicit Movement of Underwater Cultural Heritage: The Case of the* Dodington *Coins*, in *IJCP*, 2002, p. 267

Foster, *Validity, Construction and Application of Abandoned Shipwreck Act of 1987 (§§ 43 U.S.C.A. 2101 et seq.)*, in *American Law Reports Federal*, 2000, p. 421

Papa, *Controversial Issues on Protection of Underwater Cultural Heritage in the Italian Legal System*, in Cataldi (sous la direction de), *La Méditerranée et le droit de la mer à l'aube du 21ème siècle*, Bruxelles, 2002, p. 435

Prott, *The Making of the UNESCO Convention on the Protection of the Underwater Cultural Heritage 2001*, paper presented at the 5th World Archaeological Congress, Catholic University of America, Washington D.C., 21–26 June 2003

Scovazzi, *Un remède aux problèmes posés par l'application de la salvage law au patrimoine culturel subaquatique*, in *La mer et son droit. Mélanges offerts à Laurent Lucchini et Jean-Pierre Quéneudec*, Paris, 2003, p. 565

Publications on Ocean Development

1. R.P. Anand: *Legal Regime of the Sea-Bed and the Developing Countries*. 1976
ISBN 90-286-0616-5
2. N. Papadakis: *The International Legal Regime of Artificial Islands*. 1977
ISBN 90-286-0127-9
3. S. Oda: *The Law of the Sea in Our Time*. Volume I: *New Developments, 1966–1975*. 1977
ISBN 90-286-0277-1
4. S. Oda: *The Law of the Sea in Our Time*. Volume II: *The UN Seabed Committee, 1968–1973*. 1977
ISBN 90-286-0287-9
5. C.O. Okidi: *Regional Control of Ocean Pollution*. Legal and Institutional Problems and Prospects. 1978
ISBN 90-286-0367-0
6. N.S. Rembe: *Africa and the International Law of the Sea*.A Study of the Contribution of the African States to the 3rd UN Conference on the Law of the Sea. 1980
ISBN 90-286-0639-4
7. R.P. Anand: *Origin and Development of the Law of the Sea*. History of International Law Revisited. 1983
ISBN 90-247-2617-4
8. A.M. Post: *Deepsea Mining and the Law of the Sea*. 1983
ISBN 90-247-3049-X
9. S.P. Jagota: *Maritime Boundary*. 1985
ISBN 90-247-3133-X
10. A.O. Adede: *The System for Settlement of Disputes under the UN Convention on the Law of the Sea*. A Drafting History and a Commentary. 1987
ISBN 90-247-3324-3
11. M. Dahmani: *The Fisheries Regime of the Exclusive Economic Zone*. 1987
ISBN 90-247-3374-X
12. S. Oda: *International Control of Sea Resources*. Reprint with a New Introduction. 1989
ISBN 90-247-3800-8
13. D.G. Dallmeyer and L. DeVorsey, Jr. (eds.): *Rights to Oceanic Resources*. Deciding and Drawing Maritime Boundaries. 1989
ISBN 0-7923-0019-X
14. B. Kwiatkowska: *The 200 Mile Exclusive Economic Zone in the New Law of the Sea*. 1989
ISBN 0-7923-0074-2
15. H.W. Jayewardene: *The Regime of Islands in International Law*. 1990
ISBN 0-7923-0130-7
16. D.M. Johnston and M.J. Valencia: *Pacific Ocean Boundary Problems*. Status and Solutions. 1990
ISBN 0-7923-0862-X
17. J.A. de Yturriaga: *Straits Used for International Navigation*. A Spanish Perspective. 1991
ISBN 0-7923-1141-8

Publications on Ocean Development

18. C.C. Joyner: *Antarctica and the Law of the Sea.* 1992 ISBN 0-7923-1823-4
19. D. Pharand and U. Leanza (eds.): *The Continental Shelf and the Exclusive Economic Zone: Delimitation and Legal Regime/Le Plateau continental et la Zone économique exclusive: Délimitation et régime juridique.* 1993 ISBN 0-7923-2056-5
20. F. Laursen: *Small Powers at Sea.* Scandinavia and the New International Marine Order. 1993 ISBN 0-7923-2341-6
21. J. Crawford and D.R. Rothwell (eds.): *The Law of the Sea in the Asian Pacific Region.* 1995 ISBN 0-7923-2742-X
22. M. Munavvar: *Ocean States.* Archipelagic Regimes in the Law of the Sea. 1995 ISBN 0-7923-2882-5
23. A. Strati: *The Protection of the Underwater Cultural Heritage: An Emerging Objective of the Contemporary Law of the Sea.* 1995 ISBN 0-7923-3052-8
24. A.G. Oude Elferink: *The Law of Maritime Boundary Delimitation.* A Case Study of the Russian Federation. 1994 ISBN 0-7923-3082-X
25. Y. Li: *Transfer of Technology for Deep Sea-Bed Mining.* The 1982 Law of the Sea Convention and Beyond. 1994 ISBN 0-7923-3212-1
26. T.O. Akintoba: *African States and Contemporary International Law.* A Case Study of the 1982 Law of the Sea Convention and the Exclusive Economic Zone. 1996. ISBN 90-411-0144-6
27. J.A. Roach and R.W. Smith: *United States Responses to Excessive Maritime Claims.* Second Edition. 1996 ISBN 90-411-0225-6
28. T. Treves (ed.): *The Law of the Sea.* The European Union and its Member States. 1997 ISBN 90-411-0326-0
29. A. Razavi: *Continental Shelf Delimitation and Related Maritime Issues in the Persian Gulf.* 1997 ISBN 90-411-0333-3
30. J.A. de Yturriaga: *The International Regime of Fisheries.* From UNCLOS 1982 to the Presential Sea. 1997 ISBN 90-411-0365-1
31. M.J. Valencia, J.M. Van Dyke and N.A. Ludwig: *Sharing the Resources of the South China Sea.* 1997 ISBN 90-411-0411-9
32. E.C. Farrell: *The Socialist Republic of Vietnam and the Law of the Sea.* An Analysis of Vietnamese Behavior within the Emerging International Oceans Regime. 1997 ISBN 90-411-0473-9
33. P.B. Payoyo: *Cries of the Sea.* World Inequality, Sustainable Development and the Common Heritage of Humanity. 1997 ISBN 90-411-0504-2

Publications on Ocean Development

34. H.N. Scheiber (ed.): *Law of the Sea*. TheCommon Heritage and Emerging Challenges. 2000 ISBN 90-411-1401-7

35. D.R. Rothwell and S. Bateman (eds.): *Navigational Rights and Freedoms and the New Law of the Sea*. 2000 ISBN 90-411-1499-8

36. M.J. Valencia (ed.): *Maritime Regime Building*. Lessons Learned and their Relevance for Northeast Asia. 2001 ISBN 90-411-1580-3

37. A.G. Oude Elferink and D.R. Rothwell (eds.): *The Law of the Sea and Polar Maritime Delimination and Jurisdiction*. 2001 ISBN 90-411-1648-6

38. Robert Kolb, *Case Law on Equitable Maritime Delimitation/Jurisprudence sur les délimitations maritimes selon l'équité*: Digest and Commentaries/Répertoire et commentaires. 2002. ISBN 90-411-1976-0

39. Simon Marr, *The Precautionary Principle in the Law of the Sea*: Modern Decision Making in International Law. 2002. ISBN 90-411-2015-7

40. Sun Pyo Kim: *Maritime Delimitation and Interim Arrangements in North East Asia*. 2003. ISBN 90-411-3669-X